FORECASTING FINANCIAL MARKETS

FORECASTING FINANCIAL MARKETS

The Psychology of Successful Investing

5TH EDITION

TONY PLUMMER

KOGAN PAGE

London and Philadelphia

To Glenys

First published in 1989
Revised edition 1990
Second edition 1993
Third edition 1998
Fourth edition 2003
Fifth edition 2006

120 Pentonville Road
London N1 9JN
United Kingdom
www.kogan-page.co.uk

525 South 4th Street, #241
Philadelphia PA 19147
USA

© Tony Plummer, 1989, 1993, 1998, 2003, 2006

ISBN 0 7494 4749 4

British Library Cataloguing in Publication Data

A CIP record for this book is available from the British Library

Library of Congress Cataloging-in-Publication Data

Plummer, Tony.
  Forecasting financial markets : the psychology of successful investing / Tony Plummer. – 5th ed.
    p. cm.
  Includes index.
  ISBN 0-7494-4749-4
  1. Stock price forecasting. 2. Investment analysis. 3. Investments. I. Title.
HG4637.P57 2006
332.63'2220112–dc22

                             2006013221

Typeset by Saxon Graphics Ltd, Derby
Printed and bound in the United States by Thomson-Shore, Inc

Contents

Part Four: The trader at work

Foreword

The last two decades have witnessed dramatic changes in the behaviour of the free world's financial markets. The fundamental causes of these changes must embrace both the end of fixed exchange rates in the early 1970s and the progressive removal of controls on international financial flows. However, whatever the precise reasons may be, the symptoms are evident:

▌ a very marked increase in the volatility of prices and volumes in most markets;

▌ sharp and growing clashes between short-term developments and long-term trends;

▌ striking contradictions between market sentiment and economic fundamentals.

The practical consequences have sometimes daunting and sometimes humiliating challenges for forecasters but, far more importantly, much greater risk and uncertainty for businesspeople and traders. Despite the vast flow of data and major advances in computing and applied statistics, conventional forecasting and economic analysis are all too often not providing the guidance market operators need. So, it is clear that we should now ponder on why this is and consider, in an open-minded way, what can be done to broaden and strengthen the techniques we rely on. We need to widen our horizons so as to be able to heed the methods and results of technical analysis. The minimum argument for doing so is the cynical or expedient one that many professionals in the financial markets draw heavily on technical analysis in one way or another in their dealing as well as their writing and advising. A stronger argument is that technical analysis involves a serious attempt to reflect phenomena such as peer-group pressure, fashion, crowd psychology and much else, which are ignored or assumed unreliable by conventional theory. Regrettably, there has been little common ground sought between conventional forecasters and technical analysts. Tony Plummer's book is, in part, a contribution to that debate. However, it is also a serious attempt to state systematically the basis of technical analysis in a way that should interest not only other practitioners and sceptical economists, but also countless thoughtful managers who are rightly impatient with expert 'forecasts', which are, alas, not always worth the paper they are printed on.

Sir Adam Ridley
Director General, London Investment Banking Association
Special Adviser to successive Chancellors of the Exchequer 1979–85

difference between a technical reaction to an impulse wave and the emergence of a new trend. A wonderful, organized and essentially predictable world emerged from the apparent chaos. This fifth edition clarifies and expands on these findings. In particular, new sections demonstrate how comparisons of cyclical patterns – both over time and between markets – can yield extraordinary insights and conclusions. And the technique has been extended both to cover trends in inflation and to make some forecasts for the next decade. There are some interesting – and worrying – conclusions.

Tony Plummer
Little Walden, Essex

Acknowledgements

Very few authors can have had their work published without the assistance and encouragement of other people. This one is certainly no exception.

My sincere thanks still go to Michael Hughes, who patiently read the manuscript of the first edition and provided sound advice on how to recreate it in a more acceptable form. Needless to say, any subsequent errors remain my own.

My thanks also to my former colleagues at Hambros Bank, especially David Tapper and John Heywood. Their support and advice over the years were major influences on my interest in the workings of financial markets; and some of David's wisdom in particular has found expression in the following pages, albeit in ways that he might not immediately recognize!

My thanks also to my wife and family. They accepted my commitment and provided complete support for the task, even when I persistently spent long evenings and weekends hunched over a word processor.

Finally, my thanks must also go to my travelling companions on the 7.30 am from Audley End. It was their dedication to either sleep or crossword puzzles that enabled the earliest version of the manuscript to be written in the first place.

Introduction

Making money by trading in financial markets is a formidable task. This is a great truth that is almost impossible for one person to teach to another. It can only be realized by the very act of trading. Accordingly, very few people enter the trading arena with their eyes fully open to the psychological and financial risks. Indeed, they approach markets in the same way that they might approach a lake containing a fabled treasure. They feel that all they have to do is set up appropriate pumping equipment and the treasure is theirs. What they do not realize is that – as in all good fairy stories – the lake has magical properties, designed to protect the integrity of the treasure. Most people who touch the sparkling water of the lake are doomed to be transformed by it: they become treasure protectors instead of treasure hunters.

The problem is that there is an energy in financial markets (and, indeed, in economic activity) that somehow coerces and organizes investors into a single-minded unit. There is nothing sinister in this: it is just nature 'doing its thing'. However, the force is a psychological one, and it is so powerful that investors do not recognize it until they are finally caught in a disastrous bear market that wipes out months, if not years, of hard work.

The corollary of this is that truly great traders are very rare – only a few have the special clothing that protects them from the secret effects of the lake. Jack Schwager's books on 'Market Wizards' would not otherwise be best-sellers.[1] What is it, though, that separates such traders from the rest of us? How can some traders make regular and large profits, while others are unable to string two successive winning trades together? The traditional answer is that the quality of the trading system may not be good enough. Much time and money is therefore spent on developing trading systems in order to generate improved entry and exit signals. The problem, however, is that a good trading system – while absolutely essential – is only part of the solution. It is also necessary to be able to implement the signals on a consistent basis.

This may seem like a trivial statement, but it is not.[2] The reality is that successful trading requires a certain psychological competence to do the job and, unfortunately, nature has chosen not to wire up the human psyche with automatic access to this competence. The point here is that financial markets can have a direct and dramatic effect on wealth and on associated living standards. Most people are therefore likely to experience an emotional response as the market adds to, or subtracts from, the value of their assets. This is not necessarily bad in itself, but it does mean that when a system generates a buy or sell signal, the investor will still feel obliged to decide whether or not to implement that signal. Investment thereby moves away from the objective realm and into the subjective realm.

On this analysis, success or failure hinges critically on the ability to penetrate the 'emotional gateway' between the generation of a 'buy' or 'sell' signal and the implementation of that signal. Penetrating this gateway is, in essence, what this book is about. However, success is not just a case of heavy armour and battering rams. Such methods can work for short periods of time, but they require a heavy expenditure of energy and, inevitably, exhaustion sets in. A much more rewarding approach is to see the gateway as a learning opportunity. For the truth is that, once the necessary learnings have been completed, the gateway simply disappears.

Nor are the learnings particularly difficult. We are not talking about a lifetime of struggle that then enables a magnificent and heroic investment decision to be made from the deathbed. We are talking about relatively small adjustments in understandings, attitudes and responses, so that a large number of successful decisions can be made on a continuous basis. In fact, it is not too idealistic to say that we are talking about a commitment to the truth of the situation. Such a commitment encourages flexibility, without which we cannot respond effectively to unexpected information: that is, we cannot admit to our mistakes, we cannot be free of other people's opinions and we cannot make appropriate decisions.

Ultimately, it doesn't matter what economic theory predicts or what you believe ought to happen or what other people believe will happen. All that matters is that you have aligned yourself with the actual market trend, and if this involves changing your investment position, your belief system or even your drinking companions, then so be it.

The argument of this book, then, is that flexibility in the decision-making process can be attained by generating three interrelated skills. The first of these is an ability to understand the market in logical terms. That is, an investor or trader should have a philosophical approach to markets that incorporates a genuine understanding of the forces at work. The point is that markets fluctuate – regularly and, according to traditional theory, unpredictably. If an investor does not clearly recognize this, then they will be unprepared for the reality – the terror – of the situation.

The second skill, in a sense, follows from this. An investor needs to be able to understand their own emotional response to market fluctuations. This is a part of what Daniel Goleman calls 'emotional intelligence'.[3] If market participants understand their own vulnerability to the influences of financial markets, and if they can recognize those associated behaviours that are potentially self-defeating, then they can do something about it. In particular, they can adopt responses that are appropriate to market trends rather than responses that are hostile to them. The alternative, quite simply, is to become a victim.

Finally, of course, an investor needs to be able to design an investment process, or trading system, that generates objective 'buy' and 'sell' signals. In other words, the signals must be based on pre-determined criteria. This approach has two advantages:

▌ first, it focuses attention on critical factors that tend to recur through time;

▌ second, it helps to reduce the influence of any emotions that occur at that point in time.

Such a system need not be mechanical: it can have a facility to incorporate signals that cope with unusual circumstances or with investor preferences. The only criterion that ultimately matters is that the investor/trader is sufficiently confident about the signals that they will not continuously be doubted. Market participants should, therefore, be directly involved in the system testing procedures, so that they are aware of both the successes and the limitations. This, of course, also facilitates a creative response to unexpected market developments.

These three skills – the ability to understand market behaviour in logical terms, the ability to know the effects of the market in emotional terms and the ability to decide what to do in objective terms – are the basis of successful wealth creation in financial markets. Further, they enable investors and traders to be detached from the results of each individual investment position in a way that enables them, literally, to enjoy the whole process. In this way, wealth creation and personal fulfilment become a way of life.

This book explores each of these three dimensions to successful trading in some detail. The first step is to analyse the phenomenon of the 'crowd' in financial markets. Crowds come into being because of the existence of common beliefs and because of the need for protection from opposing beliefs. It is the dynamics of the crowd that cause markets to fluctuate as they do. Over the course of a pronounced market trend, investors become increasingly unable to penetrate the emotional gateway that we described above. Instead, they tend to do the same things at the same time in order to obtain psychological support. Eventually, a significant price reversal occurs simply because the majority are effectively 'one-way'. By definition, therefore, most investors will be on the wrong foot when a reversal occurs. It is this fact, more than anything else, that explains traumas such as the stock market crash of 1987 and the bond market crash of 1994. Once prices start to accelerate in the opposite direction, investors and short-term traders are induced to close off old positions and open new ones. Such behaviour maximizes losses and minimizes profits. The result is that very few investors make consistently high returns over and above bank deposit rates or outperform their benchmark indices.

The idea that people have a tendency to herd together is, of course, not a new one. What is not yet clearly understood, however, is that group, or crowd, behaviour is an unavoidable feature of the human condition. The crowd is a potent force because it encourages individuals to subsume their own needs to those of others. This transference of responsibility introduces a very large non-rational, and emotional, element to behaviour. Of course, very few people actually recognize the influence of the crowd because, as the saying goes, 'fish don't know that they're swimming in water'. However, the baleful influence of the crowd permeates all economic and financial behaviour, and is particularly noticeable in financial markets.

This means that it takes only a small adjustment in our assumptions concerning the nature of human motivation to generate a huge leap in our understanding of observed human behaviour. Specifically, if we accept the assumption that individual behaviour is influenced to some degree by the need to associate with – and obtain the approval of – other people, then all economic and financial behaviour can be seen as being ordered rather than chaotic. The uncertain behaviour of the individual transmutes into the more certain behaviour of the crowd. As a result, economic and financial activity become more explicable and predictable.

Importantly, though, this predictability is inherent in the process itself. For example, it is not necessary to look at outside forces to forecast the rhythm of breathing; once one cycle has been measured, it is possible to forecast the next cycle. This is the essence of the idea that market trends can be forecast with a high degree of accuracy by focusing attention, not so much on external economic trends and values (although these are important), but on what other investors themselves are actually doing about these economic values. In this way, it is possible to arrive at decisions about the position of the market within the context of its trend, and it is possible to make associated investment decisions that are relatively uncontaminated by the pressure to conform to group beliefs.

The idea that market trends can be anticipated by analysing the actual activity of investors is the central tenet of the trading discipline known as 'technical analysis'. Such analysis assumes that all financial markets follow specific behavioural laws, the influence of which can be observed in price–time charts and in associated indicators of investor activity, such as volumes and momentum. Over the years, a wide range of trading techniques has been developed to take advantage of these laws. However, the problem has always been to explain why the laws exist in the first place. Technical analysts might be prepared to assume that the laws are a fact of (and a gift from) nature, but others – especially academic economists – have tended to dismiss the laws as being 'accidental' and in conflict with common sense. While it would be an arrogance to claim that the analysis contained in this book is complete, it nevertheless demonstrates that the phenomenon of the crowd is a justifiable theoretical basis for technical analysis.

Importantly, many of the ideas that are involved in demonstrating this point can be explored using the language of natural systems theory. This discipline was originally developed to deal with biological phenomena, but has since been found to have wider implications. The exploration will necessarily be highly simplistic, but it will be demonstrated that natural processes create a specific (and continuously recurring) price pattern, which is essentially the blueprint for market movements. For ease of exposition, we have called this pattern 'the price pulse'.

Despite the apparent novelty of the price pulse, it must be emphasized that it does not supplant other techniques. Indeed, it can be argued that not only does the price pulse completely validate traditional technical analysis (which incorporates phenomena such as 'trend lines' and 'head-and-shoulders' reversal patterns), but that it is also the basis of the important 'Elliott wave principle'.

It will be shown that the price pulse is subject both to simple mathematical relationships between its constituent phases and to regular rhythmic oscillations. Hence, it is possible to create a workable, and often uncannily accurate, 'map' of likely future movements. Such maps are able to show the likely:

❙ profile of price movements;

❙ extent of those price movements;

❙ timings of price reversals.

Furthermore, it will be demonstrated that expected price reversals can be confirmed in real time by direct reference to certain simple measures of investor behaviour. Price maps can therefore be used as part of an effective trading system.

An intellectual understanding of the forces at work in financial markets, and the creation and use of a structured decision-making process, provide an extraordinarily powerful basis for trading markets. As already indicated, however, intellectual and technical rigour are only part of the challenge. Truly successful investment requires a certain degree of psychological competence. Without this, even a system with 20/20 foresight might be doomed to failure. A significant part of this book is therefore devoted to explaining how such psychological competence can be attained. Unfortunately, a book – any book – cannot 'teach' psychological competence: it can only point the way. That way is not easy for the vast majority of us; but the effort can bring untold rewards.

The overall aim of this book, then, is to enable the investor to understand the dynamics of financial markets, to understand the associated personal competencies that are required for investing in them and the essential format for an objective decision-making system.

The only way, however, to know whether or not these guidelines actually work is for you to try them. Good luck.

NOTES

1.   Schwager, Jack (1992) *Market Wizards*, Wiley, New York.
2.   Indeed, in a sense, all great truths are essentially simple to comprehend. Complexity is a characteristic of the periphery of a system; simplicity is a characteristic of its centre.
3.   Goleman, Daniel (1996) *Emotional Intelligence*, Bloomsbury, London.

Part One

The logic of non-rational behaviour in financial markets

Wholly individual or indivisibly whole

INTRODUCTION

Western culture places a great deal of emphasis on the rights of the individual. The concept of freedom of expression and the right of self-determination are enshrined in the democratic political systems of North America and Western Europe. Indeed, they are so familiar to us that most of us do not give them a second thought. Nevertheless, single-minded concentration on the needs and desires of the individual has encouraged an arrogance that is at once both an asset and a liability. It is an asset because it has catapulted humankind on a voyage of discovery through the universe that is within each of us, but it is also a liability because it has encouraged us to place ourselves above the cosmos of which we are a part.

Many scientists and philosophers now believe that future progress will depend on our ability to recognize and accept that the independence of each individual is a relative condition rather than an absolute one. Humankind takes great pride in its control and direction of certain aspects of the environment, but it still remains true that ultimately we are all dependent on that environment in the crucial sense of being a part of it. In fact, one of the most exciting features of scientific research during the last 50 years is the recognition that there is a deep interrelatedness among natural phenomena. Quite simply, everything in nature depends on everything else.

THE RELATIONSHIPS IN NATURE

This finding has significant implications for the development of human knowledge, because it suggests that the most important aspect of the world is not the individual parts of nature so much but the relationships in nature: the relationships define the parts, and no single part can exist independently of other parts.[1] Hence, it becomes possible to visualize the world in terms of multilevel structures that start at the subatomic level and then extend upwards in ever-increasing layers of complexity. As an example, electrons combine to form atoms, atoms combine to form molecules, molecules combine to form organs, organs combine to form organ systems, organ systems combine to form animals and humankind.

THE BREAK WITH TRADITION

These concepts have been explored in some detail in recent years,[2] and have even given a strong impetus to a new discipline known as 'systems theory'.[3] However, the ideas are not yet widely understood. Part of the difficulty derives from the fact that systems theory marks a distinct break from the traditional analytical procedures that have been favoured ever since the pioneering work of Isaac Newton and René Descartes. These procedures presume that it is possible to understand all aspects of any complicated phenomenon by 'reducing' that phenomenon to its constituent parts.

The process of dividing nature into progressively smaller units (a process that is known as 'reductionism') works very well in the context of everyday life. Indeed, the fund of knowledge is actually enhanced as differentiation increases, and so the process is self-justifying. However, in the 1920s, physicists found that the process was totally inapplicable at the subatomic level.[4] Specifically, it was found that electrons do not exist with certainty at definite places and do not behave predictably at definite times.[5] In other words, there was a critical level where 'certainties' disappeared, and where the concept of basic 'building blocks' seemed to become invalid.

The practical solution to the problem was to step back and assign characteristics to electrons that accounted for both the uncertainty of the unobserved state of existence and for the certainty of the observed state. It was hypothesized that electrons had a dual nature: on the one hand, the behaviour of an individual electron could not be forecast with any degree of certainty; on the other hand, the behaviour of groups of electrons could be forecast with a high degree of certainty. In other words, the solution[6] lay within the mathematics of probability theory, where a large number of uncertainties produce a certainty.[7] Probability theory can, for example, determine with 100 per cent accuracy the half-life of any radioactive substance,[8] despite the fact that the point in time when one particular radioactive atom will disintegrate is totally unpredictable.

THE CONCEPTUAL REVOLUTION

The search for basic building blocks in nature will undoubtedly persist.[9] In the meantime, the revelations of the New Physics (as it is called despite the fact that it is well over half a century old) are generating major structural changes in the natural and social sciences.[10] Each discipline, essentially, is having to absorb two related ideas:

▌ 'wholes' are something greater than the simple arithmetic sum of their 'parts';

▌ each 'part' has a tendency to have both a separate identity and to belong to a greater whole.

THE PROBLEM OF MOTIVATION

In the social sciences, the changes are leading towards a revolution in our understanding of human behaviour. In economics, for example, the traditional approach has been to assume that human beings are essentially mechanistic in their behaviour patterns. This assumption is based partly on introspection and partly on research. First, even an elementary level of self-analysis reveals that a large part of our behaviour involves an automatic response to particular stimuli. Second, statistical analysis can also be used to show that groups of people tend to respond in a predictable way to given stimuli. It is, therefore, only a small step to infer that individual behaviour is definitely mechanistic and to use that inference as the basis for economics analysis and forecasting.

It is certainly true that a great deal of our behaviour is mechanistic. This is, in part, due to fundamental biological and 'social' drives that

are common to many species that inhabit this planet. Indeed, anthro-
pologists such as Desmond Morris[11] have been able to identify a large
number of parallels between human behaviour and that of animals.
However, mechanistic behaviour is also due to a type of habit
formation that is a particular feature of the human subconscious mind.
The point is that, because individual histories differ, everyone's habits
are going to be different to some degree, no matter how small. This, of
course, leaves an inconsistency between habitual personal behaviour
and predictable group behaviour.

There is, however, a more telling criticism. This is that human
beings have a type of awareness that specifically transcends automatic
behaviour. As Fritz Schumacher[12] observed, the structure of living
organisms is a progression of increasing complexity and power: plants
have life; animals have life and consciousness; people have life,
consciousness and self-awareness. Self-awareness here means the
ability to be conscious of one's own existence,[13] and it encourages
each individual to choose between alternative responses to a given
situation. Self-aware decisions are not forecastable by outsiders. Nor
is there any reason to believe that one person's decisions will be the
same as anybody else's. As a very simple example, if someone was
given a windfall sum of money, it would be very difficult for another
person to predict precisely how that money would be used: it could be
saved, spent, lent, given away or even destroyed.

THE DUALISTIC NATURE OF MOTIVATION

Economists have tended to ignore the inconsistency between individual variety and group conformity for two reasons. First, it is often
argued that the assumptions in a theory are less important than the
conclusions of that theory.[14] Although there are some circumstances
where this may be true,[15] it is by no means always correct. In
particular, assumptions are all too often reflections of biased beliefs
about the world. Second, and perhaps more importantly, economic
theoreticians have tended to resist the idea that a paradox actually
exists. The reason for this seems to be that it presents a very real threat
to the logical structure of modern economic theory (this point is
covered in more detail in Chapter 6).

The solution to the dichotomy between individual variety and group
conformity lies in the concept of a duality of characteristics, comparable to that used for subatomic phenomena. People have both the

ability to be individuals and the tendency to belong to groups. The actual mix of the two characteristics varies over time depending on circumstances. Sometimes a person will be relatively individualistic, while at other times the same person will be relatively willing to conform to behavioural patterns pursued or imposed by others. The important difference between the two sets of circumstances is the degree to which a person accepts other people's belief systems, thereby limiting their personal room for manoeuvre.

CONCLUSION

The idea that motivation has a dual nature represents a major breakthrough in our understanding of human behaviour. Each person simultaneously has a tendency to be an individual with a unique and 'personal' view of the world and a tendency to belong to groups. Individual behaviour is not easily predictable, but group behaviour is. This duality of character is of the utmost importance to our analysis of investor behaviour in stock markets.

NOTES

1. The interconnectedness of nature is actually such that it can sometimes be very difficult to see where each 'part' of a structure starts or where each 'whole' ends. See Bohm, David (1980) *Wholeness and the Implicate Order*, Routledge & Kegan Paul, London.
2. See, for example, Jantsch, Erich (1980) *The Self-organizing Universe*, Pergamon, Oxford.
3. See Chapter 4.
4. The findings of the New Physics are truly remarkable. It is suggested that interested readers refer to, for example, Zukav, Gary (1979) *The Dancing Wu Li Masters*, William Morrow, New York.
5. Electrons can be viewed as being very abstract packets of energy that have a dual aspect: sometimes they adopt the characteristics of a single entity or particle, but sometimes they adopt the characteristics of continuous waves. Hence, prior to observation, it is impossible to determine whether an electron is particle-like or wave-like. Furthermore, during observation, it is impossible to determine both the position and the velocity of an electron.
6. Heisenberg, Werner (1971) *Physics and Beyond*, Allen & Unwin, London.
7. This point is well made by Arthur Koestler (1978) in *Janus: A summing up*, Hutchinson, London.
8. The half-life of a substance is the time required for half the atoms in the substance to disintegrate.

9.   The search for basic building blocks of matter has recently focused on smaller phenomena called 'quarks'. However, even ignoring the difficulties regarding the status of electrons, it is not certain that the concept will be validated. See, for example, Hawking, Stephen W (1988) *A Brief History of Time*, Transworld Publishers, London.

10.   Capra, Fritjof (1982) *The Turning Point*, Wildwood House, London.

11.   Morris, Desmond (1967) *The Naked Ape*, Jonathan Cape, London.

12.   Schumacher, E F (1977) *A Guide for the Perplexed*, Jonathan Cape, London.

13.   The term 'self-awareness' can be used as a generic term, which incorporates all the factors that enable the human mind to create an inner world that mirrors the outer 'reality'.

14.   See, for example, Friedman, Milton (1953) *Essays in Positive Economics*, University of Chicago Press, Chicago.

15.   The argument that assumptions are not as important as the conclusions (or predictions) of a model has some validity under two circumstances. It is acceptable when the assumptions are designed to neutralize external interferences. In this way, it becomes possible to analyse the response of specific variables to changes in a limited number of other variables, with outside influences being held unchanged. The argument is also acceptable when the assumptions simply affirm the 'truth' of previous research. Serious philosophical problems arise, however, when the assumptions are used to neutralize complications within a particular system because, by definition, these complications are part of the system.

Two's a crowd

INTRODUCTION

Investors who have been involved with financial markets for any length of time will readily identify with the concept of a conflicting two-way pull on their decisions. On the one hand, their own 'personal' approach to making an investment decision may suggest one course of action; on the other, the lure of the 'herd instinct' may be pulling entirely in the opposite direction. Even seasoned professionals, who make a living by anticipating and outwitting the rest of the participants in financial markets, will sometimes find themselves caught up in a common hysteria at just that time when contrary thinking is truly appropriate. It is a rare trader who can honestly say that they have not bought stock at the top of a price movement or sold stock at the bottom of a price movement.

This two-way pull on each individual is actually a natural result of the intrinsic relationship between individual integrity and group membership. On the one hand, each person has a self-assertive tendency or ability to behave in a self-determined, individualistic way. On the other hand, however, each individual also has an integrative tendency,[1] which involves a psychological drive to belong to groups of all kinds. Membership of a group involves the adoption of behavioural patterns that are consistent with the group's objectives.

THE INFLUENCE OF GROUPS

It is important to recognize that group behaviour is not, in itself, unusual. In fact, groups emerge as a result of the same basic laws that apply to the rest of nature. As Erich Jantsch[2] has shown, building on the implications of quantum physics, all of nature consists of multi-levelled structures. Each level in this hierarchy has the power to organize its lower levels and use them for its own purposes.[3] Consequently, each level is able to perpetuate itself or maintain its identity despite changes in its individual components.[4] This hierarchical structure applies to human society:[5] individuals become members of groups, groups merge to form societies and societies merge to form civilizations (see Figure 2.1).

THE INSIGHTS OF GUSTAVE LE BON

One of the first people to analyse the phenomenon of human groups in any detail was Gustave Le Bon.[6] He was fascinated by the influence and role of a very particular type of group – namely, the crowd – in the unfolding of the French Revolution. His seminal book *The Psychology of Crowds* was written in 1895, but it still stands out as a classic of social psychology. Its analysis has been validated by subsequent analysts such as Sigmund Freud and Carl Jung, as well as by theorists such as Arthur Koestler. Its conclusions have been found to be applicable to such diverse historical phenomena as the Nuremberg Rallies and the Holocaust in Nazi Germany; the attempted destruction

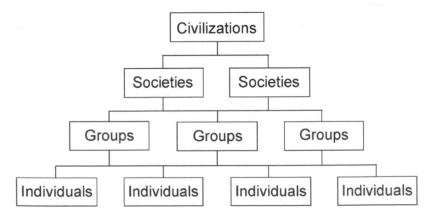

Figure 2.1 The hierarchical structure of human groupings

of 'bourgeois' and reactionary values during the Cultural Revolution in China; and the attempted elimination of individualism by the Khmer Rouge in the Killing Fields of Cambodia.

Le Bon saw a crowd as being primarily a psychological phenomenon rather than a physical one (although the two concepts are not necessarily mutually exclusive). He considered that any number of otherwise independent and spatially separate individuals could form a crowd, provided that the members had a common cause. This, of course, confirms the idea that 'crowd'-type pressures can be found in a large range of groupings. They can, for example, be found in companies, football teams, armies, religious sects and patriotic nation states, as well as riotous mobs. As we shall see, they can also be found in financial markets. Le Bon himself argued that:[7]

> The most striking peculiarity presented by a psychological crowd is the following: whoever be the individuals that compose it, however like or unlike their mode of life, their occupations, their character, or their intelligence, the fact that they have been transformed into a crowd puts them in possession of a sort of collective mind that makes them feel, think, and act in a manner quite different from that in which each individual of them would feel, think, and act were he in a state of isolation . . .
>
> What really takes place [in the formation of a crowd] is a combination followed by the creation of new characteristics, just as in chemistry certain elements, when brought into contact . . . combine to form a new body possessing properties quite different from those of the bodies that have served to form it.

This profound insight into the nature of crowds used two important concepts:

- a crowd is something other than the sum of its parts – in particular, a crowd has an effective 'mind' of its own;

- each individual's behaviour is altered by their membership of a crowd.

These two concepts are now central to the general theory of group behaviour. Within this theory, the phenomenon of the crowd presents itself as a special, and extreme, case.

THE GROUP'S ABILITY TO ORGANIZE ITSELF

From the group's point of view, it is crucial to its own autonomy that it can 'organize' its own membership. This is the only way that energy can be directed towards the overall objectives of the group. Such 'self'-organization operates through the group's belief system. To be a member of a group, an individual has to accept uncritically the same beliefs as other members of the group. In 1961, the psychoanalyst Wilfred Bion proposed that these beliefs were 'basic assumptions' held by group members.[8] In 1976, Richard Dawkins called the beliefs/assumptions 'memes'.[9] A meme is a simple, self-replicating idea (or habit, or feeling, or sense of things) that spreads from mind to mind. The presence of a particular meme does not necessarily exclude other memes, so a group member can belong to more than one group. However, whatever term might be used for the commonly held beliefs, group members will necessarily suppress behaviour that might cause them to be excluded from the group.[10] In other words, a person's individuality – or self-assertiveness – will be modified by group membership.

This situation obviously means two things:

▌ the more intense is the integrative pull of a group, the less is the degree of individuality that is allowed (we shall deal with this in Chapter 3);

▌ it is the like-mindedness of group members that gives the group its cohesion.

A group therefore organizes its members via a unifying belief system. In this way, a group becomes something more than just the sum of its parts and group members will reveal a sense of altruism towards one another in the context of group activity. Hence – whether they overtly recognize it or not – group members will act in the interests of the group as a whole.

MIND AS A DYNAMIC PRINCIPLE

This analysis has necessarily been very brief and hardly does justice to the concepts involved. Nevertheless, we now have the tools to enable us to look a little more closely at the idea of a group 'mind'. This idea is not an easy one either to grasp or to convey. Part of the difficulty lies in our language itself. As commonly used, the word 'mind' is taken to refer to that part of the physical structure of the brain that is capable of self-aware, rational thought. According to this view, people have minds, but animals do not. However, this usage not only ignores the role of the so-called 'subconscious' mind, but assumes that the physical structure of the brain is identical to, and provides the defining limits for, the inner processes of the mind.

The best way to understand the difference between the concept of 'brain' and the concept of 'mind' is to recognize that the brain is the structure, while the mind is the processing capabilities that are originated within that structure. Importantly, however, the processes of the mind are not confined to the boundaries established by the physical brain: laterally, the processes extend through the living body, dealing with automatic functions, physical movement and emotions; and, vertically, they extend (layer upon layer) into the depths of the personality. These processes are known generically as 'mentation'.

The essential point to grasp at this stage is that mentation is primafacie evidence of the phenomenon of life. This was the profound insight of the great philosopher and biologist Gregory Bateson.[11] Bateson found that exactly the same characteristics that define mentation in the human brain can be found both in all the other processes of the human body and in every aspect of nature. Mentation is actually a logical process – a single dynamic blueprint – that is the very hallmark of life on this planet. It does not, therefore, have to be encased in any particular physical structure and, conceptually, can extend beyond all physical structures. The difference between mentation in the human mind and mentation in other aspects of nature is in the quality, or depth, of consciousness. Only human mentation allows for thinking to be aware of itself.[12]

Bateson's own criteria for the existence of mind (that is, the existence of 'life') in any system were essentially four-fold, namely:

▌ the ability to control functions that were internal to the system;

▌ the ability of the system to process information;

▌ the presence of fluctuations in the processing of that information;

▌ the existence of a continuous exchange of energy and information between the system and its environment.

As we shall see, these criteria produce some very important insights into human behaviour.

THE GROUP MIND

Bateson's criteria for the existence of mind extended the concept to include all aspects of the living universe and, it may be said, added an important new dimension both to the conclusions of the New Physics and to the framework of the scientific process. Hence, the concept of mind can be used not only to describe the phenomenon of life, but also to describe and explain any particular 'unit' of life. It can be found in both the most simple and the most complicated of processes. In terms of human society, it can be found in the dynamics of people's relationships with one another: it can be found in a small group of people, in a physical crowd, in a nation state or in a whole culture. An individual's mind may (in a non-self-assertive state) be regarded as a subsystem of a greater whole. Each whole, in turn, has a 'collective mind' that organizes its own parts. From this analysis we could say that each and every human grouping may be said to have a collective consciousness.[13]

THE TRIUNE HUMAN BRAIN

As already observed, however, the collective consciousness of a human grouping is qualitatively different from the consciousness of an individual human being. The former is essentially simplistic and is not usually recognized, while the latter is not fully understood, even though it is accepted. The essential difference between the two phenomena is that a group does not have the ability to be aware of its own existence, whereas an individual does have such an ability. And it is this difference that is so important to our study of the influence of a crowd. The fact is that, as described by Le Bon, crowd behaviour involves a dramatic suppression of self-awareness by individuals and an increase in the power of the group entity that is, by definition, not self-aware in the first place. The 'total' quality of consciousness therefore deteriorates. As Scott Peck put it, 'groups are, from a psychological standpoint, less than the sum of the parts'.[14]

We can isolate two aspects to this important phenomenon. First, when an individual adopts a group belief, then, by definition, they also accept a reduction in self-awareness. This is so because the boundaries between the individual and the group become blurred. However, a reduction in self-awareness necessarily happens in all group behaviour. What makes crowd behaviour so distinctive is the degree to which an individual's self-awareness is suppressed. It seems almost as if there is a switch somewhere in the brain that flicks self-awareness to 'off' whenever a crisis arises.

This brings us to the second aspect of the deterioration in the quality of consciousness that accompanies the crowd phenomenon. There does seem to be something of a fault-line within the structure of the human brain. The problem stems from the fact that the brain consists of three main processing areas that can, to some extent, operate independently of one another. Each part is structurally and chemically different from the other parts, and appears to have its own intelligence, its own memory and its own separate functions. The brain stem (the innermost part of the brain) is concerned primarily with instinctive behaviour patterns, biological drives and compulsive behaviour. Surrounding this part is the limbic system, which is mainly involved with the recreation of external experiences in the 'inner' world, and with emotional activity. Importantly, it is also the area of the brain that is most concerned with group activities. Finally, the neocortex (the outermost part of the brain) deals with the ability both to be aware of the thought process itself, and to anticipate the future and recreate the past. It also contains the areas of the brain (the so-called 'frontal lobes') that are most involved with concern for humanity.[15,16] Because of its three-fold nature, the American neurophysiologist Paul D Maclean[17] has called the human brain the 'triune' brain.

THE NEOCORTEX

Of the three areas, it is undoubtedly the neocortex that (among other things) separates humankind from other mammals. The evolutionary history of the neocortex is, however, uncertain. No one really knows when (or how, or why) it first appeared. Current guesswork suggests it developed only during the last 50 million years or so. This compares with more than 150 million years for the limbic system, and more than 250 million years for the brain stem. Importantly, evidence from the evolution of civilization[18] suggests that the specific abilities associated with the neocortex have only developed within a very recent period. The modern ego – that is, the tendency of mental processes to organize themselves in such a way as to assert themselves as an independent entity – seems only to have arisen some four thousand (or so) years ago. The ego, therefore, is very young in terms of evolution.

We can therefore hypothesize that the operation of the neocortex can easily be overwhelmed for two related reasons:

- the neocortex has still not yet been properly integrated with the other two parts of the brain;

- the capability of 'self'-awareness is still likely to give way to more archaic states of consciousness when an 'external' authority is favoured.

THE AMYGDALA

In fact, research initiated by Joseph LeDoux at New York University has found that the main problem almost certainly rests with a tiny part of the human brain known as the 'amygdala'.[19] The amygdala is a small neural cluster lying between the brain stem and the limbic system. It is responsible for scanning the environment for threats. If a threat is perceived, it immediately triggers an emotional and physical arousal in the limbic system and brain stem. The critical point is that this arousal begins to happen before the neocortex has even had a chance to register an incoming signal. If the threat is significant, then the neocortex is allowed very little chance to intervene. As a result, we might jump out of the way of an oncoming car or remove our hand from something hot, say, and only recognize what has happened after the event. If, however, the threat is below some (subjective) threshold level of significance, the arousal starts, but is regulated to some extent by the left pre-frontal lobe.

The amygdala, therefore, acts as a trigger to an emergency neural circuit that generates an emotional arousal. Its evolutionary function is obviously to enhance survival prospects, but it is arguable that the trigger is too sensitive and requires positive intervention to 'retrain' it (we shall deal with this in a little more detail in Chapter 22). In the meantime, we need to register the fact that the amygdala is influential in the formation of crowds.

THE RESPONSE TO A THREAT

Significantly, a crowd is most likely to emerge in the presence of a threat of some kind. A group of people can have a common cause, but will not be regarded as a crowd, as such, until a threat appears. A crowd has a certain urgency and immediacy to it, which is not necessarily present in a group. Hence, there are two possibilities:

▌ a number of individuals will feel threatened in some way and then form a crowd;

▌ a group already exists that is then sufficiently threatened to transmute into a crowd.

In either case, it is not fanciful to suggest that crowd members' emergency amygdala circuits will be triggered. As a result:

▌ group survival needs overwhelm individual self-assertiveness needs;

▌   group beliefs replace personal beliefs;

▌   the influence of the neocortex is overwhelmed by the influence of the brain stem and the limbic system.

Crowds are, accordingly, involved primarily with instincts, biological drives, compulsive behaviour and emotions. Hence, their behaviour is essentially non-rational (and is, in fact, often irrational). To paraphrase Arthur Koestler:[20]

> emotion and intellect, faith and reason, [are] at loggerheads. On the one side, [is] the pale cast of rational thought, of logic suspended on a thin thread all too easily broken; on the other, [is] the raging fury of passionately held irrational beliefs, reflected in the holocausts of past and present history.

THE 'INTELLIGENCE' OF CROWDS

This certainly helps to explain the popularly held delusion that all members of a crowd are unintelligent: it is not that they are unintelligent as such – it is that their ability to remain self-aware and think logically becomes suppressed in the face of a threat. This is as true of pairs of individuals confronted with a challenge (such as a couple whose child-rearing abilities are criticized) as it is of a large group of people facing a physical threat (such as a military unit under fire).[21]

Whether or not the challenge to a crowd is physical, it almost certainly involves a threat to its underlying belief system. As a result, the strength of this belief system becomes intensified and severe limitations are accordingly imposed on the quality of data that the crowd will recognize as genuine information. Gregory Bateson defined information as 'differences which make a difference'.[22] A crowd mind can usually only perceive differences that are relatively large and that occur over very short periods of time. In other words, a crowd will only recognize obvious changes. Slow changes can be observed only by the lengthy process of continually, and rationally, scanning all the potentially relevant data. Crowds are incapable of such analysis: they think in terms of simple images and communicate with slogans. As they emerge in times of crisis, they are all too often the main vehicle for historical 'progress'.

NOTES

1. The terms 'self-assertive tendency' and 'integrative tendency' were coined by Arthur Koestler.
2. Jantsch, Erich (1980) *The Self-organizing Universe*, Pergamon, Oxford.
3. For a very straightforward commentary on this process, see Schumacher, E F (1977) *A Guide for the Perplexed*, Jonathan Cape, London.
4. This is called 'homeostasis', and is the source of the phrase *plus ça change, plus c'est la même chose.*
5. The hierarchical structuring, and therefore the crowd phenomenon, obviously also exists in the non-human world. It exists, for example, among birds, fish, ants, bees and lemmings. One of the more unusual examples concerns the ability of single-cell amoebae to form themselves into a so-called 'slime mould' in order to search for food as a group. See Tyler Bonner, John (December 1959) 'Differentiation in social amoebae', *Scientific American*.
6. Le Bon, Gustave *Psychologie des Foules*, reprinted (1922) as *The Crowd*, Macmillan, New York.
7. Ibid.
8. Bion, Wilfred (1961) *Experiences in Groups*, Tavistock Publications, London. Bion distinguished three types of 'basic assumption': 1) basic assumption dependency, where the group behaves as if its primary task is only to provide for the needs of its members and where the group leader is expected to help members to feel good; 2) basic assumption fight–flight, where there is an enemy that has to be dealt with and where, without concern, group members do as they are told by a leader; and 3) basic assumption pairing, where the group believes that a direct relationship between members and a leader will trigger a future solution to a current problem. If any, or all, of these assumptions are present, it is obviously important that individuals do not question their validity.
9. Dawkins, Richard (1976) *The Selfish Gene*, Oxford University Press, Oxford.
10. Bion, Wilfred, op. cit.
11. Bateson, Gregory (1979) *Mind and Nature: An essential unity*, Wildwood House, London.
12. It is arguable, however, that the specific ability to be aware of one's own thinking is hardly ever used. See Bennett, J G (1964) *Creative Thinking*, Coombe Springs Press, Masham, Yorkshire.
13. See Capra, Fritjof (1982) *The Turning Point*, Wildwood House, London.
14. Peck, M Scott (1983) *People of the Lie*, Rider, London.
15. The frontal lobes require continuous stimulation in order to activate the specifically human qualities of empathy and compassion. Not only is this stimulation applied irregularly, but the activity of the frontal lobes is all too often suppressed by alcohol and drugs. See, for example, Franck, Frederick (1991) *To Be Human against All the Odds*, Asian Humanities Press, Berkeley, California.
16. Erich Jantsch distinguishes three different types of mental activity, each of which corresponds to one of the different areas of the brain:

    'organismic' mental activity is the function of the brain stem: 'reflexive' activity is the province of the limbic system: 'self-reflexive' activity is conducted by the neocortex. (See Erich Jantsch, op. cit.)

17. Maclean, Paul D, 'A triune concept of the brain and behaviour', in Boag, T, and Campbell, D (eds) (1973) *The Hincks Memorial Lectures*, University of Toronto Press, Toronto.
18. Wilber, Ken (1983) *Up from Eden*, Routledge & Kegan Paul, London. See also Jaynes, Dr Julian (1976) *The Origin of Consciousness in the Breakdown of the Bicameral Mind*, Houghton Mifflin, Boston.
19. Goleman, Daniel (1996) *Emotional Intelligence*, Bloomsbury, London.
20. Koestler, Arthur (1978) *Janus: A summing up*, Hutchinson, London.
21. Scott Peck, op. cit., effectively aligns crowd-type behaviour with the concept of evil. His examples range from co-dependent couples involved in child abuse to the My Lai massacre. The central point in his analysis is the one made by Paul Maclean: compassion for others is effectively eliminated.
22. Bateson, Gregory, op. cit.

3

The individual in the crowd

THE INTEGRATIVE TENDENCY

We can now look at the crowd phenomenon from the individual's point of view because it follows that, if a crowd is to form, individual members must, in some sense, 'want' to join and be willing to conform to behavioural standards imposed by others. No group – and especially not a crowd – can exist unless each group member alters their behaviour to conform to the will of the majority. In other words, there must be a basis for the integrative tendency, or the tendency to devote oneself to a group.

Theoretically, we can observe three aspects to this phenomenon,[1] namely:

▌ identification with the crowd;

▌ acceptance of the crowd's belief system;

▌ submission to the authority of a leader.

IDENTIFICATION

There is, indeed, a well-researched predisposition for individuals to reject individuals in other groups, to accept the judgement of the majority in the group to which they belong, and to accept the instructions of a person (or persons) representing authority. In a series of experiments by Henri Tajfel[2] at Bristol University, it was shown that groups of schoolboys aged 14 to 15 could have their behaviour altered merely by telling them that they belonged to a particular group – even an unknown group. Specifically, the schoolboys would automatically associate themselves with other members of the same group, would provide active support for that group and would take every opportunity to disadvantage members of other groups. These phenomena occurred despite the fact that no indication was given to the schoolboys about the purpose or qualities of the groups.

BELIEFS

It seems that uncritical acceptance of group assumptions/beliefs has its foundation in the subconscious need to belong, or not to be seen as different. For example, experiments conducted in 1956 by Solomon Asch at Harvard[3] showed that, when matching the length of a line with one of three other lines, subjects could have their performance measurably altered by group pressures. When asked to match the length of a line with one of three other lines in isolation from others, participants made a mistake less than 1 per cent of the time. However, when placed in a group that had been instructed beforehand to claim that mismatched lines were actually the same, 75 per cent of participants agreed with the majority. This was true even when the actual difference between the lines was very significant. Worryingly, Asch also found that although some participants lacked the nerve to disagree with the majority, some maintained that they had actually seen the mismatched lines as being equal and some doubted their own perceptions.

SELF-AWARENESS AND CONFORMITY ENFORCEMENT

These general conclusions have been confirmed by research conducted at the University of Illinois by Ed Diener. He found that the most important factor in group behaviour was the suppression of self-awareness and, therefore, of self-regulation. In one particular piece of research, Diener compared behaviour under three different laboratory test conditions:[4]

■ where individuals were self-aware and isolated from group influences;

■ where individuals were non-self-aware, but were still isolated from group influences; and

■ where individuals were both non-self-aware and involved in a group environment.

It was found that individuals in the third situation generally acted spontaneously, had little sense of personal identity and related closely to other group members. Indeed, the experience was found to be very enjoyable. Quite clearly, conformity enforcement within the group goes hand in hand with reduced self-awareness by individuals.

THE CROWD LEADER

Identification with other members of the crowd and an acceptance of the crowd's belief system is stimulated by each member's willingness to obey a crowd leader. The importance of a leader for crowd dynamics was Sigmund Freud's major contribution to the debate,[5] and is based on his idea of a 'parent substitute'.[6] Specifically, Freud argued that a large group (or crowd) would follow its leader because that leader personified certain ideals and objectives for the group. Group members would essentially disable themselves by projecting their own capacities for thought, decision making and responsibility taking on to the leader.

The crowd leader acts as the main interpreter of new information from the environment, determines the appropriate tactical response and directs strategy. Leaders may be dictatorial or democratic, they may be constructive or destructive, but they will always command the attention of each of the crowd members. However, leadership may manifest in a number of different guises. On the one hand, it may be obvious, in the sense that it is vested in a particular individual or in a subgroup of people (such as a committee or board of directors). On the other hand, it may be covert. It may, for example, be vested in the democratic decision of the group itself or in the shared system of beliefs held by members of the crowd, and the code of conduct it engenders. Covert leadership, however, almost certainly requires some form of 'totem' on which the crowd can focus its attention. Throughout history, crowds have been responsive to national flags, figureheads, icons and statues.

THE FINDINGS OF STANLEY MILGRAM

The classic experiment to discover the limit to which people would be obedient to authority was conducted by Dr Stanley Milgram of Yale University.[7] In the experiment, the subjects were ordered to inflict pain on an innocent victim in the interests of an important cause. Authority (or the leader and representative of a group belief system) was represented by a scientist in a white coat who would continually urge the subject to proceed with administering electric shocks to a third person. In fact, there was no electric shock involved at all: the subject did not know it, but the third person (the victim) merely behaved as if there had been one.

At all stages throughout the experiment, the subject was made aware of the effect of their actions, both by a dial on the electric shock machine (which indicated the voltage being administered and the degree of danger involved therewith), and by the screams and protests of the victim strapped into a chair. Milgram found that over 60 per cent of the subjects were prepared to obey instructions to administer the highest and most lethal dose of electricity, even after the victim had given up screaming and was, to all intents and purposes, comatose.

ALTRUISM AND CONFLICT

In the previous chapter, it was noted that the structure of the human brain lends itself to the emergence of non-rational responses to perceived threats of any kind. In particular, the brain stem and the limbic system are subject to a significant stimulus. Significantly, the arousal of these two subsystems at the expense of the neocortex can degrade human behaviour to the extent that some degree of animal-like 'herd' behaviour materializes. This is the phenomenon of the crowd.

There are, obviously, different degrees of intensity of crowd behaviour, but its hallmark is non-rational and emotional behaviour, common to a number of individuals acting together. It follows, too, that once a crowd has been catalysed, the left pre-frontal lobe of the neocortex is even less likely to operate effectively. As a result, the amygdala of each crowd member is given an even freer rein.

The results – as researchers such as Diener and Milgram have verified – can be frightening. A crowd led by a strong leader can be a truly potent force. First, people within a crowd develop a sense of altruism towards other crowd members that is very strong. (Sometimes, indeed, it is so strong that, as Emile Durkheim found, it can result in suicide.[8]) Second, the crowd can achieve objectives using methods that more self-aware individuals would regard as being totally unacceptable. It is not surprising, therefore, that people are more likely to be involved in states of conflict as group members than as individuals. Third, and as a corollary, it follows that conflict (or stress) is a perfect catalyst for the formation of a crowd. If, for some reason, an imbalance develops between two groups, each group member will have common cause with other members of the same group in protecting the autonomy of that group. The paramount need of each group may then release the aggressiveness in, or relax constraints on, each individual.

SPLITTING AND PROJECTION

There is a broad question about what encourages, or allows, individuals actively to participate in aggressive, destructive crowd behaviour when they might not otherwise do so. One factor is the need to belong. For many, if not all, crowd participants, the sense of belonging totally to a higher psychological construct is a transcendental experience: ego boundaries collapse and are invaded by group beliefs, personal responsibility is removed and anxiety is eliminated.[9] A second factor is the way that the human psyche deals with potentially conflicting emotions. Here, an individual disowns the unacceptable side of his or her psyche and projects it out on to others.[10] The result is a toxic combination of infallibility on the one hand and hatred and fear of an 'enemy' on the other, and it is all too easy to kill and maim 'subhuman others'.[11] Unfortunately, the fact that these processes occur in the subconscious mind makes it all too easy to deny that they exist in the first place.

CONCLUSION

The conclusions of this chapter are simple, but profound. Membership of a group in general, or of a crowd in particular, involves the abrogation, to some degree, of personal responsibility – that is, people act differently as crowd participants than they do as independent individuals. A crowd as a whole tends to behave in a non-rational, emotional way in pursuit of its objectives and forces its members to do likewise. The ability of a crowd to organize its members in this way is particularly pronounced under conditions of conflict when the autonomy of the crowd is in some way threatened.

These observations go some way towards explaining some of the less attractive features of the human condition. They explain, for example, why armies of otherwise rational and humane men are prepared to go to war; they offer an explanation of why avowedly religious groups have tortured and murdered in pursuit of doctrinal purity; they explain why trade union members have been willing to destroy the companies that they work for rather than surrender any union 'rights'. The list is endless, and is the more depressing for it.

However, the purpose of this book is other than to bemoan the fate of humanity. Up to now, Part One has presented a body of theory that explains, essentially, why group behaviour is a ubiquitous feature of the human condition. For the vast majority of people, some form of group pressure provides a major motivating force in all their social, economic and political activities. Such pressure exists in such diverse structures as friendly societies, corporations and religions. It is more intense in sports teams and is at its most intense under combat conditions. As we shall demonstrate, the crowd phenomenon also exists in financial markets.

So far we have only explained why crowds exist. We have not yet shown how crowds behave. Let us, therefore, take one further step towards the primary purposes of this book by analysing the dynamics of a crowd system.

NOTES

1. Koestler, Arthur (1978) *Janus: A summing up*, Hutchinson, London.
2. Quoted in Arthur Koestler, op. cit.
3. Asch, Solomon (1956) 'Studies of independence and conformity', *Psychological Monographs*, **70** (9).
4. Diener, Ed, 'Deindividuation: the absence of self-awareness and self-regulation in group members', in Paulus, P B (ed.) (1980) *The Psychology of Group Influence*, Erlbaum, Hillside, New Jersey.
5. Freud, Sigmund (1959) *Group Psychology and the Analysis of the Ego*, Norton, New York.
6. Freud and others have argued that the willingness of individuals to respond to a leader is based on the experiences of early childhood. Under normal circumstances, each baby not only learns about its individuality, but also gains security from transactions with its parents. Hence, a need for both a parent substitute and the company of others is learnt and carried through into adult life.

7.   Milgram, Stanley (1975) *Obedience to Authority*, Harper & Row, New York.
8.   Durkheim, Emile (1970) *Suicide: A study in sociology*, Routledge & Kegan Paul, London. Durkheim differentiated between altruistic suicide, where individuals die for the group, and anomic suicide, where they die because of separation from the group.
9.   See Neumann, Erich (1990) *Depth Psychology and a New Ethic*, Shambhala, Boston, Massachusetts. See also Chapter 6, note 8.
10.   See Klein, Melanie (1946) 'Notes on some schizoid mechanisms', in (1997) *Envy and Gratitude*, Vintage, London.
11.   The psychology of the suicide bomber, for example, involves splitting and projection. However, it also involves a combination of Durkheim's anomic suicide and altruistic suicide (that is, the bomber is simultaneously cut off from the wider community and committed to protecting the integrity of a specific group or idea). Logically, the only solution to the problem is directly to address the initial sense of alienation.

4

The systems approach to crowd behaviour

INTRODUCTION

The insights of analysts such as Le Bon, Freud and Koestler take us a long way towards an understanding of the basic crowd phenomenon. However, this does not complete the process. There is one last step to take because, in order to demonstrate the importance of the crowd within the context of financial markets, it is necessary to understand how the crowd generates 'fluctuations'.

It is possible to do this thanks to the theoretical developments that have taken place in the analysis of living organisms during the last 20 years. Crucially, we can analyse the dynamics of crowd behaviour within the framework of the philosophical approach known as 'systems theory'. Such an approach – which stems from the pioneering work conducted by analysts such as Ludwig von Bertalanffy,[1] Ervin Laszlo,[2] and Erich Jantsch[3] – proceeds to a new understanding of nature by focusing on processes rather than on structures as such. Hence, each living organism is seen as being a self-organizing system, with a hierarchical structure. Each such structure is responsive to disequilibrium, open to the environment for the exchange of information and energy, and able to process information and energy. These characteristics broadly mirror Gregory Bateson's criteria for the existence of 'mind'.

In Chapter 2, it was established that – theoretically – a crowd could be regarded as having a 'mind' of its own. Furthermore, a crowd is created from living organisms. Logically, therefore, a crowd can be seen as a natural phenomenon. This, in turn, implies that a crowd is likely to be much like all other natural phenomena, in the sense of being a dynamic, fluctuating system while it is in existence. Crowd behaviour is therefore susceptible to analysis using systems theory.

NON-EQUILIBRIUM CONDITIONS

The basic catalyst for the formation of a crowd is a condition of stress, conflict or competition being experienced by more than one person simultaneously. The catalyst is a condition of 'non-equilibrium' that produces a threat of some sort. This non-equilibrium condition then provides the purpose for the creation of a crowd – namely, the alteration of the disequilibrium in order to benefit the crowd's membership. The targeted change may merely be the attraction of additional resources away from the environment (as in the case of a profit-making corporation) or it may be a more fundamental attempt to impose creative evolution on the environment (as in the case of social revolution). A crowd will continue to respond to the implicit non-equilibrium until either the crowd's purpose is achieved or (in extreme cases) the environment itself dampens down the crowd. Obviously, when a crowd's purpose is fulfilled, equilibrium exists and the crowd members will go on their way.

OPENNESS TO THE ENVIRONMENT: THE EXCHANGE OF ENERGY

In order to achieve its objectives, however, a crowd must be 'open' to the environment for the exchange of both energy and information. Energy is continually being used up by crowd members. Consequently, the loss of useful energy (known as the build-up of entropy), as individuals leave for whatever reason, has to be surmounted by continuously attracting new members to 'the cause'. The rate of addition may be greater than, equal to, or less than the rate of exhaustion or departure. Obviously, the crowd's ability to survive cannot continue if the rate of arrival of new members is less than the rate of departure. This is one of the reasons 'spontaneous' street riots rarely persist for any extended length of time, even in the absence of large-scale law enforcement.

OPENNESS TO THE ENVIRONMENT: THE EXCHANGE OF INFORMATION

This exchange of energy is complemented by an exchange of information.[4] The crowd's need to change, or manipulate, its environment for its own ends involves a continuous process of information transfer and analysis. The crowd needs to know how its achievements relate to its objectives and how the environment is responding so that counter-vailing adjustments can be made if necessary. This process therefore involves two levels of analysis:

■ the nature of the mechanism for transmitting information;

■ the inter-relationship between a crowd and its environment.

THE MECHANISM FOR TRANSMITTING INFORMATION

The nature of the information transmission mechanism is very important. Often the receipt of information from the environment, and transmission of this information, is the prerogative of whoever (or whatever) constitutes the crowd 'leader'. Essentially, however, any individual within a crowd can receive information on behalf of the whole crowd and can transmit it to the other members of the crowd. As Gustave Le Bon originally argued,[5] crowd members are in a constant state of expectant attention and are therefore vulnerable to suggestion. Moods, feelings and ideas in such an environment are, of course, very contagious and they spread rapidly. Modern, high-tech communications now ensure that the same effects can be quickly achieved even if the crowd is not assembled in one place.

However, the processes of contagion are not necessarily simplistic. Each person not only receives information and transmits it to others: they can also alter it before transmission. The alteration need not only apply to the quality of the information, it may also apply to the emotions that accompany the transmission of the information. Hence, even where the information is 'hard' data that cannot be directly altered, it will be interpreted by individuals, and will almost certainly be retransmitted in the context of an emotion (anger, greed, sadness, indifference, optimism, pessimism and so on). The end result is that crowd members all experience the same beliefs and emotions about the information that is being transmitted.

FEEDBACK LOOPS AND THE TRANSFORMATION OF INFORMATION

The idea that a crowd can process, and respond to, information in this way can usefully be described in terms of what are called 'feedback loops'. Feedback loops transform information. The process of transforming information means that there is a difference between the input of information at any stage in the loop and the output of information from the same stage (see Figure 4.1).

The resultant, changed output then becomes an input of information for the next stage. Thus, part A may affect part B, part B may affect part C, and C may feed back the (transformed) information to A. Each input of information therefore triggers a process that generates new information.[6] Interestingly, there are two possibilities here (see Figure 4.2):

Figure 4.1 Information transformation

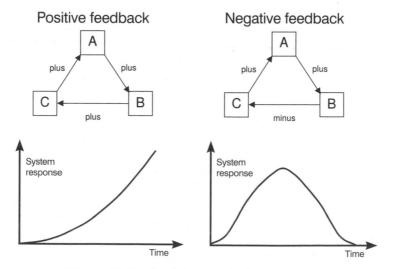

Figure 4.2 Feedback loops and adjustment paths

▌ information is given a positive gain at each stage, thereby leading to a 'runaway' system;[7]

▌ information is given a negative influence (usually by some form of 'governor') at some stage in the chain, thereby leading to an 'oscillating' system.

OSCILLATING SYSTEMS

Although the presence of a negative feedback loop always creates oscillations, it does not necessarily generate stable ones. In fact, it may generate one of three types of oscillation – namely, damped, stable or unstable. These three possibilities are shown in Figure 4.3.

THE ROLE OF THE CROWD LEADER

Within any group, the role of the 'governor' is essentially performed by the group leadership. The leadership ensures (or tries to ensure) that group behaviour is either magnified by means of positive feedback or damped down by negative feedback. Where the leadership acts to damp down the oscillations of a group, that group

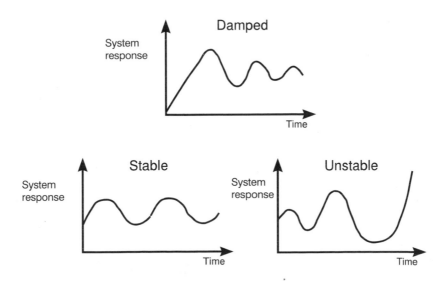

Figure 4.3 Oscillations found in negative feedback loops

operates harmoniously with its environment. Such behaviour is typical of bureaucratic organizations. Obviously, however, there are occasions when the leadership attempts to magnify the oscillations of the group. This is, perhaps, the defining characteristic of a 'crowd'. The leadership will have a vested interest in magnifying the friction created by members under its control simply because the intention is to change the environment in a fundamental way.

Under circumstances of destabilizing oscillations, the environment (that is, society) itself will attempt to protect its own autonomy by suppressing the 'runaway' behaviour of the crowd: this is the basis of police riot control. However, at an extreme, a mob may enforce evolution via revolution.

THE INTERRELATIONSHIP BETWEEN A CROWD AND ITS ENVIRONMENT

In this sense, change and 'progress' come about as a result of a dynamic interplay, both between individuals and the group to which they belong, and between a group and its environment. Any conflict creates compensating adjustments. First, therefore, it is true to say that the progressive development of any overall system is determined partly by the creative components within it. For example, cultural development in any society is the result of the interplay of creative free thinking and conservative traditions. The larger whole will invariably seek to damp down the smaller parts, but ultimately the smaller parts must have an impact on the whole if any form of progress is to be achieved. Recent cases in point are the Women's Movement and ecologically oriented groups such as Greenpeace.

Second, independent fluctuations in the environment itself can lead to a number of different responses by a crowd. Initially, a change in the environment imposes stress on the group or crowd. The group is therefore unable to respond properly and it seeks to stabilize itself by changing its metabolism.[8] Hence, for example, an established company faced with falling sales will respond by accepting lower profits, an increase in bank overdrafts and a rise in stock levels.

Subsequently, of course, the group will 'acclimatize' itself to enduring changes in the environment by adjusting its operating ability without actually changing its structure.[9] Hence, a company faced with falling sales would eventually need to take positive action in terms of a cutback in its operations if it was to survive.

Ultimately, the group may adapt to permanent changes in the environment as a result of 'revolutionary' changes. The group moves to a new, but stable, operating structure; in particular, the objectives of the group are altered.[10] Inevitably, therefore, a company that either anticipated, or was faced with, a permanent decline in demand for its products would have to diversify its operations if it were to stop itself from going out of business. The importance of timing in this process is covered in a little more detail in Chapter 9.

It is interesting to note the relationship between chance and necessity in this view of evolution. According to the old Darwinian view, chance mutation is followed by the survival of the fittest. However, from the newer systems viewpoint, chance and necessity are complementary principles. The initial perturbation that creates the instability in the system may appear to be random from the system's point of view,[11] but the need to survive forces the system to adapt. The system, in a sense, makes its own decisions about the nature of its new structure. Evolution is thus the unfolding of order and complexity in the process of learning.

CONCLUSION

To summarize the analysis of this chapter, we may argue as follows: any human grouping – specifically, a crowd – is part of the hierarchical structure of nature; and each crowd can be defined in terms of its processes rather than its physical characteristics. Theoretically, these processes are triggered by differences (or non-equilibrium conditions), utilize feedback loops and therefore involve oscillations. The processes are continually energized by the crowd's access to the environment and are sufficiently complicated to facilitate some degree of 'self-knowledge'. Energy and self-knowledge, in turn, contribute to the crowd's ability to be self-organizing. Self-organization involves the control of the crowd's members, and this enables the crowd to maintain its autonomy as well as to learn, adapt and evolve. In somewhat technical language, we have described the behavioural characteristics of Le Bon's 'crowd'.

NOTES

1.   von Bertalanffy, Ludwig (1968) *General Systems Theory: Foundation, development, applications*, Braziller, New York.
2.   Laszlo, Ervin (1972) *Introduction to Systems Philosophy: Towards a new paradigm of contemporary thought*, Gordon and Breach, New York.
3.   Jantsch, Erich (1980) *The Self-organizing Universe*, Pergamon, Oxford.
4.   The environment 'recognizes' a crowd by responding both to the difference made by that crowd's initial presence and to the difference made by its subsequent activities; while the crowd itself 'recognizes' its own existence by responding to the resulting differences in the environment.
5.   Le Bon, Gustave, *Psychologie des Foules*, reprinted (1922) as *The Crowd*, Macmillan, New York.
6.   Such systems are called 'autocatalytic'.
7.   The growth may be either exponential or hyperbolic. Exponential growth results in increases that are proportional to the amount present and in which the doubling time remains constant. Hyperbolic growth results in increases that are the square of the amount present and in which the doubling time is halved with every doubling.
8.   Metabolism means those chemical changes occurring in living organisms that are essential to sustain life.
9.   Such 'somatic' changes, however, are not necessarily permanent because they are reversible. Consequently, the changes generally amount to an internalization of stress.
10.   Fluctuations in the components, caused by environmental changes, are reinforced by feedback loops. The system is then driven into a new structure by 'order through fluctuation'. Jantsch, Erich, op. cit.
11.   The perturbation is usually part of a larger cyclical fluctuation. However, it appears to the lower-level structures as a shock (see Chapter 5).

5

Cycles in the crowd

INTRODUCTION

The important feature of any self-organizing system, whether it be a crowd or a living organism, is that it oscillates during the transfer of energy and information. Indeed, the presence of continuous fluctuations can be taken as prima-facie evidence of the presence of 'mental' activity (as defined by Gregory Bateson). There are, however, different types of oscillation that need to be distinguished, and we shall look at each of these in turn.

THE LIFE CYCLE

The first point to make is that every crowd has both a beginning and an end. There will be a time before the crowd existed and there will be a time after it has disappeared. In other words, each crowd has a life cycle. Life cycles essentially consist of three phases (see Figure 5.1):

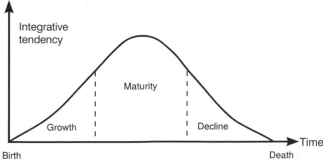

Figure 5.1 The life cycle of a crowd

▌ growth;

▌ maturity;

▌ decline.

Birth and growth

Crowds initially come into being as a result of both a change that creates a change (that is, an item of information affects a group of people) and an ability to respond purposefully to that change.[1] Once a crowd with common values and a common objective has been established, it will then respond positively to the input of new items of information from the environment. In particular, it will draw a dynamic response from the most creative elements of the crowd, especially from the crowd leadership.[2] During the growth stage of its life cycle, a crowd is completely able to maintain its integrity, even in the face of a hostile environment.

Maturity

At maturity, however, the crowd becomes self-orientated and therefore inflexible. It is able to feel comfortable, basking in the glow of its achievements, and will therefore seek to control the creativity of its smaller parts rather than the other way round. Consequently, low-level fluctuations are quickly suppressed.

Decline and death

Eventually, however, this rigidity will mean that the crowd is unable to adjust any further to changes in the environment. The expectations of the crowd are unchanging, and increasingly become divergent from actual events. There then begins a decline that is marked by internal discord, uncertain leadership and hostility towards that leadership. Ultimately comes the shock that causes the crowd members to part from each other entirely.

The life cycle is thus complete, and individuals are released to participate in other groups, or crowds. Hence generation and degeneration are succeeded by regeneration in a continuous process.

Information and the life cycle

It is apparent that the receipt of an item of information by a crowd will have a different effect depending on the stage of its life cycle. Bad weather, for example, may stimulate the resolve of pickets in the early stages of a dispute or it may encourage them to pack up and go home if the cause already appears to be lost. Invasion of one country by another may stimulate heroic resistance or passive acceptance. Innovations may be enthusiastically embraced (as in the case of microchips) or vehemently opposed (as in the case of the Luddite riots).

CO-EVOLUTION

We have seen that natural dynamic systems process information by using feedback loops. The essential feature of life (as we know it) is that it uses negative feedback loops and therefore generates continuous fluctuations. In essence, negative feedback loops are designed to allow any self-organizing system (including a crowd) to cope with changes in its environment so that it can survive. Indeed, there are two options open to it:

▌ it can seek to correct the original change in the environment directly;

▌ it can change itself to meet the change.

In either case, there is a mutual development in the system and the environment.

This mutual development involves an interesting and important concept – namely that of 'co-evolution'. The early work on the subject was conducted by Vito Volterra in 1926, and was then extended by Alfred Lotka[3] in 1956. Their basic theory centred on the existence of a complementary development between predators and their prey: predators respond to changes in both the quantity and quality of their prey, but the prey species constantly introduce countervailing measures to outwit the predators' developments. Hence, neither side wins, and both survive.

The theory was subsequently developed into a more complete theory of co-evolution by the American biologists Paul Ehrlich and Peter Raven[4] in 1965. They argued that there is a mutual complementarity between different levels of any hierarchical structure: lower-level changes could not occur without higher-level changes, and higher-level changes could not develop without lower-level changes.

In 1979, James Lovelock[5] sought to extend the basic analysis to the idea that the whole of the Earth's biosphere has developed into its current form by virtue of co-evolution between living organisms and their environment. For example, life could not have been created by the so-called Big Bang if the necessary fundamental elements had not already been in existence, yet neither could it have been created out of the basic elements if the Big Bang had not occurred. Now, of course, oxygen-breathing/carbon dioxide-creating animals could not live without oxygen-creating/carbon dioxide-using plants. The eternal 'chicken and egg' paradox is resolved by the concept of complementary and simultaneous development.

LIMIT CYCLES

The theory of co-evolution relies on the fact that the relevant feedback loops generate stable fluctuations between a particular system and a higher-order system. Actually, and more precisely, this relationship exists between a particular system and a niche in the higher-order system. Mathematicians have a name for these stable fluctuations – 'limit cycles'.[6]

The term 'limit' relates to the fact that the system oscillates within specific parameters, and the term 'cycle' refers to the fact that the oscillations continually return to the same point of departure.[7] If the limit cycle is stable, the oscillations will spiral on to the solution path from a wide range of initial states. If, on the other hand, the cycle is unstable, a disturbance will cause the oscillations to spiral away from that solution path. It follows that co-evolving systems utilize stable limit cycles (see Figure 5.2).

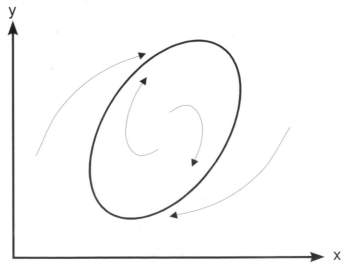

Figure 5.2 Idealized stable limit cycle

Each limit cycle expresses the relationship between two specific variables: as one variable moves, so does the other. In Figures 5.2 and 5.3, the variables are represented as x and y. However, within the context of our current analysis, we could assume that the y axis represents an index of crowd behaviour and that the x axis represents an index of environmental change. As presented, the limit cycle does not actually take a circular shape on the two-dimensional x–y surface (known as the 'phase plane'); nor does it need to do so. It may be oval or elliptical, as well as circular. The important point is that the oscillations occur between predetermined upper and lower limits, and these limits determine the amplitude of the cycle.

LIMIT CYCLES THROUGH TIME

A moment's reflection will reveal that the two-dimensional limit cycle relating x and y (or the environment and the crowd) actually unfolds over time. In other words, the cycle effectively operates in three dimensions. Let us assume that the limit cycle unfolds at a constant rate over time and so include 'time' as the third dimension in a diagram. Then the solution path takes the form of a cylinder (see Figure 5.3).

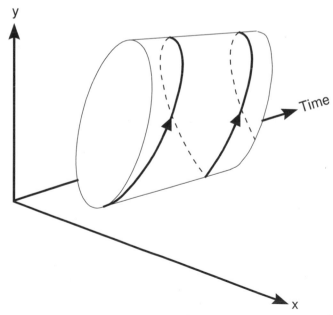

Figure 5.3 Three-dimensional limit cycle

Furthermore, if we now change the perspective of the diagram, and collapse one of the x–y dimensions (say x, which corresponds to the environmental change), then the resulting solution path yields a regular cyclical pattern in the other variable (y, which corresponds to crowd behaviour). Successive peaks will occur at regular intervals, as will successive troughs (see Figure 5.4). The regularity of the intervals between peaks and troughs defines the periodicity of the cycle. However, because a limit cycle can take any number of forms, there is no reason for the shape of the cycle to be balanced around the peaks and troughs: the up phase of the cycle may be longer or shorter than the down phase. If we collapse the time dimension, of course, we are returned to the basic limit cycle.

LIMIT CYCLES IN NATURE

There is, in fact, substantial evidence that limit cycles occur throughout nature. The human body, for example, literally pulsates with the rhythms of limit cycle fluctuations: the heart beats regularly; the neural activity of the brain proceeds in bursts of pulses;[8] the activity of breathing is rhythmical. Furthermore, Professor Rex Hersey of the University of Pennsylvania found that each individual has a personalized emotional cycle lasting for an average of 35 days.[9]

In each case, lower-level systems are oscillating regularly in harmony with each other and with the higher-level system (which is

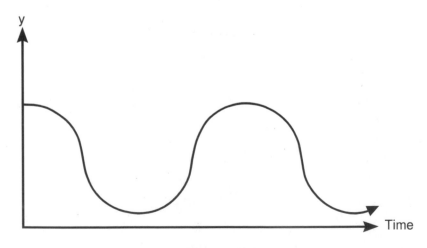

Figure 5.4 Two-dimensional limit cycle

the body itself). In turn, the metabolism of the body is integrated with the wider environment. There is, for example, a natural metabolic rate of activity and rest that harmonizes with the day/night cycle. Hence, the rate of urine production peaks each day at around the same time,[10] and the ability of the blood to coagulate on a wound is lowest in the morning. Furthermore, the rate of body metabolism is generally higher during the spring and summer than it is during the autumn and winter. It appears, in fact, that subtle electromagnetic changes in the geophysical environment induce electrochemical changes in the human body.[11]

MULTIPLE LIMIT CYCLES

There are three important features of all natural cycles. First, cycles at all levels of the hierarchy will harmonize with one another as the processes of nature do not allow discord. Second, each different hierarchical level has a different time dimension attached to it, so that higher-level cycles take longer to develop than do their lower-level counterparts. Third, the trend of each lower-degree cycle is formed by a higher-degree cycle. The situation can be presented as in Figure 5.5. For simplicity, it is assumed that only two levels of limit cycle exist, although in theory any number of levels could be included. Figure 5.5

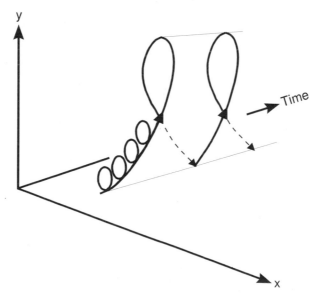

Figure 5.5 Two-limit cycles in three dimensions

shows a small, short-term cycle integrated with a larger, longer-term cycle in three-dimensional space. As before, the three dimensions could be an index of crowd behaviour, of environmental change and of time. The short-run fluctuations continue throughout each complete long-run cycle.

MULTIPLE CYCLES IN TWO DIMENSIONS

In order to obtain a clearer picture of this theoretical construct, we can visualize it in two dimensions: first, by collapsing the 'time' dimension while keeping the other two dimensions unchanged; second, by collapsing the x (or 'environment') dimension while keeping the other two dimensions unchanged (see Figure 5.6). The effect of higher-level fluctuations on the lower-level fluctuations should be perfectly clear.

THE IMPACT OF SHOCKS

Although limit cycles are the main mechanism whereby a self-organizing system copes with fluctuations in its environment, they do not fully represent the adjustment processes that are involved. By definition, items of information become available only in discontinuous or discrete time intervals. The adjustment process depends on whether or not the recipient system is prepared for the information. If the information is expected, then the system can adjust very quickly to

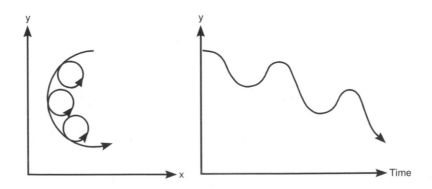

Figure 5.6 Two-limit cycles in two dimensions

suit the changed circumstances. If, however, the information is unfamiliar to the system when it is received,[12] then that information impacts as a shock and the system may have to change its dynamic structure in order to cope.

The concept of shocks as applied to group behaviour is not a new one. As early as 1933, Ragnar Frisch[13] sought to show that business cycles could be simulated by subjecting a linear model to random shocks. However, the theme being developed in this book presents a substantially different view of the world from that visualized by Frisch and many subsequent economic theorists. In particular, cyclical behaviour is here seen as an intrinsic part of nature, whereas the classical view of economics assumes linear behaviour that would converge on a 'steady state' if it were not upset by exogenous changes, such as strikes, crop shortages, changes in government policy, changes in tastes and so forth.

In practice, then, shocks are delivered to systems that are already oscillating in a limit cycle pattern with their niche in the environment. The situation can be viewed as a 'family' of limit cycles operating in three-dimensional space. Each subsystem bears a limit cycle relationship with a higher system; each higher system has a limit cycle relationship with its local environment; the local environment has a limit cycle relationship with the global environment. Divergences between lower-level cycles and higher-level cycles are rectified by shocks, and the lower-level cycle will then move to meet the upper-level cycle.

THE PROFILE OF SHOCKS

The important feature of the analysis of shocks is the form taken by the subsequent adjustment process. First, a shock delivered to a lower subsystem destabilizes the relationship between that subsystem and a higher-level system. Second, every attempt by the subsystem to re-establish its original relationship will now be met by a countervailing response from the higher system. Third (and as a consequence), every adjustment by the higher system will result in an additional response from the subsystem. Fourth, these fluctuations will continue at least until the limit cycle of the next higher degree is able to reassert control.[14]

This process of adjustment in three-dimensional space reveals itself as a spiral (see Figure 5.7). Such a spiral could, for example, materialize after a crowd had initially been 'born' and was moving towards a stable relationship with its environment. Alternatively, it could

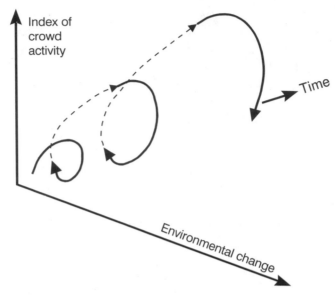

Figure 5.7 The spiral adjustment process

represent the adjustment processes within the crowd as it responded to an externally imposed shock.

SHOCKS IN TWO DIMENSIONS

If we now review the solution path in two dimensions, two familiar patterns emerge (see Figure 5.8). First, we have a spiral formation between x (which could be, for example, an index of environmental change) and y (which could be an index of crowd activity). Second, we have an unstable cycle, involving either x or y through time. As we shall see in Part Two of this book, these two patterns are of profound importance to our analysis.

SOME INSIGHTS INTO SOCIAL CHANGE

The dynamics of hierarchical crowd systems therefore involve three types of oscillation:

▮   the life cycles of the crowd systems involved;

▮   the limit cycles;

▮   the unstable fluctuations.

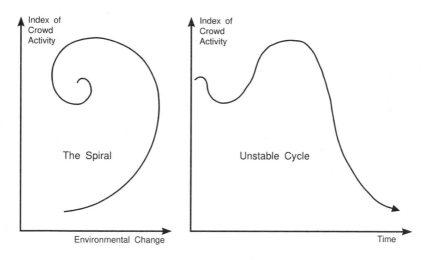

Figure 5.8 The adjustment process in two dimensions

During the life cycle of any particular crowd, its own internal cycles are bound by the requirements of higher-level oscillations, and divergences are rectified by shocks. This conclusion leads us to a number of important insights into social and economic developments. The first is that, because higher-level cycles are often so slow to develop, the social and geophysical environments usually appear static and immutable to the majority of participants. Individuals do not therefore recognize that changes have taken place until some form of catastrophe occurs. Revolutions, large-scale population migrations and wars are invariably the results of complicated changes that have been developing over long periods of time. However, they are often triggered by apparently 'local' causes or even by relatively insignificant events. The resulting gap between personal expectations and the reality of the situation invariably adds to the chaos by imposing stress and uncertainty on individuals in unfamiliar circumstances.

The second implication is that some of the events that are usually assumed to be random (such as the 'acts of God' invoked by insurance companies) may, in fact, be predictable. It will always be difficult to forecast the exact timing and location of some events, but this does not mean it is impossible to forecast that they will occur within specific time frames. There is now substantial evidence to suggest that such diverse occurrences as wars,[15] earthquakes and climatic changes exhibit cyclical behaviour. Most individuals do not recognize the rhythmic nature of the phenomena because they are exposed to their consequences irregularly, if at all, in the course of a single lifetime.

However, the concept of cyclical fluctuations in the hierarchy of nature implicitly confirms that apparently irregular events are more regular than we care to suppose.

Third, the analysis highlights the fact that short-term and long-term developments are intricately related to one another. Evolution occurs at all levels, and in all degrees, in a largely complementary fashion. Consequently, the difference between short-term cycles and long-term trends is not one that only involves quantity, but one that also involves quality. In other words, dynamic structures are continually changing in a largely irreversible fashion between one situation and another. As each short-run cycle swings down, the quantitative retracement of the previous rise is not entirely matched by a reversal in qualitative changes. Even in the case of a simple heartbeat, for example, there is a subtle ageing process between one beat and another. In the case of economic activity, each quantitative cycle in inventories (or stock levels) is accompanied by important changes in the quality of the investment. 'All change,' it is said, 'is growth; and growth is life!'

NOTES

1. This raises an interesting point. A crowd can only form in response to the receipt of information that gives the crowd a purpose; but the concept of purpose presupposes that individuals are in some way pre-programmed to recognize the validity of a specific objective. Each individual has to be able to place the information in a context that triggers their integrative tendency: the one is impotent without the other. Contexts are essentially learnt either directly or through genetic transmission. This confirms the need for learnt common values to ensure that societies survive. It also confirms the 'biological' nature of crowd behaviour.
2. If necessary, new common values and traditions will emerge that will ensure the stability of the crowd.
3. Lotka, Alfred J (1956) *Elements of Mathematical Biology*, Dover Publications, New York.
4. See Jantsch, Erich (1980) *The Self-organizing Universe*, Pergamon, Oxford.
5. Lovelock, James E (1979) *Gaia*, Oxford University Press, Oxford.
6. A limit cycle is defined as the (isolated) periodic oscillation between two variables, and is represented graphically by an (isolated) closed non-linear path. See, for example, Jordan, D W, and Smith, P (1977) *Non-linear Ordinary Differential Equations*, Oxford University Press, Oxford.
7. The time between successive troughs or successive peaks is known as the periodicity of the cycle.
8. Freeman, Walter J (1975) *Mass Action in the Nervous System*, Academic Press, New York.
9. Hersey, R B (1931) 'Emotional cycles of man', *Journal of Mental Science*. Hersey found that the cycle of each individual, taken separately, varied quite markedly from the average: some had cycles of 16 days, others had cycles of as

long as 63 days. The important point, however, is that each individual had a personalized cycle that persisted over the sampling period.

10.   Watson, Lyall (1973) *Supernature*, Hodder & Stoughton, London.

11.   There is an expanding body of literature that records the striking correlation between electromagnetic fluctuations in the solar system, electromagnetic fluctuations in the Earth's biosphere and electrochemical changes in the human body. The implication is that we are more influenced by events such as sunspot cycles and lunar cycles than we sometimes care to believe. See, for example, Gaugelin, Michael (1973) *The Cosmic Clocks*, Granada, London.

12.   That is, there is no previous context within which to place the information.

13.   Frisch, Ragnar, 'Propagation problems and impulse problems in dynamic economics', in (1933) *Essays in Honour of Gustav Cassel*, George Allen & Unwin, London.

14.   During the adjustment process, the upper-level cycle does not therefore accurately reflect the trend of the lower cycle.

15.   Some of the evidence for the striking phenomenon of cycles in warfare is discussed in Dewey, Edward R, with Mandino, Og (1971) *Cycles: The mysterious forces that trigger events*, Hawthorn, New York.

6

Approaches to forecasting crowd behaviour

INTRODUCTION

The idea that behaviour in financial markets is essentially a crowd phenomenon is the basis of a comprehensive approach to accurate forecasting in equity, bond and foreign exchange markets. At one extreme, a self-aware individual is potentially unpredictable except within the very broadest of guidelines. However, at the other extreme, people, as a group, are predictable. This is the essence of the crowd phenomenon, and it implies that price movements in financial markets are also intrinsically predictable.

RANDOM OR NON-RANDOM

First, however, it is necessary to demonstrate that price movements in financial markets do display some form of underlying order – that is, it is necessary to demonstrate that price movements are not always and everywhere just random fluctuations. This is a difficult task, because the issue of randomness or non-randomness in financial markets is still the subject of academic debate. But we need to get a general sense of the phenomenon in order to assess whether there is a case for assuming that tradable price trends exist and forecastable price patterns reproduce themselves. At this stage of the analysis, however, all that is necessary is that we look at the subject pragmatically, without going into a detailed discussion of statistical theory, in order to get a sense of the underlying phenomenon.[1]

PRICE MOVEMENTS IN THE DOW

Non-random behaviour exists in a financial market if the price movement over one period of time is related in some predictable way to the price movement over a previous period of time. However, there are two elements to this statement: one is the time periods being used (for example, one day or one month) and the other is the time elapse between the periods that are being compared (for example, today with yesterday or this month with the same month last year). Here we shall only be dealing with the influence of contiguous time periods, not with the time elapse between them, because we need to focus on continuity rather than discontinuity.

The analysis that follows concentrates on the movements between the daily closes in the Dow Jones Industrial Average Index over various periods of time. The current time period will be denoted 'time t' and will be plotted on the vertical axis of each chart, and the relevant previous time period will be denoted 'time $(t-1)$' and will be plotted on the horizontal axis of each chart. The result is that movements in the Dow are plotted in what can be called 't/$(t-1)$ phase space'.

Figure 6.1 plots each day's percentage change in the Dow against the previous day's percentage change, for every trading day between 2 January 2005 and 31 October 2005. The result is exactly the sort of pattern that could be expected if daily movements were random – that is, they are scattered widely throughout the phase space. It is not possible to predict from one location where the t/$(t-1)$ price combination will move to next. So, it does not appear possible to predict what might happen tomorrow from what has happened today.

This conclusion does not change if the analysis is extended to cover longer periods of time. Figure 6.2 goes back further in time, to cover the period from January 1990 to October 2005 inclusive. In fact, the longer time period ensures that additional extreme price movements are captured. So, the more complete the data, the stronger is the apparent evidence for randomness. However, an increase in the

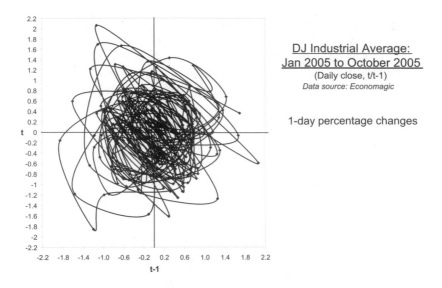

Figure 6.1 The Dow, January to October 2005

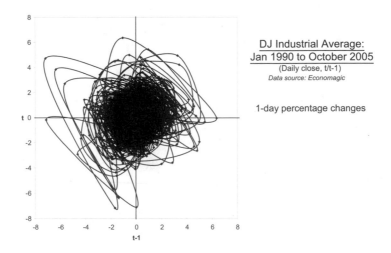

Figure 6.2 The Dow, January 1990 to October 2005

number of observations has caused something quite interesting to emerge: the price movements are tending to concentrate in a specific area in the $t/(t-1)$ phase space. In this case, by far and away the largest number of daily price movements do not exceed 4 per cent.

This conclusion becomes even more obvious if the horizontal and vertical axes of the chart are significantly extended by quadrupling the scale (see Figure 6.3). By widening our perspective in this way, it becomes very obvious that there is some form of natural limitation on day-to-day price movements. These movements tend not to move out beyond a very specific two-dimensional region in t/(t − 1) phase space. Nor does this conclusion change much if the data set is expanded even further. Figure 6.4 shows the period from January 1946 to October 2005 inclusive, with the same highs and lows on the axes as were used in Figure 6.3. This time period therefore includes the Equity Crash of October 1987. The chart clearly picks out the

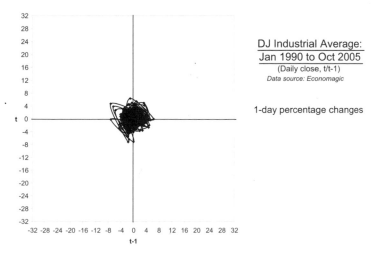

Figure 6.3 The Dow, January 1990 to October 2005

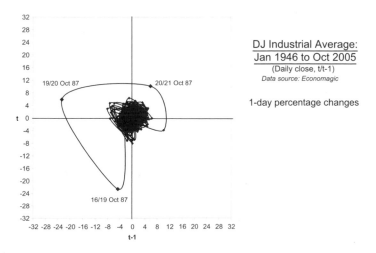

Figure 6.4 The Dow, January 1946 to October 2005

experience of 16 to 20 October; but it also emphasizes the fact that the change in prices was quickly pulled back into the central mass. In this context, the 1987 Crash event looks idiosyncratic. Hence, not only are there natural boundaries to price changes in a particular market but also, if price movements break those boundaries, they are pulled back within them. In a sense, therefore, randomness could be defined in terms of price movements that break beyond natural boundaries.

One important inference from this is that randomness has something to do with perspective: the longer the time perspective being taken (or, if you like, the broader the context), the less likely it is that fluctuations will seem random. Anyone who has traded in financial markets for any length of time will know when a price movement is 'unusual', based on his or her experience.

STRANGE ATTRACTORS

The areas in phase space that exert some form of gravitational pull on activity are now called 'strange attractors'.[2] A strange attractor is a pattern in phase space that is traced out by a dynamic system. The centre of the pattern is analogous to the centre of an orbit, and the pattern itself has the potential to be mathematically defined. Hence, a strange attractor is the stable path of behaviour within an apparently turbulent system. As James Gleick observes, in the short term any point in phase space can represent a possible behaviour for the system, but in the longer term the only possible behaviour is the attractor itself.[3]

There is a strong sense, therefore, that the boundaried behaviour of price movements in the Dow is consistent with the presence of a strange attractor. So let us take the argument a stage further and look at the price changes over periods that are longer than one day. Figure 6.5 shows an example of the five-day percentage changes in the Dow, in $t/(t-1)$ phase space. Here, the five-day percentage change for a particular day (at time t) is compared with the five-day percentage change the previous day (time $(t-1)$). What is clear is that the formerly circular 'bubble' containing price movements begins to spread out along an upward-sloping diagonal line. The 1987 Equity Crash is still obviously there and, again, it stands out as being unusual. But by far and away the largest number of the $t/(t-1)$ data points are contained within a price change range of 8 per cent.

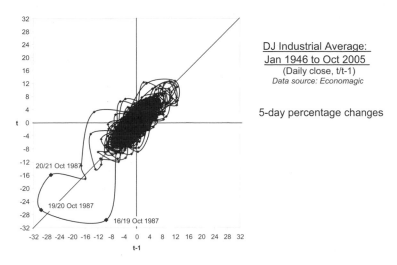

Figure 6.5 The Dow, January 1946 to October 2005

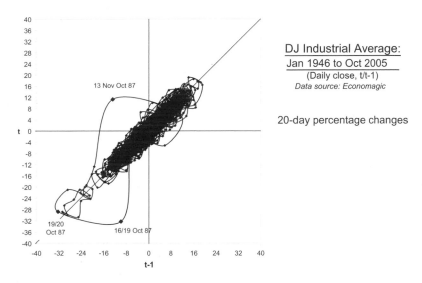

Figure 6.6 The Dow, January 1946 to October 2005

This phenomenon then becomes even more pronounced over longer time periods. Figure 6.6 shows 20-day percentage changes in the Dow, in $t/(t-1)$ phase space. Here, although the upper and lower boundaries for the price changes increase to 16 per cent, the deviation from the diagonal line contracts. Again, the 1987 Equity Crash stands out as being an unusual event, but the vast majority of $t/(t-1)$ relationships stay within a boundaried area. In other words, 20-day price changes for time t tend towards equivalence with price changes at time $(t-1)$.

PREDICTABLE PRICE MOVEMENTS

This conclusion is profound. It means that, despite short-term turbulence, movements in the Dow tend towards a stable path of change over longer time periods. In other words, price movements in the Dow do have a basic element of predictability in them. But there is another – equally important – point that emerges from the analysis. This is that price movements are persistently induced to accelerate and decelerate along their equilibrium path. We can hypothesize that investors chase the market higher until some form of upper boundary is reached, and then chase the market down until some form of lower boundary is reached. Not only is this highly suggestive of a deep-running ordered process at work, but it is also consistent with the idea that oscillations in financial markets have a cyclical rhythm. In other words, price movements are theoretically predictable.

METHODS OF PREDICTING PRICE MOVEMENTS

However, deciding that financial markets are predictable is not the same thing as deciding how such prediction may be arrived at. In essence, there are two main lines of thought. The first is that financial market prices ultimately reflect fundamental values in the economy. According to this view, financial prices are determined by actual and expected developments concerning these values, and forecasting financial prices is therefore a matter of forecasting fundamentals.[4] The second view is that most of the actual and expected information concerning fundamental values is already discounted by the market at any given point in time. Hence, market price movements tend to forecast developments in fundamental values, and forecasting financial market prices therefore becomes a matter of deciding what the market is already 'saying' about itself.

ECONOMIC FORECASTING

Despite the fact that political and social trends often have to be taken into account, forecasting financial markets on the basis of fundamentals is essentially the province of economics.

Economic theory argues that the price of any asset is determined by the interaction of demand and supply – that is, the price will rise if demand rises or supply falls; and the price will fall if demand falls or supply rises. Hence, the main task of an economist is to isolate the forces that will influence the demand for, and supply of, financial assets over time. The main tools are economic theory itself and statistics – the former to provide the logical framework and the latter to provide some form of quantification to the analysis and conclusions.[5]

PROBLEMS WITH ECONOMIC FORECASTING

The different theories concerning the specific relationships involved will not be discussed here as they are beyond the scope of this book. However, it is worthwhile commenting briefly on the methodology involved.

The analytical procedures used in economics are still steeped in the traditions of 'reductionism' (which we discussed in Chapter 1). These procedures presume that it is possible to understand all aspects of a complicated economic system by breaking it down into its constituent parts. As a result, economic models tend to be simple aggregates of mathematically independent equations and 'closed' systems that are divorced from the wider environment in which they operate. However, even if such models are accurate descriptions of the area of activity that they seek to represent, there are two immediate sources of forecasting error. First, there are no automatic feedback loops between the model and its environment.[6] Consequently, the internal relationships in the model gradually break down over time. Second, the assumptions about the environment – which are made by the forecaster to drive the model – are, of course, subject to human error.

These 'technical' problems with forecasting are, of course, clearly recognized by economic practitioners and great efforts have been made to compensate for them, both by building increasingly bigger (computer) models to embrace 'the environment' and by introducing ever more complicated submodels to deal with apparent idiosyncracies. Unfortunately, however, it is not yet clearly recognized that the fault can lie not in the incompleteness of the models, but in the structure of those models.

PROBLEMS WITH THE CONCEPTUAL FRAMEWORK

The essential problem is that economic models reflect a particular belief system (or view) about the way that the world operates. They incorporate a conviction that objects that can be differentiated from one another are also dissociated from one another unless a significant relationship can immediately be observed.[7] The problem, therefore, is not just one of inadequate techniques that can be justified on the grounds of simplicity; the problem is specifically one of understanding.

Unfortunately, the conviction that boundaries can only be perceived because the delineated objects are independent of one another is so embedded in the 'Western' way of thinking that it is difficult to see how it can be properly superseded; and the results are turning out to be disastrous:

▌ the mind becomes separated from the body and its emotions;[8]

▌ the body is separated from the wider environment and the latter is therefore seen as a potential threat;

▌ because of the role of memory,[9] the psyche not only uses static concepts to describe the world but also sees all relationships as being essentially linear and uni-directional.

The human ego therefore faces a dual illusion. On the one hand, its sense of isolation induces fear and a desire to control the environment. On the other hand, its conceptual tools encourage a belief that it can control the environment. It is in no way surprising, therefore, that economic models – the prime purpose of which is to assist in controlling the material environment – intrinsically incorporate the problems that stimulate the desire to control. Indeed, economic models do not always help with understanding reality. They instead only reflect pre-established beliefs about reality. Structural assumptions are regarded as being the 'truth' and the map is therefore mistaken for the territory.[10]

As a result, there are three significant criticisms that can be levelled against modern economic theory:[11]

▌ it tends to believe (and not just assume) that individuals behave mechanistically and, therefore, in a linear fashion;[12]

▌ it does not recognize that individuals are profoundly influenced by the activities of other people;

▌ it denies the influence of swings in sentiment.[13]

As a result, modern economics fails to recognize clearly that the combination of all economic activities transmutes into a cohesive, oscillating system with its own set of characteristics.

THE RATIONAL EXPECTATIONS HYPOTHESIS

The central point at issue here is economics' belief in the dominance of rational behaviour in human affairs. Indeed, in the last 20 years or so, this belief has been progressively refined into the hypothesis of rationally formed expectations.[14] This hypothesis is based on three interlinked assumptions:

▌ individuals do not behave irrationally – for example, they will not ordinarily put their hand in a fire;

▌ individuals learn from their mistakes – that is, if they burn themselves by putting their hand in the fire, then they will not willingly put their hand in again;

▌ individuals arrive at their decisions independently of one another – that is, they do not put their hands in the fire simply because someone else does so, or tells them to do so.

According to this analysis, group behaviour is simply the aggregate of rational behaviour by all individuals.

However, it does not take much insight to realize that the rational expectations hypothesis fails to provide a rigorous analysis either of economic booms and slumps or of speculative excesses in financial markets.[15] Rational expectations cannot, by virtue of its central assumption of independent decision making, explain why people's expectations converge on a common consensus that is inherently destabilizing. There must be a reason for people to do the same thing at the same time. And there must be a reason for people to do strange things at the same time. How, for example, can events such as the Dutch 'tulip mania' of 1634[16] be regarded as the outcome of rational decisions made by independent individuals? There must, in short, be a very good reason for markets to diverge from perceived fundamentals for sustained periods of time.

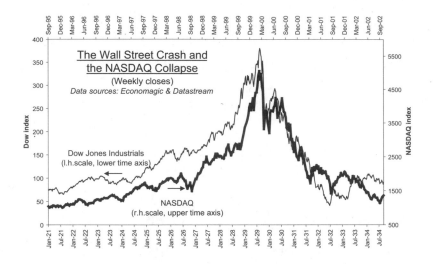

Figure 6.7 Bubble and crash in the Dow and the NASDAQ

BUBBLES AND CRASHES

Part of the answer may be found in the similarities between markets that have 'bubbled' and then crashed. Figure 6.7, for example, shows the loci of price action in both the Dow Jones Industrial Average from January 1921 to July 1934 and the NASDAQ Index between September 1995 and September 2002. The time periods involved are obviously different: the former covers a period of over 13 years, while the latter covers a period of seven years. However, when the time elapse relating to the Dow is placed on the lower horizontal axis and the time elapse of the NASDAQ is placed on the upper horizontal axis, the pattern of acceleration into their respective peaks and the patterns of their subsequent collapses are very similar. The collapses are the Wall Street Crash of 1929–32 and the NASDAQ Crash of 2000–02.

Importantly, this similarity is not an isolated event. Figure 6.8 shows the performance of the Nikkei Stock Index between January 1970 and April 2004 and then overlays on it the behaviour of the NASDAQ Index between November 1984 and October 2005. The long, slow build-up is readily apparent in both indices. Then comes the clear start of an acceleration that takes both markets into a peak. And then comes the collapse. The patterns are almost identical – at least in terms of the big moves. It is only after the collapse that the markets start to produce divergent patterns.

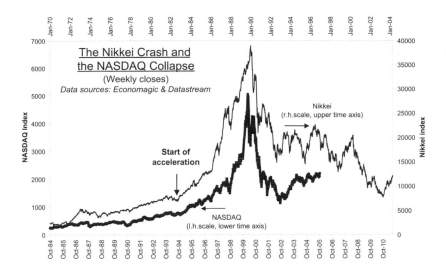

Figure 6.8 Bubble and crash in the Nikkei and the NASDAQ

NON-LINEAR MATHEMATICS

These similarities have been recognized by Didier Sornette, a professor of geophysics at UCLA. In 2003, Sornette demonstrated how non-linear mathematics can track a stock market bubble and predict the subsequent crash.[17] He arrived at two distinct conclusions: 1) the price acceleration into the final peak of a bubble is curvilinear, and the time elapse of oscillations around that accelerating trend gets progressively shorter; and 2) this phenomenon only works because of the impact of 'cooperative self-organization'. In other words, non-linear mathematics can predict the timing of the peak (because oscillations become so fast that they effectively converge on zero), but such non-linear mathematics only work because stock markets are 'natural' systems, derived from the influence of the crowd.

THE CHALLENGE TO ECONOMIC THEORY

Didier Sornette's analysis provides a direct challenge to economic theory, not only in terms of providing a mechanism that explains stock market excesses, but also right down at the level of basic assumptions about personal motivation. And he is not alone. In recent years, the subject has received detailed attention from a host of psychologists, and the conclusions are not in accord with the assumptions (and beliefs) of theoretical economists. The rich variety of potential responses, processed through the dimensions of logic and intuition, is now well attested. How then can economists assert that people acting independently of one another will tend to respond, on average, in a scientifically reproducible way to particular stimuli?

Economics' own (technical) answer is statistical. According to the so-called 'law of large numbers', which we mentioned in Chapter 1, a large number of apparently random and unrelated events produces an outcome that is predictable. Interestingly, however, the reason the law of large numbers actually works is usually ignored. It is taken as being a law of nature and left at that. However, the law hints at something both amazing and important: it suggests that order develops out of random fluctuations. In other words, unpredictable behaviour by individuals converges on predictable behaviour by groups, not because of the mechanistic workings of mathematics, but because of the controlling influence of the groups themselves.

This implies that economic theory necessarily needs to face up to the prospect of a revolutionary 'paradigm shift' – a shift in the structure of its beliefs and underlying assumptions about the way the world works.[18] At best, it can be argued that economic theory does not really understand the nature of economic fluctuations in any meaningful way; at worst, that the inability of economic theory to solve the apparently intractable problems of the current era – unemployment, price instability, global pollution and environmental destruction – is actually the consequence of a complete misunderstanding of the forces of nature in general and the human mind in particular.

TECHNICAL ANALYSIS

It should come as no surprise, therefore, to find that economic forecasts cannot accurately predict either the levels at which market prices will turn or the time they will do so. Financial markets are fast-moving, continually oscillating, reflections of the processes of transformation and change. They cannot be defined by static concepts and linear relationships. The practical value of economics is therefore limited to providing background forecasts against which to judge the current trends in markets.

The alternative method of forecasting financial market behaviour is known as 'technical analysis', and it accepts the dynamic structure of financial markets. It has no need to take account of fundamental values because it is assumed that investors' expectations concerning those values (and a lot more information besides) are already reflected in the prices. To paraphrase Oscar Wilde's view of the cynic, a technical analyst therefore knows the price of everything and the value of nothing. This implies that financial markets will, in fact, always be trying to anticipate the future and that, therefore, changes in financial market prices precede changes in fundamental conditions. In many cases, it should be possible to use price behaviour to forecast fundamentals, rather than the other way around.

THE PAST AND PRESENT AS A GUIDE TO THE FUTURE

This, in itself, would be a sufficient reason for focusing attention on the behaviour of financial asset prices. However, the claim of technical analysis is that it is actually possible to forecast the future performance of a particular market entirely by reference to the actual and historical performance of that market. In other words, no external factors need to be included in the analysis.[19]

For many years, analysts have recognized that certain price patterns have a predictive value, that the extent of some price movements can be calculated in advance and that there are regular price cycles operating in some markets. More recently, the use of technical analysis has become an increasingly large part of the investment decision-making process because it is both simple and profitable. The big problem, however, is that very few people understand why the forecasting techniques actually work. This has created tremendous difficulties of communication within the investment industry. On the one hand there are those who know that technical analysis works, but cannot explain why it does; on the other hand there are those who know that fundamental analysis does not work to the required degree of accuracy, but continue to use it because it is at least explicable.

THE RATIONALE BEHIND TECHNICAL ANALYSIS

The book up to now should have given a strong indication of the *raison d'être* of technical analysis. Natural forces encourage people to indulge in group behaviour. Groups behave as single organisms: they therefore respond in a predictable way to information shocks, have metabolic (emotional) cycles and follow a definable path of growth and decay. Unlike any other crowd, however, the behaviour of financial market crowds is clearly reflected in simple and specific indicators. These are the price movements themselves and certain mechanical indices of the underlying activity and energy of the crowd, such as trading volumes.[20] Logically, these indicators should reflect the operation of the appropriate 'natural' laws.

We shall therefore now demonstrate that price movements and indices of investor activity actually do behave in accordance with the analytical framework presented so far. We shall show that all price movements are part of a very simple pattern that is the response to information shocks, and that prices oscillate rhythmically in response to the metabolic fluctuations of the crowd. We shall show how the cohesiveness of the crowd ensures that each price movement is mathematically related to preceding price movements. We shall therefore show that it is very easy to differentiate between trends and turning points.

NOTES

1.   The following method of analysis was suggested by economists William Baumol and Jess Benhabib. See Baumol, William and Benhabib, Jess (1989) 'Chaos: significance, mechanism, and economic applications', *Journal of Economic Perspectives*, 3.

2.   The term was first coined by David Ruelle and Floris Takens in 1971. See Gleick, James (1988) *Chaos: Making a new science*, Sphere Books, London.

3.   Gleick, James, op. cit.

4.   Because, on the face of it, new information tends to become available randomly and investors are assumed to make their decisions independently of one another, current economic analysis tends to accept the hypothesis that stock prices are randomly determined (the so-called 'random walk hypothesis'). In fact, stock price movements can appear to be uncorrelated with one another over particular time periods. However, the hypothesis is essentially no more than a truism: price movements appear to be random because of the prior assumptions of random information shocks and random individual behaviour. The hypothesis fails to recognize the ordered nature of the underlying process and take account of actual investor behaviour. Furthermore, it has been shown that an unusually long run of correlated price changes occurred during the October 1987 'crash' in the United States (see Santoni, G J (May/June 1988) 'The October Crash', *The Federal Reserve Bank of St Louis Review*). The random walk hypothesis cannot therefore explain the crash.

5.   See, for example, Christ, Carl F (1966) *Econometric Models and Methods*, John Wiley, New York.

6. This exacerbates the problems of trying to forecast the effects of shocks. Shocks are continually occurring and, indeed, they are the main catalyst for change. They can be caused by events such as wars, bad weather, interruptions to supplies of raw materials, labour disputes and strikes, and bankruptcies. However, 'closed' linear economic models cannot be used to forecast the effects of such shocks with any degree of accuracy. Not only is each shock associated with a change in the environment within which economic and financial activities have to take place, but people's attitudes to such activities are likely to vary. Therefore, it is usually possible to calculate only the direction of economic changes caused by a particular shock.

7. The tendency of the modern human mind to equate differentiation with disso-ciation is carefully explained in Wilber, Ken (1983) *Up from Eden*, Routledge & Kegan Paul, London.

8. The ego itself fragments into an acceptable 'persona' and an unacceptable (and therefore deeply repressed) 'shadow'. The distinction between the accepted persona and the unaccepted shadow is one originally made by Carl Jung. The shadow consists of potential behaviour patterns that are suppressed by cultural imperatives. The problem is that the shadow still asserts its power in the form of negative emotions and habitual patterns of denial. A breakdown of the mechanism of suppression (for whatever reason) can result in apparently psychotic behaviour. It is, for example, arguable that the social disorder in Eastern Europe in the 1990s had its roots in suppressed cultural needs. See Neumann, Erich (1990) *Depth Psychology and a New Ethic*, Shambhala, Boston, Massachusetts.

9. See Whyte, L L (1950) *The Next Development in Man*, Mentor, New York. The point here is that the past is static to us. Once in our memory, it re-presents itself to us as unchanging and immutable. Thought processes that rely on memory, therefore, naturally adopt static constructs.

10. Alfred Korzybski used the analogy of a map being equated with the territory to explain the tendency people have of associating themselves directly with their mental constructs rather than with the object of their mental constructs.

11. Modern economics theory is broadly referred to as 'neo-classical' economics. It is based on two hypotheses: rationally formed expectations (after J F Muth) and the existence of a natural rate of unemployment (after M Friedman). See Tobin, James, 'Stabilization policy ten years after', in (1980) *Brookings Papers on Economic Activity*, **1**.

12. Linear relationships are usually used even in those mathematical models that are able to create cyclical fluctuations. A great variety of linear relationships allows for oscillations. These include derivatives, integrals, fixed delays and lags of various distributed forms. See Allen, R G D (1967) *Macro-economic Theory*, Macmillan, London.

13. Economic theory assumes that (uncontrollable) sentiment is not a critical feature of economic behaviour. The assumption is, of course, part of a belief system that denies that the human psyche is subject to (unacceptable) passions. It follows, therefore, that economics regards mass mood swings as being psychotic and abnormal. It is true that excesses of optimism and pessimism occur relatively infrequently and so it is certainly consistent with the evidence that emotional upheavals are unusual. However, manias and panics are actually special examples of a general phenomenon rather than idiosyncrasies as such.

14. See note 11.
15. In the late 1980s, much academic energy was spent trying to integrate the 1987 equity crash with the rational expectations hypothesis. One of the main lines of thought was to argue that the preceding 'bubble' was based on irrelevant information. No one thought to ask why the majority of market participants – many of whom spend large amounts of money on research – did not recognize that the information was irrelevant in the first place. See Diba, B T, and Grossman, H I (September 1988) 'The theory of rational bubbles in stock prices', *The Economic Journal*, **98**. The fact is that market participants were receiving very relevant information – namely, the behaviour of the market itself. (See also Chapter 7.)
16. It is almost impossible to visualize a craze for owning rare tulips occurring in a country that actually produces them *en masse*, but it happened. Homes and properties were sold to take advantage of the speculation. See Mackay, Charles (1980) *Extraordinary Popular Delusions and the Madness of Crowds*, Harmony Books, New York.
17. Sornette, Didier (2003) *Why Stock Markets Crash*, Princeton University Press, Princeton, New Jersey.
18. See Kuhn, Thomas (1962) *The Structure of Scientific Revolutions*, University of Chicago Press, Chicago. Our understanding of reality usually only progresses as a result of common consensus. Experiments are formulated within the context of this consensus, and data are interpreted according to its beliefs and injunctions. There is therefore always a limitation on the flow of genuinely new ideas, and existing theories are not easily replaced. Paradigm shifts therefore usually only occur after a crisis of understanding.
19. In practice, some knowledge of fundamental influences is clearly important in determining the validity of any longer-term forecasts that are produced by technical analysis. In Chapter 22, it will be argued that the golden ratio provides a crucial link and boundary between technical and fundamental influences.
20. Financial markets are therefore an ideal source of information about all crowd behaviour.

Part Two

The dynamics of the bull–bear cycle

7

The stock market crowd

INTRODUCTION

The physical structures of any financial market and the institutional arrangements for settling transactions in that market vary throughout the world. Many markets are centred on physical arenas known as 'exchanges'; others are established purely by telephone conversations between willing buyers and sellers. All, however, have common characteristics. The first of these, strangely enough, is that it is actually very difficult to identify a physical body of people that constitutes the market 'crowd'. The investment community is a far larger, far more amorphous and far less tangible construct than the group of people who are physically on the floor of an exchange or actually transacting bargains over the telephone at any given time.

THE INDIVIDUAL INVESTOR

The basic unit in the investment hierarchy is the individual investor. Essentially, an investor is anyone who has a 'market exposure'. In this context, the term 'market exposure' has two meanings because it may reflect a view either that market prices are going to rise or that market prices are going to fall. In the former instance, an investor will be a 'bull' (or will be 'long') of a market, while in the latter instance an investor will be a 'bear' (or will be 'short') of a market. Hence a 'bullish investor' will either own an equity, bond or commodity or have a 'right' to own an underlying security at some future date.[1] On the other hand, a 'bearish investor' will have either a direct holding of cash (or its equivalent, such as a bank deposit or a building society account) while awaiting an opportune moment to purchase a security (or securities) or will hold an investment that confers the 'right' to sell stock at some future date.[2]

The individual investor may be dealing on their own behalf (as a private investor) or be dealing on behalf of an organization (as an institutional investor). The investor's objective is to maximize total returns, subject to a preferred split between capital and income. The reasons for the separation of capital and income need not concern us unduly here. Suffice to say that each investor faces a fixed tax regime and a future set of liabilities (dependent on their age[3]), and has a natural attitude towards the acceptance of risk. The tax regime will help to determine whether or not capital is preferred to income over short periods, and the future liabilities will help to determine whether capital is preferred to income over longer periods. However, the most important consideration will be the extent to which an individual is prepared to accept the possibility of uncertain capital gains as opposed to the probability of a certain income,[4] whatever the time period concerned.

THE DEALING STRATEGY

The strategy used by the individual investor to achieve a maximum total return is that of buying securities before the market price rises and selling them after the price has done so. There are slight variations on this theme, depending on whether performance is judged against the rate of return on short-term money deposits or against a 'fully invested' position. Private individuals fall into the former category and will simply aim to buy at low prices and sell at high ones. Some institutional investors employed by pension funds and insurance companies, on the other hand, fall into the latter category. These individuals may simply hold up purchases within limited time frames to ensure that they are at least buying cheaply. Alternatively, they may switch investments from underperforming securities to better-performing securities. For all groups, however, the basic philosophy remains exactly the same: 'buy cheap and sell dear'.

THE FINANCIAL MARKET CROWD

The next higher level in the investment hierarchy consists of two groups of investor: those who are bullish and those who are bearish.

As we have seen, bullish investors expect prices to rise, while bearish ones expect prices to fall. Obviously, time plays an important part in these expectations. Investors who trade intra-day may have a time horizon of minutes or hours, while long-term investors are likely to have time horizons measured in months. So, in principle, we can also postulate a time-based hierarchy of bull and bear groups. For simplicity, however, we shall hereafter in this chapter assume that only one time horizon exists – a long-term, multi-month, time horizon. In this way, we can keep potential complications to a minimum without jeopardizing the essential message.

Now, expectations about the future trend in prices necessarily exist within the context of the most recent trend in the market. On the one hand, there will be a critical mass of participants who have taken advantage of that most recent trend and will therefore consider themselves well placed to take advantage of a continuation of the same trend. These investors will be a 'successful' group. On the other hand, however, another group of people will have missed a significant part of the trend and will not be well placed if that trend continues. These people will constitute the 'unsuccessful' group. The unsuccessful group will necessarily consist of two subgroups – namely, those who are actually holding 'losing' investments because they have been positioned against the market trend and those who are 'disinterested' in so far as they currently have no intention of participating in the trend (although they may nevertheless do so at a later date).[5]

Note, therefore, that it does not matter whether prices have been rising or falling. The critical issue is whether or not investors have been correct in anticipating the trend. It is the relationship between expectations and outcomes that not only determines individual investor attitudes, but also determines the psychological environment within which investment is taking place.

We have seen that crowds are not necessarily physical assemblies, but are psychological phenomena. This is especially true of financial market crowds. Actual and potential market participants are all linked to each other via the national and international communication networks. Newspapers, television, telephones and market reports all supplement the sort of direct contact that habitually occurs in daily professional and personal life. This network of contacts ensures that price-sensitive information is speedily disseminated and assimilated and that interested individuals are, in some way, brought into contact with each other. Understandably, however, the psychological reaction of each individual is going to depend on whether or not they are being successful.

THE INFLUENCE OF EMOTIONS

When an individual buys or sells securities, an emotional commitment is being made. Initially, of course, this commitment is being made to a trading position. The decision to deal may have been arrived at rationally, but the act of dealing creates a financial involvement and an associated need to 'get it right'. The investor will have a trading position, the market value of which is outside their control. There will be a feeling of pleasure as the price goes in their favour, but there will be a feeling of displeasure (dismay, anger, depression, fear) if the price does the opposite. These feelings of pleasure or displeasure will be associated with physiological changes in the body – the heartbeat changes, the rate of respiration alters and the palms sweat.

THE HERD INSTINCT

These feelings are intensified when an individual associates with other people. If the trading position is 'right', the personal advantages in terms of wealth and self-esteem are supplemented by communicating with other investors who have similar trading positions. Conversations with others will confirm both the validity of the trading position and the decision-making process that preceded it; satisfaction will be felt when newspaper articles or brokers' reports provide supportive evidence; members of the same group will engage in a continuous process of congratulating each other; attention will be focused on the immediate future, where critical analysis is less necessary, rather than on the longer term.

More than this, however, members of the 'successful' crowd will tend to emphasize the weakness of the arguments of the 'unsuccessful' crowd, and there will be a continuous propaganda stream aimed at the latter. Those members of the unsuccessful crowd who have wrong (losing) positions will already feel at a disadvantage and will be very vulnerable to negative information. Initially, they will feel the need to associate with others who made the same decision for protection. They will try to confirm each other's views as being correct and will emphasize the ultimate errors of the 'successful' crowd's case. Indeed, there will be a tendency to ignore the 'successful' crowd's arguments altogether. Members of the 'losing' crowd will commiserate with one another and emphasize the longer term rather than the immediate future.

Meanwhile members of the 'disinterested' subgroup will merely watch from the sidelines. It would be wrong to apply the term 'crowd' to this group because there is no emotional commitment to investment positions. Nevertheless, this group contains an important source of psychological and financial resources that can subsequently be utilized by the 'successful' crowd. Ultimately, therefore, this group is also susceptible to propaganda.

It is apparent from these comments that a commitment to a trading position is only the beginning of the story. No matter how rational the original decision to enter into a trading position may be, the very act of dealing moves an individual into a less rational, crowd-type environment. Specifically, the investor accepts a specific belief about the future trend in prices (that is, that they will go either up or down) and identifies strongly with those who hold the same belief. They, in so doing, become committed crowd members.

THE MECHANISM OF PRICE FLUCTUATIONS

The presence of two crowds – the bullish crowd and the bearish crowd – in a financial market, that have diametrically opposite views, ensures that a state of conflict exists within the rules of the investment game. While the conflict is balanced over shorter time periods, the market price action will tend to take the form of a gentle oscillation. The financial resources being allocated to buying and selling securities will not generate a long-term imbalance between the two groups. When the conflict becomes imbalanced, however, then one of the two crowds will start to become successful and the other will become unsuccessful. Consequently, the conflict intensifies and stress levels increase.

As we have already seen, conflict and stress are the main catalysts for the formation of a crowd mind. In fact, if everybody always thought the same thing at the same time, there would be no 'market' as such and, consequently, no graduated price movements: prices would jump up and down randomly, if they changed at all, and no one would trade. However, the influence of differing views as to the future course of prices and the fact that the conflict between the successful and unsuccessful crowds takes time to resolve ensures that prices trend through time.

THE BULL–BEAR LIFE CYCLE IN EMOTIONS

The intensity of this emotional commitment to a particular crowd seems to vary depending on the phases and duration of a particular bull–bear cycle. We shall be analysing these different phases in more detail in later chapters. However, the following comments can be made now.

In the early stages of a new price trend, the majority of investors still remain committed to the old price trend. The previous trend has already finished, but its termination has not yet been generally recognized. A minority of investors will have begun to suspect that a price reversal is at hand and will be altering the balance of their portfolios accordingly. However, even for this group, there will be some degree of uncertainty about the future course of prices: portfolio balances will be altered to only a relatively small degree and there will be a tendency to reverse profitable trades very quickly rather than take the longer-term view. At the beginning of a bull trend, the fear of making losses still predominates, while at the start of a bear trend greed (or a fear of missing further profits) tends to stop people from selling a significant proportion of their investments. Consequently, in the early stages of a price trend, the emotional commitment of the (ultimately) successful crowd to that trend is quite weak.

Subsequently, however, there comes a stage when the emotional commitment to the developing new trend becomes more intense. This is the stage when most of the investment community recognize that the movement in prices has become a trend, either upwards or downwards, and emotional conviction replaces any rational doubts that still persist. Investors therefore 'chase' the trend and open new trading positions.

This feature of investor behaviour then leads on to the next phase of the cycle. Once there has been a general recognition that a bullish or bearish price trend is in full swing, the foundation is laid for a price reversal. The trend will obviously persist for some time, but the fact remains that the more people who commit themselves to believing in a particular trend and to investing in that trend, the fewer people there are in fact left to perpetuate it. A price reversal therefore inevitably occurs when the vast majority of investors believe that it will not (yet) happen.

THE OBJECTIVES OF TECHNICAL ANALYSIS

It should be apparent from this (admittedly brief) analysis that the obvious rule for successful investment is to keep a close watch on what other investors are saying and doing and, then, when a vast majority are saying and doing the same thing, do the reverse. This is one of the most valuable aspects of using technical analysis: it is a rational approach to a non-rational phenomenon and encourages the user to stand aside from the crowd pressures.

THE INFLUENCE OF PRICE MOVEMENTS ON CROWD PSYCHOLOGY

There are two important points to remember here. The first is that crowds have objectives of their own, even if the individual members do not specifically recognize them as such. The second is that crowds respond very quickly and simply to leadership. It is an important feature of financial markets that prices play a crucial part in both of these aspects of crowd behaviour. First, it is the prime objective of the successful crowd to continue to move security prices in its own favour; second, the leadership role is partly provided by movements in prices themselves. Let us now analyse each of these forces in turn.

THE CONTEST BETWEEN THE TWO CROWDS

The ability of the successful crowd to move security prices in its own favour depends primarily on the financial resources that can be marshalled and committed to the market. Eventually, the conflict between the successful and unsuccessful crowds is resolved when the latter disintegrates and transfers its resources to the successful crowd.

The strategy used to win this conflict is, first, to ensure that every member of the successful crowd is fully committed to membership and, second, to bombard the opposition (which includes all those who are not yet participating in the market at all) with a continuous stream of propaganda. Hence, as a persistent move by prices in a particular direction develops, the integrative tendency of the successful crowd will ensure that each member's trading position is as large as possible. Rational behaviour by the individual becomes more difficult and non-rational (emotional) behaviour becomes increasingly easy. Trading positions are opened on the basis that the successful crowd's belief system (be it rising or falling prices) will continue to be correct and critical judgement wanes accordingly. Personal interest ultimately becomes subordinated to the group interest and overtrading begins to occur.

THE INFLUENCE OF PRICES ON BEHAVIOUR

As more and more resources are committed to the successful crowd's point of view, prices will continue to respond favourably. This, in turn, justifies the successful crowd's existence and excites members of that crowd further. Simultaneously, of course, the vested interests involved in keeping prices moving in one direction will be increased. Consequently, brokers, market makers and investors alike will provide a continuous stream of favourable comments to the media, and the latter will promote the cause to the widest possible audience.

Meanwhile, individuals in the unsuccessful crowd will already be vulnerable to coercion and will tend to desert to the successful crowd. As this process develops, market prices will continue to move in the direction required by the successful crowd. These changes in prices are a clear signal[6] to members of the unsuccessful crowd that their arguments are ineffectual. No matter how powerful these arguments might appear from a longer-term viewpoint, the short-term message cannot be ignored. The beliefs of the unsuccessful crowd are shown to be incorrect.

Eventually, the stress created by the combined forces of adverse price movements, shrinking numbers and unfavourable propaganda becomes too much and the trickle of deserters from the unsuccessful crowd becomes a flood. Prices will suddenly rise or fall very sharply as this change occurs: it is an emotional period, usually accompanied by high-volume turnover in the marketplace.[7] Furthermore, those investors who join the successful crowd at this stage are 'converts' and, as such, tend to be the more committed. They are therefore the least likely to change their minds quickly and so will provide sufficient finance to keep the trend intact.

THE LIMIT CYCLE BETWEEN PRICES AND BEHAVIOUR

From this analysis, it is apparent that price movements are not just a passive response to market forces: there is a feedback effect that ensures that market forces are themselves responsive to price movements. In other words, there is a limit cycle relationship between prices and investor behaviour. This observation is important and is in direct contrast to the assumptions of classical economics. (Indeed, within the classical framework, prices cannot be determined if the demand and supply functions are allowed to shift in response to a change in prices.) Crowd behaviour ensures that a price movement triggers an emotional response among members of opposing crowds and thereby helps to ensure that the most recent movement in prices is continued into the future.

BELIEFS AND LEADERSHIP

The reason behaviour is dependent on prices is that a price movement in a particular direction represents the beliefs of one of the two crowds and helps to fulfil the leadership function of that crowd. Because our experience of life through time is (apparently) linear and sequential and (for most of us) our thought processes are of the same nature, there is a natural tendency to believe that what has just happened will also continue to happen in the immediate future. If, for example, security prices have just risen, not only will the bulls feel satisfied, but there will also be a tendency to assume that the rise will continue. There is therefore a clear 'instruction' to investors to buy more stock if possible. In a bullish environment, therefore, a rise in prices is the flag to which investors flock and pledge allegiance; in a bearish market a fall in prices represents the harsh and terrible god to which cowed investors ultimately bend their knees.

INDIVIDUALS AS CROWD LEADERS

The role of price movements in the leadership function does not actually rule out the influence on crowd psychology of particular individuals. Indeed, the emergence of a spokesman to publicize the belief of the successful crowd greatly enhances the effect of recent price movements. From time to time, certain market traders or advisers do gain a reputation for 'getting the market right'. Usually this reputation comes either from making an accurate forecast (or 'call') of a market when no one believed it or from sticking to a particular view of the market trend longer than anyone else. At certain moments in a market price trend, sentiment may actually be influenced by such individuals.

However, there are two important points to be made about the people who provide this type of 'leadership'. First, attention is given only to individuals who have already earned a reputation: very few people will actually believe a new 'guru' the first time they make a forecast, no matter how accurate those forecasts subsequently turn out to be. Second, it becomes increasingly difficult for a particular individual to influence price movements on a regular basis. This apparent paradox occurs because, as was pointed out earlier, the more people who believe in a trend, the fewer people there are left to perpetuate it. Sooner or later, a successful 'call' will be self-defeating because too many people will believe in it. The price move generated by the call will be quickly reversed and a large number of people who followed the leader will actually lose money. Hard-won reputations, based on a high-profile exposure, are easily lost and can rarely be fully regained.

THE CONDITIONS FOR EFFECTIVE LEADERSHIP

The identity of those individuals who are able to influence markets therefore changes with time. Furthermore, this type of 'leadership' is certainly not exercised as an ongoing influence: it is essentially a transitory phenomenon that can only occur when market conditions are right. Specifically, there needs to be a state of tension between the opposing bullish and bearish crowds. Conditions of stress ensure that the reported comments or behaviour of a particular 'leader' can act as the trigger for the large-scale desertion of investors from the unsuccessful crowd to the successful one. 'Leadership' exercised by individuals can only be used within the context of the successful crowd.

INVESTMENT ADVISERS

Leadership of this nature needs to be differentiated from the regular day-to-day leadership provided by investment advisers to small groups of investors. Essentially, investment advisers distil the plethora of available economic, political and financial information and form an investment view that they dispense to their clients. They therefore provide positive leadership that, generally speaking, is acted on.

In relation to the phenomenon that we are analysing, however, investment advisers essentially lead subgroups within a bullish or bearish crowd. Crowd theory certainly applies to each subgroup. Nevertheless, each subgroup will remain dominated by the main crowd to which it belongs. The strategy to which each subgroup responds emotionally is the strategy of the 'parent' crowd. Successful advisers will not, in fact, usually make recommendations that are completely independent of market conditions – indeed, they will themselves be part of the crowd to a greater or lesser degree. However, even those rare individuals who are capable of both recognizing market sentiment and of remaining aloof from it, and so are capable of providing contrary opinion advice, cannot fulfil the role of leader for the whole crowd. More precisely, it is because they remain aloof that they cannot be market crowd leaders. Only the happy minority will follow their advice, while the majority react either too slowly or not at all.

CONCLUSION

We have thus arrived at the following conclusions in this chapter. The pursuit of trading profits as a common objective for investors ensures that stock market behaviour is a crowd phenomenon. The emotional commitment of individual investors to a particular set of trading positions translates into an emotional commitment to a particular direction of price movement. Thus, each investor accepts a bull or bear argument, identifies strongly with others who have the same view and submits to the leadership provided by spokesmen (in so far as they emerge) for their point of view.

The existence of two points of view ensures that conditions of conflict will exist. Only one of the two points of view will, however, be successful and will reap the benefits of a price trend. Hence, the gradual emergence of a successful group in a financial market will ensure that the conditions of conflict will intensify. The associated stress works on the successful and unsuccessful groups in different ways. On the one hand, the successful crowd is encouraged to tighten its autonomy as well as intensify the pursuit of its strategic objectives with respect to prices. Consequently, an individual's integrative tendency is stimulated to ensure that trading positions are marshalled for maximum effect. Trading decisions therefore tend to become increasingly non-rational as a price trend develops. As crowd members' resources are thereby committed, the internal strength of the crowd transmutes itself into external strength. Propaganda against the losing crowd intensifies.

Obviously, the stress levels within the losing crowd will be intensifying. Eventually, members will respond by joining the successful crowd. New trading positions assist in fulfilling the successful crowd's primary objective of ensuring that security prices move favourably. Ultimately extremes of euphoria or pessimism occur, and the conditions for a price reversal are created.

This analysis provides only the most basic framework for understanding the behaviour of financial markets, but, even as far as it goes, it has a number of far-reaching implications. First, it provides a theoretical framework that helps to explain both normal and abnormal behaviour in financial markets. The same concepts can be used to explain last week's movements in share prices as well as the South Sea Bubble of 1720 or the Wall Street Crash of 1929.

Second, it provides the theoretical basis for the dynamics of behaviour in financial markets that result in excesses of overtrading and create the conditions for price reversals. In other words, it explains the internal mechanism by means of which the bull–bear cycle operates.

Third, it treats behaviour in financial markets as a natural phenomenon that is subject to natural forces. (This raises some interesting possibilities as to the role of external influences – such as the weather – on crowd psychology.) The analysis has therefore moved a long way from the simplistic view that price movements in financial markets are the wholly unpredictable outcome of wholly rational decisions made by completely independent people.

NOTES

1. This involves the purchase of a call option or a futures contract. There is an important difference between the two. If held to expiry, an option is a 'right' to buy or sell an underlying security that need not be exercised. However, if held to expiry, a futures contract is a legal commitment to buy or sell an underlying security. Delivery of the underlying security can only be avoided if the futures contract is closed off before delivery date.
2. This would involve either the purchase of a put option or the sale of a futures contract. In some markets, it is also possible to sell stock 'short' – that is, to sell stock that is not actually owned.
3. Economic theory contends that savings essentially depend on the distribution of income over an expected lifetime. Hence, savings should be a larger percentage of disposable income in the middle years of a person's life than in either the early or later years. See, for example, Farrell, M J (December 1959)

'The new theories of the consumption function', *The Economic Journal*, **69**, pp 678–96.

4.　For a description of the different concepts involved, see Tobin, James (February 1958) 'Liquidity preference as behaviour towards risk', *Review of Economic Studies*, **25**, pp 65–86.

5.　The usefulness of seeing the stock market in terms of three groups was suggested to me by Alexander Elder, MD. See his book (1993) *Trading for a Living*, John Wiley, New York. For simplicity, however, I prefer to include non-participants as part of the 'unsuccessful' group.

6.　Changes are differences, and differences are items of information.

7.　This is a good example of what became known as 'catastrophe theory'. See, for example, Postle, Denis (1980) *Catastrophe Theory*, Fontana, London. This theory deals with 'discontinuities' in systems that otherwise change only gradually. The discontinuities allow a system to move to a new status without necessarily changing the structure of the system. Catastrophe theory postulates the existence of only a limited number of discontinuity 'types' and has therefore been seen as providing a possible insight into evolutionary changes.

8

The shape of the bull–bear cycle

INTRODUCTION

We are now in a position to be able to look at the internal dynamics of a complete bull–bear cycle in more detail. We have seen that the objective of any crowd, taken as a whole, is to change the environment for its own ends. The objective of a crowd in a financial market is to change prices in a particular direction: the bullish crowd will try to force prices up, while the bearish crowd will try to force them down. Each crowd has its own life cycle. During periods when the market is in the process of reversing direction, the two crowds may coexist. However, once a trend has become established, only one crowd may dominate (see Figure 8.1).

Hence within a full cycle, first the bullish crowd will dominate, then there will be a period of uneasy coexistence with the bearish crowd, then finally the bearish crowd will dominate. This means that between any two given points in time, there will be a successful crowd and an unsuccessful one.

Individuals within one of these crowds will experience different emotions from individuals in the other crowd. Members of the successful crowd will be motivated by greed (or fear of missing further profits), will obtain pleasure from their success and will feel integrated with like-minded investors. Members of the unsuccessful crowd, on the other hand, will experience fear (either of losing capital

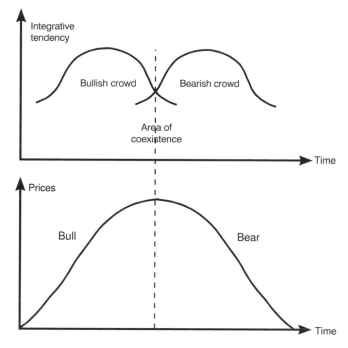

Figure 8.1 The bull–bear life cycle

or of not making any profits), will be prone to feelings of displeasure and will ultimately feel divorced from other members of the same crowd. Eventually, the stress becomes unacceptable and members of the unsuccessful crowd desert to the successful crowd.

THE LIMIT CYCLE BETWEEN PRICES AND SENTIMENT

The final arbiter of success, of course, is whether or not prices are moving in the 'right' direction. We have already seen that price movements are the outcome of the conflict between the bulls and the bears, and that price trends (once started) tend to continue because price movements transmit information and contribute to the leadership function. We have also seen that price reversals tend to occur when the investment community as a whole is more or less fully committed (financially) to one of the two points of view. Essentially, therefore, there is a limit cycle relationship between changes in prices and investor sentiment.

Investor sentiment has two aspects:

▌ expectations about the future trend in prices;

▌ the confidence with which these expectations are held.

Expectations obviously relate to whether the balance of sentiment is bullish or bearish, confidence to the willingness of market participants to translate the expectations into actual transactions.[1]

Investor sentiment is reflected in such indicators as volume and momentum. For the moment, we shall use a very simple proxy for sentiment – namely, a ratio of the number of bullish people to the number of bearish people. In Figure 8.2, this index is shown on the horizontal axis. A move to the right reflects a relative increase in the numbers expecting prices to rise, while a move to the left reflects a relative increase in the numbers expecting prices to fall. This index is directly influenced by both the direction and the size of the change in prices. The former has already been discussed. The latter is discussed below because crowds are more influenced by large price changes than by small ones.

THE BIAS IN THE LIMIT CYCLE

Figure 8.2 shows the percentage change in prices against an index of sentiment. Hence, the absolute price level will be rising above the zero

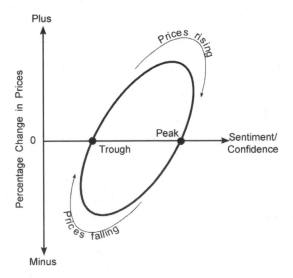

Figure 8.2 Stock market limit cycle

per cent line, and falling below the zero per cent line. As presented, the limit cycle is biased to the right. This reflects an important fact, which is particularly useful as an indicator of an imminent turning point – namely, that the confidence with which a view is being held usually turns prior to price reversals. Hence, just prior to market peaks, sentiment will begin to deteriorate as the percentage increase in prices falls. On the other hand, just prior to market troughs, sentiment begins to improve as the percentage fall in prices decreases.

It is, in fact, possible to relate this rightward-biased price–sentiment limit cycle directly to the relationships expressed in Figure 8.1. Figure 8.3 therefore shows the bull and bear life cycles, the associated periods of rising and falling prices, and the limit cycle itself. All that remains to be done is to convert the cycle of absolute price changes into the cycle of percentage price changes. Turning points in the percentage changes precede turning points in the absolute price level.

THE INFLUENCE OF 'EXTERNAL' FACTORS

The limit cycle between the prices of financial assets and sentiment does not, of course, exist in isolation: market prices are determined by

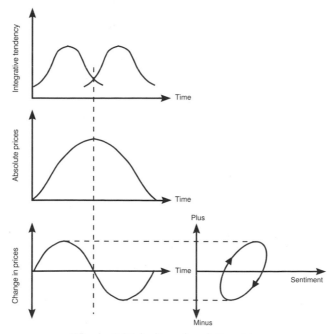

Figure 8.3 Limit cycle relationships

the physical supply of, and demand for, assets, which in turn are dependent on general financial conditions. In addition, sentiment in financial markets is very dependent on the general mood that pervades the economic, social and political environment.

In particular, changes in financial markets reflect, and create, a general change in wealth within the whole community. Equity prices, for example, may rise because of improved economic circumstances, but economic circumstances may then be improved because of the wealth effect of higher equity prices. Quite simply, more people have more capital that can be converted into current spending. Hence, rising stock prices become associated with optimism because they suggest improved employment and income prospects for the future. However, falling stock prices create general feelings of pessimism because they have adverse implications for future employment and incomes. In this way, the emotions of one area of activity spill over into another.

THE LIMIT CYCLE BETWEEN EQUITY MARKETS AND THE ECONOMY

We can express these interrelationships, if only in part, by means of limit cycles that correlate financial asset prices with general economic trends. Such a correlation is shown in Figure 8.4. As it is usual to

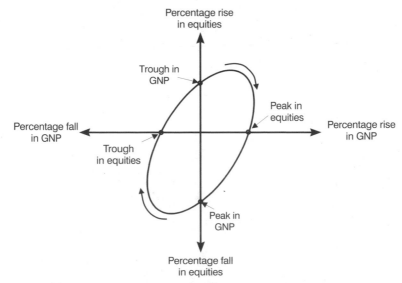

Figure 8.4 Limit cycle relating equities to the economy

analyse economic activity in terms of changes, the limit cycle relates percentage changes in gross national product (GNP) to percentage changes in equity prices.[2]

The limit cycle could take one of a number of different shapes. As shown in Figure 8.4, however, it is biased to the left. This bias reflects the important phenomenon to which we have already referred briefly, which is that security prices effectively anticipate the future by turning before fundamentals do. When the investment community as a whole is fully committed to a particular point of view, it can no longer respond to news items that confirm that point of view. The emergence of profit-taking after a price rise, or of 'bear closing' after a price fall, then creates the initial phases of a price reversal. Economic fundamentals will turn at a later stage.

Limit cycles may actually be used to explore the relationships between any two economic variables you care to look at. It is apparent from the shape of the cycle in Figure 8.4 that there are four possible interactions between a pair of economic variables: two involving a direct relationship and two involving an inverse relationship. Economic theory normally only pays close attention to the former. It follows that the narrower the shape of the oval in the diagram is, the better will be the results of any correlation and regression analysis. This naturally 'confirms' the apparent validity of linear analysis, but, of course, ignores the dynamics of continuous negative feedback.

THE INFLUENCE OF SHOCKS

This analysis confirms that the price–sentiment limit cycle operating in a financial market is also integrated with limit cycles relating that market to the wider economic, social and political environment. However, although accurate as far as it goes, the analysis implicitly assumes that financial markets are in complete harmony with their environment and that, therefore, there is nothing new to learn about that environment. As we have already seen, this assumption is ultimately incorrect:[3] fluctuations that are intrinsic to a particular level of the hierarchy are inevitably modified by fluctuations imposed from a higher level. Equity and bond prices therefore have to respond to new information about the environment at all levels of the hierarchy. In other words, they have to respond to shocks.

Shocks occur because of a sudden divergence between current price movements and expected price movements and may derive from two sources:

▌ they may be triggered by an unexpected movement in prices themselves;

▌ they may be precipitated by unexpected changes in the social, political or economic environment.

Furthermore, the shocks may be of either a pro-trend nature or a contra-trend nature.

PRO-TREND SHOCKS

The influence of pro-trend shocks can be very profound. For whatever reason, market participants suddenly find that expected prices are further away from the current levels than was originally thought. Pro-trend shocks are therefore usually sufficient to destroy the unsuccessful crowd and are always adequate to stimulate the integrative tendency of the successful crowd. Such shocks also involve a reduced lag between changes in sentiment and changes in prices, so that the associated price movements are particularly dynamic.

Almost by definition, pro-trend shocks in a financial market materialize because of independent developments in the politico-economic environment. This implies that the shock has evolutionary implications for the financial market and, therefore, has implications for the subsequent pattern of price behaviour. We shall look at this in a little more detail in the next chapter. First, however, we need to look at contra-trend shocks.

CONTRA-TREND SHOCKS AND ENERGY GAPS

At some (late) stage in a price trend, a financial market will necessarily experience a shock in the form of a contra-trend price movement. In principle, there are two ways in which this contra-trend movement can arise:

▌ there may suddenly be an unexpected[4] contra-trend movement in prices themselves;

▮ there may be an unexpected item of information concerning economic, social or political circumstances.

In either case, the successful crowd will experience a sudden divergence between actual and expected price movements. That crowd will then start to revise its expectations concerning future price movements. Indeed, some investors will actually consider that the trend in prices has changed. This revision will inevitably weaken the integrative tendency of the successful crowd and thereby undermine the existing price trend.

It is important to recognize, however, that price shocks occurring independently of environmental data are more destructive than price shocks occurring because of environmental data. This is true because, in the former case, the market will have entered an 'energy gap' that cannot be bridged. In the latter case, however, pro-trend energy is likely to still exist and prices may quickly recover from the shock.

The role of energy gaps is, unfortunately, still not fully appreciated. It is directly related to the degree to which available financial resources are already committed to the prevailing trend. Once 'all' the liquidity is in the market, there is no energy left in the trend – a fact that explains the old market saying that prices peak on good news or trough on bad. The last item of pro-trend news inevitably encourages participants to commit themselves to the final series of trades that takes the market into its terminal juncture. Genuine price reversals therefore occur because of energy gaps.

Importantly, however, the price shock created by an energy gap is usually only the first part of a price reversal rather than the complete reversal itself. The fact is that all natural systems respond to information shocks in a way that involves some retracement of the shock. There is an archetypal pattern of adjustment. As a result, there is usually a chance for knowledgeable investors to reverse their positions in the market before it is too late. We shall now look at this pattern in some detail.

SHOCKS AND THE LIMIT CYCLE

As already described, the initial shock registers as a change in the direction of price movement. Putting this another way, we can say that the shock occurs as the change in prices moves either from positive to negative or from negative to positive.

Usually, however, it is possible to get a warning of an imminent price shock from the behaviour of price momentum and investor sentiment. The relationship between either of these variables and the level of prices depends, of course, on the shape of the limit cycle. However, if we assume that the standard relationship between prices and sentiment is as shown in Figure 8.2, then we can deduce the following (see Figure 8.5).

If market prices are in a bull trend then, as that trend approaches its terminal juncture, the rate of change in prices begins to drop. At the same time, sentiment (however measured) will become less positive. Then the shock occurs as the change in prices moves through the zero change line. This is shown by the movement from A to B in Figure 8.5. The relationship between prices and sentiment 'jumps' inwards, away from the solution path defined by the limit cycle. Simultaneously, of course, sentiment turns negative.

THE RETURN TO THE LIMIT CYCLE

As the limit cycle is essentially stable, however, behaviour will try to return to the solution path. If we continue to assume that prices are

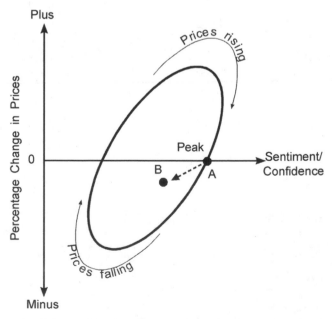

Figure 8.5 The effect of a bearish information shock

entering a bear phase, then, essentially, the sequence of events is as shown in Figure 8.6. Initially prices may fall further after the shock, and this causes sentiment to do the same. However, the fall in prices begins to slow and, eventually, lower prices encourage 'bear closing'. This, in turn, causes prices to rise. The rise in prices then stimulates a reversal in sentiment.

The improvement in sentiment can be quite dramatic in relation to the change in prices. Indeed, the strength behind the rise in prices may even be sufficient to take the market to a new high.[5] In the absence of other influences, however, the shock itself should be sufficient to preclude this.

Meanwhile, it is highly unlikely that either the rate of change in prices or the level of sentiment will achieve their previous highs. Eventually, higher prices encourage some profit-taking activity and prices begin to slip again. At first, sentiment may actually continue to improve slightly as investors search for 'cheap' stock in anticipation of the 'next' rally. Unfortunately, however, the vast majority of investors now hold stock and so their ability to buy any more is strictly limited. Indeed, the subsequent price collapse is thereby assured. It is this collapse that brings prices back to the solution path of the limit cycle.

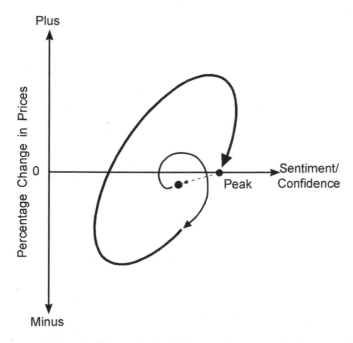

Figure 8.6 The price–sentiment spiral after a peak

PRACTICAL IMPLICATIONS

There are three important conclusions that we can draw from this analysis:

▋   the adjustment process following a shock takes the form of a spiral;

▋   the price peak that occurs just prior to the shock is re-tested during the operation of the spiral – the re-test is 'successful' if market prices move to a new high and 'unsuccessful' if they do not;

▋   sentiment appears to improve dramatically during the re-test, but, in most cases, falls short of that which was attained during the original peak.

THE PATTERN OF ADJUSTMENT AFTER TROUGHS

Obviously, the whole analysis can be repeated for situations when a market is turning from being bearish to bullish. This is shown in Figure 8.7. As the market comes to its reversal point, the rate of fall

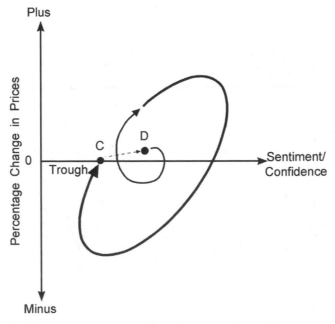

Figure 8.7 The price–sentiment spiral after a trough

in prices will initially slow and sentiment will become less negative. Then the shock occurs as the change in prices turns positive. The locus of the price movement jumps upwards and inwards, away from the limit cycle (from C to D in Figure 8.7). Then, the market spirals back to the path of the limit cycle. During the spiral, absolute prices are normally unlikely to make a new low, but nevertheless may do so.

THE REVERSAL PROCESS

1. The shock

We have thus established an idealized model for the way that financial markets behave, and from this model we can isolate three distinct stages to a price reversal. In the first stage, the market reacts to being either overbought or oversold. As the market approaches its turning point, the vast majority of investors will, because of the integrative tendency, have the same (long-term) view about the future trend in prices. As the market begins to reverse, some individuals, who are trading on relatively short time horizons, will be likely to develop negative (short-term) views and will start to neutralize all or part of their commitment to the market. Hence, an overbought market will encounter profit-taking on the part of investors and will fall, while an oversold market will encounter a bear squeeze and will rise. In both cases, the market enters an energy gap.

There are, however, insufficient financial resources in the system to offset the effects of short-term position-taking. What happens, therefore, is that prices adjust by a much larger amount than even the majority of short-term players are expecting. This adjustment therefore presents itself as an information shock to the majority of market participants.

2. The re-test

The second stage of the reversal process essentially consists of the re-assertion of the sentiment of the previously successful crowd. The first stage is seen as being technical rather than fundamental by market participants.[6] It is, however, a trap for the unwary. Very often, the only way to recognize that this is part of a reversal pattern, rather than part of a fully fledged bull or bear move, is to analyse the actual behaviour of the crowd in terms of underlying commitment to the market (that is, to analyse their behaviour in terms of the volume of transactions, their willingness to deal in the majority of securities trading in the market and their ability to open up new trading positions and stimulate fast changes in prices). During this second stage of a reversal pattern, these technical indicators of crowd behaviour will almost certainly not confirm either the apparent dynamism of the price movements or the sense of invincibility exhibited by traders.[7]

3. The new trend

The third and, in a sense, final stage of a reversal pattern is the actual change in crowd sentiment as the fundamental news itself begins to alter. It is this stage that finally triggers an ever-increasing number of people from the now unsuccessful crowd into changing their minds and their trading positions.

The stress and tension of seeing fundamentals confirm the move in prices is finally reflected in an acceleration of buying (in a bull market) or of selling (in a bear market). This third stage, therefore, generates a sharp change both in price movements and in the volume of transactions. It establishes the trend of the market, until a change in fundamentals is once more on the horizon.

THE IDEALIZED THREE-STAGE REVERSAL PATTERN

This analysis generates the concept of a three-stage reversal process. Idealized patterns are shown in Figure 8.8.

The important point to grasp is that the derived patterns are reflections of the influence of a spiral. Stage 1 of the pattern (which may in practice be more complicated than that shown in Figure 8.8) reflects the influence of a shock, and stages 2 and 3 reflect the spiral generated by that shock.

Figure 8.8 highlights the relationship between actual price levels and price changes. The lower part of the diagram makes explicit that:

▮ the rate of change in prices turns before the actual change;

▮ the reversal from an overbought or oversold condition creates a shock;

▮ re-tests of the initial reversal point are achieved at less extreme rates of change in prices.

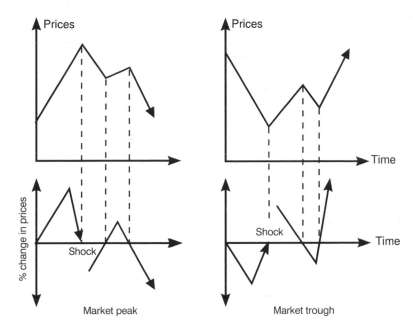

Figure 8.8 Idealized reversal patterns

THE INFLUENCE OF FEAR

It is important to note the extent to which fear plays a role in these patterns. Fear is associated with feelings of isolation, inadequacy and uncertainty. It develops suddenly when expectations diverge from actual events, and is only relieved by evasive action. In financial markets, therefore, fear persists until unsuccessful trading positions are neutralized. Hence, as a market enters stage 1 of a reversal pattern, it is likely to be overextended, either because of fear of missing further profits (in a bull market) or of making any losses (in a bear market).

There then follows the shock of an unexpected price change. This creates an atmosphere of fear, but generates only a limited degree of evasive action.

In stage 2, the re-test of the former peak or trough tends to assuage the fears created by the shock, but always leaves a residue of intangible doubts.

However, in stage 3, prices move persistently against the beliefs of the majority until naked fear triggers a widespread neutralization (and/or reversal) of bad trading positions.

It follows from this, of course, that the main indicators of investor sentiment (such as price momentum and volume) will show strong increases during periods when fear is being heightened, and will subside when fear is being reduced.

THE BIAS IN THE BULL–BEAR LIFE CYCLE

This analysis of fear implies that the disintegration phase of either a bull or a bear life cycle will occur very quickly. The relevant life cycle is therefore biased to the right because the decline phase is most closely associated with fear. However, it is obvious that the fear of not making profits is of a different order of magnitude from the fear of actually losing money. This implies, therefore, that the whole bull–bear cycle is biased to the right.

ASYMMETRIC INVESTMENT ATTITUDES

This rightward bias is assisted by another aspect of the effects of fear. The intensity of the fear of losing money means that most investors actually have an asymmetric attitude to investment positions: they prefer to hold stock rather than short positions.[8] If something goes wrong with a purchase of stock, it is at least possible to regard it as a long-term investment that will eventually come right. However, if something goes wrong with the sale of something that is not even owned, the short-term pressures to try again when the circumstances are more favourable are irresistible. This whole process is, of course, made worse by the stock-based investment policies of the savings institutions.

Bull markets therefore develop on the back of a gradual accumulation of stock, and a consequent reduction in liquidity. Furthermore, top patterns often take a long time to develop, because investors will continually take advantage of weaker prices to buy stock. However, when a bear market begins, not only do very few investors actually anticipate the fall, but there are insufficient bear positions to be closed. There is therefore very little resistance to falling prices – indeed, liquidity can only be raised by selling, and this, by definition, forces prices down further. Bear phases therefore generally take a shorter period of time than do bull phases, and are very effective in destroying wealth. Not surprisingly, bottom patterns tend to develop quickly because so few investors actually have stock.

THE PRICE PULSE

We are now in a position to combine the two reversal patterns shown in Figure 8.8 above into one single pattern representing a complete cycle. This is done in Figure 8.9. For simplicity, each wave of the pattern is given a different notation. Hence the initial upswing is denoted wave 1, the subsequent re-test of the low is wave 2 and the bull impulse wave is wave 3. Then the initial drop from the high is wave A, the re-test of the high is wave B and the main bear run is wave C. This notation will be used in the remainder of the book.

The pattern is asymmetrical: stage 1 of the pattern is longer than stage 2 because, as noted, bull markets generally take longer to develop than do bear markets. From our knowledge of the operation of limit cycles, we know that the peaks and troughs will occur on a regular basis. This implies that the basic three-wave pattern of Figure 8.9 will repeat itself continuously, thereby representing an archetypal 'heartbeat' in a particular financial market. We propose to call this the 'price pulse'.

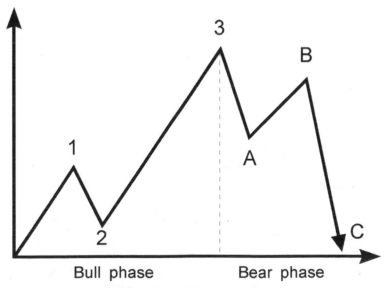

Figure 8.9 The price pulse

THE TIME HIERARCHY

It is necessary to register, however, that the price pulse is time frame-specific. That is, in any financial market, there will be a specific price pulse that is applicable to each level of the market's hierarchy of time frames. The problem is determining what time frames constitute different levels in the hiearchy.

This means that there will, in an ultimate sense, be a 'mega-pulse' that will coincide with, and therefore trace out, the life cycle of the whole financial market. The existence of such a pulse is the inevitable deduction from the theory of growth via evolutionary shocks. Eventually, therefore, there will be a financial market crash that will be associated with a fundamental alteration in the currently accepted methods of production, distribution and exchange. At present, however, the concept is purely hypothetical and so is not meant to be a specific forecast of the demise of the capitalist system. Its purpose is purely to help illustrate the interdependence of the relationships that we have so far established.

PRICE–SENTIMENT LIMIT CYCLES

The concept of an identifiable life cycle for each and every financial market also implies the presence of identifiable metabolic price–sentiment cycles. Once a life cycle has begun, it will trigger off a whole series of metabolic cycles in exactly the same way as the birth of a human being triggers off the rhythmic metabolic processes in the body. Life cycles are separate concepts from metabolic cycles, but they are dependent on one another. Hence, the movements of prices over time will reflect the influence of both the life cycle and natural price–sentiment fluctuations.

LIMIT CYCLES AND THE TRANSMISSION OF SHOCKS

The important point is that the highest-level cycles have an impact at the lower levels of the hierarchy. For periods, the lower-level cycles will operate in harmony with the higher-level cycles. Gradually, however, divergences arise. Eventually, higher-level metabolic cycles will transmit shocks to the lower levels because of the discrepancies.

These shocks create turning points. Each of them will create a specific lower-level bull–bear life cycle and will then have its own internalized metabolic rate. This process continues down through the hierarchical levels until we reach the smallest of daily fluctuations. Hence, metabolic fluctuations at a higher level create life cycles at a lower level. Simultaneously, however, the combination of all lower-level cycles within the hierarchy constitute the 'mega-pulse' of the highest-level cycle. In this way, the system becomes completely integrated.

THE HIERARCHY OF FLUCTUATIONS

From these comments, we can make three deductions:

▌ the movements in prices will consist of both a hierarchy of metabolic cycles and a hierarchy of shock-induced fluctuations;

▌ we can confirm that all oscillations will harmonize with one another, both because the lower-level oscillations are triggered by the highest-level oscillation and because the highest-level oscillation is constructed from the effects of all the lower-level oscillations;

▌ the patterns traced out by shock waves are reflected in the pattern registered by life cycles.

CONCLUSION

Let us now summarize the conclusions of this chapter by redrawing Figure 8.1 to include the greater detail that we have since uncovered (see Figure 8.10).

The top part of the diagram again consists of two life cycles – that of the bullish crowd and that of the bearish crowd. Now, however, the early stage of each life cycle is adjusted to reflect a three-stage reversal pattern, and each life cycle is biased to the right.

The second part of the diagram focuses attention on absolute prices. It incorporates the three-stage reversal pattern at both the bottom and the top of market movements, and the bear phase is shorter than the bull phase.

The third part of the diagram converts the absolute price changes into percentage price changes.

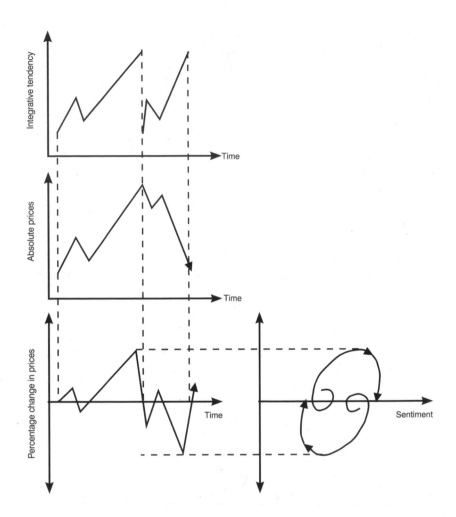

Figure 8.10 The bull–bear cycle

The final part of the diagram shows the controlling influence of the limit cycle. This cycle is the metabolic cycle that is 'handed down' from a higher level of the hierarchy. As the rate of change in prices turns from negative to positive, or from positive to negative, a shock is delivered to the system. The result is the emergence of a lower-level spiral adjustment at the point of inflection of the absolute price level.

We thus have a graphical representation of the basic features of crowd behaviour in financial markets. These are that:

▌ bull phases alternate with bear phases;

▌ each reversal pattern at the peak or trough of an oscillation consists of three phases;

▌ rates of change in prices oscillate between upper and lower limits;

▌ rates of change in prices oscillate rhythmically over time.

We have already dealt in some detail with the fact that the bull and bear phases alternate with one another. We shall develop each of the other three features throughout the rest of this book. The next few chapters will deal with the shape of the oscillations in more detail. Then we shall deal with the information provided by the technical indicators of investor sentiment. Finally, we shall deal with the implications of rhythmic oscillations.

NOTES

1. Confidence is, of course, an internal feeling. However, for market analysis, it is the external signs of internal confidence that are important. For one thing, confidence may be reflected in a certain type of complacency where no more activity is being generated because participants are so certain they are right. As we shall see, this is a warning sign for markets.

2. Among other things, it is also possible to construct a limit cycle relating the bond market to economic activity. This implies the existence of a limit cycle between bonds and equities. Generally speaking, reversals in the bond market tend to lead reversals in the equity market by between three and six months within the context of the 3¼-year business cycle.

3. It is valid only if it is applied to (relatively) high levels of the hierarchy over (relatively) short periods of time.

4. Unexpected, that is, by the majority.

5. Mathematically, absolute prices will rise above the previous high if the rate of change in prices above the zero per cent line is greater than the negative rate of change implicit in the shock.

6. In truth, it is essentially the other way round. The first stage of a reversal pattern is often the sign of changing fundamentals, while the second stage is a technical response to fundamentals being discounted far too early.

7. This conclusion adds weight to the argument that market peaks do not necessarily occur at points of extremes in sentiment. Sometimes they do, but mostly they do not. Usually, sentiment will deteriorate before prices start to fall. The idea that market peaks occur at points of massive euphoria is probably created from an illusion. During re-tests of market peaks, market traders are always very confident, particularly as the market moves into new territory. The market has now finished 'climbing its wall of worry'; it has had a correction, and has thereby satisfied the fears of the traders; now the latter can relax in the face of apparently improving fundamentals – even to the extent of buying into weakness. The error, however, has been to mistake the change in sentiment

(which is quite noticeable) for the absolute level of sentiment (which remains depressed). Another way of saying this is that players still left in the market regain their confidence without realizing that the total of the new resources that are likely to be committed to the market has been reduced. The majority of investors will therefore fail to recognize that the structure of the market is changing, and it is usually this error that virtually guarantees the destructive nature of the subsequent bear market.

8.   This is obviously not true of foreign exchange markets where a long position in one currency automatically involves a short position in another currency.

9

Energy gaps and pro-trend shocks

INTRODUCTION

It is quite clear from the analysis of Chapter 8 that each three-wave stage of the price pulse – whether up or down – is a response to the receipt of information. As such, it reflects the process of learning. This is no accident. It has specifically been found that, when an individual is learning a new task, the ability to absorb and respond to the information passes through three distinct phases. This finding by Henry Mills[1] has not been given the credit it deserves, not least because it introduces a significant qualification to the so-called 'S'-shaped learning curve. This latter was reputedly conceived by the French sociologist Gabriel Tarde in 1890 and has been a favourite with academics ever since. The two curves are shown in Figure 9.1.

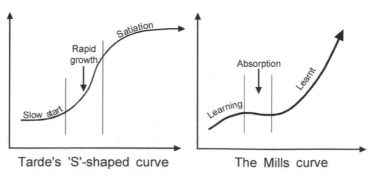

Figure 9.1 The learning curve

The insight from Tarde's curve is that it focuses on the three phases of slow beginnings, accelerating growth and satiation. Its weakness, however, is that it ignores the causes of the slow beginnings, and fails to address the consequences of satiation. Mills' findings specifically address the first of these issues. The results of satiation are a separate consideration.

In the initial phase of learning, some effort has to be applied to absorbing and dealing with the new data. The mind has to concentrate and energy is focused. As a result, the ability to respond to the inflow of data actually begins to improve quite rapidly. Hence, if a new task is being learnt, the trainee is increasingly able to do the task more quickly and with greater accuracy.

In the second phase, however, an interesting event occurs: the ability to absorb new information suddenly wanes, the task of learning suddenly becomes difficult and a sort of 'forgetting' occurs.[2] The trainee knows that they can do the task, but somehow can't quite do it effectively.

What happens is that the brain has to slow its learning process so that energy can be diverted to reorganizing the structure of memory. Donald Hebb[3] proposed that the adjustment involves the transfer of information from short-term memory to long-term memory. Short-term memory depends on the electrical impulses of the brain, while long-term memory depends on the structure of the neural network within the brain. In other words, persistent electrical activity eventually alters the connections between brain cells so that something more than just temporary learning takes place. It represents a paradigm shift.

The third phase, which follows this paradigm shift, is therefore characterized by an easy application of the learnt abilities. Thus, it does not reflect learning as such. Tasks can be carried out automatically with very little conscious concentration being applied. Short-term memory is released to cope with any other new information that might become available.

This move from an initial state of unconscious incompetence (the information shock), through the period of 'forgetting', to a final state of unconscious competence (the use of learnt skills) is directly mirrored in the oscillation of the price pulse. Initially, there is an information shock, which is reflected in either a price squeeze on the bears or a price fall against the bulls. Market prices move quickly as the crowd starts to learn that the market is changing direction. Then there comes a period of forgetting as the energy being directed towards the new trend subsides. Finally, the new trend begins to assert itself in earnest, usually accompanied by appropriate economic data. By this stage, of course, the crowd has effectively learnt that the trend is genuine and is alert to the possibility of favourable economic data.

Therefore, there is a great willingness to commit money to the new trend. This is the main impulse move – either up or down – as prices move along the path of least resistance.

ENERGY GAPS

The fact that the Mills learning curve shows the same three-wave profile as is contained in the price pulse gives even more credence to the latter. Furthermore, the logic behind both is essentially the same. What is not quite so clear, however, is the process whereby the upward-sloping learning curve converts into a downward-sloping curve and then vice versa.

The answer lies in the concept of 'energy gaps'. One type of energy gap is actually implicit in the shape of the learning curve itself. It occurs during the period of 'forgetting' when internal energy is diverted to restructuring memory. There is therefore a gap in the energy being devoted to the emerging trend. This gap is caused by the learning process and, hence, in a sense, is caused by the original 'shock' of new information. Importantly, however, the energy gap has an underlying support that links the initial information shock to permanent learning.

In a financial market, this 'period of forgetting' occurs when the crowd denies the relevance of the information shock and accepts the re-test of the high or low. This period corresponds to either wave 2 or wave B of the price pulse. Nevertheless, the crowd will internally adjust its bias from bullish to bearish or from bearish to bullish even if it doesn't explicitly realize what is happening.[4]

There is, however, another type of energy gap. This gap actually presents a barrier to further progress and, quite simply, occurs as a result of satiation. If an input of extra energy is not received at the gap, the system will fall into that gap. As a result, the system process will reverse itself. Hence, after a day's work, both body and mind need a night's rest. There is a natural energy gap, in the form of tiredness, that converts activity into rest. As a result, the active, creative processes of the day give way to the passive, recuperative processes of the night. It is important, however, to recognize that sleep constitutes an activity in its own right: the activity is just of a different nature.[5] At some stage, the activity of sleep will become satiated and create an energy gap. Hence, when a person has had sufficient sleep, they wake up. There is, thus, a simple, straightforward oscillation between activity and rest, mediated by energy gaps.

This analysis is simple, but profound. It points the way towards an understanding of all rhythmic fluctuations in terms of polarity swings from one unbridged energy gap to another. Certainly, it can be applied to the bull and bear swings in financial markets. Hence, it is apparent that unbridged energy gaps create the contra-trend information shocks that we analysed in Chapter 8. A market becomes overbought or oversold, such that no new resources can be committed to a trend and so a reversal begins. Unbridged energy gaps therefore create reversals (see Figure 9.2).

BRIDGING ENERGY GAPS

The only way that this rhythm of activity and rest can be altered is by bringing in energy from an external source to 'bridge' the gap. For example, excitement or stimulants may extend the activity of the day, while illness or sleeping pills may extend the passivity of the night. However, given the character of life as we understand it, these 'extensions' can only be temporary. Furthermore, the reaction to an extension can be quite dramatic: somebody who extends a work project through the night is likely to find that the subsequent period of sleep is longer than usual.

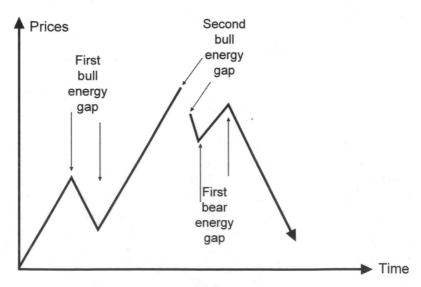

Figure 9.2 Energy gaps

Hence, an energy gap that is bridged will extend the trend. As we have already observed, the first energy gap is, in fact, a reflection of a bridge being formed. It is experienced during re-tests of highs and lows, when the market is in the process of learning that the direction of energy has changed. Such learning may be termed 'first-order' learning, because the deep structure of the market remains unaltered.

On the other hand, however, the second energy gap is not automatically bridged. Such a bridge only occurs when a suitable external shock informs the market that the quality of available energy has changed. After this shock, the trend extends itself. The bridge is thus a form of learning and it can be classified as 'second-order' learning because the deep structure of the market alters. As already indicated in our activity/sleep example, extensions after the shock are likely to be followed by a greater-than-usual reversal as the organism seeks to return to its normal pattern.

BRIDGING THE FIRST ENERGY GAP IN FINANCIAL MARKETS

It is important to understand the underlying adjustments that take place during first-order learning, when the crowd is learning that a trend change is occurring. The first point to make is that the adjustment process is associated with a great deal of confusion. On the one hand, sentiment is still being influenced by the previous trend but, on the other, there may well be fundamental evidence that a change in trend is justified. The integrative tendency of the new crowd is very weak at this stage, while the integrative tendency of the old crowd is weakening.

The second point actually follows from this. It is quite apparent, during this first energy gap, that the market participants have a great deal of difficulty actually accepting a change in outlook. Consequently, commitments to both the old and new trends, taken together, tend to drop. Uncertainty increases. Energy indicators – such as momentum and turnover – tend to drop.

Underneath, however, the actual flow of investible funds is changing direction as investors switch from one view of the market to another view. Thus it is that the first energy gap – the re-test of the high or low – provides the linking mechanism between the original contra-trend shock and the inevitable phase of 'learnt response' price movement.

What happens next is quite important. There will inevitably be a point where the market itself registers that the trend has changed.

Obviously it is a very significant point for investors, although the way it reveals itself is sometimes so subtle that it may be missed. Nevertheless, prices themselves signal that they are reversing away from the first energy gap. Sometimes the reversal will occur on a specific item of news and sometimes the reversal will just occur as a result of a build-up of trading pressure. In either case, the signal is likely to be a greater-than-usual or unexpected price move, which may be accompanied by an increase in the energy indicators such as volume. The price move may be a break out of the downtrend that formed while the energy gap was being negotiated, or it may be a break out of the trading range that the energy gap has helped to form. In either case, however, the market will register the impact of an information shock (see Figure 9.3). We shall look at the implications of information shocks in much more detail in Chapter 22.

BRIDGING THE SECOND ENERGY GAP IN FINANCIAL MARKETS

As already mentioned, however, there is a limit to price movements based on 'learnt responses'. In other words, there is a natural limit to the amount of environmentally neutral growth that is possible. Inevitably, the limit cycle relationship between price movements and the environment will begin to diverge. In principle, therefore, an energy gap that is sufficiently large to form a barrier will arise. The organism or system, or (in this case) financial market crowd, will have been moving along the line of least resistance in relation to the environment. During the move, energy (or data) has been transferred from

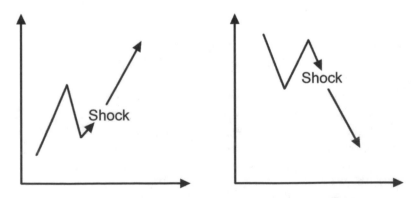

Figure 9.3 Information shocks and the first energy gap

the environment to support the movement, but the market is not actually 'learning' anything new. Eventually, however, satiation sets in – the organism reaches the limits of this phase of its growth and finds that old learnt responses no longer work.

In principle, this stage can be defined as the point of inflexion in the life cycle of the system. After this point, the life cycle switches from expansion mode to contraction mode. In financial markets, this means a switch from a bull phase to a bear phase (this was shown in Figure 8.1 in the previous chapter).

Suppose, however, that an influx of external energy occurred that was sufficient to override the system's predisposition to switch from growth to decline. This would mean a change in the quality of the life cycle. In fact, it would be represented graphically by a jump to a new life cycle (see Figure 9.4). This jump represents change in the form of revolution: the system metamorphoses to a higher level on the spiral of evolution.

However, it is important to recognize that the jump to a new life cycle represents a fundamental change in the quality of the system. As it stands, the diagram is drawn only in two dimensions, so it is all too easy to misinterpret the move from the lower life cycle to the higher one as just involving a quantitative jump. In fact, what the diagram represents is an irreversible shift in the subjective meaning of the system: there is an innovation, a paradigm shift, structural adjustment or shift in purpose. One of the clearest examples of the depth of change that is involved is that of the fertilization of an ovum by a spermatozoon. Both the ovum and the spermatozoon have a specific life cycle: if they don't meet, they

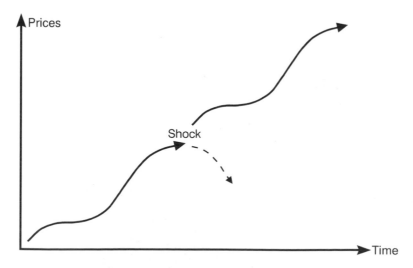

Figure 9.4 Evolutionary metamorphosis

both die; if they do meet, each jumps from its old life cycle to a new life cycle. The latter, which is the formation of an embryo, includes but transcends both the ovum and the spermatozoon.

So, the complementary ideas of 'transcending the old' and of 'irreversibility' are the ones to keep in mind when using life cycle transformations. Providing this is done, the concept is extremely powerful and can be applied to all aspects of economic, financial and social development. In 1979, for example, the German economist Gerhard Mensch used the concept to demonstrate that an economy evolves by means of a series of intermittent impulses of innovation – a process that he called 'evolutionary metamorphosis'.[6] In more recent years, the concept has been used by Charles Handy[7] and Andrew Grove[8] to demonstrate that, in order to avoid personal or corporate deterioration, there comes a stage when an evolutionary jump has to be made. To put the same thing another way, if individuals or companies are not prepared to transcend old limitations, and are not prepared to adopt new paradigms and new purposes, then a process of collapse sets in.[9]

THE IMPORTANCE OF TIMING

One point that is almost invariably missed in this type of analysis is that there is only a very narrow time window in which the transformation can occur. If that time window is missed, then either the change cannot occur or the change is just too much and it becomes destructive. In other words, evolutionary jumps can only occur at specific points in an evolutionary process. This conclusion may be difficult to accept, but the phenomenon can be clearly recognized in a number of simple examples: children enter puberty at predetermined times; water becomes steam at predetermined temperatures; and the quietude of winter becomes the vigorous stirring of spring during a specific period in the relationship between the Earth and the Sun.

In fact, if we look a little more closely at the earlier example of the ovum and the spermatozoon, a further dimension of the mysterious phenomenon of evolution reveals itself. This is that the moment of revolutionary change can only manifest under very specific conditions of synchronicity. That is, not only must the active transforming energy (the spermatazoon) be able to make exactly the right impact, but the passive receptive system (the ovum) also has to be 'ready' to receive the energy. Under any other circumstances, no change can occur.

How, then, can we determine when the recipient system is properly receptive to change? Nature, of course, has its own solution to this particular problem, but, in the context of our analysis here, the theoretical answer to the question reveals one of the great secrets of life on this planet. A system becomes properly receptive only at the point of inflexion of its life cycle. That is, it becomes properly receptive at an energy gap. Therefore, in Figure 9.4, the jump to a qualitatively different life cycle effectively circumvents the collapse of the old life cycle.

Note what will happen in other circumstances. If active energy is input into a system prior to the point of inflexion, it might either be rejected or create changes that are incompatible with the wider environment.[10] On the other hand, if energy is input into a system after the point of inflexion, the system will already be reversing so that its condition is inappropriate for the new energy.[11]

PRO-TREND SHOCKS IN FINANCIAL MARKETS

We can now look in a little more detail at the impact of structural (or second-order) change in financial markets. The important elements are shown in Figure 9.5, which traces out the initial phases of a bull market. The rally starts (1^1–2^1–3^1) with the first three waves of the lower-order price pulse (1–2–3). However, a pro-trend information shock occurs that enables the market to jump the energy gap. As a result, the market metamorphoses to a higher level (1^2–2^2–3^2), and experiences the remaining quantitative movements of the lower-level pulse (A–B–C) from a higher qualitative level. As presented, the lower-level price pulse continues to exert an influence on the market pattern, even after the pro-trend shock. Consequently, the pro-trend shock merely causes the market to delay its downturn. However, there are other alternatives. First, as already indicated, a pro-trend shock has to be absorbed, and this involves some form of retrenchment, which, in theory, need not be perfectly aligned with a downturn in a lower-order price pulse. Second, if the pro-trend shock is particularly powerful – which could well be the case if it emanates from a sufficiently high level – then the influence of the lower pulse may be all but eliminated. We shall revisit these issues in Chapter 22.

The corresponding pattern at the beginning of a bear move is shown in Figure 9.6. Here, the fall (A^1–B^1–C^1) starts with the last three waves

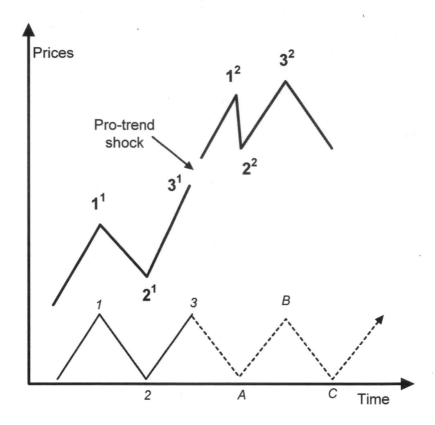

Figure 9.5 Evolutionary metamorphosis during a bull move

of a lower-order price pulse (A–B–C). However, a pro-trend information shock forces the market over the energy gap that would otherwise turn prices higher. As a result, the market aligns itself with a qualitatively different structure, and experiences a further three waves $(A^2–B^2–C^2)$ down. The effectiveness of the shock is confirmed by the fact that wave 2 of the next cycle (which should be a re-test of a trough) makes a new low. This is a very common occurrence but, it needs to be added, the timings need not automatically be determined by the lower-order price pulse. On the one hand, some form of rally after the pro-trend shock is an inevitable consequence of the shock and may not necessarily tie neatly into wave 1 of the lower-level price pulse. On the other hand, if the pro-trend information shock is significant enough, the influence of the lower-level pulse may be washed away. As already mentioned, we shall take another look at these phenomena in Chapter 22.

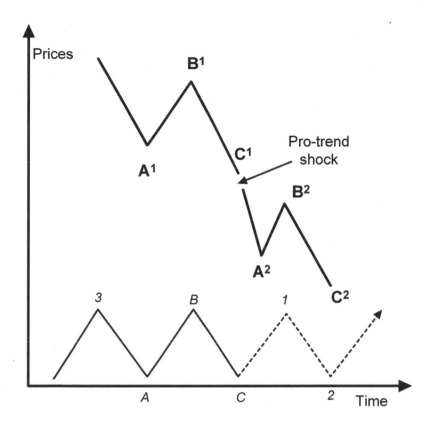

Figure 9.6 Evolutionary metamorphosis during a bear move

ENERGY GAPS AND INFORMATION FLOWS

This analysis reveals the genuine importance of information at critical moments in the evolution of a price trend in a market. First, there is the information shock of an unbridged energy gap. Then, during the re-test of the reversal point, the market 'learns' that the trend is, indeed, changing. Some of the data that occur during this period will strongly suggest that a reversal is justified. Finally, the market moves away from the reversal pattern and follows the line of least resistance up as far as the next energy gap. During this third phase, information flows confirm the market trend.

During this whole process, it is apparent that the information flows are either lagging behind market sentiment or are merely consistent with it, but they are not leading market sentiment. Nevertheless, there will come a point in the evolution of a trend when the market can go no further on the basis of information that just confirms the trend. There is, for example, a limit to the number of people who can invest solely on the news that company earnings improved during the last quarter. Unless the flow of news includes an item that is qualitatively different, the market will reverse.

If such an item of information emerges, the second energy gap will be bridged and the market will jump to a new structure. This item of information will, in a sense, be ahead of the market. There may, for example, be an official announcement that changes the responsibilities of the central bank. There may be an unexpected fiscal announcement. There may be an 'act of God', such as an earthquake in a major financial centre, or there may be a drought or flood. There may be an outbreak of war. There may even be a small item of information that finally gives critical mass to a whole matrix of related information. The list is potentially infinite. However, there are criteria that identify items of information that are pro-trend shocks:

▌ they are unexpected;

▌ they significantly alter the market crowd's 'mind map' for the future – in other words, expectations are radically adjusted as a paradigm shift emerges;

▌ the shock is most likely to occur when the market is otherwise naturally overextended and when price action may be flashing warning signals for a reversal.

CHANGES IN THE QUALITY OF INFORMATION

This last point is extraordinarily important. It is usually (and correctly) argued that reacting to news can be dangerous. Specifically, it encourages traders to buy at high prices and sell at low prices, thereby creating an energy gap. Nevertheless, it is absolutely essential to know when the quality of incoming data has changed. Awareness of such changes can give an investor the critical edge. It enables them to respond with confidence to the news. Indeed, information shocks – and, hence, market extensions – actually occur when most market participants least expect it. That is, the market is considered to have 'moved too far'. Under these circumstances, many short-term traders will have taken profits and longer-term investors will not feel confident about committing themselves further.[12] This means that financial resources will be available to respond to the shock.

IDENTIFYING THE SHOCK POINT

An information shock that bridges the second energy gap will almost certainly impact during a very short period of time. As such, there will be a 'shock point', definable in both price and time, that will be likely to leave certain distinguishing features in the pattern of price behaviour and in indices of investor behaviour.

First, the shock point will be associated with a sharp movement in prices. This may occur either as a large expansion in the width of the trading range for a given time period or as a gap in the price trading range between one period and another.

Second, momentum indicators (such as a rate of change indicator) will be likely to show signs of acceleration.

Third, investor volumes will jump and open interest in the futures market will adjust sharply[13] as the implications of the information shock sink in.

Importantly, the information shock has implications for the generation and measurement of cycles. It is part of the extraordinary mathematical coherence of markets that the shock point can usually be calculated from the pattern of the price movement that follows the shock. We shall discuss this phenomenon in Chapter 22.

THE PATTERN OF A TREND

The bridging of the energy gap is probably the only time that data genuinely 'inform' and lead the market. Furthermore, its occurrence is important because the subsequent market price action is predictable – at some stage shortly after the information shock, a contra-trend move will materialize as the cycle finally snaps in.

The most obvious conclusion from the patterns is that, following a genuine pro-trend shock, traders should buy weakness in a rising market or sell strength in a falling market. However, there are other, quite profound conclusions to be drawn from the analysis.

First, the presence of five waves in a trend – that is, three in the direction of the trend and two against the trend – is a clear indication of structural change. Five waves (or more) are the hallmark of evolution (this is shown in Figure 9.7).

Second, the third wave within a five-wave movement is likely to be the longest. This is because it consists of two parts – namely, the eventual movement along the path of least resistance after the contra-

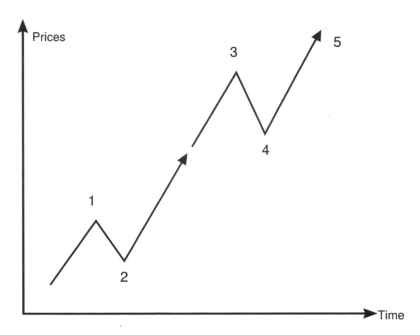

Figure 9.7 The five-wave pattern of evolution

trend information shock plus the initial response following the pro-trend shock.

Third, the fourth wave is unlikely to penetrate beyond the extreme of the first wave in the move. This is because the system has evolved and there are constraints on the subsequent ability of the system to regress.

Fourth, the correction following the fifth wave is likely to be greater than the corrections that preceded it. This is because it emerges at a higher level of the market's price–time hierarchy.

As many people now know, the five-wave pattern is the basis of Ralph Nelson Elliott's 'wave principle'. We shall therefore analyse Elliott's own work in a little more detail in Chapter 21.

CONCLUSION

Market oscillations are created by energy gaps. The first type of energy gap occurs where energy is being diverted to cope with the process of learning that a reversal has indeed taken place. The gap is, as it were, a 'pause for thought'. Information becomes available that confirms the possibility that the reversal is genuine. However, sentiment is still coloured by the previous trend.

The partial retracement of the new trend – the re-test of the original high or low – provides the platform for the subsequent impulse move. There is, therefore, a bridge across the energy gap that links the initial learning situation to the impulse move. During this impulse move, the market 'knows' that it is in a trend. All data will be understood in this context. Data that do not confirm the trend will be dismissed or ignored, while data that do confirm the trend contribute nothing new in terms of information. Prices will move along a line of least resistance.

The second type of energy gap arises when a market is satiated or overextended. In this case, no more resources can be committed to a trend. Consequently, the gap cannot be bridged and a reversal sets in. The reversal constitutes the contra-trend shock that was analysed in Chapter 8.

The combination of energy gaps therefore creates a basic three-up, three-down oscillation in financial markets. This is the basis of rhythmic cycles.

However, this basic wave pattern is subject to qualitative evolution. The second energy gap is both the point of satiation and the point at which a market is susceptible to revolutionary pro-trend shocks. Such shocks have the ability to project the market into a new paradigm. They need to be recognized by market participants because they create a jump to a new life cycle. The emergence of such a life cycle creates a market price pattern that can best be described as a five-wave pattern. Five waves are the hallmark of evolution.

NOTES

1. See Mills, Henry (1967) *Teaching and Training*, Macmillan, London.
2. Mills, Henry (1967) *Teaching and Training*, Macmillan, London.
3. Hebb, Donald (1949) *The Organisation of Behaviour*, John Wiley, New York.
4. A similar phenomenon occurs following the intake of food. Some of the existing energy has to be diverted to digest the food. As a result, the body initially experiences a period of lethargy before recovering into a period of higher energy.
5. The fact that passivity is an active energy is usually missed and therefore causes much analytical confusion. In financial markets, of course, the passive stage is a bear market. The larger bear markets destroy wealth rather than just give everybody a period of rest and recuperation.

6. Mensch, Gerhard (1979) *Stalemate in Technology*, Ballinger, Cambridge, Massachusetts. Mensch was particularly forceful in arguing that depressions occur because of the absence of basic innovations. Although he didn't specifically say so, this is an energy gap.
7. Handy, Charles (1994) *The Empty Raincoat*, Hutchinson, London.
8. Grove, Andrew S (1996) *Only the Paranoid Survive*, Doubleday, New York.
9. We shall deal with the process of personal change in a little more detail in Chapter 22.
10. If, for example, an ovum is fertilized before it reaches the womb, severe problems are created for the mother.
11. An ovum cannot be fertilized when it is being expelled from the body during menstruation.
12. Obviously, the definition of short-term and long-term investment is highly subjective.
13. Open interest will eventually rise sharply. However, it may initially contract as losing positions are unwound.

10

The spiral and the golden ratio

INTRODUCTION

We have seen that the price adjustment process following an information shock can be represented by a spiral. The adjustment spiral occurs over time, so it can be viewed in three dimensions. In a financial market, these dimensions may be described as the rate of change in prices, the level of sentiment and time. As an example, Figure 10.1 reproduces the theoretical adjustment process during the movement from a bull market to a bear market. The left-hand part of the diagram represents the spiral relationship between the change in prices and sentiment, but with no 'time' dimension, while the right-hand part represents the corresponding 'shock wave' adjustment of prices over time, but with no 'sentiment' dimension.

THE MATHEMATICS OF THE SPIRAL

From this it follows, of course, that price patterns should reveal the presence of the spiral. We shall discuss this in more detail in Chapters 11 and 12. However, there is another implication that is of profound importance. This is that price movements should be mathematically related to one another. The reason is that the spiral itself can be defined using mathematics.

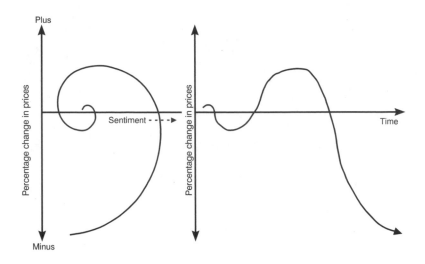

Figure 10.1 The price–sentiment spiral in two dimensions

The source of all spirals is a geometric expansion of some form. Each number in a geometric expansion is obtained from the number that precedes it by multiplying it by a constant ratio. The most obvious is the so-called 'doubling sequence' where each term in the series is double that of its predecessor – namely,

$$2, 4, 8, 16, 32, 64, 128, \text{ and so on.}$$

Here, the constant ratio is 2. It is readily apparent, even from this simple example, that the higher the ratio, the more explosive will be the result. It therefore follows that if a spiral is actually a 'natural' phenomenon (in the literal sense of being a part of nature), the ratio must be relatively small, although greater than unity.[1]

THE FIBONACCI NUMBER SEQUENCE

Of all the geometric expansions that can, and do, occur in nature, there is one in particular that stands out above the others as being important. This is the Fibonacci sequence, which is based on the ratio 1.618. This sequence is named after Leonardo of Pisa who, writing under the name of Fibonacci, published his famous *Liber Abaci* (or *Book of Calculations*) in 1202. This book introduced the decimal system (which includes zero as the first digit in the sequence and which is sometimes referred to as the Hindu–Arabic system) to Europe. Although Fibonacci was undoubtedly the greatest mathematician of the Middle Ages, it is perhaps ironic that he is remembered today mainly because the nineteenth-century analyst Edouard Lucas attached his name to a sequence that appears in a trivial problem in *Liber Abaci*.

FIBONACCI'S RABBIT PROBLEM

The problem was presented in terms of the reproductive capabilities of rabbits – namely, how many pairs of rabbits could one pair produce in a year?[2] The first pair are allowed to reproduce in the first month, but subsequent pairs can only reproduce from their second month onwards. Each birth consists of two rabbits. Assuming that none of the rabbits dies, then a pair is born during the first month, so there are two pairs. During the second month, the first pair reproduces, creating another pair. During the third month, both the original pair and the first-born pair have produced new pairs. Consequently, there are three adult pairs and two young pairs. If the analysis is continued, the results are as shown in Table 10.1, and it is apparent that the basic sequence (the Fibonacci sequence) is:

1, 1, 2, 3, 5, 8, 13, 21, 34, 55, 89, 144, and so on.

Table 10.1 Growth of a rabbit colony

Month	Adult pairs	Young pairs	Total
1	1	1	2
2	2	1	3
3	3	2	5
4	5	3	8
5	8	5	13
6	13	8	21
7	21	13	34
8	34	21	55
9	55	34	89
10	89	55	144
11	144	89	233
12	233	144	377

THE FIBONACCI SEQUENCE AND NATURE

Now, on the face of it, this sequence is of no interest to anyone other than a student of mathematics or a rabbit breeder. However, mathematicians and scientists have discovered that the Fibonacci sequence can be found throughout nature, defining both the appearance of physical structures and the progress of change in dynamic structures. Indeed, it appears that human beings find those phenomena that are overtly related to the sequence intrinsically pleasing, both to sight and hearing.[3] Before pursuing these observations any further, however, it is necessary to have a closer look at the properties of the Fibonacci sequence.

THE PROPERTIES OF THE FIBONACCI SEQUENCE

There are, in fact, three important properties of the sequence. The first is that each term in the sequence (after the second) is the sum of the two terms that immediately preceded it. That is:

$$2 = 1 + 1$$
$$3 = 2 + 1$$
$$5 = 3 + 2$$
$$8 = 5 + 3$$
$$13 = 8 + 5$$

and so on.

Such sequences – in which every term (after a certain point) can be represented as a linear combination of preceding terms – are called recursive sequences. The Fibonacci sequence is the first-known recursive sequence.

The second important feature is that each term in the sequence, when divided by the term after it, approximates the ratio 0.618. To be more precise, the ratio of successive terms oscillates around the limit of 0.618. The divergence from 0.618 is much greater for earlier values than for later ones. The inverse of 0.618 is 1.618. Not surprisingly, therefore, the ratio of each term in the sequence, divided by the term before it, approximates 1.618.

The third feature of the sequence is that alternate terms are related to one another by the ratio 0.382 and by its inverse, 2.618. Hence, if any term in the sequence is divided by the next-but-one number after it, the result is 0.382, while if it is divided by the next-but-one before it, the result is 2.618. Again, the ratio is more accurate for calculations applied to later terms in the sequence than it is to earlier ones.

Finally, the same procedure can be repeated with numbers that lie increasingly further away from one another. For example, numbers that are three terms away from one another in the Fibonacci sequence yield the ratio 0.236 and its inverse 4.236; numbers that are four terms away from one another produce the ratio 0.146 and its inverse 6.853; and so forth.

THE IMPORTANT RATIOS

There are thus several ratios that can be derived from the Fibonacci sequence and various ways in which these ratios are related. For example:

$$0.618 \times 0.618 = 0.382$$
$$1.618 \times 1.618 = 2.618$$
$$2.618 \times 1.618 = 4.236$$
$$1 - 0.618 = 0.382$$
$$1.618 / 0.618 = 2.618$$
$$0.618 / 1.618 = 0.382$$
$$0.382 \times 0.382 = 0.146$$

It is apparent, however, that the two primary ratios are 0.618 and 1.618. The others are essentially derivatives of these.

THE GOLDEN RATIO

The number 0.618 and its inverse, 1.618, are both known as the 'golden ratio', and are usually denoted in the literature by the Greek letter phi (= Φ), which is the twenty-first letter of the Greek alphabet. It is of some significance that the golden ratio is functionally related to $\sqrt{5}$, which is equal to 2.236. Specifically:

$$0.618 = (\sqrt{5} - 1) / 2$$
$$1.618 = (\sqrt{5} + 1) / 2$$

THE GOLDEN RATIO IN GEOMETRY

The important role of 0.618 and its inverse, 1.618, becomes even more explicit when the idea is extended to geometry. Any straight line may be divided in such a way that the ratio of the smaller part to the larger part is equivalent to the ratio of the larger part to the whole. That ratio is always 0.618. This is shown in Figure 10.2, where

$$BC/AB = AB/AC = 0.618$$

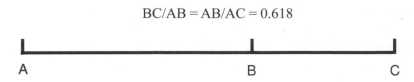

A   B   C

Figure 10.2 The golden ratio

In other words, the relationship between successive lengths – moving upwards from the smallest, through the largest, to the whole – is constant. This means that, if the length AC is given as 1 unit, then since AC = AB + BC,

$$AC = 0.382 + 0.618$$

And it also means that

$$0.382/0.618 = 0.618$$

The number 0.618 is the golden number, the associated ratio, 0.618:1, is the golden ratio, and the constant proportion between the lengths, 0.382:0.618 = 0.618:1, is the golden proportion. The generic term for the phenomenon is the golden measure.

THE GOLDEN MEASURE AND THE HUMAN BODY

Now, this is not just a rarefied exercise in mathematics or logic. The importance of the golden measure lies in the fact that it appears everywhere in nature. For example, it can be found throughout the human body.[4] The length from the base of a person's foot to the navel is, on average, 61.8 per cent of that person's total height. The distance from the navel to the middle of the neck is then 61.8 per cent of the distance from the navel to the top of the head; and the distance from the navel to the knee is 61.8 per cent of the distance from the navel to the base of the foot. Meanwhile, computer analysis of a so-called 'ideal' face, made from an amalgam of a large number of faces, confirms that the width of the head is 61.8 per cent of the height of the head; that the distance from the centre of the eyes to the tip of the nose is 61.8 per cent of the distance from the eyes to the mouth; and that the distance from the tip of the nose to the chin is 61.8 per cent of the distance from the eyes to the chin. Furthermore – and by no means finally – each bone of a person's finger is 61.8 per cent of the length of the adjoining bone.

Of course, there will be significant individual divergences from all of these calculations; but the larger the number of individuals whose structural proportions are measured, the more likely it will be that the average of the ratios will converge on the golden measure.

THE GOLDEN MEASURE IN NATURE

This is not the place to go into all the evidence for the presence of the golden measure, but the point to be clear about is that it is ubiquitous in living systems. This raises very important questions, such as: Why is this so? What does it imply about the laws of life? And should we actually be paying more attention to it? Unfortunately, although Western culture recognizes the presence of the golden measure,[5] it nevertheless tends to treat it as something of an accident, or evolutionary genetic outcome, and leave it at that. Very few take the time to ponder some of the deeper implications.

However, this was not always the case. It is not known when the presence of the golden measure was first recognized by humankind. There is certainly evidence that it was known about in the third millennium BCE because it was incorporated into the building of the pyramids at Giza.[6] However, what is clear is that, when one of the older civilizations came to know about it, it was treated with a particular degree of reverence. Specifically it was treated, not as an *outcome*, but as an *influence* – not as an effect, but as a cause. It was considered to be, in some way, inherent in the blueprint of creation and therefore 'prior to' the structures of this world. In short, the golden measure was considered to be a direct reflection of the essential nature of God.

THREE TERMS FROM TWO

The mathematics of the golden measure give us some indication of why this was considered to be the case. The main point is that the golden ratio is the only ratio that allows the proportional relationships between three terms (AB, BC and AC in Figure 10.2) to be expressed by the relationship between two of those terms (AB and BC). In other words, if BC is to AB as AB is to AC, and if AC = AB + BC, then

$$AB/(AB + BC) = BC/AB = 0.618$$

THE GOLDEN RECTANGLE AND THE GOLDEN RATIO

Moreover – and this is important – the relationship stays constant, no matter what absolute quantity is involved. That is, the golden proportion operates in (and despite) the processes of growth and decay. So, in Figure 10.2, AC can get bigger or smaller, but the internal integrity of the relationships remains unchanged. A very basic diagram can demonstrate this idea. In Figure 10.3, a rectangle ACDF is constructed on the line AC, derived from Figure 10.2. However, the dimensions of the rectangle are such that the width of the rectangle (ie, CD or BE) is equal to the length of the line AB. In other words, the rectangle is drawn so that ABEF is a square.

THE SPIRAL OF RECTANGLES

Next, we can draw a square within the smaller rectangle BCDE, with one side on, and equal to, the line DE. See Figure 10.4. Two things have now happened. First, since by construction DE/EF = 0.618, then the perimeter length of the square DEHG is 61.8 per cent of that of the

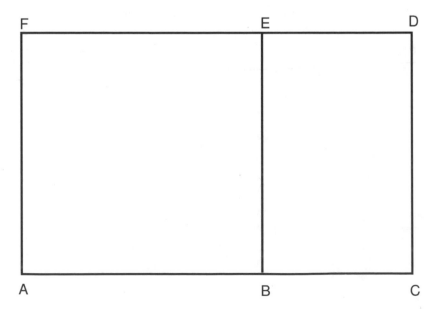

Figure 10.3 The golden rectangle

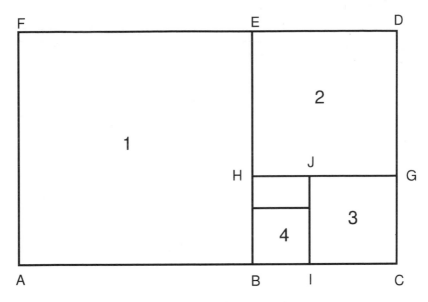

Figure 10.4 Golden rectangles

square ABEF. Second, we have simultaneously created a rectangle GHBC. Since GH/CD = 0.618, then the perimeter length of the rectangle GHBC is 61.8 per cent of that of the rectangle DEBC.

The process can then be repeated. See Figure 10.4 again. This time the new square is drawn with one of its sides on, and equal to, GC. The rectangle GHBC then consists of a square GJIC and a rectangle JHBI.

THE GOLDEN SPIRAL

It can immediately be seen that we are constructing a series of contracting squares, whose boundaries are touching in such a way that they appear to be spiralling towards some infinitesimally small amount. Indeed, the points A, E, G, I, etc can be linked together by an appropriate spiralling arc. See Figure 10.5.

Logically, of course, we could have constructed the diagram differently, drawing ever-*increasing* squares on the sides of rectangles. The process would represent a spiral towards some infinitely large figure.

PROPERTIES OF THE GOLDEN SPIRAL

The golden spiral is a logarithmic spiral and, as such, it has two distinctive features:

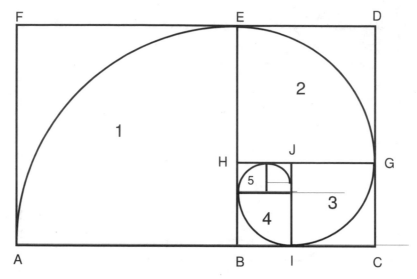

Figure 10.5 The golden spiral

▌ it starts and ends in infinity – therefore it has no boundaries and its centre can never actually be reached;

▌ it does not change shape – any straight line drawn from the centre intersects the spiral at the same angle (in Figure 10.6, therefore, the angle between the tangent at any given point and the radius drawn from the centre is a constant).

Because the golden spiral is defined by the ratio 0.618, and its inverse 1.618, there are two further characteristics that are worth highlighting:

▌ each radius drawn from the theoretical centre of the spiral is related to the radius that precedes it at 90° by 1.618;

▌ each diameter of the spiral is related to the diameter that precedes it at 90° by the ratio 1.618.

THE GOLDEN MEASURE AND ANCIENT RELIGIOUS INSIGHT

We thus have a specific type of spiral – known as a logarithmic spiral – that is constructed using the ratio 0.618:1. It starts and ends in infinity, and thereby identifies the unattainable point where the infinitely large is harmonized with the infinitesimally small. This,

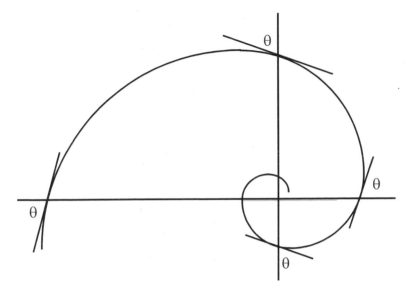

Figure 10.6 Constant angles and the golden spiral

together with the other attributes of the golden measure that have already been discussed, encouraged ancient religious authorities to consider the validity of three inter-related propositions.

First, since the larger of the elements in equation 1 is equal to the sum of the other two elements, the golden number 0.618 was an expression of the way that *The Source of All Things* divided itself into *The Many*. Or, to be even more esoteric, as the way that *The One* divided itself into *Two*. Specifically, the larger of the two portions was the passive, receptive, power; while the smaller portion was the active, generative, power. Horizontally, this meant female and male respectively; vertically, it meant spiritual and mental respectively. But note the extra element in this: the two lower-order (passive and active) polarities were balanced and harmonized by the higher-order whole.

Second, the proportional relationships made no claim about the *cause* of change. Change could be initiated from above (ie, from the whole), through either the active pole or the passive pole (ie, the parts); or it could be initiated from below by either the active part or the passive part, and the whole adjusts. Since the mathematical relationships required only that proportions remain constant, change anywhere in the system was automatically supplemented by change in other parts. Among many other things, therefore, the golden ratio 0.618:1 implied both that Man's decisions were validated by God and that God's Will was implemented by Man.

And third, because of the constancy of the relationships, the golden proportion $0.382:0.618 = 0.618:1$ was an expression of the fact that change can occur without involving chaos.

The golden measure was thus both the mathematical reconciliation between the Whole and Its Parts and the archetypal mathematical formulation of the ancient saying, 'As above, so below.'

THE 'LAWS' OF LIFE

On the face of it, these interpretations might be seen as extraordinarily arcane and, accordingly, as having little or no relevance to the modern world. But if we look a little deeper, there is a logic contained within them that not only bears consideration but also has a direct correspondence to modern scientific thought. Contemporary analysis is gradually coming to terms with three aspects of life on this planet. First, life is a self-organizing, constantly changing process that is stimulated by (and therefore learns from) information 'shocks'. Second, life interacts with itself via circulation between opposite polarities. And third, life is attracted either to expansion or contraction. These are fundamental 'laws' for the existence of life; and there are no exceptions. However, by definition, these laws have certain mathematical requirements, not the least of which is the need to reconcile random fluctuations with stable processes. And the point is that the golden measure may actually be part of the context within which this reconciliation can take place. Let's just take a brief look at this.[7]

INFORMATION AND THE HUMAN MIND

The first area to look at is the human mind. The mind is a self-organizing system that learns by its interactions with the environment. Obviously, a part of this learning involves conscious reasoning. It is relevant, therefore, that the concept of ratios is directly involved with this process. Indeed, the words *rational* ('of the reason') and *ratiocination* ('to reason') are derived from the same Latin root as *ratio*. Older civilizations than ours had therefore obviously spotted the importance of ratios to humankind's ability to think clearly. To them the ability to reason meant the ability to use ratios. Suppose, therefore, that we wanted to present a ratio, or set of ratios, that simultaneously represented the abilities of the human mind to perceive, reason and conclude.

What ratio(s) would we use? Put another way: what would be the characteristics of a ratio (or ratios) that best represented the various types of information that a human mind can receive and generate?

RECOGNIZING INFORMATION

First, the human mind needs to be able to 'recognize' information. This means that it needs to be able to recognize a change, or difference, between one state and another. This is the basis of *analytical* reasoning. In its simplest form, therefore, if we denote one state as being A and the other as being B, and the human mind recognizes and responds to the difference between A and B, then the situation could be represented by the ratio A:B. But note what happens if A = B. There is no 'difference' as such, and the ratio A:B becomes equal to unity. Without difference, there is no information and no response. Hence, a ratio that represents analytical reasoning needs to consist of unequal numbers so that it is not equal to unity.

UNDERSTANDING BY ANALOGY

Second, however, the ratio A:B does not in itself need human intelligence in order to create a reaction. The ratio could, for example, represent an amoeba's response to a change in its environment. So a simple number is a necessary, but not sufficient, part of the representation of human intelligence. In fact, human intelligence has a specific additional dimension. This is the ability to understand by *analogy* – ie, by comparison. The ability to make comparisons facilitates attraction and repulsion. Consequently, a ratio that represents the human mind and its abilities would need to include *three* terms. That is, the appropriate ratio would have to be able to compare not just A with B, but also B with (say) C. Hence, the appropriate ratio would be something like A:B = B:C. Providing that A and B are not equal, this allows for perception via both analysis and analogy. The ability to reason analytically and analogically will ensure survival.

CREATIVE INSIGHT

Even so, there is a third element. The proportion A:B = B:C does not allow for the absolutely critical part of human intelligence that goes beyond ensuring survival. This is the faculty of *creative insight*, or intuition, that encourages evolution. The very real problem, however, is that we do not really know where such insight (or intuition) comes from. It is one thing to collect pertinent facts, but it is yet another thing to claim that the critical insight based on those facts was purely the result of analytical and analogical reasoning. Or, to put the same thing another way, we can create the right quantitative conditions for insights, but the essential ingredient of putting it all together and 'seeing' a different qualitative dimension within a data set lies somehow beyond our ordinary everyday abilities.

Now, some of the greatest philosophers in the world – including more recent ones such as Alfred North Whitehead and William James – have suggested that intuition arises from a level of the mind's organizing power that is not easily accessible. Specifically, they have suggested that accessing intuition is very much a case of becoming passive and allowing an insight to 'drop through' in one whole piece, as it were. The 'effort' therefore needs to go towards relaxing the mind, rather than exciting it. If this is correct, then it suggests an intriguing possibility. This is that the mind is in a feedback loop with its own higher levels of organization.

SELF-ORGANIZING HIERARCHIES

This possibility is, in fact, not too different from the idea that was inherent in religious attitudes to the golden measure. This is that the lower-order parts are organized by higher-order levels, but that higher-order levels consist of lower-order parts. The difference between the two levels in this 'hierarchy' is that the whole is greater than the sum of its parts. And modern scientific thought now absolutely accepts the presence of such hierarchical organization in the phenomenon of life. So, if we wanted to represent this hierarchical, self-organizing aspect of the human mind, what set of ratios would we use? Amazingly, the most appropriate set is the golden proportion $A:B = B:(A + B)$! Indeed, it is only this set that allows for the whole to consist explicitly only of its parts.

So, despite the apparently arcane origins of the golden measure, it precisely contains within itself the important features of a self-organizing system. The golden measure recognizes information in the form of differences; it accommodates responsiveness to that information by allowing comparison; and it allows for feedback within a system by recognizing the presence of hierarchical levels of self-organization. We are back to the three conditions for the existence of life on this planet: self-organization stimulated by information, circulation between opposite polarities, and attraction to growth or decay.

These are profound conclusions that raise equally profound questions about the insights of those who originally worked with the golden measure. After all, only the terminology has changed. But, as we have already seen in relation to the human body, the golden measure does not appear to be just a metaphor. There seems to be something quite practical about it.

METAPHOR AND REALITY

The first point to make is that metaphors and symbols are too often taken to be an irrelevance to 'modern' life. However, psychologists are now very aware of the profound impact that metaphors and symbols can have on the individual psyche – not only as representations of inner realities, but also as triggers for inner change. Metaphors and symbols activate the right-hand side of the brain, which is non-linear and 'holistic'. In fact, the right side of the brain has to be harmonized with the left side for the faculty of creative insight to be enabled. It is therefore hubris to consider that the left-hand, linear side of the brain is more important, more creative and more useful. And, as a corollary, it is immensely misguided to consider that historically early insights into the nature of being were incomplete or irrelevant. They may well have been complete: it is just that they may not necessarily have been packed out with a modern degree of scientific detail.[8]

The second point, however, is possibly more important. This is that the golden measure is not just a right-brain symbol. It is also clearly defined by left-brain mathematical equations. The science of mathematics rightfully belongs to the realm of ideas, but its ultimate value lies either in the accuracy of its description of known reality or in its implications for unknown reality. So, mathematics can, like metaphors, point towards a truth that lies beyond the boundary of known experimental techniques. Hence, one inference that could be drawn from the mathematics of the golden measure is that, if it is relevant to life on earth, we really should be able to identify its presence in indices that, in some way, reflect the behaviour of living systems. And it is arguable that one such system is a financial market.

FINANCIAL MARKET CROWDS

This idea holds water because the phenomenon of self-organization is universal. If every part of life has its own individuality but belongs to a larger group, then it follows that there are forces at work in human behaviour that originate from beyond each individual person. There is nothing esoteric about this (although that, too, is an option). All it means is that human beings come together in various ways and create groupings whose influence is greater than the sum of their parts. At a simple level, there is 'family' or 'tribe'; at a larger level, there is 'society'; and at a meta-level, there is 'civilization'. And these groupings incorporate the influences of history, so self-organization extends over time. The point is that these groupings are psychological and not necessarily physical. They are based on beliefs, understandings and codes of behaviour that are transmitted from one person to another, and from one sub-group to another. And they are discriminatory: an individual is either in a particular overall grouping or out of it. This is the basis of all forms of group competition and group violence. Individuals behave differently in groups than they do in isolation.

Within financial markets, the outcome of group behaviour is measurable by the fluctuation in prices. Indeed, financial markets therefore form a wonderful laboratory for testing out ideas about group behaviour. Moreover, simple observation of market prices confirms that they oscillate – ie, they go up and down – so it is probable that some form of swing between opposite polarities is at work. Consequently, a practical working hypothesis includes three features: a) financial markets are a part of a wider socio-economic environment and are therefore 'organized' by the latter; b) a market 'organizes' its parts to conform with developments in the higher socio-economic environment; and c) the various hierarchical levels are linked by the transfer of information that creates oscillations. Under this hypothesis, a group is a part of the natural order of things and, as such, its behaviour should reveal the influence of the golden measure.

THE GOLDEN MEASURE AND FINANCIAL MARKETS

In fact, the presence of the golden measure in financial markets has been known about since the early part of the last century. R N Elliott[9] was the most celebrated exponent but others such as H M Gartley[10] also utilized it very effectively. Elliott saw that corrections during a mature trend would tend to remain above 61.8 per cent of that trend; both he and Gartley saw that a re-test of a high or low would be limited to 61.8 per cent of the initial breakaway from that high or low. To put the same thing another way, both saw that corrections were somehow constrained by the golden proportion $0.382:0.618 = 0.618:1$.

One inference is that corrections are not random and chaotic events that materialize out of nowhere. They somehow bear a natural relationship to the cyclical process of which they are a part. We shall explore this in more detail in the following chapters.

NOTES

1. If the ratio is less than unity, the series will consist of progressively smaller numbers.
2. Quoted in Vorob'ev, N N (1961) *Fibonacci Numbers*, Pergamon, New York.
3. See, for example, the analysis by Huntley, H E (1970) *The Divine Proportion*, Dover Publications, New York.
4. The presence of the golden ratio in the human body is discussed in Ghyka, Matila (1977) *The Geometry of Art and Life*, Dover Publications, New York.
5. The recognition is also sub-conscious. It has been shown that if people are presented with a large number of four-sided shapes ranging from a square to a very long, thin rectangle, most of them will choose the shape that corresponds to the golden rectangle. See Borissavlietch, M (1958) *The Golden Number*, Tiranti, London.
6. See, for example, Michell, John (1983) *The New View Over Atlantis*, Thames and Hudson, London.
7. See, for example, Lawlor, Robert (1982) *Sacred Geometry: Philosophy and practice*, Thames and Hudson, London.
8. Metaphors and symbols – particularly those that 'work' – point to great truths, even though they are not themselves *the* truth. Since the ultimate truth (whatever that may be) is – by definition – unchanged and unchanging, old metaphors and symbols may still be applicable, provided that we can understand them.
9. Elliott, Ralph N (1946) *Nature's Law: The secret of the universe*, Elliott, New York, reprinted in Prechter, Robert (ed.) (1980) *The Major Works of R N Elliott*, New Classics Library, New York.
10. Gartley, H M (1935) *Profits in the Stock Market*, reprinted (1981) by Lambert-Gann, Pomeroy, Washington.

11

The mathematical basis of price movements

INTRODUCTION

It follows from the analysis of the previous chapter that the golden ratio is intricately linked to the growth of dynamic systems. As a crowd is a dynamic system, and financial markets exhibit crowd behaviour, it follows that the golden ratio should be found in financial markets. So, the next question is: how does the ratio actually reveal itself in financial markets?

We have already confirmed that all the points along a logarithmic spiral are mathematically related to one another. It therefore follows that spiral adjustments in financial markets should exhibit the same relationships. It will be remembered that when a financial market spiral is translated into two-dimensional space, the result is an 'unstable' cycle. Each swing of this cycle is related to its predecessor by a logarithmic ratio. In the case of the golden spiral – to which we have paid special attention – the relevant ratio will be 1.618 and its derivatives.

In Figure 10.5 of the previous chapter, rectangles were used to construct a golden spiral.[1] The important point is that the length of each rectangle measures a 'width' of the spiral, and that alternate rectangles reflect opposite 'swings' of the spiral. Hence, if we transfer the spiral into the two dimensions of price and time, it follows that successive swings will be related to one another by the ratio 2.618:1.[2] This relationship is shown in Figure 11.1, where:

$$CD/BC = 2.618$$

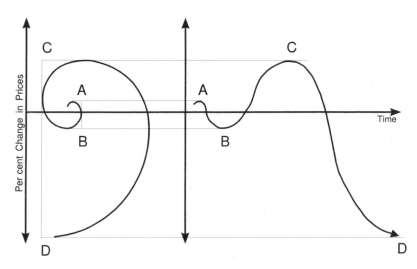

Figure 11.1 The golden ratio in price fluctuations

THE CALCULATION OF PRICE TARGETS

This implies that if we can identify the presence of the 'unstable' cycle in price movements, we should also be able to calculate precise price targets from the number 2.618. Initially, the market responds positively to a shock (which may be suggestive of either a new trend or a resumption of an old one). It then reverses direction under the influence of the spiral mechanism. Finally, it jumps in a dynamic move – the extent of which is determined by the ratio 2.618:1. In other words, the target level for the thrust is 2.618 times the arithmetical length of the last wave of the base or top pattern that preceded it. Hence, in Figure 11.2 the target price (P_t) is given as:

$$P_t = P_2 + (P_1 - P_2) \times 2.618$$

for rising markets, and:

$$P_t = P_2 - (P_2 - P_1) \times 2.618$$

for falling markets.

Despite the general accuracy of this calculation, it is worth noting that the mathematics sometimes need to be conducted in percentage terms. This is particularly true of bond markets, which are particularly susceptible to the psychological influence of percentage changes. Here, the relevant formulae are:

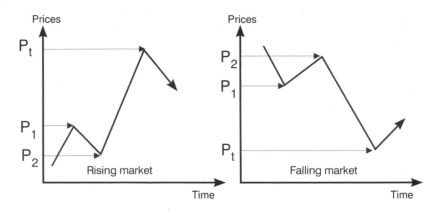

Figure 11.2 The 2.618 calculation

$$P_t = P_2 \times (1 + (1 - (P_2/P_1))) \times 2.618$$

for rising markets, and:

$$P_t = P_2 \times (1 + (P_1/P_2) - 1)) \times 2.618$$

for falling markets.

It is a simple exercise to conduct a few calculations on historical data to see if a particular market is responding to percentage changes or to absolute changes.

THE APPLICATION OF THE TARGET FORMULA

One of the most important demonstrations of the target formula dates back to the Wall Street Crash in the United States. Between the stock market high in 1929 and the low in 1932, the Dow Jones Industrial Average Index collapsed from 386 to 42 – a fall of 344 points. Multiplying 344 by 2.618 gave a targeted rise of 901 points. This meant an Index target of 942, just 58 points short of the psychologically important 1000 level (see Figure 11.3). This target was achieved almost 34 years[3] later in 1965–66, after which followed a multi-year correction. In fact, the level of 1000 was not seriously penetrated until early 1983.

However, the 2.618 'spiral' formula works in falling equity markets as well. Figure 11.4 shows the chart for the Hong Kong stock market, as represented by the Hang Seng Index. During the spring and early summer in 1997, the Hang Seng rallied to an intra-day high of

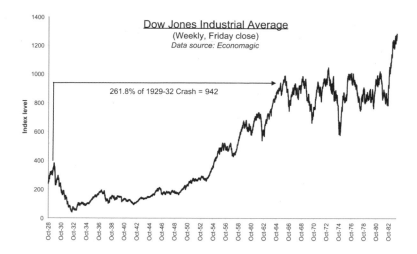

Figure 11.3 The Dow, 1928 to 1982

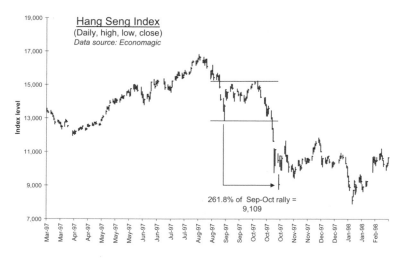

Figure 11.4 The Hang Seng stock market crash, 1997

16820.31 on 7 August. There then followed a sharp 23.3 per cent drop into early September. The next move, however, was a standard re-test of the high. The rally amounted to 2342.84 index points (that is, 18.16 per cent). Accordingly, when the next phase of the sell-off began in the wake of the Asian liquidity crisis, the projected fall was one of 6133.56 points, to an index level of 9109. This was a fall of 47.5 per cent (or a total fall of 54 per cent from the August high). On 27 October 1997, the market closed at 9059.89, having been somewhat lower during the day.

EXAMPLES FROM THE UK GILT-EDGED MARKET

We shall now look in some detail at government bond markets. They are highly liquid markets in the sense that willing buyers and sellers can be matched in large numbers within a relatively narrow range of prices, and they are efficient in so far as information is transmitted very quickly. Furthermore, bond markets are particularly applicable to the subject matter of this book because they are also very responsive to a wide range of economic, political and social influences.

Bond markets are also useful markets to monitor for purely practical reasons. They can be very simply represented by a general index, by the price of a single bond or by the yield of a single bond. First, apart from slight nuances with regard to coupons, one treasury bond is much the same as any other within a particular maturity range. Second, in all fixed interest markets, yields are inversely related to prices. Therefore, a chart history of any bond price over any given period would not only be representative of a whole range of stocks within a market, but would also be a mirror image of a chart history of yields over the same period.

Hence, Figure 11.5 shows the price movements of the UK treasury bond market (called the 'gilt-edged' market) between 1970 and 1994. Here, the gilt market is represented by an ultra-long-dated stock, Treasury 2½ per cent, redeemable on or after 1 April 1975.[4] This particular stock has been chosen because it provides a long and

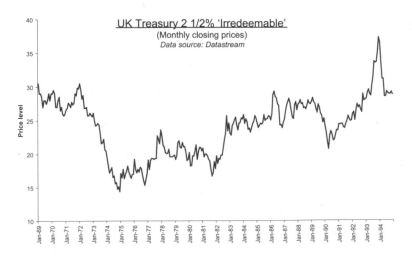

Figure 11.5 The UK gilt-edged market, 1970 to 1994

consistent history, without suffering distortions provided by the 'pull to redemption'.[5] The chart shows the massive collapse in prices between January 1972 and January 1975, followed by the volatile rise from 1975 to the high in January 1994. It also shows the so-called 'crash' of 1994. Roughly, we can identify three major bull phases over the period: October 1976 to January 1978, September 1981 to November 1982, and April 1990 to January 1994. Importantly, and persuasively, each of these bull phases – measured in percentage terms – was 2.618 times the correction that immediately preceded it.[6]

The years of 1972, 1973 and 1974 were dark years for both the gilt market and the UK equity market. Inflation was rising rapidly and the government boosted the economy when it should have been pulling in the reins. Between January 1975 and January 1976, however, there was a sharp rally in asset markets. In the case of Treasury 2½ per cent, the rally was one of 33 per cent. This rally was sufficient to convince even the most committed bears that a change in trend had taken place. However, between January 1976 and late 1976, when the IMF became involved with the state of Britain's finances following a sterling crisis, the market reversed. Treasury 2½ per cent fell by 20.13 per cent. If the spiral hypothesis is correct, then the subsequent rally should have amounted to 52.7 per cent (that is, 20.13 × 2.618), giving a target of 23.47. Between the end of October 1976 and the major peak in January 1978, the market rallied by 54.5 per cent to bring the price of Treasury 2½ per cent to 23.75 (see Figure 11.6).

There then followed a lengthy, and frequently interrupted, bear market down into September 1981. The last phase of this fall – from

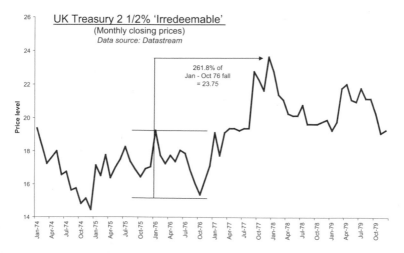

Figure 11.6 The UK gilt-edged market, January 1974 to October 1979

July 1980 to September 1981 – was a steep decline of 23.44 per cent (see Figure 11.7). The calculated target after this low involved a rally of 61.4 per cent to a price of 27.03. The actual close on 2 November 1982 was 27.00.

The following six and a half years were very volatile, to say the least. In particular, they covered the period leading up to and following the equity crash of 1987. The price of Treasury 2½ per cent rallied into a high (of 30.0) in April 1986, fell (to 24.63) prior to the equity crash, then rose into a re-test high (of 29.50) in March 1989. However, between March 1989 and April 1990, the bond fell by 29.5 per cent (to 20.81), taking the total fall since the high of April 1986 to 30.63 per cent (see Figure 11.8). The calculated upside target was 37.5, representing a rise of 80.2 per cent. The actual high in January 1994 was 37.63. The subsequent fall is now referred to as the bond 'crash of 1994'.

ADDITIONAL EXAMPLES

Before moving on to the US Treasury market, it is perhaps just worth commenting a little further on two specific episodes shown in Figure 11.5. These are the fall in gilt prices between January 1972 and January 1975 and the sharp rally into the high of April 1986. For this analysis, we shall use a different gilt stock – namely, Treasury 5½ per cent 2008/12. This stock has been chosen in order to highlight the fact that price targets may be calculated in arithmetical terms as well as in percentage terms.

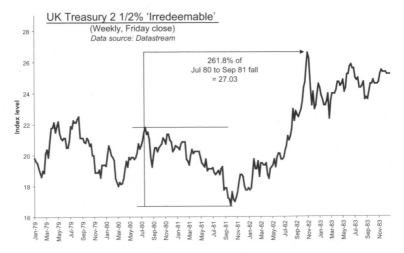

Figure 11.7 The UK gilt-edged market, January 1979 to November 1983

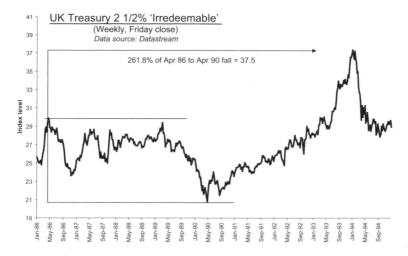

Figure 11.8 The UK gilt-edged market, January 1986 to September 1994

In the early 1970s, Chancellor Barber (under Prime Minister Heath) injected a massive dose of inflation into the UK economy. Long bonds were very badly hurt. Between January 1972 and January 1975, the price of Treasury 5½ per cent 2008/12 fell by 40.37 points – that is, from a price of 73.25 to a price of 32.88 (see Figure 11.9). This was a fall of 55.1 per cent. In the price action prior to the collapse, Treasury 5½ per cent 2008/12 rallied by 15.25 points. Using the arithmetical formula, the targeted fall was 33.33 (that is, 73.25 – (2.618 × 15.25)). The difference between forecast and outcome was therefore just over 1 per cent. The incredible implication of this calculation is that, although the fall was directly attributable to the policy errors made by Heath and Barber, it was actually foreshadowed by market behaviour in the period 1969–71.

Between February 1985 and April 1986, the gilt-edged market had a sharp rally into a peak that was not subsequently exceeded until 1993. The rally consisted of an initial base, lasting from February 1985 to February 1986, followed by a sharp impulse wave. Within this, the last phase of the base pattern between 29 July 1985 and 31 January 1986 was a fall of 5.25 points. Using the arithmetical formula, the projected rally for Treasury 5½ per cent 2008/12 was for a rise of 13.75 points to a level of 71.75. This level was hit precisely on 17 April 1986 (see Figure 11.10).

These calculations are very compelling. Critics may justifiably argue that not all of them are absolutely precise to the nearest two decimal places. However, the fact is that the forecasting errors are normally very small in relation to the huge moves that are being analysed.

Figure 11.9 The UK gilt-edged market, January 1970 to January 1975

Figure 11.10 The UK gilt-edged market, July 1984 to April 1986

EXAMPLES FROM THE US TREASURY BOND MARKET

These findings can be confirmed by an analysis of the US Treasury bond market. Figure 11.11 shows an index of Treasury bond prices, calculated by deducting the constant maturity yield on 20-year bonds from 100. The period covered in Figure 11.11 runs from the secular low of 1981 to just prior to the Equity Crash of October 1987. Within this pattern, we shall be looking at price behaviour in the autumn of 1981, then from late 1981 to late 1982, and finally from the summer of 1983 to the spring of 1987.

Figure 11.12 shows the dying phase of the great inflation-generated bear market of the 1970s and early 1980s. In October 1981, the market rallied in early October, and then fell to make a final – albeit marginal – new low. The last fall on the 30-year index was 1.1 per cent. Multiplying this by 2.618 indicated a rally of 2.9 per cent, or an index target of 87.25. The index closed at 87.24 on 27 November.

The market then fell steeply, as it re-tested the October 1981 low. By February 1982, the index had fallen by 2.4 per cent. However, the base pattern continued for some months and was not finally terminated until June 1982 (see Figure 11.13). When the market broke out of the base pattern in August 1982, it was possible to anticipate a total rally from the June turning point of 6.27 per cent. This corresponded to an index target of 89.62. The market peaked at an index level of 89.65 on 19 November 1982, formed a top pattern, and collapsed again into May 1984.

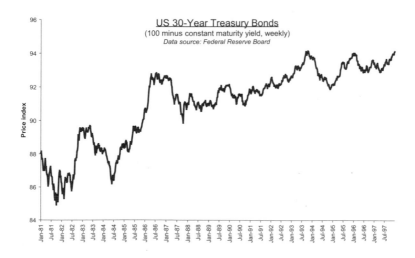

Figure 11.11 US Treasury bonds 1981 to 1987

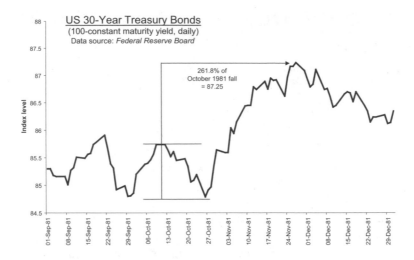

Figure 11.12 US Treasury bonds, October to November 1981

Figure 11.13 US Treasury bonds, November 1981 to November 1982

Figure 11.14 draws attention to the last phase of this fall. Between October 1983 and May 1984, the index fell by 2.56 index points or by 2.89 per cent. Applying the spiral formula to these two figures, the former predicted a rise of 6.70 index points to 92.76, while the latter anticipated a rise of 7.56 per cent to 92.57. The market peaked at 92.84 in April 1986.

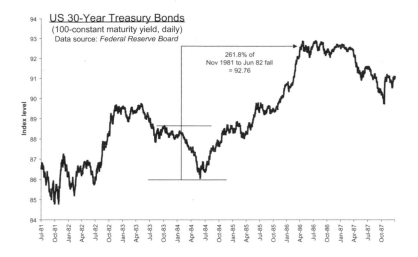

Figure 11.14 US Treasury bonds, October 1983 to April 1986

In this last example, there is obviously a slight difference in accuracy between the two targets: the arithmetic calculation was more precise than was the percentage calculation. In fact, it needs to be remembered that the implied fall in long-dated bond yields between May 1984 and April 1986 translates into a massive rise in actual bond prices, and that the resulting error is actually quite small for those who played the long side. Nevertheless, the difference obviously highlights the advantages of conducting the calculations in both arithmetical and percentage terms. It also confirms that some leeway has to be allowed in generating targets, particularly if the market is accelerating sharply (as was the case with US bonds in 1986). Targets are likely to be temporarily penetrated as traders panic but this, in itself, creates the conditions for a reversal and underscores the effectiveness of the target calculations.

CONCLUSION

We have looked closely at price swings in two of the world's major bond markets over relatively long periods of time. We have also picked out two important examples from equity markets. There is strong evidence that the main impulse wave of either a bull market or bear market is related to the base or top pattern that preceded it by the ratio 2.618:1. This confirms the theoretical implications of the golden spiral that we explored in Chapter 10.

The 2.618 formula can be calculated either in terms of simple price changes or in terms of percentage changes. The situation depends on the market being tracked and circumstances. The point, however, is that the formula provides a phenomenally accurate forecast of potential turning points.

NOTES

1. This is mathematically equivalent to saying that each diameter is related to the one that precedes it at 180° (that is, the next smallest diameter along the same straight line) by the ratio 2.618.
2. Note that the first wave is excluded from the calculations because it does not involve a full diameter.
3. The number 34 is a Fibonacci number.
4. Treasury 2½ per cent (redeemable on or after 1975) is called an 'irredeemable' on the assumption that yields will 'never' fall to 2½ per cent again. Only at this stage would the stock actually be redeemed. In the interim, it constitutes cheap funding.
5. The pull to redemption is the tendency of a stock to gravitate towards its redemption price (100.00) as it nears the maturity date. This obviously does not reflect what is happening to the whole market.
6. The calculations are all conducted using closing prices. The results are usually even more accurate using intra-day highs and lows.

12

The shape of things to come

INTRODUCTION

In the analysis of the last chapter, a definite price pattern emerged. In bull markets, there was a base pattern followed by a rapidly rising impulse wave, while in bear markets the pattern was reversed. Insofar as the patterns were deduced from bond markets, we can also infer that the pattern applies both to prices and to yields. In other words, the pattern is symmetrical. There is thus a basic three-wave pattern that uses, or is controlled by, the ratio 2.618:1. We shall now look at the relevant patterns in more detail.

EXAMPLES

Figure 12.1 shows the monthly price pattern in UK gilts that started off the great disinflationary bull market way back in 1975. The bond used is an ultra-long-dated low-coupon stock, Treasury 2½ per cent with a maturity date on or after 1 April 1975. It is known as an 'irredeemable' because it is unlikely to be redeemed until redemption yields fall below 2½ per cent. Otherwise it remains cheap funding for the government. The stock is a useful one to use because its long maturity ensures that its price patterns are not distorted by the pull to redemption. This influence normally causes the price of a stock to move towards a price of 100 as it approaches final maturity.

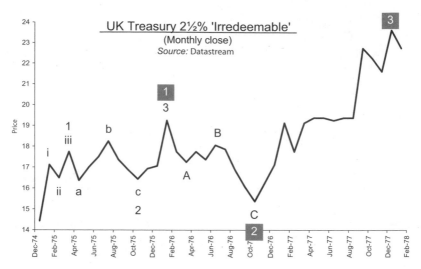

Figure 12.1 The UK gilt-edged market, December 1974 to February 1978

The pattern shown in the chart consists of a base formation and an impulse wave. The primary waves are denoted by the white numbers with the dark background – namely 1, 2 and 3. However, it is relevant, and important, that the base formation in the pattern consists of six waves. These are denoted by the unblocked lettering, 1–2–3 up and A–B–C down. Finally, even the base formation within this pattern (ie, waves 1 and 2) consists of six waves. These are denoted by the Roman numerals and lower case letters, i–ii–iii up and a–b–c down. We thus have a nested set of patterns that completely confirm the more theoretical analysis of earlier chapters.

This example is by no means unique. Figure 12.2 shows the price of Treasury 2½ per cent between February 1983 and February 1994. This was the long pattern that ran into the bond 'crash' of 1994. Again, a base formation (ie, 1–2) precedes an impulse wave (ie, 3). And, again, the base formation consists of six waves and the base formation within this base formation consists of six waves.

Just to show how the wave patterns nest within one another, Figure 12.3 compares the up-phase of the 1983–90 base pattern in Figure 12.2 with the whole pattern of Figure 12.2. That is, the period February 1983 to April 1986 is compared with the whole period February 1983 to August 1993. Obviously the time elapse of each of the patterns is different. However, they can be equalized – or made comparable – by separating the time axes and making them geometrically equivalent. Hence the shorter period (1983–1986) is shown on the lower horizontal axis and the longer period (1983–1993) is shown on the upper

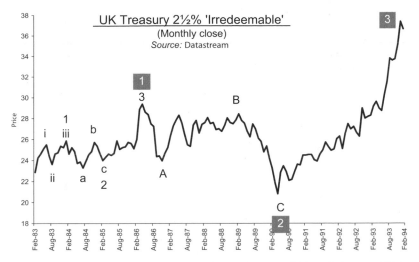

Figure 12.2 The UK gilt-edged market, February 1983 to February 1994

horizontal axis. In order to show how well the two patterns mirror each other, both time periods are extended to catch the initial drop after their respective wave 3 highs.

The first thing to notice is the way that the three-up/three-down base patterns of both formations, and the subsequent up-wave, coincide. The second thing to notice, therefore, is that the timings of the turning points within the patterns display a constant relationship to the whole

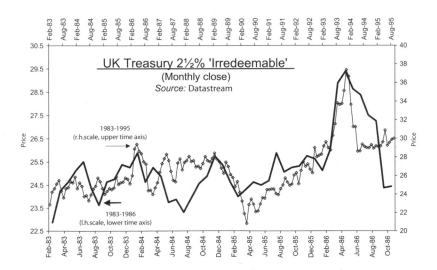

Figure 12.3 Pattern comparisons in the gilt market, 1983 to 1986 and 1983 to 1995

pattern of which they are a part. The patterns are therefore repro-
ducing themselves.

PRICE AND MOMENTUM

One of the difficulties with this sort of analysis is that the patterns are
usually very clear when a market is oscillating sideways, or is not
being subjected to economic shocks. However, as soon as a sustained
trend emerges, or a significant information shock appears, the shorter-
term pattern tends to become obscured. Hence, for example, while it
has been possible to identify the 1–2–3–A–B–C pattern in the UK gilt-
edged market during the price oscillations of 1975–1985, it becomes
increasingly difficult to do so once the effects of disinflation started to
set in. In other words, we need a method of de-trending the data.

Historically, a great deal of attention has been paid to this aspect of
analysis and different analysts will have different ideas on the subject.
However, by far and away the simplest solution is to use a straightforward momentum indicator, such as a percentage rate of change.
A percentage rate of change has the dual advantage of being independent of the level of the market and being easy to calculate. Under
some circumstances, an analyst may want to smooth the data by using
some form of moving average before applying the momentum calculations. However, this is by no means essential.

The advantages of using a momentum indicator can be demonstrated with reference to the US Treasury bond market. Shown in
Figure 12.4 is a weekly price index of constant maturity 10-year
T-bonds between May 1988 and April 1990. The index is calculated
by the simple expedient of deducting the yield (which is available
from the US Federal Reserve Board) from 100. Using constant
maturity bond yields has the advantage – as with Treasury 2½ per cent
above – of avoiding the problems of the pull to redemption. It can
immediately be seen that the price index pattern is very similar to
those generated by the UK gilt-edged market. Further, because the
pattern applies to a relatively short and undistorted period of time, the
archetypal six-wave (1–2–3–A–B–C) pattern can very clearly be
discerned.

Now look what happens (see Figure 12.5) when a 13-week
percentage rate of change is calculated from the index. The six-wave
pattern actually becomes clearer. There is an issue about the fact that
the momentum low in March 1990 precedes the price low; but this
phenomenon will be dealt with in Chapter 13.

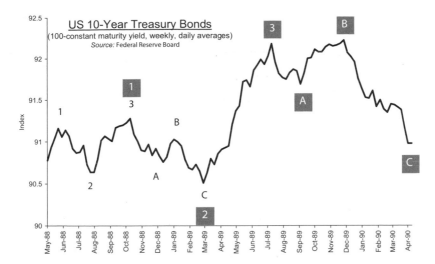

Figure 12.4 The US Treasury bond market, May 1988 to April 1990

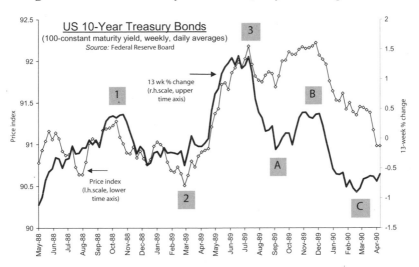

Figure 12.5 T-bond price and momentum, May 1988 to April 1990

MOMENTUM EXAMPLES

Having made the adjustment to momentum patterns, we can now look at some additional charts of the US T-bond market. Hence, Figures 12.6 to 12.9 show the 13-week percentage change in the price index of 10-year constant maturity bonds for March 1990 to April 1992, April 1992 to May 1994, May 1994 to May 1996 and May 1996 to May 1998. In each case, the six-wave pattern (which, as before, is denoted 1–2–3–A–B–C) is clearly visible.

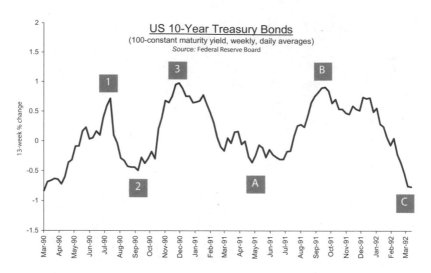

Figure 12.6 T-bond momentum pattern, March 1990 to April 1992

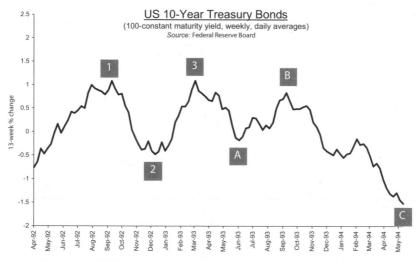

Figure 12.7 T-bond momentum pattern, April 1992 to May 1994

INTIMATIONS OF CYCLICALITY

It may already have been noticed that the sequence of charts showing momentum in the T-bond market are contiguous. The five charts reveal a six-wave pulse for a succession of (roughly) two-year periods. We therefore have some evidence that not only does each pair of up- and down-waves evolve according to an archetypal pattern but

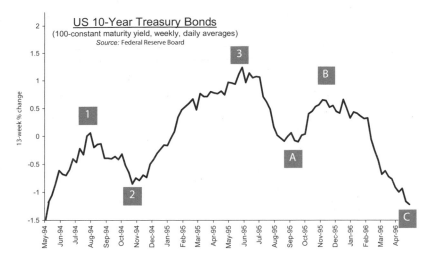

Figure 12.8 T-bond momentum pattern, May 1994 to May 1996

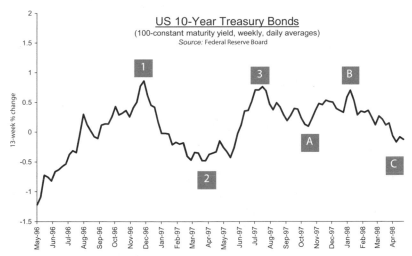

Figure 12.9 T-bond momentum pattern, May 1996 to May 1998

that the period between successive lows is not random. In other words, the T-bond market appears to be driven by structured rhythms.

We need to leave a more detailed analysis of this until later, because we are here dealing specifically with patterns. However, we can already see that the theoretical framework of the price pulse that was explored in earlier chapters has some grounding in the evidence. Price fluctuations contain a six-wave pattern and are subject to regular periodicities.

STYLIZED PATTERNS

The six-wave pattern that we have so far analysed is very simple. In general, a recovery from a low is partially retraced. This is then followed by an impulse wave. Eventually, prices fail to make any further headway and drop. This drop is partially retraced. Then there is a dynamic impulse wave downwards.

It follows, however, from what has previously been said, and then demonstrated in the examples from the UK gilt market, that lower-level oscillations will basically reflect the patterns of higher-level oscillations. Hence the base and top patterns will themselves consist of six waves and will thus be a smaller version of the larger pattern of which they are a part. This is a good example of 'fractal geometry'.[1] A stylized version of the net result is shown in Figure 12.10.

ASYMMETRY

The unfolding of lower-level patterns is continuously being modified by the influence of higher-level patterns. This results, from time to time, in clear distortions. These distortions can be particularly profound in bear markets, where top formations may sometimes be suppressed and where the downward-flowing impulse wave may be very short in time but long in price. This is due to the asymmetric

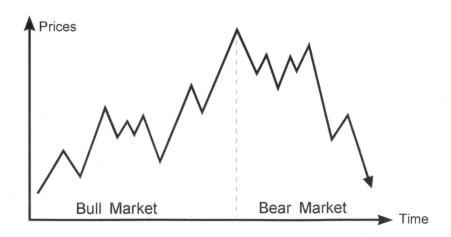

Figure 12.10 Stylized T-bond price cycle

influence of fear. Specifically, the fear of losing money will often encourage long base patterns and create a slowly rising impulse wave. However, it will also encourage quicker reactions when things start to go wrong.

CONCLUSION

It is apparent from this analysis that the actual shape of the price pulse will be distorted by higher-order trends. These distortions give an illusion of randomness to what is actually an ordered process.

The archetypal pattern is a three-phase movement, whether up or down. The first two phases constitute the top pattern or the base pattern. The third phase consists of a dynamic impulse wave. What is more, the pattern repeats itself as the market evolves through time. This pattern is central to the phenomenon of cycles.

NOTE

1.   Fractal geometry, which reflects the idea that lower-degree details of a natural phenomenon are identical to higher-degree details of the same phenomenon, receives a great deal of support from the scientific community. The idea of fractal geometry was pioneered by Professor Mandelbrot at the IBM Research Laboratories. It suggests that, no matter how much an object is magnified, the new details appearing on the smaller scale are always the same as the old details on the larger scale. See Mandelbrot, Benoit (1982) *The Fractal Geometry of Nature*, W H Freeman, New York.

Part Three

Forecasting turning points

13

The phenomenon of cycles

INTRODUCTION

One of the most difficult questions facing a technical analyst is how to differentiate a signal that requires a minor portfolio adjustment from a signal that necessitates a major re-appraisal of a strategic view. The traditional answer has been that it doesn't matter insofar as accurate short-term decisions will ensure that the long-term decisions are largely unnecessary. This answer is probably correct for day-traders and small-scale investors. However, reliance on the short-term is largely incorrect for strategic investors and large-scale money managers: the movement of large sums of money can incur penal transaction costs, is often disallowed under management agreements and inevitably exposes funds to huge performance risks against competitors. Long-term managers have to take long-term decisions, so even the most enthusiastic of technical fund managers will cast more than a passing glance at so-called economic 'fundamentals'.

This – and the fact that technical analysis still does not have a satisfactory theoretical underpinning amongst academics – helps to explain why economic analysis continues to have such an intractable hold over investment decisions. Of course, it wouldn't matter if economic forecasting was accurate but – as we argued in Chapter 6 – it isn't. First, the intellectual framework of economics is still largely incapable of placing accurate time frames on turning points in relevant variables. Second, economic forecasting is based on data that are both out of date and inaccurate. Indeed, at the point where major investment decisions are likely to be made, economic analysis often provides no more than an intellectual comfort for an emotionally based guess.

So we're left with a situation where short-term technical analysis may not be clear about the importance of a signal and where long-term economic forecasting may not be clear about the imminence of a turning point. Is there any way that the resulting uncertainty can be reduced? The answer is: yes. And it comes from the realm of time cycle analysis.

THE INFLUENCE OF GROUPS

In the earlier chapters of this book, it was argued that the conflict between random fluctuations and ordered process in markets is essentially resolved by the influence of the group. That is, the inherent desire of otherwise independent individuals to participate in greater wholes allows the 'whole' to devolve order onto the participants. The influence of the whole is psychological, emotional and, accordingly, powerful: individuals are eventually induced to do what everyone else is doing. This is why large numbers of people simultaneously buy dotcom stocks or second houses to rent, when reason suggests that caution might be more appropriate.

So, if we can allow that each person has a tendency both to be an individual and to be part of a group, then two of the fundamental assumptions of economic theory fall flat on their face. First, aggregate behaviour is not just the sum of the parts; it is something significantly more. Second, this augmented behaviour involves an important non-rational (and sometimes even *ir*rational) dimension. In effect, what economic theory ignores is that each of us has an impulse to create 'meaning' for ourselves, where meaning is measured by our inner world of feelings, and where feelings are stimulated by, and integrated with, our relationships with others.

Of course, it can be argued that the simplifying assumption of rational behaviour by independent individuals just makes the forecasting models easier to use. The problem, however, is that it also runs the risk of making the forecasts less accurate. Critically, the simplifying assumption that behaviour is rational and non-affective does not allow for the simple reality of human behaviour that lies at the heart of cyclical behaviour – the emergence of satiation. Indeed, in economics, satiation is treated as an aberration: the unspoken presumption is that we never have enough 'goods' (note the terminology). Hence, growth can – and should – continue persistently and indefinitely, subject only to the birth rate (which creates new entrants to the consumer market) and the ability of the system to generate new 'goods' (through innovation).

SATIATION

In nature, however, every living system oscillates between a state of activity and a state of rest. Indeed, rest is essential in order to re-energize an organism and delay entropy. Without rest, life (as we know it) could not exist. So, cycles are the signature of life. The question is, how does an organism 'know' when to switch from activity to rest, or back again? As indicated in Chapter 9, the answer is satiation: 'enough' of activity causes an organism to switch from activity into rest, while 'enough' of rest causes an organism to switch from rest into activity. As we approach satiation at the end of a day, we begin to lose energy, our body heat drops and our metabolism slows. Then, suddenly, we fall asleep. We traverse a *process gap*. Conversely, when we've had enough sleep, our energy potential is re-established, so our organ systems start to speed up and our body temperature rises. Again, we experience a process gap; and, suddenly, we are awake. Every living organism regularly, and at some infinitesimal moment in time, passes over the cusp that delineates sleep from rest. Moreover, these moments in time are *entrained* across nature. Most of us, for example, go to sleep before midnight and wake up in the early morning (give or take a late night out!). The harmonization of activity and rest throughout the biosphere reduces interference and allows total energy usage to be minimized.

TRANSFORMATION OF ENERGY AND INFORMATION

There is, however, another element here, which is also critical to our understanding of oscillations in living systems. Living systems respond to the input of energy and information. The interesting point, however, is that when a system receives new energy or information, it has to divert existing energy to deal with it. A simple example is eating.

Food provides new energy to our bodies. The first thing that happens, however, is that energy resources are diverted to deal with the transformation and absorption of the food. That is, our freely available energy tends to drop and, while this is happening, we actually tend to slow down and feel sleepy. In a sense, this slowdown revisits the drop in energy that initially signalled the need to eat. But there is a huge qualitative difference: the slowdown without food marks the end of a phase, while the slowdown with food marks the transition to a new phase. Having eaten, our energy is eventually considerably enhanced and we can go about our activities with some degree of vigour.

Obviously what we have here is a three-phase process that proceeds through input, absorption and application. Importantly, this pattern does not just apply to energy; it also applies to information. As discussed in Chapter 9, the diversion of energy to deal with the transfer of information from short-term memory to long-term memory momentarily interrupts the ability to apply new learnings. So, the three-wave pattern is also the signature of 'learning'. The first two stages are the true learning stages (where information actually alters the qualitative structure of the organism) and the third stage constitutes the confirmation that learning has occurred.

There are thus four ideas that can be used to produce a model of oscillations that mirrors what happens in financial markets. These ideas are: 1) individuals combine into groups; 2) groups respond to the input of energy and information from their environment; 3) the associated absorption of new energy and information involves a pause in activity; and 4) satiation causes a polarity switch between activity and rest. One inference, of course, is that a financial market crowd or an economically active group can be treated *as if* they were living organisms.

THE PATTERN THAT CONNECTS

These four ideas are the basis of the price pulse, with its six-wave (1–2–3–A–B–C) pattern. The important implication, therefore, is that a full theory of cyclical behaviour needs to take into account the fact that rhythmic oscillations have both a definite mechanism and a precise pattern. Historically, great effort has been spent in identifying time windows and precise dates when a cycle inflexion might be expected to occur. Great additional effort has then been spent in trying to identify the internal and external influences that might validate precise periodicities. Almost inevitably, however, the efforts have only been partially successful and, as a consequence, analysts have tended either to give the influence of time a very low priority or to ignore it altogether. But, as already argued, fluctuations are essential to the existence of life.

A potential solution, therefore, to the problem of variable periodicities is to track directly the *pattern* of the oscillations through time. If the pattern reflects (or is consistent with) the influence of the satiation-and-energy gap mechanism, then there is a good chance that we can know where we are in the cycle. The average historical periodicity of the market's heartbeat can be used to estimate when an inflexion point might arise. Ultimately, however, it is the pattern that determines the imminence of, and confirms the passing of, a turning point.

We shall be developing this theme in far more detail in the chapters ahead. In the meantime, it is worth noting that the existence of an archetypal pattern in cycles can be used to cross-correlate cycles with one another. Short-term cycles can be compared with long-term ones, adjacent cycles can be compared with one another, and cycles from different markets can be compared with one another. The point is that, as a new cycle is evolving, it can be compared directly and (more or less unambiguously) with appropriate cycles that have already completed. The price pulse is, to use Gregory Bateson's phrase,[1] the pattern that connects.

TRACKING THE CYCLE

The first consideration, therefore, is: how can the pattern of a cycle best be tracked? In Chapter 12, we had a brief look at the pattern of the price pulse in the context of bond markets. It was quite clear from the analysis that the pattern can be deduced directly from the behaviour of prices (or yields). The problem, however, is that, when a market is strongly trending, then the pattern may be difficult to see. The solution, obviously, is to de-trend the data. Traditionally, the preferred method for doing this is to use deviations from some form of moving average. The simplest method, however, is to use a momentum index.

MOMENTUM INDICES

A momentum indicator measures the rate of change in prices per unit of time. It therefore measures the *speed* of a market. The nature and time period of the indicator that is used are, to some extent, a matter of personal preference. However, there are two simple guidelines that can be used. First, it is better to use a percentage rate of change if there has been a large change in levels of the underlying index. A 10-point move in an index means something different if the base is 25 points rather than 100 points. Otherwise a simple difference can be used, calculated by subtracting one term in the data series from another.

Second, the time period that is used should be as short as is convenient. Long time periods have a tendency to iron out short-term fluctuations and short time periods have a tendency to emphasize them. However, the period should not be more than 25 per cent of the time period being tracked. Hence for a four-year cycle (for example), a one-year rate of change indicator is about the longest that should be used.

MOMENTUM AND THE CYCLE

One of the strengths of a momentum indicator is that it can provide a good indication of the actual status of a cycle in 'real' time. There is a very good theoretical reason for this. Figure 13.1a shows the position of a regular cycle with respect to time. Note that the slope of the cycle varies with the stage of the cycle. At point A, the slope is flat because the cycle is in the process of turning down. At point B, the slope is steep and downward (or negative). At point C, the slope is flat again because the cycle is turning up. And at D, the slope is steep and upward (or positive).

Now, the steepness of the curve represents the rate at which the position changes. It is the velocity of the cycle and is known to mathematicians as the first derivative of the cycle with respect to time. The velocity is shown in Figure 13.1b. The important point to note is that the resulting curve is the same shape as the original cycle but it is displaced a quarter-cycle back from the original.

The analysis can be taken a stage further. The slope of the velocity cycle represents the rate at which velocity is changing. It is therefore the acceleration/deceleration of the cycle and is known to mathematicians as the second derivative of the cycle with respect to time. The acceleration/deceleration cycle is shown in Figure 13.1c. Note that this cycle is displaced a quarter-cycle ahead of the velocity cycle. It is therefore a half-cycle back from the original cycle.

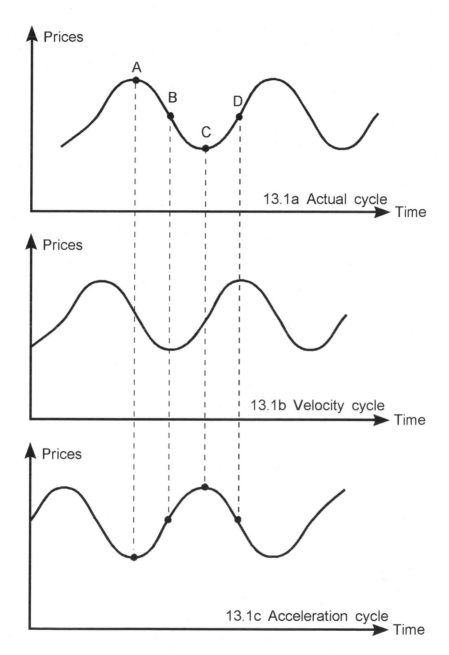

Figure 13.1 Change, velocity and acceleration

ANTICIPATING INFLEXION POINTS

This is not, of course, the whole story, because price cycles do not take the smooth curvilinear form shown in Figure 13.1. Nevertheless, it does give us access to some important information. First, a 'spike' in momentum will occur at least a quarter-cycle ahead of the cycle being tracked. This can give us an estimate for the timing of the absolute turning point. If we are tracking a 3.25-year cycle and an 'oversold' reading occurs in the momentum indicator, we can estimate that the absolute low might occur approximately 42 weeks (a quarter of the 3.25-year cycle) later. As a corollary, the time elapse between the point when a market becomes 'oversold' (or 'overbought') and the point where a reversal in the absolute price level occurs can be used to estimate a possible periodicity for a new cycle. All that needs to be done is to multiply the time elapse by four. Finally, a distinct warning about the possible presence of speculative – or, at least, highly emotional – activity in the market can be given if prices continue to trend well beyond the time elapse that normally follows a momentum reversal.

Hence, in Figure 13.2, the Dow momentum reversals in January 1983 and August 1989 were followed 10 or 11 months later by price inflexions on weaker momentum. This was consistent with the operation of an underlying 40- to 44-month cycle. In between these two dates, there was another momentum reversal followed by a price inflexion. However, the quality of the relationship was very different. The absolute momentum peak occurred in March 1986. There was then a lower momentum peak 12 months later. But it was not accompanied by a price peak. This could have been taken as indicating that a problem was developing. The 12-month time elapse between the momentum peaks was actually consistent with a 48-month cycle rather than a 40- to 44-month cycle, and was therefore suggesting some distortion. In the event, prices continued to rise into a high in August 1987, which was 17 months after the initial momentum inflexion. What followed was the 1987 'crash'.

VELOCITY AND NON-CONFIRMATION

Following on from this, the relationship between prices and velocity helps to explain the idea of 'non-confirmation' that is so important to market analysis. It is apparent from Figure 13.2 that upward

Figure 13.2 Momentum and price in the Dow Jones Industrial Average,
1981 to 1990

momentum tends to be weakening at a price high and that downward
momentum tends to be fading at a price low. In fact, for longer
cycles, the pattern is likely to be quite clear cut. There will be a
preliminary spike in short-term momentum as the market becomes
overextended. This will be followed by a sharp correction in the
market. Prices then move back towards the level at which they
became overextended. As prices move out into new territory, there
will be a second spike in the momentum indicator, which will not
usually be greater than the first one.

Consequently, the second higher peak or lower trough in prices is
'not confirmed' by the associated momentum indicator. Under normal
circumstances, this warns that the reversal is important.

ACCELERATION AND THE CYCLE

Finally, the acceleration/deceleration cycle provides us with a potentially powerful tool for confirming when a cycle has actually reversed.
There are occasions when momentum stretches out to exceptional
levels (positive or negative) immediately after a reversal in absolute
prices. As we have seen, the cycle of acceleration occurs in opposition
to the cycle in absolute prices and a surge in momentum is therefore
prima-facie evidence that a high-level cycle has reversed direction.

It is important, however, to be clear that the acceleration in momentum is not just a result of mathematics – for example, the momentum index was previously 'oversold' and is now 'overbought'. Sometimes, therefore, there will be some doubt. However, if the acceleration in momentum occurs after a non-confirmed price extreme, then the chances are that the signal is genuine. An example is shown in Figure 13.3. Here the low in the Dow in late 1975 was not confirmed by a two-month rate of change indicator. The subsequent surge in that rate of change indicator was strong evidence that a turn had occurred.

CONCLUSION

This chapter has recapitulated the influence of the three-wave pattern that regulates the processes of learning and energy absorption in the evolution of price–time cycles. The basic pattern applies both to phases of expansion and phases of contraction. Importantly, behavioural cycles switch polarity between expansion and contraction when they transit into an energy gap. This simple mechanism – which, unfortunately, is usually ignored simply because it is so simple – applies to all cycles. This, in turn, means that it is the pattern of the cycle that is the critical element in timing the turn, not the actual

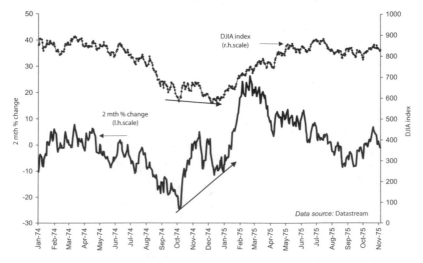

Figure 13.3 Non-confirmation and accelerating momentum in the Dow, 1974 to 1975

passage of time itself. The latter is important insofar as previous beats of a cycle have established a periodicity of some sort. This will enable the analyst to calculate time windows in which a reversal can be expected. However, the periodicity will be variable and, ultimately, the periodicity is subordinate to the pattern.

The pattern of the cycle can be tracked in real time, using a simple momentum indicator. Once the three-up/three-down pattern has been identified, it should be possible to anticipate the pattern of an evolving cycle beat, both directly and by comparing it with historical precedent. We shall now look at this process in more detail.

NOTE

1.   Bateson, Gregory (1979) *Mind and Nature: An essential unity*, Wildwood House, London.

14

The threefold nature of cycles

INTRODUCTION

We can now look at some of the evidence for the existence of specific cycles in financial markets. This will also give us the opportunity to explore the basic characteristics of such cycles and to draw conclusions that can be used for wider analyses. To start, therefore, we shall concentrate on the US Dow Jones Industrial Average. There are very strong reasons for doing this, not the least of which is that it is the most well-known index within the context of history. Modern markets, with their widespread use of futures and options, may be more directly orientated to other indices. However, it was the Dow that was followed during the Wall Street Crash of 1929; it was the Dow that hit the headlines in the Crash of 1987; and it is the Dow that is treated as the pre-eminent index on the TV news channels and in the daily press. The point is that the Dow Jones Industrial Average is the one that has reflected investor emotions in the equity market over a long span of history. If there is a rhythm in the US stock market, it should exist in the Dow.[1]

THE 11-YEAR CYCLE IN THE DOW

There is a great deal of evidence, which is borne out by the detailed work of many others,[2] that one of the dominant cycles in the Dow

Jones Industrial Average has an average duration of about 11 years. The cycle seems to have undergone a big distortion during the Second World War – which is not surprising – so there is some doubt about whether the correct timing of the low that was due towards the end of the war actually occurred in the autumn of 1943 or in the autumn of 1946. Despite this, subsequent lows occurred in winter 1957, summer 1970, autumn 1981, autumn 1990 and autumn 2001.

The 11-year cycle in the Dow can be tracked using a six-month percentage rate of change in the monthly closes. Figures 14.1 to 14.5 therefore show the resulting profile over successive periods of approximately 11 years, starting in November 1943. Figure 14.1 covers the 158 months from November 1943 to February 1957. Figure 14.2 covers the 160 months from February 1957 to June 1970. Figure 14.3 coves the 135 months from June 1970 to September 1981. Figure 14.4 covers the 110 months from September 1981 to November 1990. And Figure 14.5 covers the 131 months from November 1990 to October 2001.

In each of the figures, an initial attempt has been made to identify the archetypal six-wave pattern that defines a complete beat of the price pulse. The resulting conclusions will be subject to alteration on closer consideration; but it is exactly the sort of approach that an analyst might make when first confronted with the patterns. Hence, in each figure, the archetypal pattern is distinguished by the 1–2–3–A–B–C notation that has already been used. The only allowance that has been made at this stage is for the fact that, after

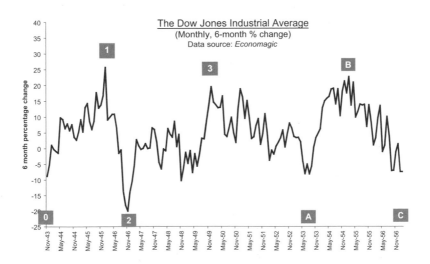

Figure 14.1 The Dow, November 1943 to February 1957

deep momentum lows at the end of a cycle, the initial upswing may be particularly dynamic. This means that the top of this initial surge will not necessarily mark the peak of the cycle. This consideration applies to Figures 14.2 and 14.3.

In the last cycle – ie, 1990–2001 – the pattern is obviously more complicated than that of its predecessors. This is due to the fact that the pattern evolved during a particularly dynamic period of economic growth, where one of the underlying themes is trial and error.

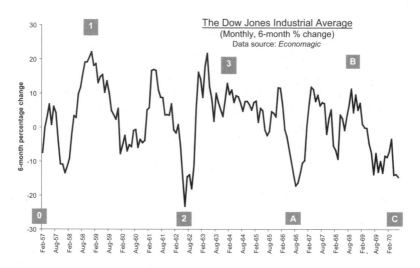

Figure 14.2 The Dow, February 1957 to June 1970

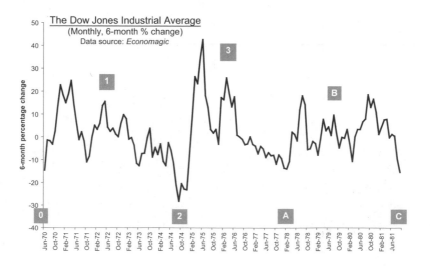

Figure 14.3 The Dow, June 1970 to September 1981

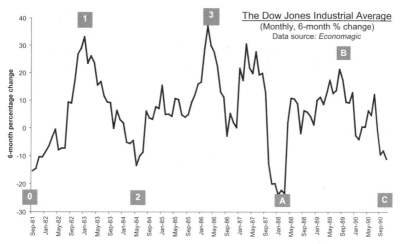

Figure 14.4 The Dow, September 1981 to November 1990

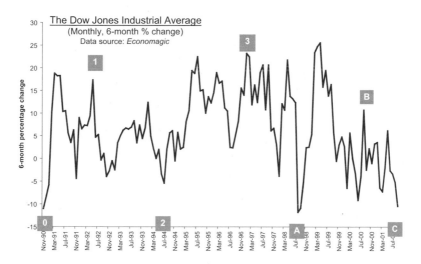

Figure 14.5 The Dow, November 1990 to October 2001

Increased risk often means increased volatility because things can – and do – go wrong. We shall analyse the pattern in more detail at a later stage. In the meantime, the initial labelling of the 1990–2001 pattern is as indicated in Figure 14.5.

IDEALIZED CYCLES

A useful starting point for analysing these charts is the construction of an 'idealized' timing pattern, which might apply to them all. Figure

14.6 shows such a pattern. The whole (higher-level) cycle is represented by the move from 0 to C – ie, 1–2–3 up and A–B–C down. It
then consists of three lower-level (sub-) cycles, each of which itself
contains the archetypal six-wave pattern. In theory, each of these
lower-level cycles will itself consist of three cycles. In other words,
the cycles are nested within each other. In all cases, significant lows
can be expected to occur one-third and two-thirds along the time
elapse of the next higher cycle that contains it. Similarly, important
highs occur at one-sixth, one-half and five-sixths along the time
elapse of that higher-level cycle.

COMPARING THE CYCLES

We can now compare each of the cycles shown in Figures 14.1 to 14.5
to the idealized version shown in Figure 14.6. This is done in Figures
14.7 to 14.11. In each figure, three things are held constant: the
vertical scale that measures the six-month percentage rates of change;
the vertical lines that represent the idealized timings of the peaks and
troughs relative to the total time elapse of each cycle; and the ideal
behavioural pattern of each cycle, shown as the dashed line. In this
way, we have a blueprint on to which we can overlay each complete
Dow cycle.

   Figure 14.7 shows the period from November 1943 to February
1957. The first peak seems clearly defined inasmuch as it is followed
by a large fall. However, the end of that fall probably does not mark

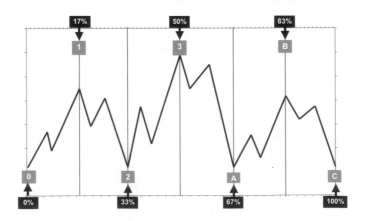

Figure 14.6 Idealized triadic cycle pattern

the proper end of the sub-cycle. The ideal behavioural pattern suggests that the actual low was in February 1946. Next, the sharp rally into the wave 3 peak seems to have begun on time but it probably ended a little early, in December 1949. Then there was the sequence of the initial drop in momentum, the recovery into early 1951, and the downswing to the base of wave A. Obviously, there is some doubt about the exact timing of the low of wave A because the ideal location is straddled by two momentum lows – one in early 1952 and one in mid-1953. However, the ideal shape of the subsequent rally into the peak of wave B suggests that the former is the correct one. Finally, momentum falls into early 1957. Hence, although this cycle was undoubtedly distorted by its placement in relation to the war so that we have had to make some adjustments to our initial assessment of the timings within the cycle, the basic pattern was actually not too different to the blueprint.

Figure 14.8 shows the period from February 1957 to June 1970. It starts well enough in relation to the blueprint, but wave 2 is distorted by a big rally in early 1961, with the result that the effective low is delayed until mid-1962. The subsequent rally is very sharp, as it should be following a deep sell-off, so the cycle peak (on lower momentum) is placed in early 1964. Then there is the fall into the base of wave A, which – like the base of wave 2 – is delayed until late 1967. Finally, momentum has a three-wave rally into a high in late 1968, followed by a three-wave fall. The cycle thus follows the blueprint in terms of pattern, but its highs and lows regularly occur later than the ideal because of the upward distortion that occurred in early 1961.

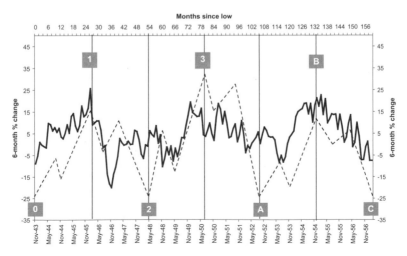

Figure 14.7 The Dow, November 1943 to February 1957

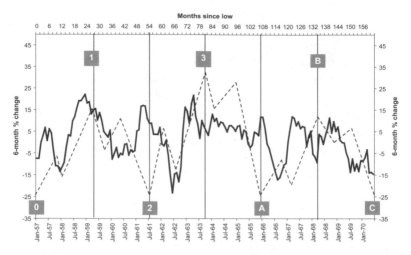

Figure 14.8 The Dow, February 1957 to June 1970

Figure 14.9 tracks the market's performance from June 1970 to the big market low in September 1981. The period started with a big jump in momentum, so the correct placement of the first high is where it should be, on the lower momentum of late 1971. The base of wave 2 was a little delayed, but the top of wave 3 arrived more or less on time. Again, the correct timing of the high is not after the initial surge from the low, but on the subsequent lower momentum peak. The low of wave A arrives on time, as does the peak of wave B and the low of wave C. The cycle thus accords very closely with the ideal blueprint.

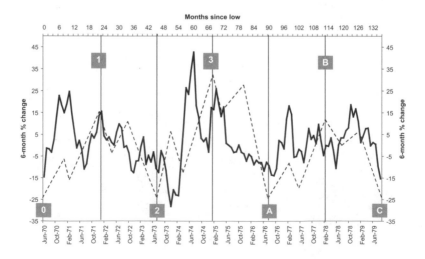

Figure 14.9 The Dow, June 1970 to September 1981

Figure 14.10 shows the momentum of the Dow from September 1981 to November 1990. Very little needs to be said about this particular cycle. Like its predecessor, it follows the blueprint very closely indeed. Even the sub-cycles seem to be in synchrony with the ideal.

Figure 14.11 tracks the momentum of the Dow from November 1990 to the October 2001 low. Unlike the cycles of its two predecessors, this cycle suffers from what seem to be distortions. The first sub-cycle follows the blueprint very closely; but the following sub-cycle is biased upwards to the right, and the last sub-cycle is

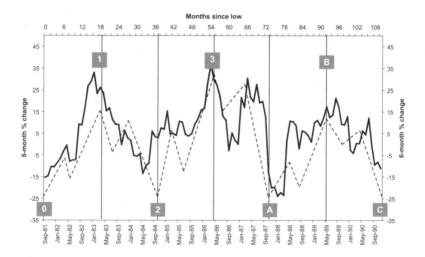

Figure 14.10 The Dow, September 1981 to November 1990

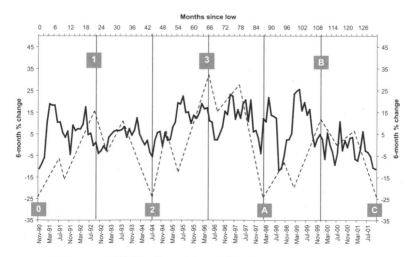

Figure 14.11 The Dow, November 1990 to October 2001

extremely volatile. In fact, the pattern is very specific. The whole pattern is related to major changes to the US (and, indeed, global) economic infrastructure. Such cycles are biased upwards to the right and are terminated by a three-wave contraction. Moreover, in general terms, the pattern of the whole cycle will be similar to the pattern of the middle cycle. Fortunately for analysts, this phenomenon does not just arrive out of the blue. It is part of the natural processes of evolution, which can be anticipated by paying attention to the economic cycle itself. We shall be looking at this in Chapters 15 and 16. In the meantime, we can anticipate the conclusions by saying that the correct low for the second sub-cycle in the 1990–2001 triad is in August 1998 and that the correct high for the third sub-cycle is in April 1999.

ACTUAL CYCLE TIMINGS

We can now conduct an analysis of actual cycle timings, based on the above observations. Table 14.1 shows the time elapses, measured in months, between the important turning points in Figures 14.7 to 14.11. It indicates that the average periodicity of the five cycles starting in November 1943 is 11.58 years. However, it is also clear that the periodicity has been contracting. The average of the last four cycles was 11.17 years, and the average of the last three was only 10.4 years. The most recent complete cycle took 10.92 years. So there is some variability in the time elapse of the 11-year cycle.

Nevertheless, Table 14.1 reveals something very interesting. Despite the variability in the overall cycle lengths, there seems to be a tendency for the peaks and troughs generated by the sub-cycles to meet the timings indicated by the blueprint shown in Figure 14.6. The main peaks and troughs occur on average at positions that are 15 per cent, 35 per cent, 51 per cent, 67 per cent and 83 per cent of the total time elapse of the cycle. These are very close to the timings suggested by the blueprint, which correspond to the percentages that arise if unity is divided into six parts. That is, one-sixth is 17 per cent, two-sixths (or a third) is 33 per cent, three-sixths (or a half) is 50 per cent, four-sixths (or two-thirds) is 67 per cent and five-sixths is 83 per cent.

In other words, peaks and troughs in a cycle tend to conform to a very simple formula: major troughs occur at around 33 per cent and 67 per cent of the total time elapse of a cycle, and peaks occur at around 17 per cent, 50 per cent and 83 per cent of the cycle.

Table 14.1 Cycle timings in the Dow

Dates	Months from start of cycle					
	1st high 1	1st low 2	2nd high 3	2nd low A	3rd high B	3rd low C
Nov 43 – Feb 57	26 (16%)	51 (32%)	73 (46%)	99 (63%)	135 (85%)	158 (100%)
Feb 57 – Jun 70	22 (14%)	64 (40%)	83 (52%)	114 (71%)	139 (87%)	160 (100%)
Jun 70 – Sep 81	23 (17%)	51 (38%)	69 (51%)	92 (68%)	110 (81%)	135 (100%)
Sep 81 – Nov 90	16 (15%)	32 (30%)	54 (50%)	76 (70%)	95 (88%)	110 (100%)
Nov 90 – Oct 01	18 (14%)	44 (34%)	74 (56%)	86 (72%)	101 (90%)	131 (100%)
Averages	21 (15%)	48 (35%)	71 (51%)	93 (67%)	116 (83%)	139 11.58 yrs

THE FOUR-YEAR CYCLE IN THE DOW

This analysis is consistent with the idea that cycles are grouped together in threes, or in balanced triads. Specifically, the main cycle consists of three lower-level cycles, each of which has a duration that is about one-third of the duration of the main one. We can confirm this conclusion with respect to the 11-year cycle. The time elapse, measured in months, of each of the sub-cycles in Table 14.1 is shown in Table 14.2. The average of the first sub-cycles in each triad is 48 months, the average of all the second cycles is 45 months, and the average of all third cycles is also 45 months. The average of all 15 cycles is therefore 46 months.[3] This is what is more popularly known as the four-year cycle in the Dow.

TRIADS, DYADS AND ENERGY GAPS

One of the conclusions that emerges from this analysis is that the pattern of the cycle is at least as important as the actual time elapse of the cycle. Another conclusion is that the mid-point of the second cycle within any triad will coincide with the mid-point of the relevant over-arching higher-level cycle. This latter is important because it means

Table 14.2 The four-year cycle in the Dow

Dates	Length (months)				
	Total	1st cycle	2nd cycle	3rd cycle	Averages
Nov 43 – Feb 57	158	51	48	59	53
Feb 57 – Jun 70	160	64	50	46	53
Jun 70 – Sep 81	135	51	41	43	45
Sep 81 – Nov 90	110	32	44	34	37
Nov 90 – Oct 01	131	44	42	45	44
Averages	139	48	45	45	46

that cycles are genuinely harmonically related to one another. If cycles were instead grouped in pairs, there would be a conflict between the upper- and lower-level cycles. Specifically, the peak of the former would coincide with a low in the latter. In terms of integrated systems, this is simply a non-starter: it would indicate dissonance. Nevertheless, there must be one or more reasons why some analysts insist that cycles arise in pairs. This needs to be addressed.

The first reason why cycles are often interpreted as being dyads is that dissonance is exactly what does seem to appear. That is, cycle lows arise at approximately the point where a high is expected. This frustrating phenomenon is taken by some to 'confirm' the presence of dyads and is taken by others as being an indication that cycles simply don't work. There is, however, the possibility that the phenomenon is an illusion, arising from a misinterpretation of the evidence. What may be happening is that the influence of an energy gap after a high is being taken as indicating the presence of a low.

Figure 14.12 demonstrates the essence of this problem. It focuses on momentum immediately after an important high. The upper chart assumes a higher-level cycle that is divided into three lower-level cycles. At the peak of the second cycle the market is satiated. It therefore falls into an energy gap, which reverses the polarity of the market into bearish mode. Prices accordingly fall sharply. In the lower chart, this fall in prices registers as a sharp drop in momentum. What happens, therefore, is that the momentum indicator registers a low. So, if the analyst is measuring cycles from momentum low to momentum low, then the data register the end of a cycle. Consequently, the whole higher-level cycle (when it finally ends) looks as if it is constructed of two sub-cycles. In fact, what has happened is that the signs of a high have been misinterpreted as a low. *Ex post*, the mid-cycle momentum

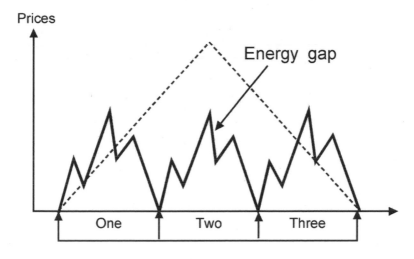

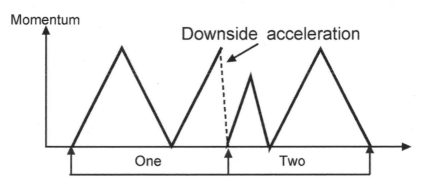

Figure 14.12 Momentum and the energy gap

low might be seen as being caused by a rightward-biased sub-cycle that inevitably had to succumb to the magnetic pull of a cycle low.

THE 1987 CRASH

A very clear example of this phenomenon occurred in the Australian equity market during the 1987 Equity Crash. Figure 14.13 shows the one-year percentage rate of change in the Australian All Ordinaries Index between late 1974 and late 1989. Looking just at the registered lows in the index, it would have been very easy to conclude that there had been two beats of a seven-year cycle, which had thereby completed a 14-year cycle. The conclusion would have been given credence by the fact that not only did the cycle begin and end after

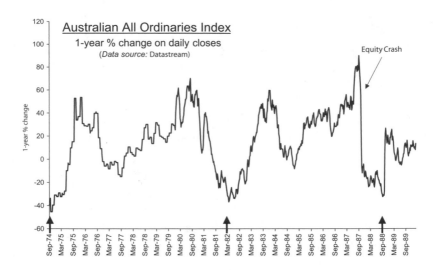

Figure 14.13 Dyadic cycles and the 1987 Equity Crash

significant bear phases (ie, the 1973–74 bear and the aftershocks from the 1987 Crash) but both beats of the apparent seven-year cycle 'look' the same.

However, let us suppose that the performance of the All Ordinaries Index can be redefined to allow for the possibility that the 1987 Crash was some form of energy gap. And let us use a three-month percentage rate of change indicator to enable us to focus more directly on short-term cycles. Figure 14.14 shows the resulting momentum in the All Ordinaries Index immediately prior to, and just after, the Crash. It can be seen that the high of 25 September 1987 occurs at the mid-point of what could be a 6.33-year cycle. Moreover, this 6.33-year cycle clearly sub-divides into three 2.11-year cycles.

A complete analysis would, of course, need to extend forward and backwards in time, in order to ensure that both the alleged 6.33-year cycle and the underlying 2.11-year cycles repeated themselves. Nevertheless, the example quite clearly indicates that using an energy gap to isolate a potential cycle peak, and then searching forward and backwards in time for momentum lows that are balanced around that peak, can produce clear evidence of six-wave cyclical fluctuations. This is a more satisfactory outcome than assuming that the low after a sharp market fall marks the end of a cycle. In fact, a confirmed energy gap is prima-facie evidence, not of a cycle low, but of a cycle peak. It is then a simple matter to find lows prior to the peak and lows after the

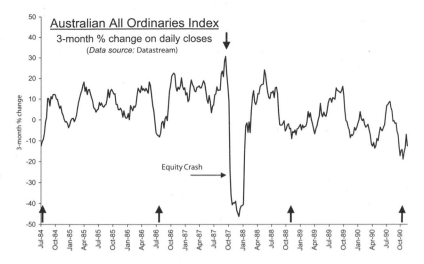

Figure 14.14 Triadic cycles and the 1987 Equity Crash

peak that are equidistant from the peak. The time elapse between any such pairs of lows will then provide an indication of what cycle periodicities are operating.

CONFIRMATION OF THE ENERGY GAP

When an energy gap actually occurs in a market, people know it because they experience it. However, when researching historical data, to establish the rhythm of a cycle, it is not possible to access emotions directly. We need a proxy of some sort. Quite obviously, an acceleration in momentum (whether up or down) is a good starting point. However, we also need an indicator that can provide independent confirmation. One such indicator is the percentage intra-day spread between price highs and lows. The important point here is that an energy gap implies an underlying imbalance between supply and demand. In extreme cases, once a market has entered a 'bubble' period, and demand literally becomes one-way, a point will arrive when long-term fundamental investors are satiated and only a small amount of short-term technical selling will burst the bubble. In other words, selling will have an unusually strong downward impact on prices, because there are no natural buyers into weakness. This important moment can usually be identified by a significant move in the spread between the daily high and the daily low in prices.

THE WALL STREET CRASH

One of the best examples is the Wall Street Crash of 1929. The start of the Crash, as reflected in the Dow Jones Industrial Average, is shown in Figure 14.15. Here daily closes on the Dow are correlated with the intra-day percentage spread between the index high and the index low. If the day is an up day the spread is positive; if it is a down day, the spread is negative. The Dow reached a closing peak for the period on 3 September 1929. It then began to fall away. There were short periods, when the index fell for a number of consecutive days. This was certainly unusual in the context of what had gone before, and was therefore a warning sign; but the daily price spread remained relatively unaffected. Note, however, the way that the daily spread ballooned out on 23 and 24 October 1929, and then did so again on 28 and 29 October. This was the energy gap.

As predicted by theory, at some stage after the market had negotiated the energy gap (and implicitly completed its task of reversing the polarity of the market), prices began to rally. In fact, after the October 1929 shock, the rally on the Dow lasted until mid-April 1930, thereby lulling investors into a false sense of security. And then the impulsive down-wave materialized. In fact, the intra-day spread did widen out as the market tipped into that down-wave but it never came anywhere near the levels experienced during the energy gap.

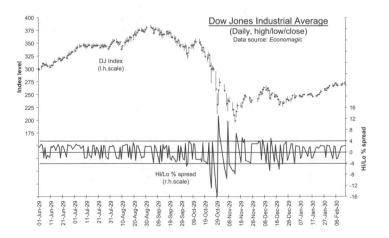

Figure 14.15 Confirmation of the energy gap

CYCLE CHARACTERISTICS

The fact that cycles cluster in triads suggests that each cycle may have a different purpose, which is in some way related to the evolution of the higher-level cycle of which it is a part. If this is correct, then it is also likely that each cycle will have specific 'footprints' that may help to identify it. There will always be significant variations, based on the essential creativity of markets. Nevertheless, certain practical generalizations are possible, particularly in relation to cycles that last for months and years. These generalizations relate to cycle functions, cycle biases and cycle behavioural traits. In the analysis that follows, it is assumed that the higher-level cycle is one that lasts for about 11½ years and that the lower-level sub-cycles last for about 46 months. This is consistent with the data in Tables 14.1 and 14.2.

CYCLE FUNCTIONS

The first set of generalizations relate directly to the *position* of a cycle in a triad (see Figure 14.16). This is, in a sense, an extension of the diagram that dealt with the momentum distortions created by energy gaps (Figure 14.12). The first cycle in a triad is likely to encompass the information shock, or energy gap, that initiates the higher-level cycle. It is also likely to encompass the initial re-test of the low. In other words, the first cycle embraces the period when the market

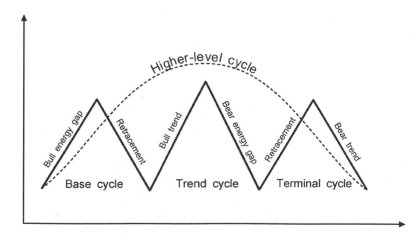

Figure 14.16 Cycle functions within a triad

learns that the trend has changed. As such, it is the *base* cycle within the context of the higher-level cycle.

The second cycle in a triad is likely to be quite dynamic during its rally phase. The market will have learnt that a reversal has occurred and will be in a natural impulse wave. At the top of the cycle, of course, the market will be genuinely overbought. Consequently, the down phase of the second cycle will likely encompass the information shock, or energy gap, that initiates the bear phase. The second cycle is therefore the *trend* cycle, although it also incorporates the start of a reversal.

The third cycle in a triad fulfils the task that follows on from this. Its rally phase will incorporate the re-test of the high as the market learns that a reversal has occurred. However, its down phase will involve the main thrust of the bear. The third cycle in a triad, therefore, is the *terminal* cycle, which unwinds the excesses of the previous cycle and leaves the market oversold.

CYCLE TRANSLATION

The second set of generalizations relating to cycles arises directly from each cycle's implicit relationship to the higher-level cycle of which it is a part. Most analysis will be done on the assumption that a cycle will peak somewhere near the centre of its periodicity. Hence, for example, a 44-month cycle might be expected to peak somewhere between months 21 and 23. However, many analysts have noted that – in contrast to cycle lows, which tend to arrive (more or less) in an expected time frame – cycle highs can arrive significantly earlier or later than expected. In other words, there is more variability in the timing of peaks. This is why it is always best to measure cycle period-icities in relation to low points.

Deviations from the central timings of cycle highs are called 'trans-lations'. A left translation means that a cycle peaks significantly earlier than the middle date, while a right translation means that a cycle peaks significantly later.

TRANSLATIONS WITHIN A TRIAD

The effects of a higher-level cycle on a lower-level triad of cycles are shown in Figure 14.17. The first cycle, which initiates the bull phase, is likely to be the subject of uncertainty and to be characterized by

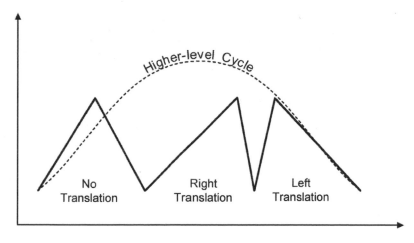

Figure 14.17 Cycle translations within a triad

slow learning. It is unlikely that it will be characterized by any great degree of urgency in either direction, up or down. In general, therefore, a base cycle is likely to be neutral in relation to its centre point, or unbiased.

The second cycle, which is characterized by bullish sentiment, is likely to incorporate the long haul into an overbought condition. At some stage, new money is no longer available from cash reserves; it will either have to be borrowed or earned before it can be committed to the market. Also, the influx of bullish data, which confirm the trend, will be spread over time. These two forces suggest that a trend cycle is likely to peak late: it is biased to the right, or is right-translated.

The third cycle in a triad is destined to unwind the excesses of the trend cycle. The fall at the end of the trend cycle will already have warned that the market was overbought and investor sentiment will have started to shift from the fear of being left out of the market to the fear of being left in the market. This shift will ensure that each rally will tend to be relatively limited in price and that falls are extended in time. Consequently, a terminal cycle is likely to peak early. It therefore tends to be left-translated.

THE INFLUENCE OF HIGHER-LEVEL CYCLES

As shown in Figure 14.17, the higher-level cycle (represented by the dotted line) is implicitly assumed to be passive in relation to the biases in its lower-level constituent cycles. However, this is far from being the case. On the basis of what has been noted about the different functions of different cycles, it is possible to hypothesize that translation of a specific level depends on two factors – namely, the position of the cycle within its triad and the influence of the higher-level cycle.

The distinction between the two influences is important. It cannot be emphasized enough that the bias of a lower-level cycle is determined by the influence of its immediate higher-level cycle; and that the latter depends on fundamental trends in the socio-economic environment. This is one of the reasons why it is so dangerous to ignore 'fundamentals'. We shall accordingly be looking at economic cycles in Chapter 15.

Some of these issues are shown in Figure 14.18. Here, the sequence of biases shown in Figure 14.17 is reflected in the likely biases of lower-level cycles. Hence, the triad in the base cycle is likely to be centred, and the triad in the trend cycle is likely to reproduce the biases of all three higher-level cycles. The triad in the terminal cycle is often less certain. The middle sub-cycle, for example, might reflect a long, slow struggle against the downtrend (ie, be right-translated) or it might be characterized by a short rally and a long fall (ie, be left-translated). Nevertheless, the first of the three should be centred, the second should allow a recovery that is limited in price but long in time, and the third should reflect the final capitulation.

CYCLE BIASES AND ENERGY GAPS

There is an underlying issue here about where precisely the critical energy gap – which reverses the polarity of a cycle from bullish to

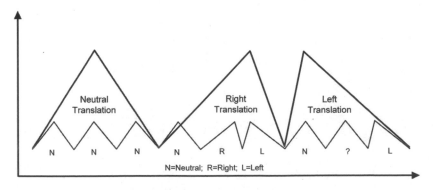

Figure 14.18 Lower-level cycle translations

bearish – will actually impact. If the trend cycle is particularly strong, and particularly rightward-biased, the late bear phase may not actually reverse the market's polarity (although it will warn of such a reversal). This will allow the market to make a new high in the first sub-cycle of the terminal cycle and, as a result, the energy gap will impact when that first cycle turns down. Often the only way to tell whether or not an energy gap has occurred is to look at the energy indicators.

CYCLE BEHAVIOURAL TRAITS

The third set of generalizations relating to cycle characteristics is that each cycle within a triad will reflect certain behavioural traits by participants. It is as if the attitudes of the many become so homogenized and condensed that they can be analysed as if they were being exhibited by just one person. This is one of the implications of group, or crowd, behaviour. As we indicated in Chapter 2, an effective crowd gains critical mass through conformity enforcement, thereby suppressing diversity generation. Hence, the capabilities of individuals within the crowd are reduced down to a common level.

In theory, all behaviour has three dimensions to it – namely, affective, somatic and cognitive.[4] With a crowd the quality of these dimensions will essentially be very simplistic, not least because they will be orientated towards fulfilling the crowd's purpose. We have just seen that each cycle within a triad has a specific purpose. So the crowd involved with the cycle will likely exhibit a blend of characteristics that reflect that purpose. Indeed, that blend will be the one that helps to bind the participating individuals together. For each of the cycles in a long-term triad, we can hypothesize that the emotional tone, the thrust of the activity and the tendency in thought processes will be as shown in Figure 14.19.

Sometimes, these traits will be easy to identify by observation and introspection. If this is so, analysts can have an even clearer understanding of what is happening. Often, however, they may not be easy to identify, particularly over short time horizons. In this case, it may only be possible to guess at, or intuit, them. Nevertheless, a general understanding of the psychosomatic basis of the crowd can provide a distinctive aid to understanding the likely consequences for finance, business and politics. So let us look briefly at each of the cycles in turn.

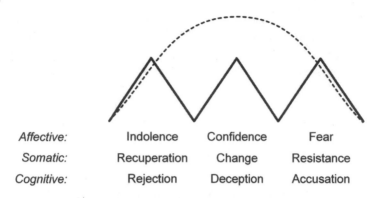

Affective:	Indolence	Confidence	Fear
Somatic:	Recuperation	Change	Resistance
Cognitive:	Rejection	Deception	Accusation

Figure 14.19 Behavioural traits within a triad

BEHAVIOURAL TRAITS IN A BASE CYCLE

Each cycle in a triad is very much influenced by – and is, indeed, a derivative of – the cycle that preceded it. Hence the first cycle in a triad is characterized by a reaction to the preceding crisis from which it was born. It is the most passive cycle because there is a need to recover from the shock. Feelings will be slow-moving and indolent; activity in terms of market transactions will be sporadic and short-lived and will reflect the overall need for rest and recuperation; and, importantly, the cognitive bias, or the mental lens through which the world is seen, will be clouded by a denial that circumstances are moving beyond a crisis atmosphere. This combination is essentially very dangerous because, under certain circumstances, despair may set in.

BEHAVIOURAL TRAITS IN A TREND CYCLE

The second cycle is the most creative. It is the one that incorporates the learning generated from the base cycle. It exhibits a recognition that circumstances have actually changed. Feelings are therefore likely to be coloured by a sense of confidence about the trend, both now and in the future; activity is likely to be orientated towards change and will be the more dynamic for it; but, strangely, the cognitive bias will incorporate a sense of deception inasmuch as attention increasingly focuses on market price movement rather than underlying fundamentals. In other words, during a trend cycle, sentiment and activity can become increasingly divorced from reality.

BEHAVIOURAL TRAITS IN A TERMINAL CYCLE

The third cycle within the triad is overtly destructive. Whereas setbacks in the previous two cycles may have been quickly reversed, in the terminal cycle they may translate into something more dramatic. In other words, the setback has the quality of a fundamental bear rather than of a technical correction. So it is no surprise that the dominant feeling tone of the third cycle is one of fear.[5] In the face of a genuine threat, the only valid responses are to fight, to flee or to freeze. Some investors will basically fight the bear by buying into weakness. Their reaction is primarily emotion-based and will, more often than not, involve an element of anger.[6] Some investors will run from the bear by selling. Their reaction can best be described as body-based since the primary motivation is physical protection.[7] The vast majority, however, will be unable either to fight or to flee. They will have been shocked by the energy gap (which may have occurred at the tail end of the trend cycle or in the first downturn of the terminal cycle) and they will freeze.[8] The somatic reaction of the crowd will therefore be one of a deep-rooted resistance to the actual ending of the trend cycle.[9] Interestingly, under these circumstances, there will be a natural tendency to blame others, or external events, for the undesired changes. The cognitive bias of the third cycle in a triad, therefore, will be one of accusation. There is, however, one consolation from this cycle. This is that, after initial shock, fear is likely to eventually translate into action. This action is explicitly focused on avoiding further damage but is also implicitly orientated towards trying to return to the wellbeing of the previous cycle. As a result, the third cycle has a tendency to be shorter than the previous pair.

A SCHEMATIC FOR FINANCIAL MARKETS

We can pull these various strands together and express them in the form of a schematic diagram (see Figure 14.20). This diagram is basically an adjustment of that shown in Figure 14.6. It takes into account the potential biases – devolved from the relevant higher-level cycle – that might be experienced by the lower-level cycles. Thus, the first (base) cycle is centred; the second (trend) cycle is biased to the right; and the third (terminal) cycle is biased to the left. The result is a pattern that hints at three types of corrective move: a deep one at the end of the

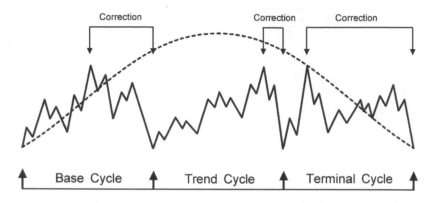

Figure 14.20 The cycle pattern in financial markets

first cycle; a short, sharp, one at the end of the second cycle; and two more within the third cycle that are interspersed with a rally. Most (ie, somewhere between two-thirds and five-sixths) of the third cycle thus presents itself as a correction to the *whole* pattern.

Interestingly, this schematic is a close reproduction of the pattern shown in Figure 14.5, which showed the six-month percentage change in the Dow Jones Industrial Average between November 1990 and October 2001. As will be demonstrated in Chapter 17, this period was dominated by revolutionary innovation. The pattern shown in Figure 14.20 is therefore one that implies change within the system. The pattern will reappear again in our analysis in due course.

LIMITED CYCLE PATTERNS

This analysis indicates that any particular cycle can only present itself as one of a limited number of patterns, based around an underlying three-up/three-down process: a balanced form, an upward rising form or a corrective form. This further means that properly specified triads of cycles will also present in the same limited number of ways. Indeed, for the bigger cycles the pattern is likely to look something like that shown in Figure 14.20.

CONCLUSION

We saw in the previous chapter that the intrinsic pattern within a cyclical upswing or downswing is the three-wave pattern of recognizing, absorbing and responding to changes in the socio-economic environment. In this chapter we have extended the analysis to show that cycles cluster in groups of three – that is, there are three sub-cycles in a higher-level cycle, each of which has a different purpose in relation to that higher-level cycle. Further, each sub-cycle is likely to reach a peak that bears a very specific relationship to the theoretical centre point of the cycle. Finally, the resulting bias almost certainly reflects a specific combination of subjective qualities based on the three characteristics of mood, 'physicality' and cognition.

There is thus an essential 'threesomeness' to cycles that manifests itself in a number of dimensions. This is further evidence of the non-random nature of the phenomenon of markets.

NOTES

1. There is also the added point that the Dow Jones Industrial Average is partnered by the Dow Jones Transportation Average. The two indices are often tracked together to establish the degree to which they are behaving in a similar fashion. This is the basis of 'confirmation' and 'non-confirmation'.
2. See Wilson, Louise (1964) *Catalogue of Cycles: Part I – Economics*, Foundation for the Study of Cycles, Pittsburgh.
3. Importantly, confirmation of a (roughly) 46-month cycle comes from other sources. First, it corresponds to the length of the short-term business cycle found by Joseph Kitchin. See Kitchin, Joseph (1923) 'Cycles and trends in economic factors', *Review of Economic Statistics*, **5**, Harvard Economic Service, Cambridge, Massachusetts. Second, and more directly, it falls into the range of periodicities between 40 months and 50 months that have been reported by Leonard Ayres, Ellsworth Huntingdon and Edward Dewey. See Ayres, Leonard (1939) *Turning Points in Business Cycles*, Macmillan, New York; Huntingdon, Ellsworth (1941) 'Effect of atmosphere electricity on business', in *The Frontier*, Armour Research Foundation, Chicago; and Dewey, Edward (1955) 'The 3½-year cycle in general business', in *Cycles*, **VI**, Foundation for the Study of Cycles, Pittsburgh. For a complete list, see Wilson, Louise (1964) *Catalogue of Cycles: Part I – Economics*, Foundation for the Study of Cycles, Pittsburgh.
4. The characteristics are derived from the work of psychologist Claudio Naranjo. Naranjo argues that there are three basic centres – affective, physical and cognitive – in each person, around which that person's character structure constellates. Since these centres operate in combination, and since each combination has a different hierarchical pattern, the result is that there are nine potential centres of gravity within the psyche. Each person will operate from one of those gravity centres. See Naranjo, C (1994) *Character and Neurosis: An integrative view*, Gateways/IDHHB, Nevada City, California. Some of the implications of Naranjo's work for individuals are explored in Chapter 25. The implications for a crowd are much simpler. All that we need to know are the basic affective, somatic and cognitive characteristics of birth, growth and decay.

5.   The higher the level at which the cycle is operating, the more pronounced and pervasive the feeling of fear will be.

6.   The anger is likely to arise because the market has confronted the investor's beliefs about himself or herself. See also Chapter 25.

7.   The physical bias in 'running' from the market is very important. Market professionals sometimes refer to it as 'gut feel'.

8.   The 'freeze' response is the one that is least understood by most people, including psychologists, and yet is the one that is most widely experienced. However, it is the most likely outcome when a person can neither fight nor flee. The resulting shock, or trauma, becomes locked in the psychosomatic system and can easily be activated (and re-lived) by apparently non-relevant events. Post-traumatic stress disorder is only the most extreme example of this. Some analysts argue that traumatic shock is a universal malady. See, for example, Levine, Peter A (1997) *Waking the Tiger: Healing trauma*, North Atlantic Books, Berkeley, California.

9.   This, of course, will ultimately be the primary reason why the bear will take a long time to resolve itself and why downward price movements will be vicious.

15

Economic cycles

INTRODUCTION

Technical analysis seeks to be objective, basing decisions on the evidence that is directly available from the markets themselves. Little or no account is therefore taken of the subjective interpretation of economic and social trends. Indeed, there is strong evidence that the attempt by investors to anticipate the future means that market prices start to turn before actual fundamentals. There is, for example, convincing evidence that major lows in the US equity markets precede major lows in the US economy by between four and six months.[1] Under these circumstances, there seems little point in analysing fundamentals.

Nevertheless, there is an aspect of the relationship between markets and the economy that needs to be taken into account. This is the fact that there comes a point in a bull or bear trend when the markets and fundamentals enter a strong feedback relationship with each other. It is the presence of feedback that generates the trend in the first place. For example, there comes a point where falling equity prices impact wealth and confidence to the extent that consumption and investment start to contract. Consequently, economic activity slows, thereby increasing unemployment, reducing spending power and further undermining confidence. So equity prices fall. And so on. Technical analysis is not necessarily very good at determining when this feedback process actually begins. This raises the question about what techniques might be used to address this deficiency.

There are two methods that can be used. The first, which will be addressed in Chapter 22, is the application of the golden ratio (0.382:0.618) to identify critical boundaries. The second, which is the subject of this chapter, is to apply the techniques of cyclical analysis to the economy itself. If we can objectively know the current status of the economy within the big scheme of things, then we have some indication of the implicit bias in a financial market cycle, we have an improved chance of anticipating official policy adjustments that might impinge on a market and we have a good chance of being invested the right way during a trend move.

NOTE ON ECONOMIC THEORY

Mainstream economic theory basically discounts the inevitability of economic cycles. There are three reasons for this. The first, which has already been alluded to in Chapter 6, is that economic theory excludes, by assumption, the controlling influence of the crowd. In economics, the rational individual reigns supreme and – like a Clint Eastwood character in a spaghetti western – does not take much account of the behaviour of others. Further, such rational behaviour is linear. Under these circumstances, economic fluctuations are essentially caused by unforeseen (exogenous) 'shocks'.

The second reason why economic theory does not see economic cycles as being inevitable follows from this. If economic fluctuations are in some way an accident, then a government can use its authority and resources to offset any undesirable developments. Hence a government is empowered to lower interest rates, reduce taxes and increase government spending in a recession and it is empowered to raise interest rates, increase taxes and reduce government spending under conditions of inflation. In theory, it is possible to offset economic fluctuations and converge on non-inflationary/high employment trend growth.

The third reason why economic theory has problems in recognizing the influence of economic cycles is that the historical evidence does not support constant periodicities for cycles. In 1923, Joseph Kitchin reported a short-term, three- to five-year, business cycle based on inventory adjustments.[2] In 1862, Clement Juglar reported a medium-term, seven- to 11-year, cycle relating to capital investment.[3] In 1930, Simon Kuznets pointed to the idea of a 15- to 25-year cycle involving the interaction of construction and demographic factors.[4] And there are even longer cycles on offer. In 1991, Brian Berry pointed to the presence of a generation-length, 25- to 35-year, cycle that was related to investment in infrastructure.[5] In 1926, Nikolai Kondratyev published his classic article on long waves of 40 to 60 years in commodity prices.[6] Finally, in 1991, social economists William Strauss and Neil Howe presented a strong case for an inter-generational, 85- to 99-year, crisis cycle.[7] However, despite the depth of research conducted by these economists, there is a tendency to ignore the role of cycles. There are two basic reasons for this. First, it is very difficult to identify appropriate causal agents, particularly within long-term cycles. Second, the variation in periodicities makes it difficult to use cycles for forecasting purposes. It is therefore much easier to ignore the research and concentrate instead on short-term control mechanisms.

AN INTEGRATIVE VIEW

The fact remains, however, that certain important cycles have been shown to exist. Suppose, therefore, that we could find the presence of a three-wave adjustment mechanism within these cycles. This mech-anism – of information shock, information absorption and infor-mation application – would be endogenous to the process and would not necessarily rely on an external timing mechanism. Nor would it necessarily require a specific internal causal mechanism. Wouldn't this mean that the *pattern* of the cycle would be at least as important as the *periodicity* of a cycle?

If this is correct, then the correct approach to cycles is to search, not just for specific cycle periodicities, but instead search for completing patterns within time windows that are defined by the variability of the periodicities. Indeed, we could even compare currently evolving economic cycles with previous completed cycles. If we thus know where we are on the economic cycle, we can have some idea about what to expect from markets. This would have the potential to signif-icantly reduce forecasting uncertainties.

Importantly, this integrative approach allows both for creativity in economic processes and for some form of constraining order in those processes. On the one hand, the intrinsic creativity of human action generates variability in the periodicity of a cycle. On the other hand, the natural processes of human life ensure that the evolution of that cycle will conform to an underlying pattern. Hence, randomness and order co-exist.

RELATIONSHIPS BETWEEN ECONOMIC CYCLES

Let us start the analysis by looking briefly at the possible timing relationships between the economic cycles that are indicated above. The
first important step here is to incorporate the research findings of other
independent analysts to see if there are any obvious 'averages' that
can be used. The second important step (given the analysis of the
previous chapter) is then to look specifically for cycles that are
grouped in batches of three. Obviously, this is something of an iter-
ative process. The basic idea is to arrive at a set of cycle averages that
incorporates all the main cycles in triads.

FROM KITCHIN TO STRAUSS AND HOWE

There is a huge amount of evidence that the central periodicity of the
short-term Kitchin cycle (or inventory adjustment cycle) is somewhere between 40 and 44 months – that is, somewhere between 3.33
and 3.67 years.[8] These periodicities can be found in indices of general
business activity and in indices relating to specific industrial sectors.
There are variations depending on the length of data that is analysed
and on the purposes of the researcher; and there are always outliers
that can distort the evidence. Nevertheless, this is the one cycle length
that, if pressed, most economists would accept as being correct.

If we then multiply this short-term business cycle by three, we find
that the next higher-level cycle has a periodicity of 10 to 11 years. This
is undoubtedly the potential range for the Juglar cycle (or capital
investment cycle). Multiplying this by three gives an outcome of 30 to
33 years. This is the range for the Berry cycle (or infrastructure cycle).
Multiplying the Berry cycle by three results in 90 to 99 years, which
coincides with the Strauss and Howe cycle (or crisis cycle).

FROM STRAUSS AND HOWE TO KITCHIN

Now, Strauss and Howe's findings are quite specific about the nature
of the 90-year crisis cycle. On the basis of an analysis that goes back
to the 16th century, they argue that 'social moments' occur every 45
years.[9] A social moment is defined as being either a secular

(economic) crisis or a spiritual (social) awakening. Hence, there is a secular crisis every 90 years. If we use this as our starting point, and now divide by three, we get 30 years, which is the Berry infrastructure cycle. If we divide this by three, we get 10 years, which is the Juglar investment cycle. And if we divide this by three, we arrive at 3.33 years, which is the Kitchin inventory cycle.

The basic outline of these simple relationships is shown in Table 15.1. There is no question that we are looking at a series of cycles with central periodicities of 3.33 years, 10 years, 30 years and 90 years.

Table 15.1 Relationships between economic cycles

Researcher	Period (years)	Average	Relationships
Kitchin	3–5	3.33	
Juglar	7–11	10	3 × Kitchin
Kuznets	20–25		
Berry	25–35	30	3 × Juglar/9 × Kitchin
Kondratyev	45–60		
Strauss and Howe	85–99	90	3 × Berry/9 × Juglar

KUZNETS AND KONDRATYEV

There are, however, two cycles that need further comment. These are the 20- to 25-year Kuznets cycle and the 45- to 60-year Kondratyev cycle.

The Kuznets cycle is no longer generally accepted as being a separate cycle.[10] A 20-year cycle was very evident prior to the First World War, but has not obviously been present since. However, Brian Berry has counter-argued that a Kuznets-type cycle does exist, but that it is longer than Kuznets thought. That is, its central periodicity is 30 years, rather than 20 years. Berry calls his 30-year cycle a Kuznets cycle. Actually, to avoid confusion and to take account of the fact that Berry shifts the emphasis from building to general infrastructure (which includes intellectual infrastructure), it is more accurate to call the 30-year cycle the 'Berry' cycle.

The Kondratyev cycle is a price cycle, not an economic cycle as such. This is an important distinction, which is often either ignored or forgotten. Kondratyev saw prices as rising and falling in long waves. It is therefore appropriate to see which groupings of economic cycles coincide with one complete beat of a Kondratyev cycle. We shall look at this in Chapter 17. In the meantime, we can point to some interesting relationships between the Kondratyev cycle and the Strauss and Howe crisis cycle. The first conclusion is that not all Kondratyev lows are major depressions because not all Strauss and Howe lows will coincide with a Kondratyev low. The second, which follows from this, is that Strauss and Howe crises will alternate between deflation (persistently falling prices) and accelerating inflation (rapidly rising prices).

ECONOMIC THEORY AND TECHNICAL ANALYSIS

The above survey hardly does justice to the massive amount of research and analysis conducted by the specifically named individuals and nor does it include the wealth of supportive information provided by other analysts. Further, the analysis has been concentrated on a particularly narrow range of cycle periodicities. However, the purpose of this exercise is not to embark on a critique of economic causation but to point out that a) impeccable research by respected economists confirms that certain important economic cycles definitely exist and that b) a simple examination of the periodicities indicates that these cycles are probably related. In other words, there is evidence that economic cycles are ordered processes and that these processes seem to adhere to an intrinsic 'rule of threesomeness'.

In a sense, this is all that a technical analyst needs to know. Once the decision has been taken to pursue an as-objective-as-possible approach to market timing, an analyst need only track the evolution of a cycle's momentum through time. The underlying economic theory and political nuances become irrelevant. It is not necessary, for example, to understand in detail the precise theoretical mechanisms behind a 60-year, or 90-year, cycle. It is only necessary to know that there is strong evidence that they do, in fact, exist.

In addition, since the analysts will be concentrating on behavioural patterns it is not necessary to use sophisticated statistical techniques to calculate either the precise periodicity, or the precise historical variability, of cycles. All we need to know is that a cycle series with approximate, but inter-related, periodicities is operating. Hence, in the cycle series outlined above, reference to a '3.33-year cycle' or a '10-year cycle' does not mean that those periodicities are precise and inviolable. The references are merely labels that point us in the direction of an important phenomenon.

CYCLE CHARACTERISTICS

Before looking at some historical data in any detail, there is one more piece of the theoretical jigsaw that needs to be put in place. This is the fact that each economic cycle within a triad is likely to fulfil a different purpose to its neighbours. This is exactly the same point as was made in Chapter 14 about financial market cycles.

Let us look briefly at the likely characteristics of a longer-term cycle (without being too precise about the definition of 'longer-term'). There are a number of points that can be made:

▌ each new cycle is born from the downswing of the previous one;

▌ the overarching longer-term cycle will begin from a recession and will end with a recession;

▌ the first sub-cycle (the base cycle) in a triad will therefore be involved in re-establishing some form of stability in the economy;

▌ the second sub-cycle (the trend cycle) in a triad will incorporate any qualitative changes that are appropriate after the re-basing;

▌ the third sub-cycle (the terminal cycle) will embrace the recession that concludes the higher-level cycle.

However, each sub-cycle obviously consists of an upswing and a downswing. So there will be two sub-cycle recessions between each of the two larger-scale recessions. This is shown in Figure 15.1.

BIASES IN CYCLES

It is thus possible to hypothesize that the higher-level cycle will be *quantitatively* affected by the lower-level cycles, and that the lower-level sub-cycles will be *qualitatively* affected by the higher-level cycle. What this basically means is that the shorter-term cycles will be the vehicle by which longer-term structural changes in the economy

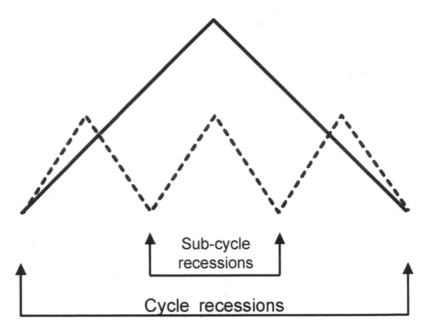

Figure 15.1 Cycle and sub-cycle recessions

are laid down. It also means that the fluctuations in each shorter-term cycle will be biased both in amplitude and time by evolutionary developments in the longer-term cycle. Consequently, each cycle in a triad is likely to have a specific type of bias that will be unique to itself. So we shall now look at each cycle in turn, building on the strands of thought that we started to develop in the last chapter.

For ease of presentation, we can present the observations graphically, as in Figure 15.2. The diagram shows a notional index of business confidence as it might develop over three contiguous cycles. The dashed line shows the overarching long-term cycle. The three sub-cycles are referred to as the 'base' cycle, the 'trend' cycle and the 'terminal' cycle respectively. These three cycles are treated as having a similar time elapse to one another. Further, each sub-cycle is shown to consist of three lower-degree cycles.

The diagram is highly schematic inasmuch as the amplitude of the economic fluctuations will be more variable than indicated and the bias in the cycles may diverge from those indicated. Nevertheless, the diagram shows clearly how a triad of cycles might relate to one another. The pattern is the same as the one shown in Figure 14.15.

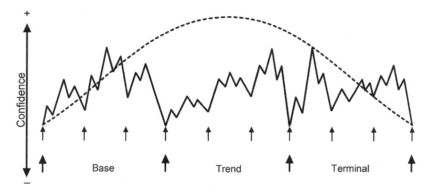

Figure 15.2 A triad of economic cycles

AN EXAMPLE FROM HISTORY

It might be useful at this stage to confirm that there is some practical logic behind the diagram in Figure 15.2. Figure 15.3 accordingly shows the Berry-length cycle in US industrial production that began in the winter of 1946 and ended in the summer of 1980. The evolution of the cycle is tracked in terms of two-year percentage rates of change. It is often useful to use two-year rates of change when searching for longer-term cycles, because it helps to cut out short-term fluctuations while still giving a good indication of the timing of important lows. The period covers just over 34 calendar years. It was characterized by restoration after the Second World War, by the Cold War and by the Vietnam War. It was therefore a period of increasing government deficit financing and rising inflation.

JUGLAR CYCLES DURING THE 1946 TO 1980 BERRY CYCLE

The first Juglar cycle in this period, measured from low to low, lasted from February 1946 to April 1958. It was basically associated with the gradual restoration of normality after the trauma of the Great Depression and the Second World War and was clearly characterized by a three-wave expansion (1–2–3) and a three-wave contraction (A–B–C). The peak of wave 3 was more or less in the middle of the cycle.

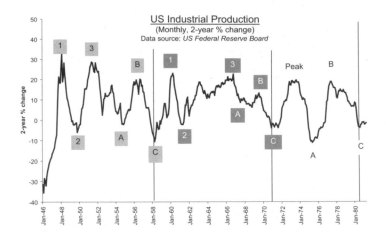

Figure 15.3 US industrial production, 1946 to 1980

The second Juglar cycle in the period lasted from April 1958 to November 1970. It was the period of social upheaval and change that is now called the 'Swinging Sixties'. It was also very inflationary. The expansion from May 1961 to October 1966 was one of the longest on record. The cycle was therefore rightward biased, with an elongated upwave (1–2–3) being followed by a short, sharp downwave (A–B–C).

The third Juglar cycle lasted from November 1970 to August 1980. The first phase was an inflationary recovery, which was halted in its tracks by a sharp rise in oil prices. The two-year percentage change in industrial production fell sharply between August 1973 and May 1975. There was then another sharp recovery into June 1977 before a final collapse into June 1980. The overall profile taken by this crisis cycle was of an initial sharp recovery followed by a slow three-wave fall.

THEORY AND FACT

We can therefore conclude from this important example that the inflationary 34-year Berry infrastructure cycle, which started in February 1946 and ended in June 1980, consisted of three Juglar capital investment cycles that lasted, respectively, for 12 years, 12 years and 10 years. Moreover, the pattern of each cycle accords with the basic model that has already been outlined – namely, the first cycle is a base cycle, the second (the 'Swinging Sixties') is a trend cycle and the third is a terminal cycle.

It is also worth mentioning that the terminal cycle was characterized by a number of unpleasant shocks, ranging from an intensification of the war in Vietnam with the invasion of Cambodia in 1971, to a hike in oil prices after the outbreak of war in the Middle East in 1973.

THE FIRST CYCLE

We can now draw some further useful general conclusions about the intrinsic nature of each of the Juglar cycles in a Berry cycle. The first Juglar cycle – the base cycle – will be heavily influenced by the trauma from which it was born. The initial recovery from the low will be quantitative, rather than qualitative. That is, output and spending levels will recover, but will not be particularly orientated towards new goods or new processes. The recovery will, in fact, be largely driven by an inventory adjustment as producers try to realign output with better market conditions. In effect, the recovery presents itself as an information 'shock' to the economy insofar as it starts unexpectedly.

However, the general economic environment will remain burdened by the effects of the previous recession. Unemployment will still be high and attitudes will be pessimistic. The over-riding need is for rest and recuperation, so the emotional tone will be indolent and mental attitudes will involve a denial that things are really improving. Under these circumstances, there is little chance of a prolonged economic recovery. Consequently, the peak will tend to be midway into the estimated periodicity of the sub-cycle. The subsequent downturn could be quite deep. It tends to be the stage when businesses start to take drastic action on costs. Old plant and machinery is scrapped and unemployment rises again. This relapse corresponds to the information absorption stage of the learning process. The economy starts to detach itself from its old methodologies.

THE SECOND CYCLE

The second Juglar cycle – the trend cycle – within a Berry cycle is like the mythical phoenix rising out of the ashes. Because surviving businesses have taken some difficult decisions, they are able to respond more freely to genuine business opportunities. If there is a new product line, a new set of ideas about business practices, or new markets to be exploited, this is when it properly starts. The over-riding impulse during this cycle is towards change. Accordingly, the feeling tone is positive and confident and the mental attitude is towards higher risk.

Quite obviously, a positive economic environment has the potential to establish a persistently high level of economic growth. If there is genuine innovation occurring, the trend rate of growth in the economy may even appear to be improving. This is the period of transition to a new structure in the economy and it means that downturns are likely to be mild and that the eventual peak of the cycle is likely to be delayed. The cycle is therefore biased to the right. Nevertheless, demand runs persistently ahead of supply, leading to a trade deficit and/or inflation. Eventually, consumer satiation sets in. Once this has happened, a process gap (ie, an energy gap) becomes inevitable.

Because of the rightward bias in the cycle, the downswing into recession appears suddenly and is a 'shock'. Interest rates, which may have been increased to stem excess demand, are quickly reduced again. Government deficits may be expanded to help bring back the good times. But the damage has been done.

THE THIRD CYCLE

The third Juglar cycle – the terminal cycle – within a Berry cycle is the one where the overspill from the innovation wave makes itself felt. Like all preceding cycles, it starts with a recovery of some sort. However, whereas the preceding upswing had a large qualitative dimension, this last upswing in the triad can only be quantitative. It is based on demand stimulation, rather than industrial innovation. As such it is potentially inflationary. The underlying constraint is that there is now market satiation and therefore resistance to further change.

This means that the lifespan of the recovery is limited. Quite apart from anything else, there is likely to be upward pressure on interest rates. Consequently, either there is a bond market collapse, or equities continue to fall, or even some combination of both of these. Eventually, therefore, the recovery is aborted and a prolonged economic recession sets in. It needs hardly be said that, the greater were the excesses of the preceding boom, the greater will be the recession. The affective tone of this period becomes one of outright fear and the mental tendency is to blame others for the problems. The important part of this process, however, is that the ephemeral is separated from the enduring. And it is the latter that is fully incorporated into the deep structure of the economy.

EVOLUTION

This analysis of the stages within a cycle has brought into focus the different stages of the evolutionary process within an economy. At its simplest, each triad of cycles is involved in adjustments in the higher-order cycle of which they are directly a part. For example, three Kitchin inventory cycles will complete one Juglar capital investment cycle; and the economy will in some way be different by the end of the third Kitchin cycle. Another way of looking at this is to say that each triad of cycles involves the creation of a higher-order structure that is more complex than the one it replaces. Hence, the information technology that was introduced in the 1990s embraces a far more complex economic 'system' than did the mass consumption that dominated the 1960s. However, the process of moving from a lower level to a higher level is not just a wild jump. Somehow the economy has simultaneously to meet two objectives: it has to detach itself from dependence on old structures so that it can identify itself with the newer, more integrated one; and it has to keep the best of the old structure while also adopting the new. So, for example, the new era of information technology has been built on the foundations created by the era of mass consumption. Or, to put it another way, mass consumption becomes a *part* of the new era, rather than being the *whole* of an era.

The relevance of this to the current analysis is that the process of adjustment to new economic structures consists of three stages: *detachment* from the old structure, *transition* to a new structure, and *attachment* to the enduring parts of the new structure.[11] These stages clearly correspond to the three phases of the triadic cycle model. The base cycle encourages detachment from the old paradigm (whatever that may be). This detachment will normally be most clearly apparent in the economic slowdown that terminates the base cycle. The trend cycle involves the transition to the new paradigm (which usually involves a change in attitudes). Importantly, the end-cycle economic slowdown is relatively moderate because the adjustment is still 'in process'. Finally, the terminal cycle is dominated by the separation of the ephemeral from the enduring (usually through the exigencies of a recession). It is only during the third, often very difficult stage that the 'new era' paradigm becomes properly established. This is because the inevitable excesses of the transition phase have to be accepted and eliminated before the economy finally 'knows' within itself what parts of the changes are permanent. Prior to this, there is too often a tendency for participants to believe that all aspects of the change are permanent. Dotcom companies are a case in point. So, the transition stage is not a permanent structure; and recessions and bear markets have an evolutionary function.

LABELLING THE CYCLES

So far, we have simply referred to the cycles in a triad as being 'base', 'trend' and 'terminal' cycles respectively. The advantage of doing this is that the terms are basically neutral with respect to the level of the cycle being discussed. Nevertheless, there are also some advantages in being more specific about the essential nature of any particular cycle. For example, a base Kitchin cycle is different from a base Juglar cycle, which is different again to a base Berry cycle, which is different yet again to a base Strauss and Howe cycle. Where it is appropriate to do so, we shall in future use the labels provided in Table 15.2.

Table 15.2 The labelling of economic cycles

Cycle	Base	Trend	Terminal
Strauss and Howe	Involution	Evolution	Revolution
Berry	Adaptation	Regeneration	Crisis
Juglar	Recuperation	Innovation	Disruption
Kitchin	Recovery	Advance	Recession

Hence a 90-year Strauss and Howe cycle will start with a 30-year period of social and political soul-searching, progress through a 30-year period of dynamic economic and social evolution, and terminate in great upheaval. A 30-year Berry cycle will be initiated by a period of adaptation to changed circumstances, continue through a period of social change, and end with a period of crisis. A 10-year Juglar cycle will begin with a period of economic recuperation, respond vigorously to a period of innovation and finish with an economic disruption. Finally, the 3.33-year Kitchin cycle will start sluggishly, eventually move into an economic upswing and terminate in a recession.

These labels are, of course, indicative only. They pick out what are likely to be the main features of any given period. As already mentioned, however, the lower levels will be strongly influenced by developments at the higher levels. Consequently, some of the subtleties of any given situation might be missed. For example, the fluctuations of the Kitchin cycle are likely to be distorted by a conjunction of terminal cycles at the Strauss and Howe, Berry, and Juglar levels. Alternatively, the Kitchin cycle might be very easy to pick out during more benign periods, such as might occur during a conjunction of base cycles at the Strauss and Howe, Berry and Juglar levels.

CONCLUSION

This chapter has established a theoretical framework for looking at economic cycles, based on the comments that were initially explored in the context of financial markets in Chapter 14. We started by looking at those cycles that respected economists have identified as being important. These cycles are the 3.33-year Kitchin inventory cycle, the 10-year Juglar capital investment cycle, the 30-year Berry infrastructure cycle and the 90-year Strauss and Howe crisis, or meta-cycle. The initial evidence was that the cycles harmonize with one another in groups of three.

We took a preliminary look at the experience of the inflationary 1946 to 1980 period in the United States. The facts seem to accord with the theory. If this relationship is also true for other time dimensions, then we can draw some profound conclusions about the nature of economic oscillations. Specifically, they are ordered rather than random; they are more predictable than is usually supposed; and this predictability applies to longer-term cycles as well as to short-term ones. We now need to look at some more evidence.

NOTES

1. We shall look at some of this evidence in Chapter 18.
2. Kitchin, Joseph (1923) 'Cycles and trends in economic factors', *Review of Economic Statistics*, **5**, pp 10–16.
3. Juglar, Clement (1862) *Des crises commerciales et leur retour périodique en France, en Angleterre et aux Etats Unis*, Librairie Guillaumin et Cie, Paris.
4. Kuznets, Simon (1930) *Secular Movements in Production and Prices*, Houghton Mifflin, Boston.

5.   Berry, Brian J L (1991) *Long-Wave Rhythms in Economic Development and Political Behavior*, Johns Hopkins, Baltimore.

6.   Kondratyev, Nikolai (1926) 'Die langen Wellen der Konjunktur', *Archiv fur Sozialwissenschaft und Sozialpolitik*, **56**, pp 573–609.

7.   Strauss, William and Howe, Neil (1991) *Generations: The history of America's future, 1584 to 2069*, William Morrow, New York. Strauss and Howe argue that secular crises alternate with 'spiritual awakenings' every 45 years. Hence there is a secular (economic) crisis every 90 years or so.

8.   See Wilson, Louise (1964) *Catalogue of Cycles, Part I – Economics*, Foundation for the Study of Cycles, Pittsburgh.

9.   Actually, the cycle is the length of two 'life phases', where a life phase is 22 years long. Some analysts might argue for a different length for a life phase. However, the length of a life phase is not regarded as being absolutely precise. It is the general influence that counts.

10. See, for example, van Duijn, Jaap J (1983) *The Long Wave in Economic Life*, George Allen & Unwin, London.

11. This view of the evolutionary process in an economy is derived from Ken Wilber's analysis of three-phase change. See, for example, Wilber, K (1998) *The Eye of Spirit: An integral vision for a world gone slightly mad*, Shambhala, Boston. Mr Wilber's extraordinary grasp of the logic of change and development, particularly in the context of human consciousness, has been a major influence on my thinking.

16

Recurrence in economic and financial activity

INTRODUCTION

In the previous chapter, we traced the theoretical evolution of a specific pattern – or, more precisely, a triad of patterns – in economic activity. If the theory is correct, then the patterns should repeat themselves in a 'fractal'-like fashion across all genuine cyclical time periods. This phenomenon is currently unknown to economic theory.

This, in turn, raises the possibility that we can compare the evolution of one beat of a particular cycle with the evolution of a previous beat of the same cycle. Indeed, we can compare the pattern that has been traced out by a particular sub-cycle in a triad with the comparable sub-cycle in an earlier triad.

This has revolutionary implications. If we know the history of a cycle, then we can track any new evolving cycle directly against that history. There will always be the danger of unexpected shocks; but, within reason, we should be able to see where we are in the context of the whole.

ECONOMIC AND FINANCIAL MARKET CYCLES

The process of comparing one cycle with another can be applied both to economic activity and to financial markets. The big advantage of drawing economic activity directly into the analysis is that it reduces the risk of making big mistakes. Specifically, if we know more or less where we are in the evolution of the economy, we should have some idea about the likely implications for financial markets.

Moreover, and as we shall demonstrate in Chapter 22, the relationship between markets and the economy is controlled by the golden ratio, 0.382:0.618. Specifically, the golden ratio can be used to estimate when a market is moving from a technical correction into a fundamental trend. So, even if the equity market turns before the economy (which is usual but not inevitable), we can know what that market might be trying to anticipate in terms of fundamentals. Further, we can know when a market trend is actually locking into feedback with those fundamentals. This latter is important because it marks the point where a trend starts to make itself felt.

SEARCHING FOR CYCLES

Figure 16.1 shows the two-year rates of change in US industrial production since just after the end of the American Civil War. The data are annual, so monthly fluctuations are eliminated. The chart covers a period of 133 years.

At first glance, there is not much obvious order in the chart. It is easy to pick out the period covering the 'Roaring Twenties', the Great

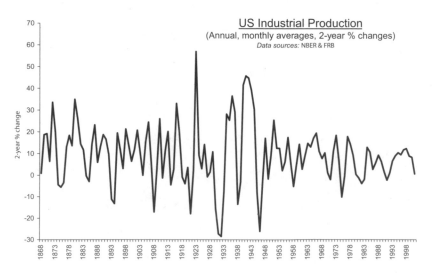

Figure 16.1 US industrial production, 1868 to 2001

Depression and World War II because the fluctuations are so massive. However, it is difficult to pick out a consistent periodicity between momentum lows. For example, it is certainly possible to pick out some of the deeper economic lows that are spaced 25 to 30 years apart (eg, 1868, 1894, 1921, 1946 and 1975). However, there are some deep lows that fell outside of the series (eg, 1908 and 1932).

What normally happens when faced with these apparent inconsistencies is that analysts assume that a) cycles of different lengths are independent of one another and that b) the deeper the low, the longer must be the cycle that is operating. They would then go through the data, searching for longer cycles centred on the Great Depression low of 1932.

In fact, the depth of the cycle is not necessarily the most important factor in determining cycle periodicities. The important consideration is the intrinsic pattern. Deep lows may occur at the *end* of a cycle but they can also occur at other points *within* a cycle. Deep lows within a cycle can occur as a result of shocks, especially policy mistakes. As will be demonstrated, the Great Depression low did not occur because it coincided with the end of an important long-term cycle. It occurred because it was part of an energy gap within the economic system. As we saw in Chapter 14, an energy gap may more accurately define a cycle high than a cycle low.

So the starting point in a search for cycles is twofold: either we can find an obvious energy gap that can be used to locate an economic peak and spread our analysis outwards around it; or we can look for the centred three-up/three-down base cycle that is normally to be found at the beginning of a triad.

THE 1868–94 CYCLE

The first obvious candidate for an important base cycle is the 26-year cycle that emerged after the end of the American Civil War. It fulfils the basic technical criterion of being a balanced six-wave (ie, three-up/three-down) cycle and it fulfils the economic criterion of being a period when adaptation to new circumstances was most likely. The momentum pattern is shown in Figure 16.2, using two-year percentage rates of change on annual data. It consists of a three-wave up move (1–2–3) followed by a three-wave down move (A–B–C). In line with the requirements of a base cycle, the pattern is balanced around a centre point.

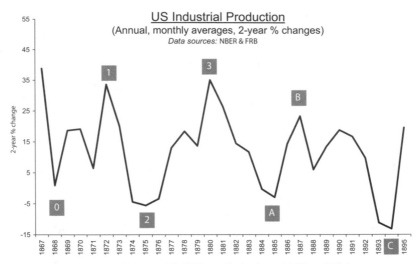

Figure 16.2 Post Civil War adaptation, 1868 to 1894

It is of some importance that this large adaptation cycle can easily be divided into Juglar-length sub-cycles. The first one (1868–75) covers the period now known as the 'Gilded Age', as emotions recovered from the tragedy of the Civil War. The second period (1875–85) was the time when cultural deepening took place, as the North and South came a little closer together. And the third period (1885–94) was the period of cultural unease and disruption known as the 'Missionary Awakening', characterized by labour violence and student evangelism.[1]

THE 1894–1921 CYCLE

The next cycle, in a sense, necessarily follows from this. After a period of rest and recuperation, creative energies re-emerge. In this case, a new generation 'comes of age'. Figure 16.3 shows the momentum of US industrial production over the 27-year period from 1894 to 1921. The period basically covers the huge adjustment in US society as it shifted to the mass production of industrial goods. As with most innovation-related cycles, this one had a strong rightward bias and did not properly peak until 1916. Hence, the pattern consists of a base pattern (1–2); a trend wave (wave 3, albeit interrupted by a crisis in 1907); an energy gap (wave A) up to the First World War; a sharp recovery into a late peak (wave B); and a short, sharp downswing (wave C). This is the classic pattern for a trend cycle.

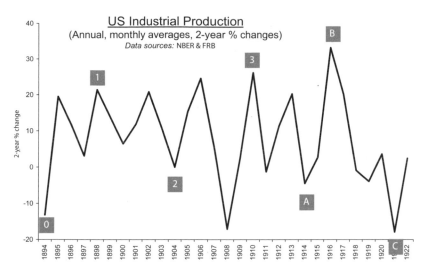

Figure 16.3 Regeneration cycle, 1894 to 1921

Like the cycle before it, this large cycle can be divided into three separate Juglar-length phases. The first phase (1894–1904) has the technical characteristics of a base cycle insofar as it has a balanced three-up/three-down look to it. The second phase (1904–14) is the period most usually associated with mass production of consumer goods such as cars and telephones. The period was, however, interrupted by a financial crisis, which was precipitated by the failure of the Knickerbocker Trust in 1907. Nevertheless, output recovered. The third phase (1914–21) was dominated by the United States' involvement in the First World War. Note how the initial war-induced surge was followed by a sharp three-wave decline into the 1921 low.

THE 1921–46 CYCLE

An adaptation cycle and a regeneration cycle are inevitably followed by a crisis cycle. The 1921–46 cycle was *the* cycle that confirmed the accuracy of this rule. Figure 16.4 shows the momentum of US industrial production over this period, measured by two-year percentage rates of change in the annual data. The chart embraces the Wall Street Crash of 1929, the Great Depression of 1929–32 and the Second World War of 1939–46. It is quite obvious that the pattern of the cycle conforms to the basic archetype that has already been described for terminal cycles: there is an early peak, and then a slow, but ultimately devastating, three-wave (A–B–C) fall into the final low.

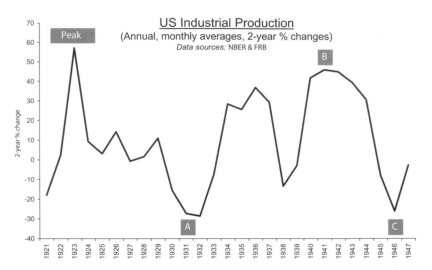

Figure 16.4 Crisis, 1921 to 1946

STRAUSS AND HOWE META-CYCLE

These three cycles are set out in sequence in Figure 16.5. Their average periodicity is 26 years, which places them in the time span appropriate to Berry cycles. The first such cycle, which covered the 26 years of reconstruction after the Civil War, was thus an adaptation cycle. The second, which covered the 27 years of innovation in electricity, electronics and cars, was a regeneration cycle. And the third, which covered the 25 years of disruption involving the Great Depression and the Second World War, was a crisis cycle.

We thus have a set of three major Berry cycles that accord to the basic blueprint – both in terms of pattern and time – that was set out in Chapter 15. This, in turn, means that we have a triad of cycles that constitute some form of higher-level cycle. The time span of the three Berry cycles, taken together, is 78 years. This is an acceptable time span for a Strauss and Howe meta-cycle. We can thus conclude that the period that lasted from just after the end of the American Civil War to the end of the Second World War was, indeed, a Strauss and Howe meta-cycle. It is no accident that the cycle was born out of a secular crisis and ended in one.

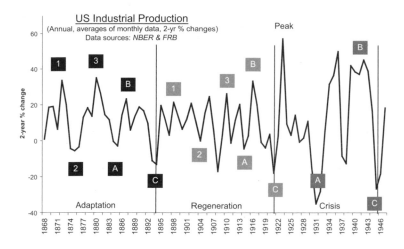

Figure 16.5 From the American Civil War to WWII

THE BERRY TERMINAL CYCLE

Although the overall patterning is entirely consistent with the triadic model, it does raise a question about why 1946 is shown as the low of the terminal cycle, rather than the more traditional date of 1932. It is important to remember that the cycle is here being defined by the patterns of group behaviour, not by specific events such as a very deep recession low. Specific events are relevant – and will give a cycle its essential flavour – but they do not define that cycle. So, we can go further and look at the shorter-term cycles within the larger-scale 1921–46 cycle. Even a terminal cycle should exhibit signs of an underlying triad of cycles. Figure 16.6 shows one-year percentage rates of change in the index of US industrial production between 1921 and 1946. The three-wave-up/three-wave-down notation that defines the locus of the whole cycle is shown in blocked alphanumerics (1–2–3/A–B–C) and the notation for the sub-cycles is shown in lower-case lettering and Roman numerals. It is quite clear that the 25-year Berry crisis cycle that lasted from 1921 to 1946 consisted of three Juglar-length sub-cycles.

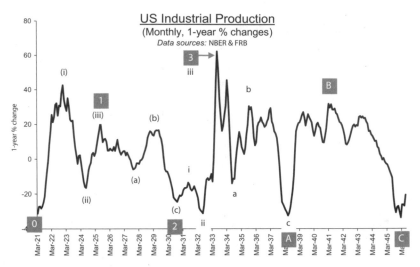

Figure 16.6 The crisis triad, 1921 to 1946

THE FIRST JUGLAR CYCLE

We can now see how this Berry crisis cycle breaks down into smaller-degree cycles. In theory, it should initially divide down into three cycles of approximately eight to nine years each. This would make them Juglar cycles. The first such Juglar cycle lasted from March 1921 to October 1930. It actually breaks down into a very clear six-wave pattern. In a terminal cycle, the momentum peak is very likely to occur in the first sub-cycle. This is exactly what happened. The momentum peak (at (i)) was high partly in response to the sharp low in 1921. Nevertheless, subsequent peaks (at (iii) and (b)) were progressively lower. Hence, although the recuperation cycle contained a very clear pattern of three waves up and three waves down, and although there was an appropriate peak in the middle of the cycle in July 1925, the cycle contained warning biases.

THE SECOND JUGLAR CYCLE

The second cycle in the triad lasted from October 1930 to June 1938. It also breaks down into a very clear six-wave pattern. It is notable that wave ii within this pattern made a new momentum low. This was essentially because the authorities had made a mistake in allowing the credit and monetary aggregates to contract. This policy mistake was a shock that distorted the cycle; it was not an essential part of the cycle. After such a deep low, it would not have been surprising to see a sharp recovery. This latter duly occurred, assisted by Franklin D Roosevelt's 'New Deal' after he was elected in November 1932. Nevertheless, the economy needed more time to re-establish confidence. Production contracted again in 1937 and early 1938.

THE THIRD JUGLAR CYCLE

The third cycle lasted from May 1938 to February 1946. It reflected the impact of the war in Europe. Its position in the triad makes it the terminal sub-cycle within the bigger cycle. Initially, the United States was not directly involved with the war. However, it became increasingly supportive of Britain's efforts throughout 1940 and early 1941. This helped to provide a boost to the cycle, which therefore had an unusually centred look to it. Nevertheless, total output subsequently contracted, first as production facilities became focused on military hardware and then as the war in Europe finished in the spring of 1945.

CONFIRMING THE 1946 LOW

Measuring from 1868, the Strauss and Howe meta-cycle lasted for 78 years. It contained three Berry cycles each averaging 26 years in duration. The last cycle in the Berry triad – the 1921–46 crisis cycle – contained three clear Juglar sub-cycles, which took the economy into its final low. These considerations are important. Had the final low been placed in 1932, then the last phase would only have consisted of two cycles that had Juglar-type lengths. Further the time elapse of that last phase (1921–32) would have been only 17 per cent of the implied Strauss and Howe meta-cycle (1868–1932), which is about half the standard percentage. And the meta-cycle itself would have been unusually short at 64 years, which is about two-thirds of the standard length.

The year 1946 therefore marked the end of an era, as measured by a Strauss and Howe meta-cycle. This is a critical conclusion, because it means that we can now start estimating where we are in the subsequent meta-cycle. As a central estimate, the new era that started in 1946 is destined to last 90 years. It could, of course, be about 10 years longer or shorter than this, depending on how the underlying Berry and Juglar cycles evolve. Nevertheless, the new Strauss and Howe cycle is scheduled to end somewhere between 2026 and 2046.

THE 1946–80 BERRY ADAPTATION CYCLE

The new era that began in 1946 started with a Berry adaptation cycle. We looked at this cycle briefly in Chapter 15. It was characterized by a large-scale government incursion into the economy and was ultimately inflationary. It lasted from 1946 to 1980. The time elapse of this cycle – at 34 years – was obviously longer than the Berry cycles that materialized in the previous meta-cycle. This is because the underlying Juglar and Kitchin cycles were longer. It might be interesting to speculate why this might have been so but, as far as this analysis is concerned, it doesn't strictly matter. All that we need to know is where we are at any particular point in time.

Figure 16.7 shows the profile of US industrial production over the period 1946–80, measured in terms of two-year percentage rates of change. Data are, however, monthly, which allows for a little more precision. The chart covers the Korean War, the social revolution of the 1960s, the Vietnam War and the great inflation of the late 1970s.

This cycle was divided into three clear Juglar-length phases. The first (February 1946 to April 1958) was a classic base cycle, with three waves into the 1951 peak and then three waves down into the 1957

Figure 16.7 The Berry adaptation cycle, 1946 to 1980

low. It covered the basic post-war reconstruction of industry and business. The second cycle in the triad (April 1958 to November 1970) spanned the period known as the 'Swinging Sixties'. It marked the transition in the economy to mass consumption. It was therefore an innovation cycle and – not surprisingly – was biased to the right. The last cycle (November 1970 to August 1980) was the cycle of disruption, related to an explosion in the prices both of consumer goods and of raw materials, especially oil. This cycle followed the classic pattern that has already been outlined – namely, an early peak, followed by a three-wave fall into a final low.

THE 1970–80 JUGLAR CYCLE

The last cycle needs a little explanation. It has traditionally been assumed that 1975 marked the major cycle low of the period. Demand had been badly hit in 1974 by a combination of higher interest rates and the sharp rise in oil prices after the 1973 Yom Kippur War. However, on the basis of the model that is being presented here, the final low of the crisis phase of the post-war adaptation cycle could not have been in 1975. For a start, it would have meant that the third cycle in the triad would have only been four years long, which is less than 15 per cent of what would then have been the whole cycle (1946–75). Second, inflationary expectations were not at that time brought properly under control because governments still did not see that public sector deficit financing was at the root of the problem. Finally, there was a second oil price shock after the Ayatollah's Revolution in Iran, which deflated the US economy into a second low. Such an event is typical of a terminal cycle. The point is that the 1975 low was created – as was the low in 1932 – by a shock to the system. It was not generated by the process that creates a normal cycle low. Hence the correct placement of the low is in 1980. This ensures that the third cycle in the post-1946 triad was 10 years in length. This is of the same order of magnitude as the previous two.

THE KITCHIN TRIAD

A closer inspection of the 1970–80 Juglar cycle, using a shorter momentum index, reveals that it sub-divides into three Kitchin cycles. Figure 16.8 shows the annualized three-month percentage rates of

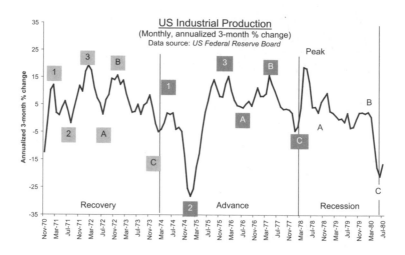

Figure 16.8 US industrial production, November 1970 to June 1980

change in US industrial production between November 1970 and June 1980. This is a 10-year cycle that breaks down into three sub-cycles, each lasting about 3.2 years, or 38 months. Moreover, the pattern of the sub-cycles contains the expected three-up/three-down profile.

The first Kitchin cycle is very clear. It peaked halfway through its eventual time elapse and finished in February 1974. The second cycle started on time, but was deflated by the impact of the huge increase in oil prices that occurred in December 1973. Wave 2 was therefore very deep and made a new low. As mentioned in Chapter 9, this is by no means an unusual phenomenon. Nevertheless, there was a wave 3 recovery into the summer of 1975. The subsequent wave A was quite mild, allowing wave B to peak at high levels. This gave a rightward bias to the middle wave. Finally, the third Kitchin cycle looks remarkably like the terminal Juglar cycle just described. It has a sharp initial rally and then a slower three-wave fall. It is also shorter than its predecessors. And note this: the pattern in Figure 16.8 is almost identical to the pattern in Figure 16.3.

Hence, the patterns of the Kitchin cycles reproduced the patterns of the Juglar cycles, which repeated the patterns of the Berry cycles, which mirrored the patterns of the Strauss and Howe meta-cycle. Cycles nest in fractal-like hierarchies.

THE POST-1980 BERRY REGENERATION CYCLE

The model suggests that, after a period of adaptation, the economy enters a period of genuine change, involving qualitative evolution in the physical and intellectual infrastructure. The Berry cycle that started in 1980 is such a cycle; and, on the basis of the average of Berry cycles since 1868, it is scheduled to finish in 2010. There is some evidence that the cycle has lengthened since the end of the Second World War, which means that it could finish as late as 2014. Normally, this spread of end dates would cause forecasters to turn to other methods. The point, however, is that we will likely be able to track the cycle into its final low just by focusing on the pattern.

THE JUGLAR RECUPERATION AND INNOVATION CYCLES

Shown in Figure 16.9 is the two-year percentage change in the monthly index of US industrial production between 1980 and 2005. It covers the initial recovery out of the 1980 low, the deep recession of the early 1990s, the long subsequent boom associated with the infotech revolution, and the 'unexpected' collapse of 2000–01.

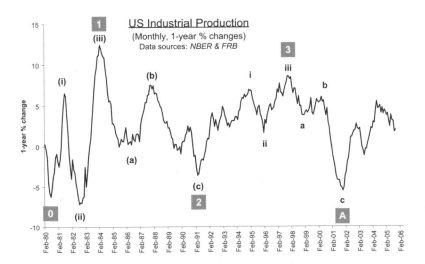

Figure 16.9 The Berry regeneration cycle, 1980 to 2005

Up to the end of 2001, therefore, the Berry regeneration cycle had spanned two of its three Juglar cycles. The first of these (July 1980 to March 1991) was a classic base cycle in its own right. It had a clear six-wave pattern consisting of three waves up ((i), (ii), (iii)) and three waves down ((a), (b), (c)). As occasionally happens, wave (ii) in this pattern made a new low. This was partly caused by the fact that interest rates were not only high, but also rose again in the early part of 1982. So there was a 'second dip' to the recession. However, the overall cycle was basically centred and, when completed, it formed waves 1 and 2 of the higher-level Berry cycle.

The second pattern (March 1991 to November 2001) was the innovation cycle proper. It incorporated the spread of personal computers, the adoption of Internet usage and the conversion to mobile telephones. The cycle was biased to the right and the recession, when it came, was sudden and seemingly unexpected.

KITCHIN CYCLES

If we look a little more closely at this Juglar innovation cycle, we can see just how closely it conforms to the archetypal triadic patterning for a complete cycle. Shown in Figure 16.10 is the three-month annualized percentage change in the monthly index of US industrial production from January 1991 to November 2001. The starting date of the cycle is slightly earlier because of the shorter momentum indicator but it demonstrates that the Juglar cycle breaks down into three smaller Kitchin cycles.

The first one (January 1991 to April 1995) was a standard base, or recovery, cycle as the economy recovered from the traumatic recession of 1990. It consisted of the archetypal centred six-wave pattern associated with such a cycle. The second cycle (April 1995 to July 1998) was the Kitchin advance cycle. It had a long upward bias and therefore peaked late. The third cycle (July 1998 to November 2001) was the Kitchin recession cycle. It peaked early and then had a long three-wave correction into the final low.

CONCLUSION

The vibrations in industrial production since the end of the American Civil War confirm that an economic cycle, of whatever duration,

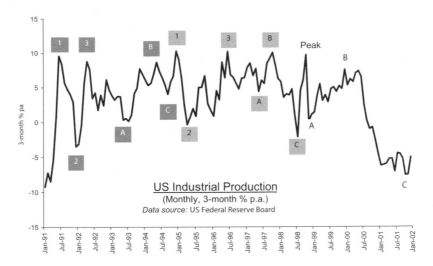

Figure 16.10 The Juglar innovation cycle, 1991 to 2001

evolves according to a basic pattern. The pattern consists of three sub-cycles. The first cycle is a base (or detachment) cycle. It consists of a balanced six-wave pattern and peaks in the middle. The second cycle is a trend (or transition) cycle that incorporates the social and techno-logical changes of the period. It, too, consists of six waves. However, it is biased to the right and tends to peak late. The third cycle is a terminal (or detachment) cycle. The underlying pattern consists of six waves, but the occurrence of shocks tends to suppress some of them. In particular, the first downturn within the early part of the cycle can act as an energy gap, or shock, that reverses the polarity of the system. The cycle therefore tends to present as a sharp rise into an early peak, followed by an extended three-wave fall into a final low.

The basic pattern has been found to exist within a series of cycles that harmonize with each other. It exists in a 90-year Strauss and Howe meta-cycle, a 30-year Berry infrastructure cycle, a 10-year Juglar investment cycle and a 3.33-year Kitchin cycle.

These are extraordinary conclusions. They mean that economic cycles are both ordered and predictable.

NOTE

1.   See Strauss, William and Howe, Neil (1991) *Generations: The history of America's future, 1584 to 2069*, William Morrow, New York.

17

Integrating the cycles

INTRODUCTION

The inference from the foregoing analysis is that group activity results in clearly identifiable patterns of behaviour. The patterns are derived from a single archetypal pattern, evolve in groups of three and oscillate rhythmically. This phenomenon, which is currently unrecognized by the social sciences, hints at the existence of a profound depth of order to social, political and economic development. In other words, although evolution is always a creative response to changing circumstances, the mechanisms by which that evolution takes place are not random.

If this is so, then we have the possibility of comparing current developments (whatever they may be and whenever they occur) with previous episodes of history, in order to see what can be learnt. This is something that historians have always attempted to do. The difference here is that we have important criteria for ensuring that we are comparing like with like.

HISTORICAL SCHEMATIC

The schematic diagram in Figure 17.1 incorporates the broad characteristics that we have been able to identify for each of the Berry and Juglar cycles that have evolved since the beginning of the 19th century. The cycles are measured from low points in economic momentum, using annual data. Since we are here looking at broad trends and essential characteristics of cycles, the use of annual data does not matter too much. However, the dating varies slightly when shorter-term momentum indicators are used. For example, in the 1930s, the US economy almost certainly moved from the adaptation stage to the regeneration stage of the Berry cycle in 1931. However, the regeneration stage was initially biased downwards such that industrial production continued to fall into 1932. Inevitably, therefore, the diagram must be used with appropriate caution.

With this qualification in mind, the diagram incorporates the basic three-phase model of cyclical behaviour that was shown in Figure 15.2, in Chapter 15. Here, each of the three phases is a Juglar cycle; and three Juglar cycles constitute a Berry cycle. Each Juglar cycle will be either a base cycle, a trend cycle or a terminal cycle. Each Berry cycle will be either a base cycle, a trend cycle or a terminal cycle. These terms will, of course, have a different quality of meaning, depending on the level of the hierarchy being considered.

Shown in the lower part of the diagram are the dates of each of the major Juglar cycle turning points that have already been identified. These turning points have been identified by the pattern of the cycle rather than by the periodicity of the cycle.

Between each pair of dates are shown the essential characteristics of the Juglar cycle in question. These characteristics are historically identifiable and will, in essence, involve recuperation, innovation or disruption. Similarly, down the right-hand side of the lower part of the diagram are the indications as to whether a specific Berry cycle is

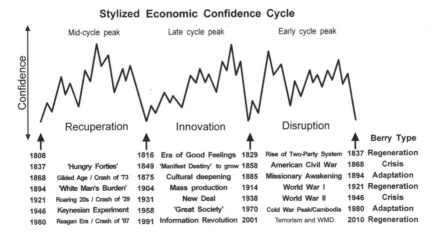

Figure 17.1 Characteristics of Berry and Juglar cycles

orientated to adaptation, regeneration or crisis. We can thus locate the essential 'flavour' of any particular time period from its position on the diagram.

SURVEY OF THE DIAGRAM

What is so striking about the diagram is the natural way in which the various distinctions can be drawn and applied. At the Berry level, it is, for example, quite obvious that the 1868 to 1894 period should have been an adaptation period following the Civil War. And it is quite obvious that the 1921 to 1946 cycle was a huge crisis cycle. The primary characteristics of the Berry cycles have therefore occurred precisely where they should have done.

Meanwhile, at the Juglar level, history is quite clear that the important periods of very active change in the last century were: the decade prior to the First World War (mass production); the Swinging Sixties (mass consumption); and, more recently, the infotech revolution (information technology). Again, periods of recognizable economic and social change occur precisely where they should. One very obvious inference is that periods of important adjustment occur every 30 years or so.

Having thus locked the diagram in place, other periods can easily be fitted in. For example, we can see how precisely the three Juglar cycles that evolved between 1868 and 1894 fitted in. First, the period 1868 to 1875 is now known as the 'Gilded Age', reflecting the relief that the Civil War was over. Then 1875 to 1885 saw something of a cultural revolution as the North and South started to integrate. Finally, the Missionary Awakening that started in 1885 embraced a period of unrest. Indeed, it was a complete contrast to the quiet deepening of the previous 10 years. There were violent labour disputes and there was an explosion of missionary activity. Both, in their way, were a confrontation with the existing order of things: the labour disputes were very much related to a desire for a radical change in the domestic culture; the missionary activity was energized by a desire to change the external world. It seems that a polarization of attitudes and various forms of unrest are part and parcel of any Juglar disruption cycle.

On this analysis, it is not therefore surprising to find that every Juglar disruption cycle in Figure 17.1 has been dominated by an intensification of aggression. Hence, the Civil War impacted during the 1858–68 Juglar disruption cycle; the First World War occurred in the 1914–21 cycle; the Second World War impacted during the 1938–46 cycle; and the US invasion of Cambodia and the the peak of the Cold War (as well as the Yom Kippur War) occurred during the 1970–80 cycle. It is, therefore, consistent with the model that the War on Terrorism has dominated the start of the terminal Juglar cycle within the current Berry trend cycle.

Where world war has dominated a disruption cycle, the room for domestic political confrontation has been reduced. Nevertheless, the potential for such confrontation is never very far away. The experience of the Missionary Awakening period has already been mentioned. There was also labour unrest in the 1970s. In 1978 in the United States, for example, the miners went on strike and newspapers were shut down for months. In the UK (which follows the US cycle quite closely), the winter of 1978/79 became known as the 'Winter of Discontent'.

Naturally enough, the traumas of a disruption cycle generate a need for recuperation. Hence the 10-year period following each Juglar disruption cycle has been very much associated with a sense of relief, especially in the first five years or so. The 'Gilded Age' has already been mentioned. The recovery from the First World War was associated with the 'Roaring Twenties'; the recovery from the Second World War was very much a period of reconstruction and generated cultural phenomena such as the 'New Look', 'Teddy Boys' and rock and roll. And the recovery from the war-peppered and inflationary 1970s was marked by a decisive shift towards conservative politics (Ronald Reagan in the United States and Margaret Thatcher in the UK) and the start of the lengthy campaign against large government deficits and rapid monetary growth.

Finally, it needs to be noted that the last phase of the recuperation cycle is usually marked by a deep recession. The need to detach from the old order means that some of its entrenched attitudes have to be eradicated. Some of these attitudes are often the outmoded methods of dealing with a crisis in the first place. The Great Depression of 1929–32, the recession of 1957–58 and the slump of 1990–91 occurred during the last phase of a Juglar recuperation cycle.

USING THE DIAGRAM

One definite inference from this summary is that the diagram can be used to assess the tone of current social and economic developments. There may be some uncertainty about precise start and end dates, and there is always the danger of unforeseen shocks. Nevertheless, it is possible to embed forecasts for the economy and financial markets in specific assumptions that will almost certainly be justified. For example, it is possible to say that the Juglar cycle that began in 2001 will be characterized by persistent international conflict and labour unrest.

In addition, we can assume that fluctuations in industrial production during this Juglar cycle will exhibit a very clear pattern. Specifically, there will be an initial recovery, which will be followed by a slow three-wave fall into a late period low. This implies that there will be at least two very difficult periods, of which the second one (into the cycle low) will probably be the worst. What we cannot yet know is how strong the intermediate recovery will be.

This is where the bigger picture may provide some help. Another way of using the diagram is to see what is *unlikely* over any particular period. In the 1990s, for example, we could validly have regarded international tension as being a low risk. Indeed, we might have concluded this even before the fall of the Berlin Wall in 1989. This did not mean that warfare wouldn't happen during the 1990s, just that it was unlikely to be a long-term dominant factor as far as the domestic economy and mass public attention were concerned. Hence, the Gulf War, which impacted at the end of the 1980–91 recuperation cycle, was quick and (from the West's point of view) effective. Oil prices fell back after the war and the global economy quickly recovered. This contrasts, for example, with the intra-cycle war events of 1970 to 1980, which resulted in a rapid expansion of money growth and an irreversible explosion in oil prices. The US economy (and other economies) suffered from these events.

What is unlikely in the current Juglar cycle is another 1930s-style recession. For a start, the current Berry cycle is a regeneration cycle, not a crisis cycle; and the Great Depression occurred in a Berry crisis cycle. Second, the tone of the current Juglar cycle is simply not the same as that which gripped the US economy during the Depression years. This needs some explanation.

THE GREAT DEPRESSION

As indicated in Chapter 16, socio-economic behaviour expresses itself in a different blend of affective, somatic and cognitive characteristics in each Juglar cycle. A Juglar disruption cycle is, of course, dominated by fear. Ultimately, however, fear evokes a response from those who are closely involved with it. The most obvious response is from investors and employers: the former sell stock and the latter lay off labour. However, the response that in many ways is the most important (in relation, that is, to the onset of an economic depression) comes from the authorities. They, too, will be driven by fear. But the quality of their policy response will be influenced by the somatic and cognitive milieu of the time.

In a Juglar disruption cycle, the dominant somatic reaction is one of resistance. Initially this takes the form of resistance to any more change (ie, satiation with innovation). Subsequently, however, it takes the form of resistance to losing the gains that were achieved during the innovation cycle. Meanwhile, the dominant cognitive reaction is one of accusation. Initially, this takes the form of passively blaming external events for changing circumstances. Subsequently, however, it can take the form of direct action against a perceived aggressor. This is one of the reasons why the prolonged economic difficulties of a Juglar disruption cycle are associated with persistent civil unrest and/or military action.

However, the combination of fear, resistance and accusation can be a powerful stimulus for governments to take action on the economy. Governments become interventionist. Monetary and fiscal policy becomes very pro-active. Tariff barriers are erected against foreign competition. Failing industries are supported by direct intervention. This action cannot bypass the economic contraction entirely but it can ameliorate that contraction.

This is in direct contrast to the matrix of indolence, need for recuperation, and loss of self-assertiveness that can bleed into business activity and policy-making during a recuperation cycle. Normally, this may not matter very much; it is just part of the ebb and flow of life. However, under particularly trying conditions – such as in a Berry crisis cycle – it can matter a great deal. The problem is that no one is able to take control once things start to go wrong. A sort of laziness and fatalistic acceptance settles over business and politics. Mistakes get made and a genuine psychological depression sets in. This is one of the aspects of the Great Depression that is least commented on – it was, above all else, a psychological phenomenon.

THE NEXT BERRY CRISIS CYCLE

One inference, therefore, is that the 10-year terminal cycle that started in 2001 will be difficult. Specifically, it seems likely to drive the economy from above-trend growth to below-trend growth. However, the pattern clearly confirms that it is not destined to have the psychological overtones that characterize a major economic depression. In fact, if any such problem were to occur, it would most likely impact during the *next* Juglar cycle. There are two reasons for this. First, the next 30-year Berry cycle will probably be a crisis cycle. Second, the next Juglar cycle, which will also start at the same time, will probably be a recuperation cycle. The implication is that the downturn of this next Juglar cycle could bring with it a depression-like trauma and thereby trigger a crisis period that could last until 2040.

The general themes for the 30-year period are shown in Figure 17.2. Taking our lead from the experience of the 1920s and 1930s, the middle of the next decade (ie, 2015 or thereabouts) will probably mark the end of a prolonged period of economic growth, and a satiated economy will drop into an energy gap. If, then, the patterns of history continue to repeat themselves, 2020–30 will see the beginnings of a revolutionary upheaval in attitudes towards politics and economic policy, and 2030–40 will be blemished by global conflict. We shall see.

KONDRATYEV WAVES

This 'forecast' raises the question of the relationship between the current cyclical pattern and the Kondratyev price cycle, which we mentioned in Chapter 15. Specifically, if a genuine crisis is going to

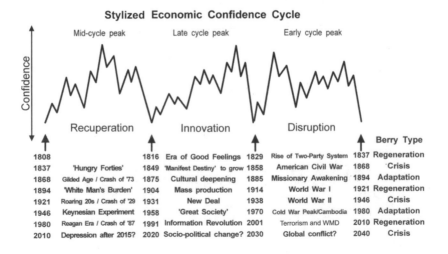

Figure 17.2 The Berry crisis cycle, 2010 to 2040

start sometime in the next decade, what might commodity prices be doing? Figure 17.3 shows the one-year percentage change in the annual closing level of the three-year average of US wholesale commodity prices. The time series starts from the late 18th century; so it is a relatively long series. What is apparent is that there is a basic oscillation, measured from low to low, that takes about 28 years. However, there are a number of other distinctive features. The first is that the cycles tend to be biased to the right, so that highs occur very late in the cycle and are followed by a sharp drop. The second is that the most dominant highs are associated with major wars. And the third feature is that each pair of oscillations is very biased upwards to the right, such that the first oscillation forms a base and the second oscillation involves a three-phase impulse wave and a final collapse. Moreover, the peaks are 28 years apart, so a double oscillation lasts for about 56 years. This is the accepted periodicity of the Kondratyev wave.

So, there certainly seems to be some ordered process at work. However, the important point is that the highs are almost certainly preludes to energy gaps, which are reflected in the sharpness of the subsequent drop. The highs are thus genuine cycle highs, but the lows are not necessarily always proper cycle lows. As was demonstrated in Figure 14.7, lows may be caused by shocks to the system. On this basis, the correct version of Figure 17.3 is as shown in Figure 17.4. The periodicity is still 56 years, but the lows are now in different places. Specifically, the lows are in 1842, 1895 and 1954.

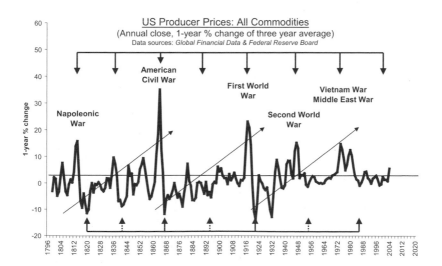

Figure 17.3 US wholesale price inflation, 1796 to 2001

Figure 17.4 The Kondratyev cycle in US wholesale prices

One important inference is that we can use these timings to identify periods of inflation and periods of disinflation. That is, the 28-year period prior to a Kondratyev peak is inflationary and the 28-year period after that peak is disinflationary.

However, we can take this analysis an important step further. One of the important ideas that we are pursuing is that historical patterns reproduce themselves over the course of comparable cycles. Figure 17.5 takes the 1841 to 1895 cycle shown in Figure 17.4 and compares

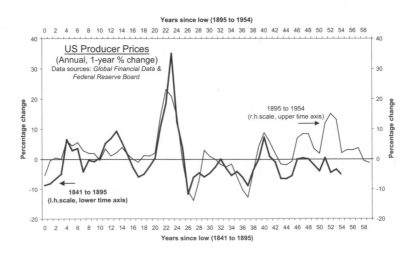

Figure 17.5 Comparison of cycles, 1841–95 and 1895–1954

it with the subsequent cycle that ran from 1895 to 1954. There is a truly remarkable correlation between the two patterns. In particular, there is a major cycle peak about 22 years into the cycle. What emerges, however, is that the later cycle was probably longer than its predecessor, by up to five years. Taking the average of the two cycles, the cycle peaks seem to occur 39 per cent into the whole cycle.

Next, we can compare the 1895 to 1954 cycle with the most recent cycle, which evolved after 1954. This time, however, it is necessary to adjust the patterns, by plotting each cycle on separate axes, so that the major turning points coincide (see Figure 17.6). Once this is done, there is another remarkable correlation between the patterns, providing it is allowed that the cycle that started in 1954 either ended in 2003 or is destined to have another sharp drop very shortly. Actually, when the most recent cycle is compared with the 1841 to 1895 cycle, it looks reasonably clear that the former has indeed ended. At the comparable stage of the 1841 to 1895 cycle, prices had already started to rise sharply (see Figure 17.7). This suggests that the time elapse of the most recent cycle is 49 years, rather than 56 years. Importantly, this would also mean that the cycle peak in year 20 would have occurred 40 per cent of the way through it, which is not significantly different to the timings for its predecessors.

If we now translate the general information from the above analysis into the terms of Figure 17.1, something very interesting emerges (see Figure 17.8). First, the main Kondratyev price lows (eg, 1895 and 1954) occur during Juglar recuperation cycles. Second, Kondratyev

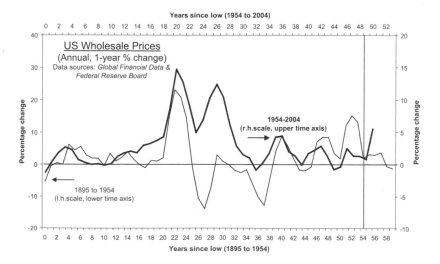

Figure 17.6 Comparison of cycles, 1895–1954 and 1954–2004

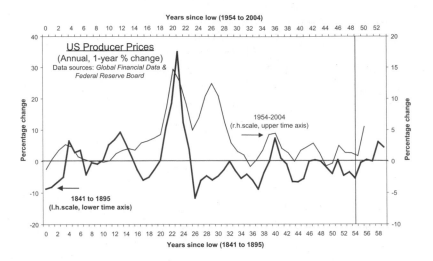

Figure 17.7 Comparison of cycles, 1841–95 and 1954–2004

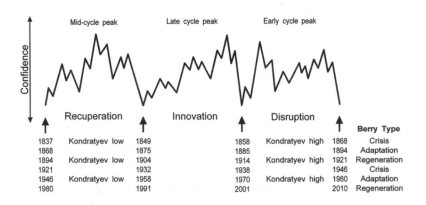

Figure 17.8 The Kondratyev price cycle

price highs (eg, 1864, 1917, 1974) occur during Juglar disruption cycles. Moreover, these highs are war-related. However, the precise timing of the price highs and price lows within the appropriate Juglar cycle seems not to be a constant. In other words, there is a slight mismatch between prices and output.[1]

What is clear is that Kondratyev price highs occur during Juglar disruption cycles and that such Juglar cycles are likely to involve serious international tension. What is also clear is that the Juglar recuperation cycle after a major price peak is particularly dangerous. There were deep recessions in 1873–75, 1929–32 and 1990–91.

KONDRATYEV WAVES AND STRAUSS AND HOWE META-CYCLES

There are now a number of additional points that can be made about the diagrams shown in Figures 17.1 and 17.8, which actually help to confirm their validity. The first point is that the Crash of 1873, the Wall Street Crash of 1929 and the Equity Crash of 1987 *all* occurred in the downwave of Juglar recuperation cycles. Further, they all occurred after a major Kondratyev price high. This is compelling evidence that the model is an accurate one.

Nevertheless, there are differences. The 1873 event occurred in a Berry adaptation cycle, and Congress limited the circulation of notes and coins. The 1929 episode occurred in a Berry crisis cycle, and the authorities made the mistake of allowing the money and credit aggregates to contract. The 1987 event occurred in a Berry regeneration cycle, and the authorities reacted with a monetary stimulus.

There is a second point about the diagrams, which is in many ways more important. The diagram quite clearly indicates that the Great Depression is not specifically a Kondratyev phenomenon. Indeed, as presented, the Wall Street Crash and Depression were part of the *beginning* of a crisis period, rather than part of the end of one. This is entirely consistent with the idea offered by Strauss and Howe that major socio-economic crises occur every 90 years or so. In the context of the basic cycle mechanism, the Crash/Depression presents itself as an energy gap in the system. In the context of the 90-year Strauss and Howe meta-cycle, such an energy gap is likely to occur in the third Berry cycle (ie, the Berry crisis cycle) in a triad of such cycles. Specifically, it is likely to occur in the first downturn of the first Juglar cycle in that Berry cycle. Measuring from 1868 in Figure 17.1, the downturn could have been expected in the late 1920s – which is precisely where it occurred.

Finally, there is the interesting conundrum of whether or not the Kondratyev wave that began in 1954 has actually finished or not. Up to 1954, the periodicity of the Kondratyev wave has actually been steadier than that of the underlying economic cycles, with a periodicity of 56 years. On the basis of simple mathematics, the next low after 1954 is scheduled for 2010; and we have already indicated that an output low is scheduled for 2010. However, a more detailed analysis of the last Kondratyev cycle suggests that it may already be moving into another upwave. This not only supports the view that the long wave is not a mechanical phenomenon, but also suggests that the economic low scheduled for around 2010 may not actually be severe.

There are two good reasons to suspect that this may be the case. The first is that the authorities are, in general terms, aware of the phenomenon of end-cycle deflation. They have moved strongly to avoid it. The second reason is that the economic confidence model shown in Figure 17.2 reveals that any end-cycle economic weakness will not be part of an energy gap. This latter is scheduled for 2015 (or thereabouts). Such a gap will necessarily arise out of excesses, and it is reasonable to assume that those excesses will be sourced in the attempts to avoid recession during the 2001–10 period. What is more, whether the low of the most recent Kondratyev cycle occurred in 2003 or is likely to impact in 2010, one thing seems certain: the next energy gap will be associated with inflation, not deflation.

CONCLUSION

Forecasting financial markets will probably never be a perfect science; but it can be a less stressful art. In this respect, the suggestion that economic activity exhibits patterned rhythms is an important asset. If an analyst can identify the current location of the economy in the context of an evolving pattern, then there is a good chance that it will be possible to distinguish a little more clearly between temporary fluctuations and important trends.

This chapter has therefore surveyed in some detail the evolution of economic cycles dating back to the end of the American Civil War. It has found that certain economic phenomena reproduce themselves periodically. Quite specifically, it has been found that the economy enters a period of innovation, or change, every 30 years or so, as the energy of a new mix of generations starts to make itself felt. This period of innovation is preceded by a period of gradual awakening and is succeeded by a period of retrenchment. Each of these phases lasts about 10 years.

The presence of this phenomenon is highly suggestive of an ordered process at work. Moreover, it confirms that economic theory's assumption of rational behaviour by independent individuals is deeply flawed.

NOTE

1.　Professor Berry assigns two 'Berry cycles' to one beat of the Kondratyev wave. This means that each Kondratyev price low and price high is accompanied by a recession. The former could be a depression; the latter is a stagflation. See Berry, Brian J L (1991) *Long-Wave Rhythms in Economic Development and Politicial Behavior*, Johns Hopkins, Baltimore.

18

Forecasting with cycles

INTRODUCTION

In the last chapter, we revealed the presence of order in the evolution of economic cycles. Importantly, this order is based on logic, and the evidence supports the theory. We thus have the capability of understanding the economic context within which financial market cycles occur, without having to resort to a detailed analysis of daily and monthly statistics. We can know, for example, when we are in a crisis cycle that is vulnerable to shocks, especially war-related shocks. We can know whether this cycle is likely to be inflationary or not. We can judge the likely pattern of the cycle over time. And we can use history to estimate when the important turning points are going to be.

This is a huge step forward. Nevertheless, the periodicity of a cycle will still vary through time. No matter how careful we are, the time elapse of a cycle can expand or contract and throw us off balance. The critical point, however, is that, despite the potential variation in the periodicity, the basic pattern of the cycle remains unchanged. The art, therefore, is to track the pattern of a cycle in real time.

One of the ways of doing this is to use a previous cycle as a blueprint and measure the evolution of the contemporaneous cycle against it.

THE CURRENT BERRY ECONOMIC CYCLE

Shown in Figure 18.1 is the two-year rate of change in the monthly index of US industrial production over two time periods. The first time period is the whole Berry adaptation cycle that evolved between 1946 and 1980. The second is the incomplete Berry regeneration cycle that started in 1980. The latter Berry cycle has so far negotiated two Juglar cycles – namely 1980 to 1991, and 1991 to 2001 – and is now in its third.

The secret of making the comparison is to track the evolution of the current cycle on a different time axis to the original cycle. This means that any variations in the time elapse of the cycle can be absorbed, while holding the pattern constant. In Figure 18.1, the 1946–80 cycle – now to be our blueprint – is tracked along the lower time axis and the subsequent Berry cycle that started in 1980 is tracked along the upper time axis.

CYCLE ALIGNMENT

The first task is to align the three-up/three-down pattern of the 1980–91 Juglar cycle with the three-up/three-down pattern of the 1946–57 Juglar cycle. This should be relatively easy to do because both cycles are base cycles and should therefore have the same clear shape. This shape normally incorporates a mid-cycle peak.[1] Once the alignment has been done, the 1991–2001 Juglar cycle then easily coincides with the 1957–70 cycle.

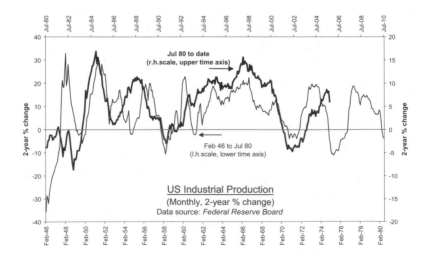

Figure 18.1 Juglar economic cycles compared

This alignment seems amazing, although it is actually quite normal. It means that it was possible to confirm both the 1991 low and the 2001 low, as they were occurring.

The second task is to estimate the likely duration of the whole Berry cycle that started in 1980. Looking at the top horizontal axis, it can be seen that, in order to make the momentum troughs on the chart coincide, the total time elapse of the post-1980 cycle would have to be 355 months, or 29.6 years. Since the cycle started in July 1980, this means that the expected low for the whole cycle is early 2010. This is a clear confirmation of the date given in the previous chapter, which was calculated using averages of previous cycle periodicities.

There is a new piece of information here. This is that the post-1980 cycle is likely to be shorter than its 1946–80 counterpart. The latter took 413 months (or 34.4 years) to complete. This confirms the value of looking at the pattern and, as a corollary, the danger of concentrating on periodicities.

SENTIMENT IN A JUGLAR INNOVATION CYCLE

Although it is more than adequate to work just with economic statistics, it is often helpful to track sentiment indicators as well. These are usually released more quickly than official data and, indeed, may actually inflect before the official data. One of the primary indices to use in relation to the US economy is the composite index of producer expectations that is produced by the Institute of Supply Management (ISM). Comparable indices are produced by the Confederation of British Industry (CBI) in the UK and by the Institute for Economic Research (IFO) in Germany.

Such indices are very sensitive. So they are particularly useful for short-term work and for comparing cycles directly with one another. Figure 18.2 compares the Juglar innovation cycle in the ISM index between January 1958 and November 1970 with the Juglar innovation cycle in that same index between February 1991 and November 2001. The ISM index has been re-based to 100 at the cycle start dates.

What is very clear is that, once the two completed cycles are aligned with one another, their basic shapes are very similar. This again means that it was possible to recognize in late 2001 that an end-cycle inflexion was occurring.

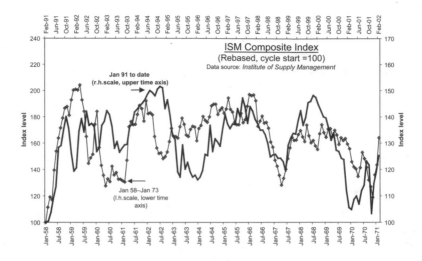

Figure 18.2 Juglar innovation cycles in the ISM index

Moreover, it was possible to do so despite the inherent difference in the time elapse between the two cycles in Figure 18.2. This is important. The original 1958–70 cycle lasted for 154 months but the 1991–2001 cycle took only 129 months. This was a difference of more than two years. In terms of history, such a difference is not unusual. However, it could have been a major problem for an analyst who was following fixed periodicities.

It was therefore possible to conclude in late 2001 that the US economy was transiting from a Juglar innovation cycle into a Juglar disruption cycle, with all the problems that such a transition would entail.

SENTIMENT IN THE JUGLAR CRISIS CYCLE

However, even crisis cycles necessarily start with a recovery of some sort. The Juglar disruption cycle that started in late 2001 was no different. However, the move from an innovation cycle into a crisis cycle involves a move from supply-led growth to demand-led growth. That is, capital investment subsides, although inventory investment recovers. So the analyst can always expect the initial upswing of any Juglar disruption cycle to be more quantitative than qualitative. This distinction is very important. It takes most people a very long time to recognize that things have actually changed and that the dynamism of the innovation cycle cannot immediately be resumed.

An analyst could then estimate the likely strength and duration of the post-2001 recovery by comparing it with the one that occurred after the 1970 low. The first thing to do, therefore, would be to extend the locus of the older cycle. The new cycle should continue to move in parallel with it. This is exactly what happened (see Figure 18.3).

COMPARISONS WITH PREVIOUS CYCLES

The next stage, quite obviously, would be to look at the whole crisis cycle, rather than just the first stage. Figure 18.4 shows the movement in the ISM index of producer expectations between October 2001 and October 2005 in the context of the same index between November 1970 and May 1980.

As already argued, the pattern of the 1970–80 Juglar disruption cycle in Figure 18.4 is archetypal. It shows the initial rally into a peak and then a long three-wave decline. Because of the danger of unexpected events, there is always the possibility of divergences from the norm, especially in the form of a shorter-than-expected cycle. Nevertheless, as of October 2002, an analyst could reasonably have concluded that the 2001–10 Juglar disruption cycle was evolving according to precedent. Furthermore, an analyst could also have

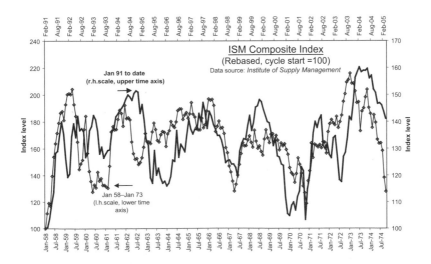

Figure 18.3 Extending into the next cycle

concluded that there was still some time left before the next serious
downleg would impact. In Figure 18.4, the real problems in the
1970–80 cycle started where shown, in early 1974.

In the event, although activity did indeed slow during 2005, it was
not a rerun of 1974 and, by October 2005, the ISM index had started to
recover. The important point, however, is that the pattern was exactly
as predicted. Just to confirm the importance of this pattern, we can
compare the 1970–80 fluctuations in the ISM index with another
period of serious dislocation. Figure 18.5 accordingly compares the
ISM index during the 1970–80 Juglar disruption cycle with movements in industrial production during the 1921–46 Berry crisis cycle.
The Juglar cycle peaked later in the context of the whole cycle than
did the Berry cycle, but the patterns were very similar.

It can clearly be seen that, despite their different time spans, the
serious problems that were specific to each cycle impacted at almost
exactly the same time location within the cycle. This is shown in Figure
18.5 by the dotted vertical line. Within the 1921–46 Berry cycle, the
equity crash happened in 1929; within the 1970–80 Juglar cycle, the
economic recession started in early 1974. Both periods of weakness
started to impact 33 per cent into the total time elapse of the cycle. This
calculation is, of course, made in retrospect. Nevertheless, it implies
that the cycle takes the shape that it does because the economy fails to
recover when it should do – namely, about one-third of the way into the
cycle. In other words, the low of the first sub-cycle fails to provide

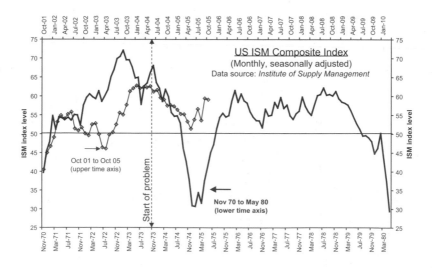

Figure 18.4 The Juglar disruption cycle

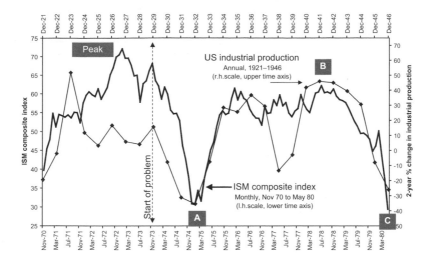

Figure 18.5 Juglar disruption cycle compared with Berry crisis cycle

support and the recovery that should initiate the second sub-cycle accordingly fails to materialize on time. This phenomenon is one of the characteristics of an energy gap. As at the end of 2005, such a gap had not impacted the US economy. It remains to be seen how closely the rest of the 2001–10(?) Juglar cycle will follow the pattern.

THE KITCHIN CYCLE

The idea that we can anticipate, and then track, a new cycle as it develops is exciting in itself. However, we can fine-tune the forecasting process by delving down into the shorter-term cycles. For example, in the context of a Juglar cycle, we can look at the 3.33-year Kitchin cycles that initiate it. This is particularly appropriate insofar as Kitchin cycles are primarily concerned with inventory adjustments. It is almost certainly the case that a Juglar cycle will end with a rundown in inventories and that the new one will therefore be triggered by a recovery in inventories. If the basic model is correct then the first Kitchin cycle in any Juglar cycle should consist of an archetypal three-up/three-down pattern.

Shown in Figure 18.6 is the profile of the ISM producer confidence index, measured in terms of three-month actual changes in that index, for the first 24 to 32 months of the Juglar cycles that began in 1970,

1980 and 1991. The oscillations in the momentum indices are marked 0–1–2–3–A–B–C. Hence the first sub-cycle covers 0–1–2, the second sub-cycle is 2–3–A and the third is A–B–C. It is quite clear that, although there is some divergence in the timing and extent of momentum in the third sub-cycle, the patterns accord to the basic model. If we now lay the Kitchin cycle that began in late 2001 on the matrix of previous cycles, we can see how closely it tracked them up to June 2004 (see Figure 18.7).

ESTIMATING THE TIMING OF TURNING POINTS

This process again suggests that we can use the timing of previous turning points to forecast future ones. This can be done using just one previous cycle, or it can be done using an average of previous cycles. Suppose that previous cycles mirrored the basic model, and registered important lows at 33 per cent and 67 per cent of their total time elapse, and registered important highs at 17 per cent, 50 per cent and 83 per cent of their total time elapse. It would be reasonable to expect that the current evolving cycle would also register the same pattern.

The unknown, however, is precisely how long the current cycle is actually going to take. It could be shorter or longer than the average, even though the turning points emerge in the 'correct' place. This

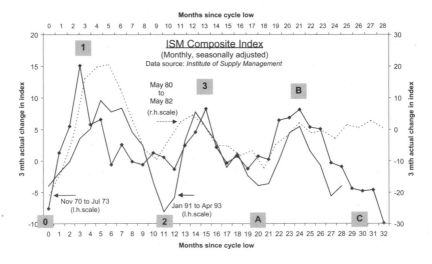

Figure 18.6 The Kitchin cycle

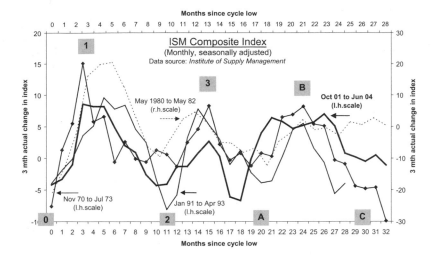

Figure 18.7 The Kitchin cycle

problem can be dealt with as soon as turning points have started to materialize. If we know that the first peak is going to occur 17 per cent into the cycle then, once we have an inflexion point that looks appropriate, we can start to calculate the eventual likely outcome. That is,

Possible cycle length = time from start of cycle to first peak / 0.17

For example, if we were tracking a Juglar cycle, we might expect the first high to arrive after about 20 months. Suppose that such a high then occurred after 22 months, the estimated cycle length would be 22 / 0.17 = 129.4 months. In other words, the estimated cycle length after the first peak would be 10.78 years.

From this, we could then start estimating the other intra-cycle turning points. We would expect the first important low to occur one-third of the way into the cycle. That is,

First low = estimated total length of cycle / 0.33

Hence, for a 10.78-year cycle, the first low would be calculated to occur after (10.78 / 0.33 =) 3.56 years, which is 42.7 months.

Then we could calculate the likely timing of the second high (ie, the mid-point) of the cycle. That is,

Second high = estimated cycle length / 0.50

So, for a 10.78-year cycle, the second high would be estimated to occur after (10.78 / 0.5 =) 5.39 years, which is 64.7 months.

CUMULATIVE ESTIMATION

We are thus starting to get quite a lot of information, just from one point of reference. Nevertheless, we know that, however close the actual outcome might be to the basic model, there are bound to be significant variations. The analysis, therefore, is cumulative – that is, it takes the variations into account as they occur. Hence, suppose that the first low of the Juglar cycle arrives on time (ie, after 3.56 years), but that the second high arrives, not after 5.39 years, but after 5.08 years (ie, 62 months). This would indicate that the cycle length might now be shorter than previously estimated. That is, since

Possible cycle length = time from start of cycle to second peak / 0.5

then calculating the cycle just from the second peak would indicate a length of (5.08 / 0.5 =) 10.16 years.

However, the implications of the first and second turning points still hold good, so the best solution is to average the calculations. Hence, the new central estimate for the total cycle length after three turning points becomes the average prediction from those three turning points. In our example, therefore, the new central prediction after two highs and an interim low is (10.78 + 10.78 + 10.16) / 3 = 10.57 years. This is, indeed, shorter than the first estimates. And we can now use the new estimated length to calculate future turning points.

It follows from this that the closer we get to the end of the cycle, the more definite we will be about the actual point at which it will end. Given that the psychological atmosphere at the last stage of any cycle is likely to be one of capitulation, such information may be absolutely priceless.

THE LEAD FROM FINANCIAL MARKETS TO THE ECONOMY

Importantly, the capitulation normally takes place in the equity market about four to six months before it occurs in manufacturers' stock levels. Hence, the closer that we get to the end of a large economic cycle, the more important it becomes to track the behaviour of the equity market as an item of information. If equities start to rally strongly, within six months of a projected low in output, then the chances are that the equity market is right. The very fact that equities might have broken loose from feedback with the economy is a valuable piece of information in its own right. The more important point, however, is that the rally will be confirming the imminence of a cyclical turn in output.

Table 18.1 Equity lead times over output

DJIA low (level)	US output low (level)	Equity lead (months)
Dec 57	Apr 58	4
Jun 70	Nov 70	5
Jul 82	Dec 82	5
Oct 90	Mar 91	6
Sep 01	Dec 01	3
	Average:	**4.6**

Shown in Table 18.1 is the relationship between a turn in the absolute level in the Dow and turning points in the level of production at the start of each of the major Juglar cycles since 1957. They confirm that the average equity lead time is about five months.

CONCLUSION

This chapter has demonstrated that, once cycles have been properly categorized, they can be used in a very powerful manner. Specifically, the pattern of pre-existing cycles can be used to track the pattern of a newly emerging one, and those patterns can be used to look into the future. The simplest method is to compare similar cycles to one another. Hence we can compare base, trend and terminal cycles with other base, trend and terminal cycles. However, we can also compare different cycles with one another. Hence we can compare a base cycle with a trend cycle or a terminal cycle. Or we can compare a Berry cycle with a Juglar cycle. Or we can even compare financial market cycles with output cycles. This can be particularly fruitful if a major economic low is expected. The point is that the basic model of economic and financial behaviour that was revealed in Chapter 16 is universal: it applies to all group behaviour, at all levels of the hierarchy.

NOTE

1.   The 1980–91 cycle made a new low in 1982. This might have created some uncertainty about the correct date for the end of the previous crisis cycle. In fact, the validity of the relationship shown in Figure 18.1 can be confirmed by using the index of producer sentiment, calculated by the Institute of Supply Management. This index did not make a new low in 1982.

19

Finding cycles: a case study

INTRODUCTION

There is, of course, no point in attempting to use cycles, if you can't find them in the first place. In fact, finding them is something of an art. Sometimes they leap off the chart at you. At other times, however, they remain tantalizingly elusive. It is like looking at a distant ship through a powerful telescope: if the focus is too close, you see only the sea; if the focus is too distant, you see only the sky. You need the correct focus to give you the desired result. With cycles, the lens is focused by adjusting the speed of the momentum indicator.

GUIDELINES

There are no hard-and-fast rules for finding cycles. Nevertheless, there are certain initial guidelines that can be used. The first point to remember is that it is the *pattern* that defines the cycle, not the precision of the periodicity (although the periodicity is relevant). So the starting point is to look for a recognizable three-up/three-down pattern. The second point to remember is that cycles operate in triads. So, if there is one easily recognizable pattern, there ought to be two others associated with it. The third point to remember is that very sharp drops could be energy gaps, which define a peak rather than a trough (see Chapter 14). So, unusual lows may not actually mark the end of a cycle.

In addition, there is a broader point. This is that the cycles are nested in hierarchical layers. Consequently, and providing the data set being analysed is sufficiently detailed, it is very helpful to look for *three* layers of cycles – namely, the immediate level, the one above it and the one below it.

PRACTICAL PROCESS

The practical process then starts by calculating a long-term picture of a market or economic indicator by using a long-term momentum indicator. One very useful indicator is a two-year percentage rate of change. This has the dual advantage of smoothing out some of the volatility in a series and providing a close estimate of the timing of most of the peaks and troughs. Sometimes, this will be sufficient, particularly with very slow-moving processes like the economy itself. Often, however, it will only provide a broad indication of where the major turning points are, and a further refocusing has to be done.

UK GILTS

Shown in Figure 19.1 is a two-year percentage rate of change of the UK government bond market ('gilts'), represented by the Treasury 2½ per cent bond, redeemable on or after 1 April 1975. As already mentioned, this bond is usually called an 'irredeemable' because it is unlikely to be redeemed until redemption yields fall below 2½ per cent. It has the big advantage for analysis of not being influenced by the so-called 'pull to redemption', whereby the price of a bond tends to be drawn towards its redemption price (usually 100) as its maturity shortens.

Shown on the same chart is the actual price performance of the bond between 1971 and late 2002. It therefore covers the tail end of the inflationary bear market of the 1970s, and the great disinflationary bull market of the 1980s and 1990s.

The first thing to notice in the chart is that, between October 1974 and January 1996, there was a huge three-up/three-down momentum pattern, marked 1–2–3/A–B–C. This was reflected in a similarly profiled price oscillation, with a slight upward bias, which started in December 1974 and ended in April 1996. This, in effect, was the

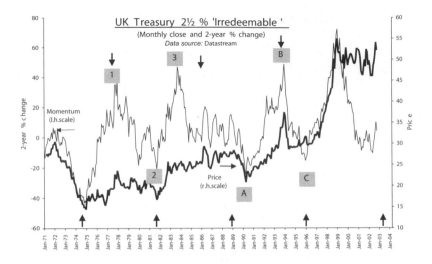

Figure 19.1 The UK gilt market, 1971 to 2002

massive pattern that formed the base for the subsequent impulse wave that occurred between April 1996 and January 1999. The base pattern has the requisite archetypal formation and took 19.26 years. So it is a good starting point.

The earlier analysis of triads in Chapter 17 suggests that the 19.26-year cycle ought to sub-divide into three approximately equal cycle beats of (19.26/3 =) 7.09 years. When this calculation is applied to the *actual* lows in bond prices, starting at December 1974, it does seem to pick out important turning points. The theoretical lows of a potential 7.09-year cycle are shown by the upward-pointing arrows in Figure 19.1. Obviously the start and end dates coincide with the arrows. However, the end dates of the sub-cycles do not. The first sub-cycle should have ended in January 1982 but it ended in September 1981. The second sub-cycle should have ended in February 1989 but it ended in April 1990. The first discrepancy is not necessarily significant in the context of a 7.09-year cycle; however, the second discrepancy is significant and will need an explanation. In the meantime, if we project this periodicity forward, out of the base pattern, the estimated date of the next low would be April 2003.

CALCULATING PEAKS

The next step is to analyse the peaks. One point to remember is that momentum peaks are often biased in relation both to the centre point of a cycle and in relation to the actual price peak. Momentum will often accelerate coming out of a cycle low and will often be decelerating at a cycle high. This helps to validate the cycle (see Chapter 13) but it is also a reminder that we might be looking for 'non-confirmed' price highs at around the middle of the cycle.

The obvious price peaks are as shown by the downward-pointing arrows in Figure 19.1. They occurred in December 1977, April 1986 and December 1993. Importantly, the second of these peaks is 'non-confirmed' by the two-year momentum, which indicates its importance. The average period is – quite clearly – eight years. Further, projecting forward gives a potential peak in January 2001. There was, indeed, a peak at that time. However, there was an even more important one in January 1999, which was two years earlier. So, there is only a loose match between the periodicities of the highs and lows.

REFOCUSING MOMENTUM

The next step, therefore, is to recalibrate the momentum indicator over shorter time periods. The most obvious one to use is a one-year percentage rate of change. This is shown in Figure 19.2, together with the actual level of prices.

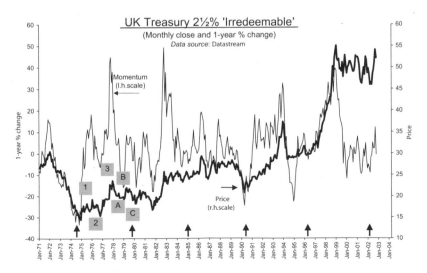

Figure 19.2 The UK gilt market, 1971 to 2002

Now, a slightly different picture starts to emerge. First, if we look for the three-up/three-down pattern, the first cycle in the sequence may have ended in February 1980 rather than May 1981. This is shown by the 1–2–3–A–B–C pattern on the chart. Second, the December 1993 to June 1994 fall in prices (the bond 'crash') looks very much like an energy gap. In this case, the momentum low that was registered in December 1994 was not a cycle low, but the low in April 1996 probably was. This latter coincides with the conclusion from the two-year momentum index. Moreover, we now also have a clearer view of the importance of the peak in late 1993.

If we now assume that February 1980 and April 1996 are valid cycle lows, then they can only be matched if the cycle periodicity is 5.34 years. This is shown by the upward-pointing arrows in Figure 19.2. The low in April 1990 now comes much closer to being properly included in the cycle, even though the theoretical timing for it was December 1990.

At this stage of the analysis, therefore, we have the possibility of the presence of either a 7.09- to 8-year cycle or a 5.34-year cycle. Interestingly, the 5.34-year cycle is just over 75 per cent of the 7.09-year cycle, which means that there is some form of harmonic relationship working. If the two cycles were separate, four 5.34-year cycles would coincide with three 7.09-year cycles. That is, they would approximately coincide every 19.25 years or so.

THE IMPORTANCE OF THREE

There are two potential solutions here. The first is to assume that the two cycles are independent of one another. The second is to look for reasons why one of the two cycles might be false. One of the clues comes from the fact that three longer cycles equal four shorter cycles. Specifically, what might be happening is that shocks and energy gaps in a genuine 5.34-year cycle may have created conditions that could be misread as lows of a false 7.09-year cycle. Figure 19.3 shows how this might occur. The upward-pointing arrows show the 5.34-year cycle lows. The downward-pointing arrows show the 7.09-year cycle lows. One of the issues is whether the low of April 1990 belongs to a 5.34-year cycle or a 7.09-year cycle. A 5.34-year cycle would divide into three sub-cycles of about 1.78 years (ie, just over 21 months); and 5.34 + 1.78 = 7.12. In other words, the 7.09-year cycle could be the shorter 5.34-year cycle with an extra 1.78-year cycle added on. In this case, unexpectedly deep lows in the 5.34-year cycle could be misread

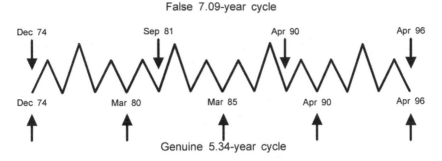

Figure 19.3 Confusion between cycles

as lows in a 7.09-year cycle. Conversely, weak lows in the 5.34-year cycle might be ignored altogether.

This may be exactly what has happened. It remains true that the price low in September 1981 was deeper, and that the low in March 1985 was weaker, than might have been expected for a 5.34-year cycle. However, the April 1990 low can be seen as the early end of the 5.34-year cycle rather than the very late end of a 7.09-year cycle.

SCANNING FOR TRIADS

The secret, obviously, is to look for triads, rather than just for periodic rhythms. So we can now take this a step further. We have already identified the 5.34-year cycle that started in December 1974 as being an archetypal three-up/three-down cycle. See Figure 19.2 again. Further, it 'looks' centred. This means that it could be a base cycle within the context of a batch of three. This makes sense inasmuch as it emerged after the traumatic bear market of 1973/74. According to the schematic model outlined in Chapter 17, the next cycle is likely to be a trend cycle, which would have a rightward bias. A glance at Figure 19.2 shows that the cycle from February 1980 to March 1985 does indeed have an upward bias, such that the March 1985 low hardly registers. What is also clear, however, is that the first 1.78-year sub-cycle creates a very deep low before the trend starts. Let us, therefore, tighten the focus a little further by looking at six-month percentage rates of change (see Figure 19.4).

This chart takes the same form as its predecessors. Now, however, we can start being clearer about the influence of the cycle groupings. The first beat of the proposed 5.34-year cycle (November 1974 to

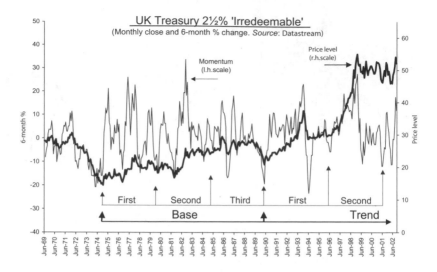

Figure 19.4 Using six-month rates of change

March 1980) is marked on the chart as 'First'. The second beat (March 1980 to June 1985) is marked 'Second'. Then there is a third beat of the cycle (June 1985 to April 1990), marked 'Third'. These three beats of the 5.34-year cycle, which in total take 15 to 16 years to evolve, form the big base pattern to which we have already referred. This is marked 'Base'. It is actually the cycle that ushered in the removal of inflationary psychology, so it is also a 'detachment' cycle.

In the triadic model, this base pattern should lead into a big trend cycle, also lasting 15 to 16 years. This latter is not scheduled to end until late 2006/early 2007. However, it can be seen from the chart that it is undoubtedly a trend cycle. This cycle is marked 'Trend' in Figure 19.4 and it is the cycle that is involved with the move to genuinely lower inflationary expectations. So it is a 'transition' cycle.

The final 15- to 16-year cycle still lies well ahead. It should start in late 2006/early 2007 and end in 2022/2023. It will be the cycle that fully embeds disinflation in the economy. Unfortunately, it is likely to have to do so in the context of falling bond prices.

THE FIRST CYCLE WITHIN THE BASE CYCLE

The first 5.34-year cycle within the base cycle (which, for simplicity, we will assume has a periodicity of 16 years) has a very clear archetypal three-up/three-down pattern in both price and momentum (see Figure 19.5). The theoretical sub-cycle lows, calculated as one-third and two-thirds respectively of the final cycle length, are indicated by the upward-pointing arrows. The first sub-cycle ends more or less on time. The second sub-cycle ends somewhat late but nevertheless allows a rally prior to the final fall.

THE SECOND CYCLE

The second beat of the 5.34-year cycle has a clear three-up/three-down pattern in momentum terms but not in price terms (see Figure 19.6). Prices basically trend upwards over the period, which confirms that the second cycle is a trend cycle within the overarching base cycle. The theoretical sub-cycle lows, calculated as one-third and two-thirds of the actual cycle, are shown as upward-pointing arrows. As already mentioned, the first such sub-cycle of this second 5.34-year cycle makes a new low in both price and momentum terms. This is not unusual. The point is that a trend cannot fully develop until the market, or economic index, has properly bottomed. This is particularly true of 'nested' base cycles – that is, lower-level base cycles within higher-level base cycles. The 1.78-year cycle was a base cycle within the 5.34-year trend cycle but was obviously still subject to the pull of the 5.34-year base cycle from which it was born.

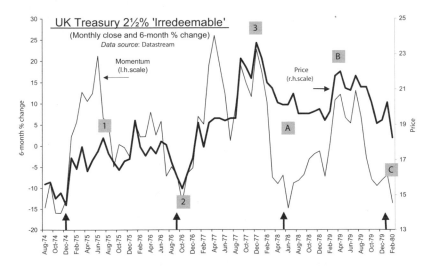

Figure 19.5 The first 5.34-year cycle

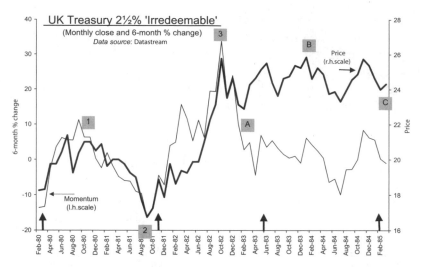

Figure 19.6 The second 5.34-year cycle

THE THIRD CYCLE

The third beat of the proposed 5.34-year cycle has a much more volatile look than either of its predecessors (see Figure 19.7). This is because it is a terminal cycle in its own right. It is therefore subject to an air of crisis and a vulnerability to shocks. The theoretical lows of the sub-cycles are indicated by upward-pointing arrows. They actually coincide with near-term lows. However, the overarching profile is an early peak (in April 1986) followed by a slow three-wave (A–B–C) fall into a relatively deep low. The peak occurs, as is usual, in the first sub-cycle. The A-wave fall is an energy gap, and is therefore quite sharp. The B-wave is a long rally, on progressively weaker momentum. The C-wave is a deep fall into the final low. It is a classic pattern.

THE 16-YEAR TREND CYCLE

After the completion of the third (terminal) 5.34-year cycle in the 16-year base cycle, a new 16-year cycle starts. This is a trend cycle and, as such, should be characterized by a strong uptrend for part of its pattern. As has already been pointed out, this is exactly what happened (see Figure 19.4 again). The period April 1990 to late 2002

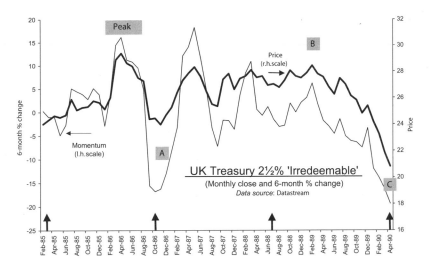

Figure 19.7 The third 5.34-year cycle

was dominated by a strong uptrend in bond prices. In principle, the trend cycle should consist of three 5.34-year cycles. Two of these appear to have completed. The first, which lasted from April 1990 to April 1996, had something of an upward bias but was in essence still the base cycle within the higher-order trend cycle. The second cycle, which lasted from April 1996 until (probably) June 2001, was the trend cycle proper. Prices moved sharply higher during this cycle. The third cycle (the terminal cycle) is scheduled to finish between April 2006 (which is 16.02 years – ie, 3 × 5.34 years – after April 1990) and October 2006 (which is 5.34 years after June 2001).

THE FIRST CYCLE WITHIN THE TREND CYCLE

The first (base) cycle within the 16-year trend cycle actually lasted six years, from April 1990 to April 1996. It was therefore longer than the average (see Figure 19.8). The theoretical timings of the sub-cycle lows, based on the completion of the whole base cycle, is shown by the upward-pointing arrows. The pattern of the first sub-cycle (which lasted about two years) is not clear from the behaviour of prices themselves. The pattern does, however, reveal itself in the associated six-month rate of change.

The pattern of the second sub-cycle was dominated by an acceleration of prices into a peak in December 1993. The peak was relatively

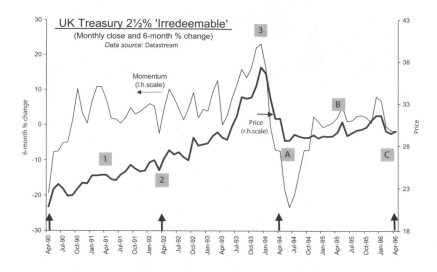

Figure 19.8 The first 5.34-year cycle within the trend cycle

late, which gave the cycle a rightward bias. This, of course, is typical of the second cycle in any triad. Moreover, the subsequent fall was a surprise – so much so, in fact, that it became known as the 'bond crash of 1994'. The crash was an energy gap.

The pattern of the third sub-cycle was very much a response to the depth of the energy gap 'crash'. It was very muted, but it helped to fulfil the archetypal pattern, by incorporating a rally and then a decline into the April 1996 low. Importantly, the market could not sustain a proper rally out of an oversold condition until the cycle was complete.

THE SECOND CYCLE

The second cycle within the 16-year trend cycle lasted just over five years, from April 1996 to June 2001. Being the middle cycle of a trend cycle, it was particularly dynamic (see Figure 19.9). In fact, the move was so strong that the underlying cycles were suppressed. The theoretical timings of the sub-cycle lows, based on the completion of the whole cycle, are indicated by the upward-pointing arrows. Quite obviously, the low of wave 2 is difficult to pinpoint.

Again, however, being itself a second cycle within a triad that is scheduled to last for 16 or so years, it peaked late and unexpectedly. The subsequent fall took the market down into a 1.78-year sub-cycle low, from where it completed the last phase of the 5.34-year cycle.

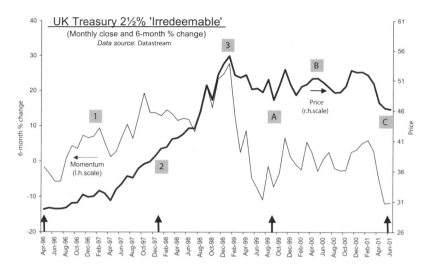

Figure 19.9 The second 5.34-year cycle within the trend cycle

CYCLE PEAKS

This simple exercise quite clearly points to the operation of a cycle that has an average beat of 5.34 years. Not only does each beat of the cycle fit reasonably closely to the calculated rhythm but – and, in a sense, more importantly – the differing patterns for each beat of the cycle adhere very closely to those predicted by the theoretical triadic model. The next question is, how do the peaks fit against this conclusion?

Figure 19.10 is the same chart as that in Figure 19.4, adjusted to show the important cycle peaks since January 1972. What is apparent is that significant peaks occur every 5.40 years. Five of the six peaks occur at the end of sharp rallies; one cycle, however, does not. This is the apparent peak in the middle of the March 1985 to April 1990 cycle, which occurred in March 1988. The important point, however, is that the actual price peak should have occurred earlier than the March 1988 date because the whole cycle was the third (terminal or detachment) cycle within the base cycle. Such cycles are usually 'left-translated'. Nevertheless, March 1988 was the centre of the counter-trend rally that resolved into the 1989–90 bear phase.

The incidence of peaks that are 5.40 years apart obviously accords well with troughs that are 5.34 years apart. So we can be reasonably sure that a cycle of five to five and a half years operates in the UK gilt market.

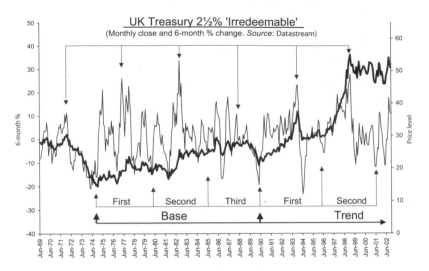

Figure 19.10 Cycle peaks, January 1972 to January 1999

FORECASTING

This gives us a starting point for forecasting future peaks and troughs. Such forecasts are dynamic (because they will be adjusted through time); nevertheless we can calculate initial estimates for future turning points. According to our model, the final peak of the disinflationary trend cycle is likely to occur before the mid-point of its terminal cycle. That is, the third cycle within the overall disinflationary trend cycle is likely to be 'left-translated'. We know that this high will be the fifth one along from the 1977 peak. Using the measured periodicity of the peaks, we can therefore estimate that the mid-point of the third cycle is likely to occur 5 × 5.40 years (or 27 years) from December 1977. This is December 2004. So the price high of the last cycle in the disinflationary trend cycle should impact before December 2004.

We can, however, be a little bit more precise. It is normal for the peak to occur in the first one-third of this last cycle (see Chapters 15 and 18). Since we are looking at a cycle that probably started in June 2001 and that will likely end by October 2006, the time period for the peak is sometime between June 2001 and March 2003.

If this last peak bears the same relationship to the whole cycle as did its April 1986 counterpart, then it is likely to impact 3 × 5.40 years (or 16.2 years) from April 1986. This is June 2002. There was an important high in September 2002.

Of course, we cannot know for certain that a particular price high is *the* high of the move. So we need to be quite clear about what may happen next. In particular, we need to know the critical level beyond which we can assume that the trend of the market has reversed. This is the subject of the next chapter.

CONCLUSION

This chapter has provided a brief case study of cyclical behaviour in a well-known financial market. The purpose was to explain how a search for cycles can be conducted, rather than to present a forecast for the future as such. Nevertheless, the case study showed that, first, price patterns in the gilt market follow the pattern predicted by the triadic cycle model of financial market behaviour; and, second, the gilt market oscillates to the rhythm of a cycle that has a central periodicity of 5.34 to 5.40 years. The periodicity can expand and contract through time – and obviously does so. However, the final arbiter of the important highs and lows is the pattern itself. The cycle is defined by its intrinsic pattern, not the precision of the periodicity.

20

Price patterns in financial markets

INTRODUCTION

Despite the potential accuracy of cycle analysis, it is impossible to be absolutely sure that a turning point is occurring, even when it is actually happening. There are a number of complementary tools that can be used to help reduce uncertainty, and we shall look at some of them in more detail in Chapter 23. However, the main task is not so much to pick the absolute high or low, but to recognize when a reversal is shifting from being a correction that needs little or no response into being a trend that requires a change in investment positions. To some extent, the difference is subjective: the boundary between a correction and a trend is different for a short-term trader from what it is for a long-term investor. For the market, however, the boundary is much more objective. The market itself 'knows' the price–time frame for which it is correcting and it 'knows' the point when it moves from one price–time frame to another (higher) price–time frame. We shall now look at this issue in more detail.

HIERARCHICAL TRENDS

As pointed out in Chapter 5, markets do not operate independently of 'fundamentals'; they operate in a limit cycle relationship with those fundamentals. Furthermore, such fundamentals are hierarchical in nature. In Chapter 15, we briefly surveyed some of the time frames used in economics. But the scope is much broader than just economics: the longer the time frames that are being analysed, the more influential are factors such as socio-political trends and the climate. Hence, we can visualize a spectrum of influences whose vibrations are very fast over short time frames and very slow over longer ones. For example, the author and exponent of 'the long view' Stewart Brand uses six layers of analysis, with each layer corresponding to a different time frame. The layers are: fashion/art; business/commerce; intellectual and physical infrastructure; governance; culture; and climate.[1] Undoubtedly, we could use others. However, we could say that the fashion cycle lasts about a year, the business cycle lasts about three years, the infrastructure cycle takes 10 years, the governance cycle may shift in rhythms of 30–50 years, culture evolves in cycles of 90–150 years, and climate oscillates in patterns that may take 500 years and more. The parallel with some of the economic cycles tabulated in Chapter 15 should be obvious.

MARKETS AND FUNDAMENTAL TRENDS

For any given hierarchical level, information from a higher level is likely to impact as a shock; and the lower-level system will have to adjust to that shock. Hence, climate changes in the form of prolonged drought or heavy rainfall can have dramatic effects on (say) a three-year business cycle. However, the emergence of a shock at the lower level does not mean that the process is random. From the perspective of the hierarchical level from which it emerges, it is part of the process. It is just that, from the perspective of the lower level with limited time horizons, the information was unexpected.

This raises some important questions about the inter-relationship between market movements and changes in fundamentals. How do we know, for example, if the market is responding to long-term deep-structure tides or to short-term surface-structure ripples? Alternatively, why should a correction that might be considered 'normal' in the context of fundamentals suddenly turn into a blood-curdling bear that can be viewed as being 'abnormal' even after the event?

ECONOMIC CYCLES, PRICE PATTERNS AND PRICE TRENDS

One important part of the answer to these questions relates to economic and social cycles themselves. If we know where we are in the bigger socio-economic cycles, then we have an idea about what to expect from them. This is why it is so important to include an analysis of economic oscillations (at least along the lines outlined in this book) in an investment decision-making process. Another important part of the answer is that markets try to anticipate turning points in fundamentals through the agency of patterned price movements. These patterns are hierarchical in nature and can to some degree be interpreted for clues about future fundamentals. The final part of the answer is that the markets will signal when they are locking into feedback with a higher level of fundamentals by penetrating certain *boundaries*.

We have already dealt with economic cycles at some length. The next two chapters will cover the implications of price patterns. Chapter 22 will cover the question of boundaries.

THE PATTERN OF A TREND

In Chapter 16 we concluded that there were always likely to be biases in the three-by-three pattern of a cycle, which reflected that cycle's position in relation to its higher-level counterpart. One way of looking at the consequences of these biases is to take the basic patterns and run a trend through them.

Figure 20.1 shows what happens if a rising trend is applied to a base cycle pattern. Quite clearly, wave B of the cycle can be sufficiently distorted upwards to make a new high. As a result the cycle appears to evolve in a five-wave format: there is a base pattern, a long, rising, impulse wave, a temporary correction, and a final high. A corollary to this is that a five-wave profile indicates that the trend is upwards. Consequently, the emergence of five waves in a base cycle can be used to confirm that the trend has changed. The signal would be given when the new high occurs within wave B. Following such a signal, the inference is that setbacks are buying opportunities.

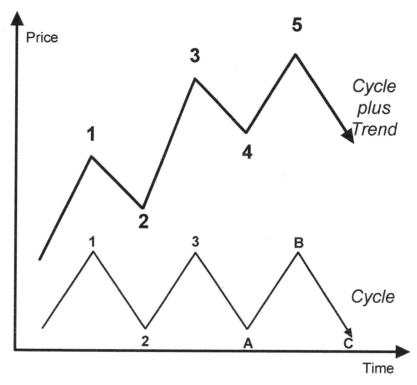

Figure 20.1 Base cycle plus trend

THE FIVE–THREE WAVE PATTERN IN COMPLEX STRUCTURES

Very importantly, however, the five-wave profile is not just confined to base cycles. It also emerges in the context of more complex structures. Figure 20.2 shows what happens if a rising trend is applied to the more complex cycle pattern that incorporates sub-cycle biases. Ignoring the very low-level fluctuations, a very important pattern emerges. First, the base cycle develops five waves (i–ii–iii–iv–v) and a short correction (from 1 to 2). Second the long, impulsive trend cycle embodies five waves (i–ii–iii–iv–v) and a limited correction (from 3 to 4). Third, the terminal cycle evolves as a sharp rally to a new high (at 5) followed by a three-wave correction (A–B–C). The whole pattern therefore seems to contain three rising impulse waves (1, 3 and 5, of which 3 is the longest), two corrections (2 and 4) and a three-wave fall (A–B–C). In other words, a bull market plus a natural correction presents itself as a five–three pattern.

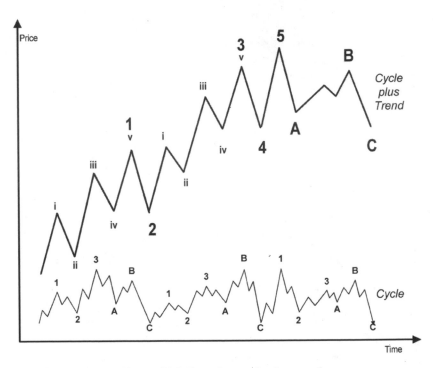

Figure 20.2 Complex cycle plus trend

THE ELLIOTT WAVE PRINCIPLE

The idea that markets move in a five–three pattern was the perceptive insight of the great stock market theorist Ralph Nelson Elliott.[2] Writing in the 1930s, Elliott concluded that the five–three profile was essentially a law of nature. He deduced that the associated patterns obeyed certain clearly defined rules that could be used in trading. He observed, however, that not all patterns actually matched the basic five–three profile, and he accordingly went to great lengths to show that any aberrations were caused by distortions to the underlying five–three pattern. In particular, he argued that the fifth wave of an impulse movement could 'fail', so that the whole movement essentially looked like a three-wave movement; and he argued that an apparent fifth wave that consisted only of three sub-waves was part of a correction.

Elliott's 'wave principle' provides a wonderfully thorough coverage of price patterns in financial markets. Indeed, there is no known pattern that falls outside of his framework. The truth, however, is that the five–three pattern is not a fundamental law of nature. It is a derivative of a much more fundamental three–three cycle pattern, which *is* a law of nature.

Nevertheless, Elliott's findings are a valid and practical philosophical approach to markets, and his 'wave principle' invokes rules that are valid interpretations of the implications of the three–three price pulse. Traders who use the Elliott wave principle will generally obtain exceptionally good results. For that reason, we shall analyse Elliott's conclusions in a little more detail in the next chapter. In the meantime, however, we need to assess the implications of the three–three price pulse in a little more detail.

INVESTMENT GUIDELINES

It should be apparent from Figure 20.2 that there are 18 waves in a complete move – namely six waves within three sub-cycles. However, distortions to the natural cycle allow variations both in the pattern of a rally and in the pattern of a fall. A rally can consist either of three waves (when the cycle doesn't have an uptrend) or of five waves (when it does). Meanwhile, a correction can consist either of one wave (if the cycle has an uptrend) or of three waves (if it doesn't). This knowledge implies four very important guidelines that can be used for investment and trading. The first is the buy signal after a low. The second is the warning that a bear phase has started. The third relates to when a correction can be expected. And the fourth involves the message that can be derived from the strength of contra-trend rallies within corrections.

THE BUY SIGNAL AFTER A LOW

We have already mentioned the importance of a five-wave rally after a low. This would be an indication that the trend has turned upwards. If this is true, then the correction immediately following the five waves, which completes the first (base or detachment) cycle, is going to be very limited. Consequently, the next new high is going to provide a clear buy signal because the implication is that the market has moved into its second (trend or transition) cycle. This latter has the potential to be the most dynamic (see Figure 20.3).

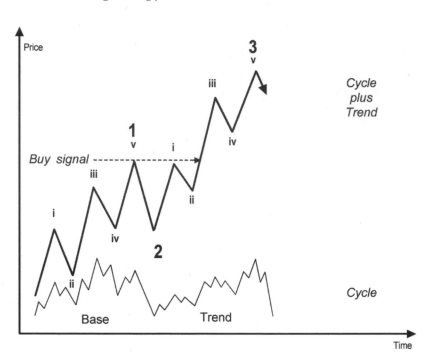

Figure 20.3 The buy signal

WARNING OF A BEAR PHASE

Because the basic pattern of the price pulse is three-up/three-down, it follows that patterns that emerge in rising markets are also likely to materialize – although in reverse – in falling markets. Hence, if the presence of five waves in an upward direction signals the possibility of a bull trend, the emergence of five waves in a downward direction will signal the possibility of a bearish one. This is demonstrated in Figure 20.4. Here, a downtrend is applied to the basic triad of cycles, starting from the peak of the first cycle in the triad. In other words, it is assumed that the market comes to a natural cyclical peak and then starts correcting downwards, but that the correction is actually for a higher-level cycle. The result is that what should have been the base phase in the second cycle is so biased downwards that it makes a new low.

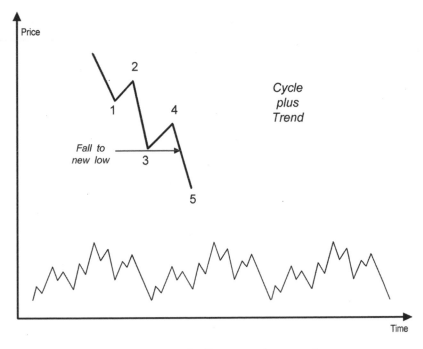

Figure 20.4 The five-wave downtrend

THE TERMINAL CYCLE

This is basically what is likely to happen in a terminal cycle. The market (or economy) peaks during the first cycle in a triad and then makes a low in the early part of the second cycle. In other words, the natural cycle low at the end of the first cycle provides support but not a final turning point. We provided evidence of this phenomenon in Chapter 18. The difficulty, however, is that the five-wave pattern may not necessarily impact quickly enough to provide a strategic sell signal. Obviously, a trading signal is given as wave 5 makes a new low; but it stands to be quickly reversed as wave 3 of the second cycle snaps in. The evidence is that there is then normally a long three-wave rally prior to a final – and often very difficult – down-wave right at the end of the third cycle (see Figure 20.5). Good examples of this phenomenon were shown in Figure 18.5 in Chapter 18.

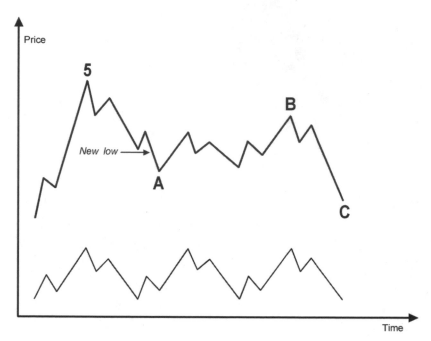

Figure 20.5 The pattern of the terminal cycle

THE LOCATION OF CORRECTIONS

The second important guideline is that a contra-trend correction will occur after a five-wave rally. In the simplest case, the correction will just consist of a simple down-wave. In the more complex case, the correction will consist of three clear waves – ie, two falling waves, interspersed with a rising wave.

The simple down-waves are likely to occur when a market is trending strongly. Moreover, because it derives from wave C of the cycle, it is likely to be larger in price terms than either of the two preceding corrections (which would have been wave 2 and wave A). It is relevant, however, that it will probably encapsulate three lower-order waves (see Figure 20.6). It will therefore take on a three-wave 'look' (ie, a–b–c).

The more complex down-waves are likely to occur within the context of big, longer-term cycles that are losing their impetus (see Figure 20.7). Since it consists of three distinct waves (A–B–C), such a correction is likely to be greater in both price and time than either of its two predecessors. Further, once account is taken of the unfolding of lower-order waves, it is easy to see that each wave within the correction will itself consist of three waves.

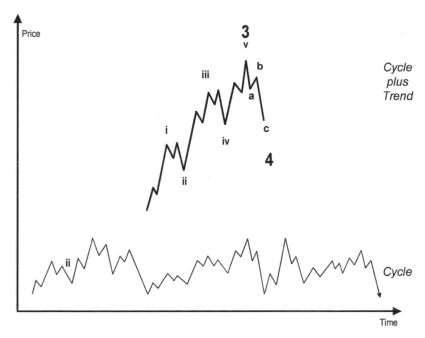

Figure 20.6 Simple corrections

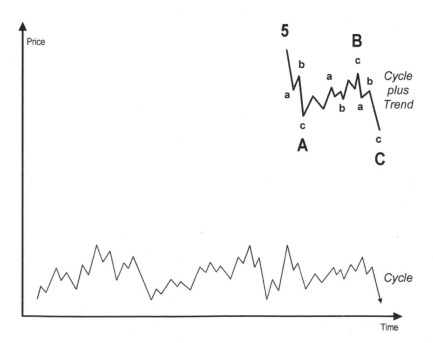

Figure 20.7 Complex corrections

THE STRENGTH OF CONTRA-TREND RALLIES

As presented in Figures 20.2 and 20.7, the final three-wave correction (A–B–C) is assumed to take on a 'zigzag' appearance. This will allow quite a deep correction. Sometimes, however, the contra-trend rally is quite strong, taking it up very close to the wave 5 high, so that it has a 'flat' appearance (see Figure 20.8). Strong contra-trend waves are prima-facie evidence that the higher-order uptrend is still intact. For example, it may be part of a higher-order base (or detachment) cycle. Hence 'double tops' are likely to be penetrated.

NON-CONFIRMATION REVISITED

It is worth at this point commenting again on the 'non-confirmation' of new highs or new lows. We referred to this concept in Chapter 13. Basically, non-confirmation means that a new price high or a new price low is not fully reflected in one or more of the auxiliary indices that measure the energy of a trend.

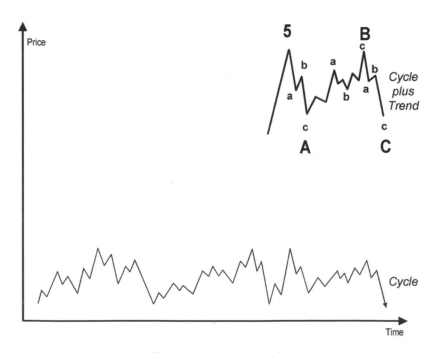

Figure 20.8 Flat correction

The foregoing analysis indicates that wave B in a rising market, and wave 2 in a falling market, may be forced into new territory for the trend. In principle, however, both are contra-trend waves and are not intrinsically energetic. Hence, a properly defined energy indicator should pick up on this flagging energy. One of the most relevant, and easiest to use, is a simple momentum indicator. Shown in Figure 20.9 is the weekly close of the US dollar in terms of Japanese yen for the period September 1999 to November 2002. It reveals a five-wave rally since the November 1999 low. Also shown on the chart is the 52-week percentage change in the weekly closes. For most of the rally, the momentum indicator moves to a peak of 3 to 4 per cent and then turns down as a contra-trend correction develops. By the time the dollar reached the final high in the five-wave move, however, the momentum indicator was dropping sharply. This was a genuine non-confirmation.

Of course, a non-confirmation using a simple rate of change indicator needs to be backed up by other tools. We shall have a very brief look at some of these extra tools in Chapter 23.

In the meantime, however, there is obviously an important inference that we can draw from this analysis. This is that a genuine non-confirmation – that will be associated with a significant correction – will only arise in a 'fifth wave'.

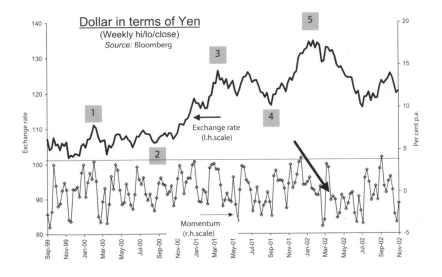

Figure 20.9 Non-confirmation in a fifth wave

ANTICIPATING TURNING POINTS

There is one further piece that needs to be added to the jigsaw puzzle. In Chapter 11, it was argued that turning points could be anticipated with the help of the golden ratio. Specifically, it was shown that impulsive movements could be related to the correction that preceded them by the ratio 2.618:1, which is a derivative of the golden ratio.

The ratio 2.618:1 is undoubtedly the most important ratio in calculating price objectives. In particular, it tends to apply to wave 3, which is often the longest wave, of a five-wave movement. However, it is not the only relevant ratio. The main point is that waves of any degree tend to be extended or damped by the influence of higher-order trends. However, even here, it seems to be a feature of nature that golden ratio influences still operate because price movements remain mathematically related to one another. One of two things may happen. First, a higher-order trend may counteract the impulse wave, so that the appropriate ratio for calculating the subsequent objective is 1.618:1. This often happens either in the last wave of a five-wave impulse movement or in the last wave of a three-wave counter-trend move. Second, a higher-level trend may complement the impulse wave, so that the appropriate ratio is 4.236:1. This latter may be found in particularly dynamic impulse waves.

These ratios are all related to each other by the golden ratio. They come from the (infinite) number series

$$... 0.236, 0.382, 0.618, 1, 1.618, 2.618, 4.236...$$

where each number in the series is 161.8 per cent higher than the number that precedes it.

THE GOLDEN RATIO FORMULAE

We have already dealt with the 2.618 formula in some detail in Chapter 11. We can now place it in a more general context. Figure 20.10 shows a schematic diagram for a bull move, whereby the depth of a correction is multiplied by 1.618, 2.618 and 4.236 and the resulting outcomes are added to the level at which the correction ended. Reversals can then be expected after a wave has travelled 161.8 per cent, 261.8 per cent or 423.6 per cent of the depth of the correction. Corresponding calculations can also be made for a falling market. Here, the extent of a contra-trend rally is multiplied by each of

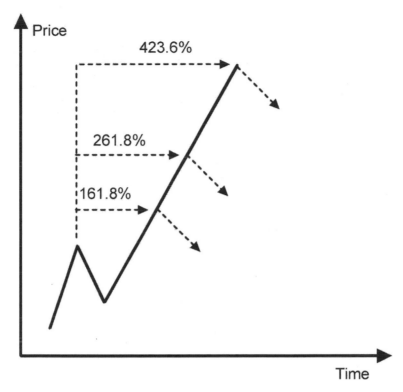

Figure 20.10 Golden ratio calculations

the numbers 1.618, 2.618 and 4.236. The resulting figures are deducted from the level that marks the top of the counter-trend rally.

SOME EXAMPLES

Shown in Figure 20.11 is the behaviour of the US dollar in terms of the Japanese yen between June 1998 and June 2002. We shall just pick out some of the main movements. Hence, the last up-wave of the top pattern between June and August 1998 was ¥13.97. Multiplying this by 2.618 and deducting the result from the high of ¥147.66 generated a target of ¥111.08. The actual temporary low in October 1998 was ¥111.58.

Between early June and early July 1999, the market traced out a mini top pattern by retracing part of the initial fall from the mid-May 1999 high. The rally was only ¥5.00. However, multiplying that by 4.236, and then deducting that from the top of the re-test at ¥120.90, produced a downside target of ¥101.75. The market reached a final low at ¥101.25.

The US dollar then formed a base between late November 1999 and late March 2000. The re-test of the low, in March, was ¥9.66. Multiplying this by 2.618 and adding the result to the re-test low of ¥102.07 produced an objective of ¥127.35. The market rallied to ¥126.85 in March 2001.

Between March and September 2001, the dollar fell by ¥11.01. Multiplying this by 1.618 and adding the result to the end of the correction produced a target of ¥133.64. The market reached ¥135.14 in late January 2002.

These examples are taken from just one market over a relatively limited period of time. It was easy to find that each of the main impulse movements bore a golden ratio relationship to the contra-trend move from which it emerged. It was not necessarily possible prior to the event to know which multiple would be applicable to the move, and there is quite obviously always some room for manoeuvre in the precision of the calculations.

Nevertheless, it would be possible to produce literally thousands of other examples of this extraordinary inter-relationship between patterns and ratios. The strong evidence is that the underlying processes in financial markets are not random.

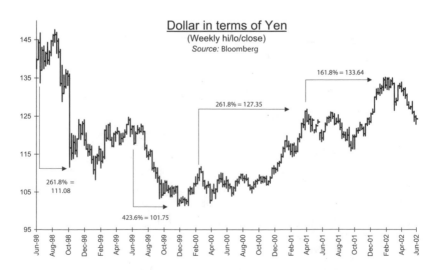

Figure 20.11 Golden ratio calculations for the dollar–yen

CONCLUSION

In this chapter, we have looked at the way that price patterns can provide a clue to the nature of the underlying trend. We have found that the emergence of a five-wave pattern is a strong indication that a trend is in force. We have also found that the price span of a five-wave trend may to some extent be predictable using the golden ratio and that a five-wave pattern is followed by a correction. Quite obviously the higher the level at which the five-wave pattern occurs, the deeper will be the associated correction. We therefore need to look more closely at the nesting of price patterns; and we shall do so by surveying Ralph Nelson Elliott's 'wave principle'.

NOTES

1.   Brand, Stewart (1999) *The Clock of the Long Now: Time and responsibility*, Weidenfeld & Nicolson, London.
2.   Elliott, Ralph Nelson (1946) *Nature's Law: The secret of the universe*, Elliott, New York, reprinted in Prechter, Robert (ed.) (1980) *The Major Works of R N Elliott*, New Classics Library, New York.

21

The Elliott wave principle

ELLIOTT'S DISCOVERY

The Elliott wave principle is a widely used, but little understood, philosophical approach to stock markets. During a long period of convalescence in the early 1930s, Elliott occupied himself by undertaking a detailed analysis of stock market movements. In the process, he discovered a unique formula that 'defined' stock market movements. This formula was based on the premise that the stock market averages rise in five 'waves' and fall in three 'waves', and it subsequently enabled Elliott to predict price movements with a degree of accuracy that astounded contemporary commentators. In 1938, he published his findings in his book entitled *The Wave Principle*.[1]

The Elliott wave principle has been popularized by Robert Prechter in the United States in recent years, and its enviable record of success has created a large following. Nevertheless, it is fair to say that the wave principle suffers from two specific problems:

▌ it is an extraordinarily complicated system to apply;

▌ no one (including, it has to be said, Elliott himself) has actually been able to explain why the central formula works.

THE PRICE PULSE AS THE BASIS OF THE WAVE PRINCIPLE

As we have demonstrated, the key to understanding Elliott's formula is the price pulse. Once this is recognized, the whole of Elliott's analysis becomes an acceptable method of analysing, and forecasting, stock market prices. Quite simply, price pulses from different levels of the hierarchy combine with one another, thereby creating the different patterns that Elliott found conformed to certain simple rules. Let us therefore survey Elliott's findings in more detail.

THE BASIC WAVE PATTERN

Elliott's primary assertion was that all bull markets consist of five waves and that all bear markets consist of three waves. These are shown in Figure 21.1. Each bull phase therefore consists of three impulse waves (1, 3 and 5 in Figure 21.1), interspersed with two corrective waves (2 and 4 in Figure 21.1). The bear phase consists of two impulse waves (A and C in Figure 21.1) interspersed with one contra-trend corrective wave (B in Figure 21.1).

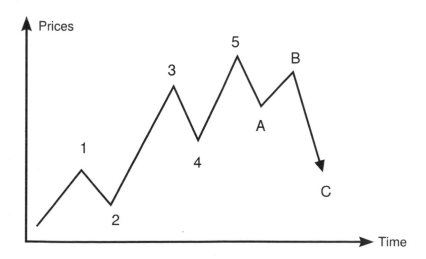

Figure 21.1 The Elliott wave

CORRECTIONS

In this simple formulation, waves A, B and C of the bear phase can be broken down into easily identifiable patterns. Waves A and C are impulse waves. Elliott considered that both would therefore consist of five waves. Wave B, on the other hand, is a corrective wave (that is, it corrects during a correction). It therefore consists of three waves, and is an inverted version of the whole A–B–C correction itself (see Figure 21.2).

A UNIVERSAL PHENOMENON

An important feature of the Elliott wave principle is that it applies to all degrees of movement. Hence, waves 1, 3 and 5 of any five-wave impulse movement each consists of five waves itself, while waves 2 and 4 of that movement each consist of three waves. Hence, each complete five–three bull–bear cycle becomes part of the cycle of the next higher degree. For example, the bull–bear formation shown in Figure 21.1 could constitute either waves (1) and (2), or waves (3) and (4), of a higher-order cycle[2] (see Figure 21.3). In this sense, Elliott's principle embraces a theory of growth: ultimately, bear market price falls will be completely reversed, and the previous bull market price peak will be exceeded.

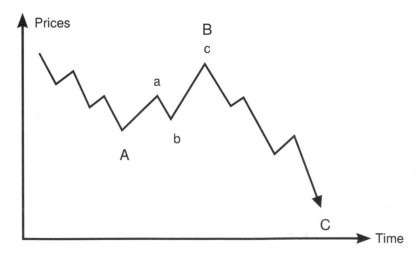

Figure 21.2 Basic Elliott corrective wave

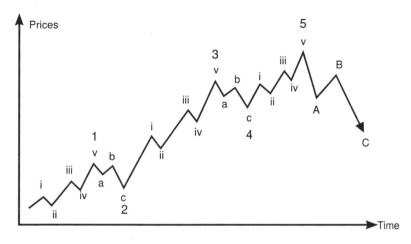

Figure 21.3 The complete Elliott wave

THE WAVE PRINCIPLE AS A NATURAL PHENOMENON

Elliott therefore made the important observation that stock market behaviour was a natural phenomenon that contained its own intrinsic patterns. This, of course, had fundamental implications for the process of forecasting stock market behaviour, because, in principle, the patterns of the lower levels should regenerate themselves at a higher level.

DERIVED RULES: TREND INDICATIONS

Elliott, in fact, established certain rules by which it would be possible to both establish the direction of the main trend in the market and determine when a market reversal, or turning point, was in the process of occurring. First, he noted that the emergence of a five-wave impulse pattern, either upwards or downwards, would provide a strong indication of the direction of the longer-term trend. Hence, a rising five-wave pattern after a sharp fall in the market would be suggestive of further rises; while a falling five-wave pattern after a sharp rise would suggest that further falls would take place.

DERIVED RULES: IMPULSE WAVES

Second, within each five-wave movement, three basic rules would apply:

▌ wave 4 will not penetrate below the peak of wave 1;[3]

▌ wave 3 is often the longest, but is never the shortest, of the five impulse waves that constitute the whole movement;

▌ two of the three impulse waves will be equal in length.

DERIVED RULES: CORRECTIONS

Third, on the question of corrections, Elliott noted three basic guidelines:

▌ no A–B–C formation will ever fully retrace the preceding five-wave formation to the same degree;

▌ each correction will be at least as large in price, and as long in time, as all lower-degree corrections that preceded it;

▌ each correction tends to return to the price range spanned by a corrective wave of one degree lower – that is, either to wave 2 or 4.[4]

COMPLICATIONS WITHIN THE SYSTEM

Elliott's basic five–three formulation, together with its associated guidelines, provided a unique view of the way that stock markets operate. Unfortunately, however, the formula is not totally comprehensive. Elliott himself found that although the basic five–three pattern applied to a large number of situations, there were, nevertheless, certain variations that had to be taken into account. When these variations were included, then indeed the analysis was complete: there is no known stock market price pattern that falls outside Elliott's framework.

FIFTH-WAVE VARIATIONS: FAILURES AND EXTENSIONS

The first set of variations that Elliott dealt with were those that apply to the fifth wave of an impulse movement. The basic formulation suggests that the fifth wave will travel beyond the end of the third wave of the same degree. However, in practice the fifth wave can either fall short of the end of the fifth wave (a failure) or extend itself in an additional dynamic five-wave movement (an extension). These are shown in Figures 21.4 and 21.5 respectively.

BEHAVIOUR FOLLOWING FAILURE OR EXTENSION

The occurrence of either a failure or an extension in the fifth wave of a movement gives a very clear indication of the subsequent behaviour

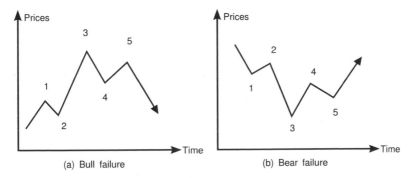

Figure 21.4 Fifth-wave failures

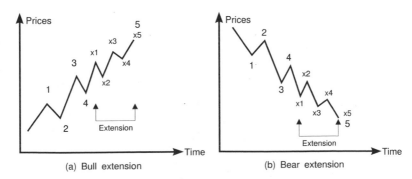

Figure 21.5 Fifth-wave extensions

of the market. A fifth-wave failure is obviously the sign of great weakness at the end of a bull run or of great strength at the end of a bear phase. Corrections following a fifth-wave bull market failure will therefore be very deep in price terms; rallies following a bear market failure will be very sharp. These are shown in Figure 21.6.

On the other hand, extensions signal a very dynamic impulse movement.[5] Consequently, in a bull market, prices will move to new high ground even after the apparent peak of the fifth wave; in a bear market, prices will drop to new lows after the apparent end of the fifth wave. These are shown in Figure 21.7. Elliott called this price action the 'double retracement principle' as prices would twice cover the ground traced out by the extension itself. The first retracement would return to the beginning of the extension (shown as ×2 in Figure 21.7), and the second retracement would move the market back past the end of wave 5.[6]

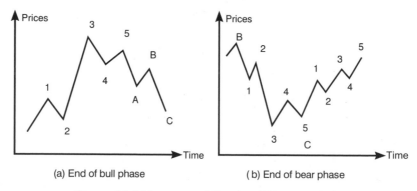

(a) End of bull phase   (b) End of bear phase

Figure 21.6 Movement following fifth-wave failure

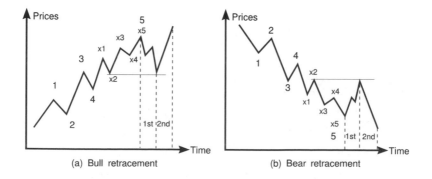

(a) Bull retracement   (b) Bear retracement

Figure 21.7 Movement following fifth-wave extension

FIFTH-WAVE VARIATIONS: DIAGONAL TRIANGLES

In addition, Elliott found that sometimes the fifth wave consists of a diagonally sloping triangular formation where:

▌ the formation consists of five waves;

▌ each wave is a three-wave movement;

▌ the fourth wave may penetrate below the peak of the first wave.[7]

This pattern is relatively uncommon, but is always followed by a dramatic move in prices in the opposite direction to the slope of the triangle. Two examples are shown in Figure 21.8.

VARIATIONS IN CORRECTIONS: THE THREE-PHASE A-WAVE

The second set of variations analysed by Elliott relates to the form of the corrective patterns. The basic pattern, which was reflected in Figure 21.2, is called a 'zigzag' – that is, it consists of two declining waves interspersed with a contra-trend rally. As explained earlier, both the A- and the C-waves of a zigzag movement consist of five declining waves, and the B-wave consists of three waves. The zigzag correction is therefore a five–three–five formation. The variations from the basic zigzag pattern relate to the fact that the A-wave often consists only of three waves, thereby yielding a three–three–five formation.[8] The B-wave following such a 'truncated' A-wave tends to be very strong –

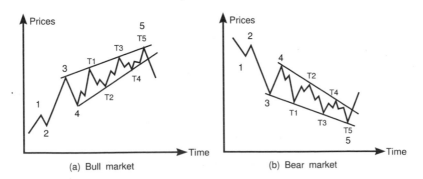

Figure 21.8 Fifth-wave diagonal triangles

so much so, in fact, that it travels at least to the point at which the A-wave started. Elliott actually found three possible three–three–five formations. These he called the 'regular flat correction', the 'irregular flat correction' and the 'running correction' respectively.

THE FLAT CORRECTION

With a regular flat correction (see Figure 21.9), the B-wave takes prices back to the level they were at at the start of the A-wave, and the subsequent C-wave returns prices to the level they were at at the end of the A-wave. In other words, prices fluctuate within a trading range before resuming their trend.

With an irregular flat, however, there are two distinct alternatives. First, the B-wave may take prices back above the level at which they were at the start of the A-wave. Second, the C-wave may either fall significantly short of the bottom of the A-wave or it may significantly exceed the bottom of the A-wave. Two of the possible combinations are shown in Figure 21.10.

In extreme cases, the relatively rare running correction occurs. Here, the B-wave substantially exceeds the start of wave A, and the subsequent C-wave also leaves prices above the start of wave A (see Figure 21.11).

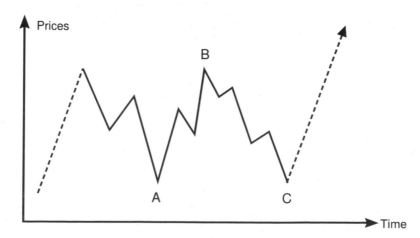

Figure 21.9 Regular flat correction

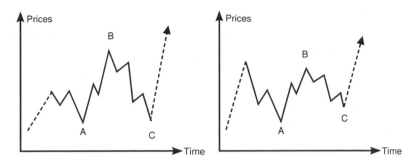

Figure 21.10 Irregular flat corrections

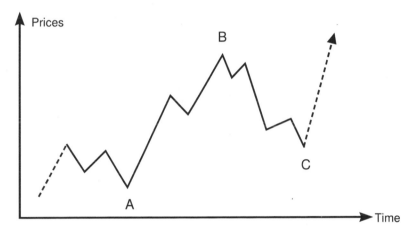

Figure 21.11 Running correction

Elliott's basic rule concerning both flat and running corrections was that they are all indicative of the fundamental trend in the market. Specifically, the strength of the B-wave is an important indication that market prices will rally very sharply following the end of a correction and that prices will probably exceed the peak of that B-wave.

COMPLEX CORRECTIONS

Obviously, therefore, corrections are potentially complicated movements. Their essential purpose is to counteract the excesses of the previous rising impulse wave of the same degree and to prepare the conditions for the next rising impulse wave. Sometimes, however, a simple zigzag or flat correction is insufficient for this task.

Consequently, the market extends the correction by combining two or more corrective patterns. In principle, any number of such patterns may be strung together, and the only restriction on the resulting complicated formation is that each A–B–C pattern is separated from the next one by another A–B–C pattern. This latter intervening pattern is usually called an X-wave. Two examples of complex corrections are shown in Figure 21.12.

TRIANGLES

One of the complex corrections that Elliott considered to be particularly important was a triangular formation. Such a formation essentially consists of five A–B–C waves or, more precisely, three A–B–C waves interspersed with two X-waves – and the extent of travel of each successive A–B–C movement is contained by boundary lines that are either contracting or expanding.[9] Relevant examples are shown in Figure 21.13.

THE IMPLICATIONS OF A TRIANGLE

The importance of the triangle lies in the fact that it gives a unique indication of the subsequent behaviour of market prices:

▌ market prices exit the triangle in the same direction as wave 2 of the triangle;

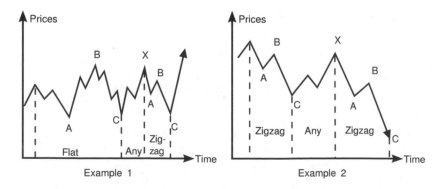

Figure 21.12 Complex corrections

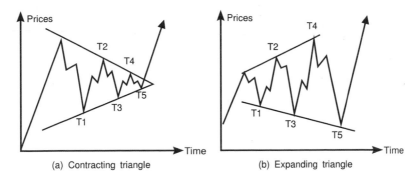

Figure 21.13 Triangular corrections

▌ the resulting impulse wave is the last such wave in the direction of the main trend;[10]

▌ in the case of contracting triangles, prices tend to move by an amount equal to the widest part of the triangle and to change trend in line with the apex of the triangle.[11]

These rules are reflected in the example shown in Figure 21.14.

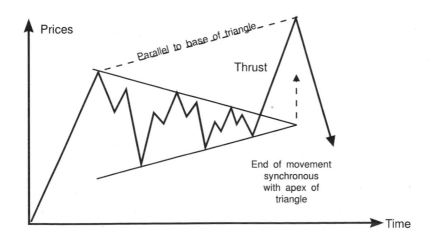

Figure 21.14 Price movement after a triangle

INVERTED CORRECTIONS

Although all these comments relate to corrections within the context of a rising market, they also apply to contra-trend movements within a falling market. Hence, they apply to waves 2 and 4 of a falling impulse wave and to the B-wave of an ordinary correction. It is usual to apply the term 'inverted' to the relevant formation. Examples of an inverted zigzag, an inverted regular flat, an inverted irregular flat and an inverted symmetrical triangle are shown in Figure 21.15.

THE 'RULE OF ALTERNATION'

In his book *Nature's Law*, Elliott argued that an essential feature of the wave principle was the 'rule of alternation'. At its simplest level, alternation can be taken to mean that bear markets alternate with bull markets. More importantly, however, Elliott argued that successive

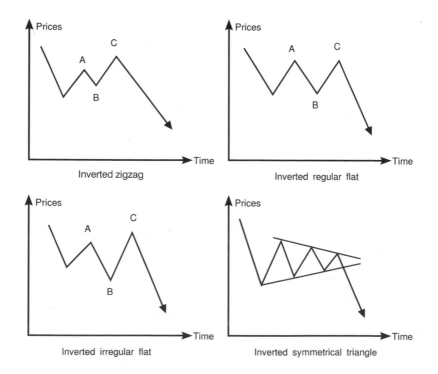

Figure 21.15 Inverted corrections

corrective patterns will be different from each other. Hence, within a five-wave impulse movement, wave 2 will differ from wave 4 both in type and complexity. Within a complicated correction, adjacent three-wave patterns will also differ from one another, both in type and complexity. Accordingly, for example, a zigzag might be followed by a flat, and a simple correction will be followed by a complicated correction consisting of two or more three-wave patterns. However, Frost and Prechter[12] suggest that the tendency for corrections to alternate should be regarded as a probability rather than an inviolable rule. There are actually numerous examples where alternation does not occur.

THE PROBLEMS WITH THE ELLIOTT WAVE PRINCIPLE

Despite the fact that the Elliott wave principle provides a complete catalogue of price patterns, many analysts find it very unsatisfactory. There are four interrelated reasons for this:

■ There has previously been no satisfactory explanation of the five–three formation. Elliott himself considered that the formation was a 'law of nature'[13] and left it at that. Unfortunately – and apart from the fact that the numbers derive from the Fibonacci sequence – the five–three pattern does not obviously appear as a regular phenomenon anywhere else in nature. It is difficult to believe that something that is supposedly so fundamental is both totally inexplicable and without parallel.

■ The integrity of the central theorem of a five–three pattern for each bull–bear cycle is only maintained by the use of the concepts of failures and irregular corrections. This suggests the absence of a unifying cause and effect.

■ The complexity of the Elliott wave (particularly in so far as extensions and complicated corrections are concerned) means that it is often impossible to establish a unique future out-turn for market prices.

■ It is possible to isolate alternatives (and therefore probabilities) in the knowledge that any actual out-turn will be a valid expression of the Elliott principle, but precise forecasts are difficult to make prior to the event.

Furthermore, even those analysts who accept the basic validity of the principle, and therefore make substantial use of it, have noted some additional problems:

▍ The principle is more difficult to apply to some markets than to others – for example, it is difficult to apply to commodity markets because wave 4 of a rising impulse wave often penetrates below the peak of wave 1 of the same degree.

▍ It is also difficult to apply to foreign exchange markets where a five–three pattern for one currency in a particular cross-rate constitutes a three–five pattern for the other currency in that cross-rate.[14]

▍ The wave principle suggests that the stock market will always rise: each upward wave is always part of a larger upward wave, and all corrections will terminate above the start of wave 1 of the preceding bull run, but this conclusion implies that dynamic systems grow quantitatively, but do not change qualitatively, which is at odds with the basic principles of natural development.

All these difficulties disappear once the implications of the price pulse are understood. Specifically, all movements unfold in three waves unless there is a qualitative (that is, second-order) change. In this latter case, the movement takes on a five-wave profile. Elliott's five–three wave principle is therefore actually a product of an evolving economy.

NOTES

1.   Elliott, Ralph Nelson (1938) *The Wave Principle*, Elliott, New York, reprinted in Prechter, Robert R (ed.) (1980) *The Major Works of R N Elliott*, New Classics Library, New York.

2.   In differentiating between movements of differing degrees, it is conventional to use different notations. For example, the lowest-level waves are usually numbered using the lower-case Roman numerals i, ii, iii, iv, v, followed by a, b, c. The next level is (i), (ii), (iii), (iv), (v), followed by (a), (b), (c). Then comes 1, 2, 3, 4, 5, followed by A, B, C. Then (1), (2), (3), (4), (5), followed by (A), (B), (C). And so forth.

3.   Except in cases of relatively rare triangular formations and commodity markets.

4.   Indeed, Elliott found that, very often, a correction would return to the lower-degree corrective wave that bore the same relationship to the larger movement. Hence, a higher-degree wave (2) would return to the lower-degree wave 2, while a higher-degree wave (4) would return to the lower-degree wave 4.

5.   Elliott argued that fifth-wave extensions were likely to occur if waves 1 and 2 were short and equal in length.

6. According to the price pulse formulation, an extension during (for example) a rising market emerges during wave 3. The double retracement is then caused by the subsequent wave A and wave B, but where wave B itself moves to a new high. The whole pattern assumes a sharply rising trend. The converse is so for a bear market.

7. In stock markets, this is the only exception to the rule that wave 4 corrections cannot penetrate below the end of wave 1 of the same degree. The evidence suggests that the rule is also sometimes violated in commodity markets.

8. This implies that all movements end on a five-wave count. However, Elliott himself was not entirely convinced by this, and he dabbled with the concept of an 'A–B base' that was a three–three construct. See Elliott, Ralph Nelson (1946) *Nature's Law: The secret of the universe,* Elliott, New York, reprinted in Prechter, Robert R (ed.) (1980) *The Major Works of R N Elliott*, New Classics Library, New York. The A–B base is a perfect reflection of the wave 1 and wave 2 base of the price pulse.

9. The boundary lines of the triangle need not converge nor diverge in a symmetrical fashion. In an ascending triangle, the top boundary line is horizontal, while in a descending triangle, the bottom line is horizontal.

10. That is, in a bull run, triangles can only occur in wave 4.

11. Frost, Alfred J, and Prechter, Robert R (1978) *Elliott Wave Principle*, New Classics Library, New York.

12. Ibid.

13. Elliott, Ralph Nelson (1946) *Nature's Law: The secret of the universe*, Elliott, New York, reprinted in Prechter, Robert R (ed.) (1980) *The Major Works of R N Elliott*, New Classics Library, New York.

14. This problem does not necessarily exist where the US dollar is being used as the base currency. This is because the dollar is an international medium of exchange and store of value.

22

Information shocks and corrections

INTRODUCTION

The pattern of prices can help market participants to gauge where they are in the context of the bigger trends. However, the art is always to be able to stay with the trend long enough to make a serious profit and then to close positions without giving too much of that profit back. This, again, means that it is important to be able to distinguish between a technical correction that need not involve the wholesale reversal of investment positions and a fundamental trend reversal that does require such a change. The great secret is not only that the market 'knows' the location of these important boundaries, but also that it conveys this information to those who are willing to look for it. We need, therefore, to look more closely at information shocks and the market's response to those shocks.

INFORMATION SHOCKS

In Chapter 9, we pinpointed two types of information shock that are relevant to the discussion. These shocks occur:

▌ when the market recognizes that it has changed direction; and

▌ when the market is accepting an extension of its trend.

The former is likely to occur at, or just after, the beginning of wave 2 in a bull phase or the beginning of wave C in a bear phase. The latter is likely to occur towards the end of wave 3 in a bull phase or towards the end of wave C in a bear phase. These shock points are likely to be accompanied by a surge in the market's energy indicators: volumes will increase, price gaps will appear, daily price spreads between highs and lows will widen and short-term momentum will rise.

INFORMATION SHOCKS AND A FIVE-WAVE TREND

Shock points indicate moments when the market accepts that a change has occurred. They subsequently become very important points of reference, which can be used to calculate entry and exit levels. We shall look at these calculations shortly. Before doing so, however, we need to explore the role of information shocks in the unfolding of the five–three pattern of price trends. First, in any impulsive five-wave pattern, there will be *three* shock points, which either initiate or restore the trend. The first shock point will signify the change in trend and will be associated with an energy gap, and the other two shock points will signify the end of contra-trend corrections and/or the beginning of an impulse wave.

Second, in any five-wave trend there is likely to be at least one pro-trend shock point, which signifies second-order change. This will likely emerge in the vicinity of what might otherwise have been an energy gap. In other words, to create a five-wave pattern, a pro-trend shock may be needed to over-ride an energy gap.

The relevant shock points in the context of a bull trend are shown in Figure 22.1. Those relating to a bear phase are shown in Figure 22.2.

SHOCKS AND CYCLES

In Figures 22.1 and 22.2, the timings of contra-trend lows that follow an information shock coincide with the natural rhythm of underlying cycles. Figure 22.3 shows such a situation in the context of the sterling–dollar exchange rate. Sterling made an important low against the US dollar in June 2001. The rate rallied until October 2001, before re-testing the low in February 2002. Using the time elapse between June 2001 and February 2002 (ie, roughly 32 weeks) as indicating the

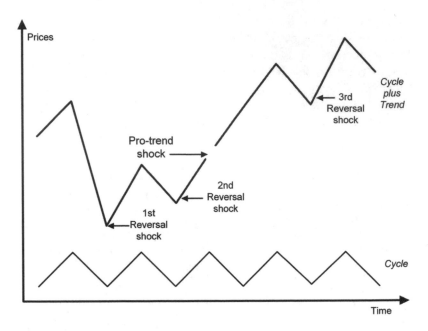

Figure 22.1 Information shocks in a bull trend

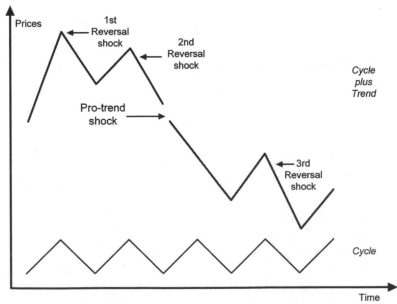

Figure 22.2 Information shocks in a bear trend

influence of a cycle, the high of cycle wave 3 was due in May 2003. However, just after getting there, the market generated an important buy signal. So, instead of entering a wave B contraction, the market jumped the energy gap and surged into a bull trend. Nevertheless, the underlying cycle seemed still to operate because lows were reached in August 2002 and April 2003. In other words, the shock that allowed sterling to jump the energy gap did not distort the underlying cycles.

On the other hand, a shock may derive from a sufficiently high level of the cycle hierarchy to upset the rhythms of the lower levels. Figure 22.4 shows the impact of a shock, in the context of a (roughly) 22-week cycle, on the Dow Jones Industrial Average. The Dow made a major low in September 2002, rallied into the turn of the year, and then made a re-test low in February 2003. The high of the cycle was due in May 2003 but that high took the market out of the trading range of the base pattern. So, the market jumped the energy gap and rose into a bull trend. This trend was sufficiently strong to damp down (but not eliminate) the underlying cycle for a long time – probably, in fact, until at least October 2004.

One way of thinking about this phenomenon is to consider what happens to the human heartbeat when the body moves from walking to running: the result is a much faster heartbeat. That is, the cycle adjusts to the information shock, rather than the other way around. In financial markets, pro-trend shocks that come from one level of the hierarchy may not have much of an obvious distorting effect on the cycles on the next lower level, other than through a slight expansion or

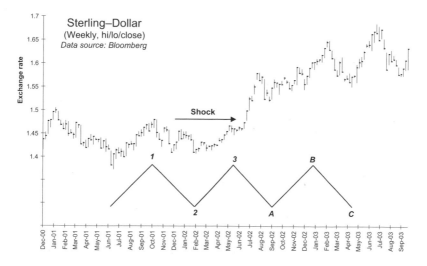

Figure 22.3 Information shock and underlying cycles

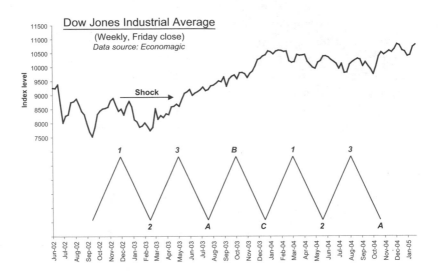

Figure 22.4 Information shocks and underlying cycles

contraction in timings. However, such shocks may have quite an effect on cycles that are two or more levels below. Hence, a pro-trend shock deriving from a 12-year cycle may not necessarily upset the basic rhythm of a 4-year cycle, but it could have quite a profound impact on underlying 1.33-year cycles and below. The beat of the 1.33-year cycle may be so extended that it hardly registers or is totally eliminated. Indeed, a large-enough information shock will need to be absorbed independently of lower-level cyclical fluctuations, and this may even give the impression of randomness. As far as the analyst is concerned, it is much more important to watch the pattern after a price shock than it is to rely on the precision of cycle periodicities.

INFORMATION SHOCKS AND BOUNDARIES

A five-wave upswing is the signature of second-order change, or of evolution, while a five-wave downswing is the signature of a break in the uptrend and/or of involution. Neither should be ignored. Despite the compelling nature of the five-wave pattern, however, there will still be some uncertainty about when the market is actually beginning to trend. Technically, a trend only really starts when the market begins to lock into a higher level of changing fundamentals. Prior to this point, the market is only correcting within the context of unchanged fundamentals.

The important point is that a market 'knows' when a higher-order trend is beginning to develop (even if analysts don't). Specifically, it will not transit through certain, well-defined points unless a higher-order trend is beginning to impact. The secret is that contra-trend movements are normally limited by their relationship to the information shocks that preceded them.

Every information shock (defined by price and energy action, not by news flows) marks a moment in price and time where the market has changed its perception about future potential (either in direction or extent). That moment is a point of learning. As we saw in Chapter 9, the learning process requires a diversion of energy to absorb new information. At the very least, this diversion of energy should not normally make the learning organism more inefficient than it was before the learning started. In the context of markets, this means that retracements should not normally fall below the price level at which the information shock occurred.[1] Consequently, a move back to the shock point should be taken as a warning sign.

However, there is more. The strong evidence is that markets will relate to the shock point through the operation of the golden ratio. Specifically, the golden ratio defines the boundaries through which a market will not go unless fundamentals are changing.

CORRECTIONS AND SHOCKS

In Chapter 10, we saw that the golden ratio – defined as 0.618:1 – is intimately bound up with the evolution of natural systems; and, in the first part of this book, we argued that, in effect, financial markets are natural systems bound together by group processes. It is not, therefore, surprising to find that the golden ratio operates in financial markets. In Chapter 11, we saw how derivatives of the golden ratio – especially 1.618 and (1.618 × 1.618 =) 2.618 – can constrain rallies. Now we shall see how the golden ratio can constrain corrections.

The first point to make is that there are two important 'types' of correction:

▌ A correction that creates the base or top pattern. For a new bull trend, the market will make a final low, rally sharply and then retrace a significant part of the rally. The converse holds true for a bear trend. This type of correction occurs in wave 2 or wave B of the price pulse. It also corresponds to wave 2 of a five-wave pattern or wave B in the subsequent three-wave corrective pattern.

■ A correction that occurs during the impulse wave. The standard explanation for this type is that it is a response to the market becoming overbought or oversold. It is therefore a 'continuation' pattern, or period of hesitation. Broadly, it corresponds to wave A of the price pulse in a bull run or wave 1 of the price pulse in a bear phase. More revealingly, it corresponds to wave 4 in a five-wave pattern or wave B of the subsequent three-wave corrective pattern.

The second point to make is that each trend move will be stimulated by a very definite shock point. Such a shock point can either be the point of inflexion in the market, or a subsequent sharp move that is accompanied by a jump in the energy indicators. The latter often occurs as a market jumps out of a trend channel or out of a short-term trading range (see Figure 22.5). Because of the nature of shocks, there may be some doubt about the exact level at which it has occurred: it may be the support or resistance level that it has penetrated; it may be the middle of any subsequent price gap or trading range; or it may even be the closing price on the day of the breakout. Some degree of leeway has to be allowed.

THE GOLDEN RATIO BOUNDARIES

The evidence is that all corrections are 'boundaried' in some way by the ratio 0.618:1. That is, if the market is reversing into a new trend, it will *retrace* 61.8 per cent of the initial impulse move from the appropriate shock point to the first point of inflexion in the new trend. And

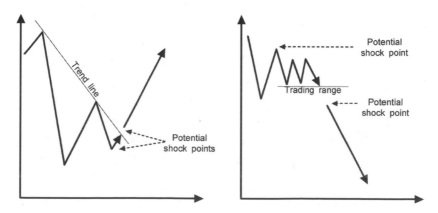

Figure 22.5 Potential shock points after a correction

if a market is only hesitating, it will *retain* 61.8 per cent of its whole movement from the appropriate shock point to the point of inflexion of the current trend. As we shall see, the appropriate shock point for the latter may be either the shock point that initiated the whole movement or the pro-trend shock point that introduced an extension of the trend.

If we assume, for the moment, that points of inflexion serve as the relevant shock points, then the golden ratio boundaries are as shown in Figures 22.6A and 22.6B. Hence, since 0.618 + 0.382 = 1, any move can be divided into two parts – namely, 61.8 per cent and 38.2 per cent.

IMPLICATIONS OF THE 38.2 PER CENT/ 61.8 PER CENT BOUNDARY

The boundary between the two proportions is of the utmost significance:

▮ If the boundary is accepted – that is, if it acts as support or resistance – then it will mean that the market has either learnt that a turning point has occurred or has continued to accept that fundamentals still favour the trend.

▮ If the boundary is penetrated, it will mean either that the market has not fully accepted the implications of an information shock (from a turning point) or is beginning to over-ride the implications of an information shock that was previously accepted.

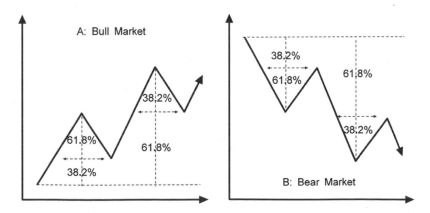

Figure 22.6 The golden ratio

TECHNICAL CORRECTIONS AND FUNDAMENTAL REVERSALS

There are two profound inferences here. The first is that a 61.8 per cent retracement defines the maximum allowable retracement during the process of learning. Indeed, a 61.8 per cent retracement is part of the signature of learning.

The second inference is that a 38.2 per cent retracement marks the boundary between a 'technical' correction and a more 'fundamental' one. After receiving an information shock and moving to a new hierarchical structure, a system must introduce constraints on its ability to regress. In the early stages after a shock, when the system is still 'learning', there is quite a lot of flexibility. However, after the market has accepted the implications of a shock, its ability to return to the level of that shock must become increasingly limited as the trend progresses. Contra-trend moves cannot significantly influence the thrust of the main trend. Consequently, prices will respond to contra-trend 'technical' factors, but they will not respond to fundamental trends that do not exist. Hence, if prices are rising because fundamentals are improving – and are expected to improve and, indeed, do improve – then prices will not suddenly start to discount Armageddon.

This makes some sense. All evolving structures carry a record of their history in whatever it is that constitutes their 'memory' (that is, in their minds and/or genes).[2] They therefore 'know' where the last set of boundaries has been established. In financial markets, such knowledge is reflected in the tacit recognition of the golden ratio limitations that are imposed on corrective movements.

TOP RETRACEMENTS

The idea that a market will retrace 61.8 per cent of the initial move away from a terminal juncture is a potential source of extraordinary profits. If, for example, there are strong grounds for supposing that the market is peaking, then a re-test of the high is likely to retrace 61.8 per cent of the fall from the top. If short positions are then opened, with a stop loss,[3] there is a good chance of catching the whole of the subsequent down-wave.

Two important examples of the operation of the 61.8 per cent retracement in the context of a top pattern were the US Dow Jones Industrial Average in 1987 and the US NASDAQ in 2000. See Figures 22.7 and 22.8.

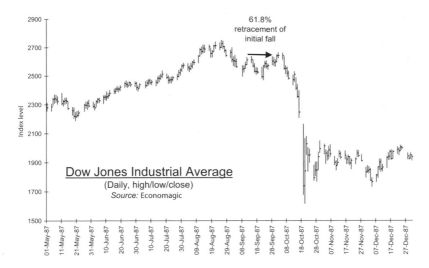

Figure 22.7 The Crash of 1987

On 25 August 1987, the Dow's intra-day high was 2,746.7. A month later, on 22 September, the intra-day low was 2,468.99. This was a fall of 277.71 points. A 61.8 per cent retracement would have covered 171.62 points, to 2,640.61. The Dow recovered to an intra-day high of 2,662.4 on 2 October but closed at 2,640.99. At the close on 19 October 1987, the market was 34 per cent lower.

Figure 22.8 The NASDAQ crash of 2000–01

On 6 March 2000, the NASDAQ touched a high of 5,132.52. By 22 May 2000, it had fallen to an intra-day low of 3,042.66. This was a fall of 2,089.86 points. A 61.8 per cent retracement would have been a rise of 1,291.53 points to 4,334.19. In fact, the market never quite got there. It stopped at 4,289.06. However, this was only 1 per cent short of target, and well within the range of error. At the close on 2 April 2001, the NASDAQ was 38 per cent lower.

BASE RETRACEMENTS

A similar analysis applies to base patterns. If there are good reasons to suppose that a base pattern might be in progress, then buying stock at (or around) the 61.8 per cent retracement level, with an appropriate stop,[4] should yield very good returns.

Good examples of this phenomenon are shown in Figure 22.9. The chart is an index of US 10-year Treasury bonds. The index is calculated by deducting the constant maturity yield (as calculated by the Federal Reserve Board) from 100. The chart shows that, at the beginning of the great disinflationary bull market in bonds that started in the early 1980s, the base pattern was defined by the golden ratio. The bond market had an initial bounce off its secular low that lasted from early October to late December in 1981. This move was retraced by 61.8 per

Figure 22.9 The golden ratio in base patterns

cent before the market started to rally again. Overall, the first impulse wave lasted from October 1981 to May 1983. Between May 1983 and June 1984, bonds retraced 61.8 per cent of this impulse wave.

THE GOLDEN RATIO AND CONTINUATION PATTERNS

Once a market has started to trend, it will normally retain 61.8 per cent of the move, unless underlying conditions are altering. Another way of putting this is to say that the market will not retrace more than 38.2 per cent of the trend unless conditions are altering. This is because $1 - 0.618 = 0.382$. Furthermore, the ratio $0.382:0.618$ is equivalent to the ratio $0.618:1$.

Good examples of this phenomenon are shown in Figures 22.10 and 22.11. The former shows the correction in 10-year US bonds in the run-up to the 1987 Equity Crash. The latter shows the fall in the Dow Jones Industrial Average index during that crash.

Figure 22.10 is part of the sequel to the story introduced in Figure 22.9. Between October 1981 and the end of 1986, 10-year US bonds rallied by 3.30 index points. A 38.2 per cent retracement of that rally was equivalent to a level of 89.67 on the chart. The subsequent fall in 10-year bonds took the index to 89.89 on 16 October 1987.

Figure 22.10 A 38.2 per cent correction in US Treasury bonds

We have already described the top pattern in the Dow that evolved in the summer of 1987. On Friday 16 October 1987, equities had a shock fall. The following Monday, 19 October, the Dow plunged by almost 23 per cent from close to close. There was further weakness the following day, but the market then started to rally. It closed higher on 20 October than it did on the 19th. Now, a fall of 38.2 per cent in absolute terms from the intra-day high on 25 August (of 2,746.7) would have taken the Dow to 1,697.46. In the event the intra-day low on the Dow on 20 October 1987 was 1,616.21. Given the trauma of the event (and the technical difficulties in calculating the correct level of the index), it is not surprising that there was an overshoot. However, this was tiny in relation to the extent of the fall. Further, the market never closed below the 38.2 per cent retracement level. The lowest close was 1,738.74 on 19 October.

The Equity Crash of 1987 was a traumatic event for market participants. Nevertheless, taken in context, it was actually just a continuation pattern. The market somehow recognized the existence of an impenetrable boundary 38.2 per cent below the August 1987 high. The importance of this boundary – and the conclusions to be drawn from it – cannot be emphasized enough. Once the market had started to penetrate beyond it, the implication would have been that very long-term fundamentals were deteriorating. In short, capitalism itself would have been at risk.[5] The point is that the 38.2 per cent/61.8 per cent boundary was calculated with reference to the impulse movement since the market was theoretically priced at zero.[6] The crash event of

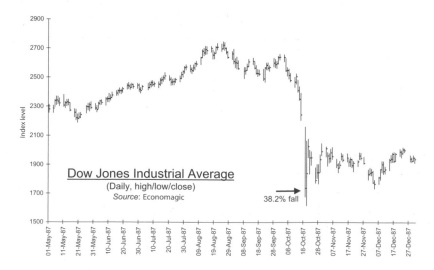

Figure 22.11 The 38.2 per cent fall in the Dow, 1987

1987 is one of the strongest pieces of evidence for the validity of the 38.2 per cent/61.8 per cent boundary.

HIERARCHICAL STRUCTURING

It is worth noting that the golden ratio boundary is hierarchical. In a bull or bear phase, the market can, in theory, retrace 38.2 per cent of the move to date, extend into new ground and then retrace 38.2 per cent of the extended move; and so on. This process sets up a series of turning points in a market, which will subsequently operate as support or resistance. In short-term trading, it is easy to see why this happens. Some segments of the market will have been wrong-footed by a reversal and will use the retracement to close off trades at a minimum loss. In longer-term investment, however, the reason for the operation of support and resistance is more opaque. It is certainly not the re-appearance of ancient fund managers who have been sitting on a losing trade for 20 years and who finally see an opportunity to get out at cost! At the simplest level, it is arguable that the market 'remembers' its boundaries. At another level, however, these boundaries are likely to implicate the golden ratio in some way.

If we assume that a market has had a series of rallies and retracements, knowledge of the golden ratio presents an opportunity to calculate future potential turning points. If the market is likely to use a recent low as support on a 38.2 per cent retracement, then the implication is that the forthcoming rally into new highs will be 38.2 per cent of the whole rally since the start of the move (see Figure 22.12). Hence, if a market has been trending from a low point at P_1 to an interim high at P_2, and has finished a correction back down to P_3, then the target high at P_t is:

$$P_t = (P_3 - (0.382\ P_1))/0.618$$

THE 38.2 PER CENT/61.8 PER CENT BOUNDARY IN A DOWN-WAVE

The boundary also operates in relation to falling markets. Figure 22.13 shows the performance of the US dollar against the Swiss franc between 1978 and 2002. There was a massive rally in the dollar between October 1978 and March 1985. Then there was a disruptive

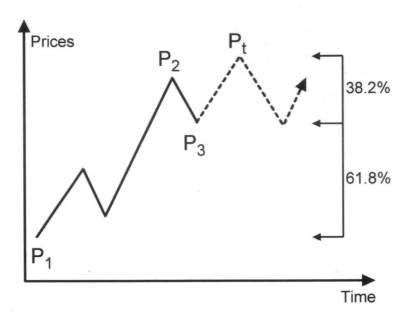

Figure 22.12 Price projections from golden ratio retracements

fall, which lasted 10 years. The most important boundary in relation to this fall was a 38.2 per cent retracement, which was equivalent to SF1.8030. The dollar took five and a half years to get there. It went through it briefly, to SF1.8298, in October 2000, and then pulled sharply back. It then rallied again in the first half of 2001, reaching SF1.8223 in the July. On neither of these two occasions, however, did the dollar close above SF1.8030 on a monthly closing basis. It subsequently fell quite sharply (see Figure 22.13).

GUIDELINES FOR CALCULATING BOUNDARIES

Quite obviously, there are different golden ratio boundaries depending on the trend that is being reversed. There are, therefore, three guidelines to take into account:

▮   take note of long-term trends;

▮   use the five-wave 'count' to define a trend;

▮   use the concept of shock points to make the calculations.

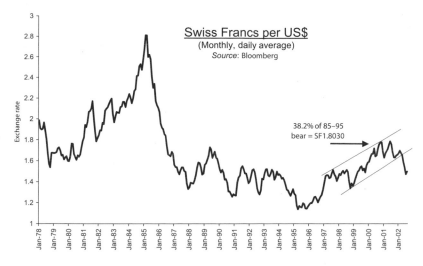

Figure 22.13 The US dollar, 1978–2002

The starting point is that the longer the trend has been in place, the more impenetrable will be the associated boundary – or the more work that a market will have to do to get through it. It is therefore important for the analysts to take account of the history of a market.

Next, a trend can be partly defined by the basic five-wave pattern that was discussed in Chapters 20 and 21. Since the five-wave pattern is basically a nested phenomenon, it is usually a simple matter to look at a chart and isolate the beginning of each five-wave movement. A schematic example is shown in Figure 22.14. Hence the first boundary to be calculated is that applicable to the last wave (wave v in the dia-gram); then the bigger wave of which that is a part (wave 5 in the diagram); and so on. Eventually the calculations will include the boundaries for the whole move from the lowest low and for the move since the price was zero.

Finally the boundaries need to be calculated in relation to the actual shock points that are relevant to the trend. This is because it is the shock point that marks the level and moment in time where the market recognizes that the trend has been initiated or renewed. Sometimes this is the reversal point itself. As already mentioned, this is some-times the break from a trend channel or trading range. Obviously, the latter occur *after* the reversal point. Consequently, the calculated retracement boundaries are going to be slightly higher in an uptrend or slightly lower in a downtrend. A schematic example is shown in Figure 22.15.

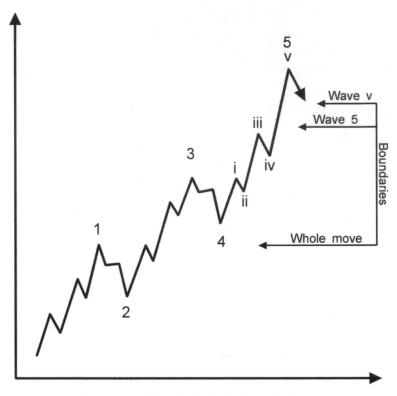

Figure 22.14 Calculating boundaries

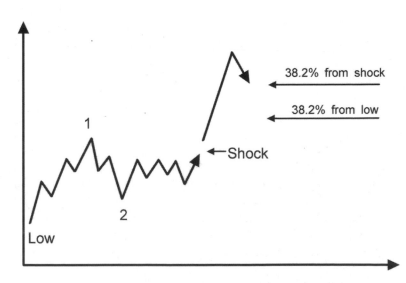

Figure 22.15 Calculating boundaries from shock points

PRO-TREND SHOCKS

There is another important aspect to this process of establishing boundaries. After a trend has been properly established, there may well be a pro-trend shock that alters the deep structure of the market. In a bull market, this is a second-order change; in a bear market, it is a recognition that a longer-term reversal is under way. These pro-trend shocks can occur relatively late in a trend. Indeed, as already discussed in Chapter 9, they are likely to occur towards the location of what might otherwise have been a cyclical peak. There are then two consequences:

▐ the onset of the correction will be delayed; and

▐ the pattern will have a five-wave structure.

There is, however, another point. This is that the pro-trend shock provides the market with extra information that needs to be absorbed and – like any learning process – this absorption will necessitate a retracement. As has already been discussed, however, retracements that are associated with learning have a maximum depth of 61.8 per cent of the move from the shock point to the subsequent inflexion point. This is demonstrated in Figure 22.16. Here, the correction will amount to 61.8 per cent of the move from the shock point to the top of wave 3 in the five-wave pattern. The calculation also applies in the context of a downtrend.

The implication is that the (delayed) correction after a pro-trend shock will constitute wave 4 in a five-wave impulse movement. This means, in turn, that there is another consideration. From the market's point of view, a wave 4 correction can only be 'technical'. It cannot lock into fundamentals. Consequently, the correction will also need to retain 61.8 per cent of the whole move from the market low. There is thus a good chance that the market will find support at a level that represents 61.8 per cent of the move after the pro-trend shock *and* 38.2 per cent of the whole move from the low (see Figure 22.16 again). If these two calculations coincide, they will provide almost impenetrable support (in a bull market) and resistance (in a bear phase).

A PRACTICAL EXAMPLE

We can now pull these strands of thought together in the form of a practical example. The market chosen is that for the US dollar in terms

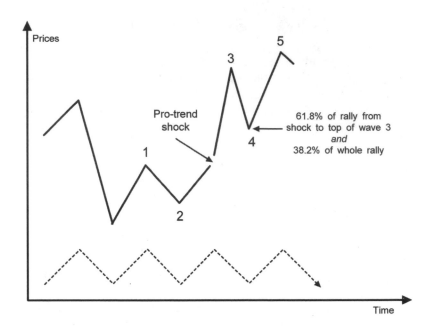

Figure 22.16 Retracements after a pro-trend shock

of the Japanese yen. The overall profile of the dollar, since its low in 1999, is shown in Figure 22.17.

To place the analysis in context, there are a number of points that can be made about the overall profile:

▌ The move since the low in November 1999 consists of five clear waves upwards, interspersed with two corrections downwards.

▌ The first correction took the form of a triangle; the second took the form of a zigzag.

▌ Wave 3 was approximately 261.8 per cent of the widest part of wave 2; wave 5 was 161.8 per cent of the depth of wave 4. We discussed the former in Chapter 11 and the latter in Chapter 20.

THE BASE PATTERN

The base formation is shown in Figure 22.18. The dollar received a bullish shock, and gave a buy signal, at SP1 (ie, about ¥102.50) as it moved out of the downtrend and cleared the trading range that had

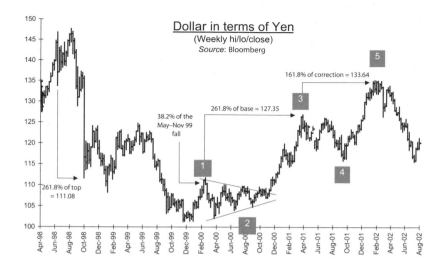

Figure 22.17 The US dollar in terms of Japanese yen

established itself in December 1999. The target was 38.2 per cent of the last fall, which was ¥110.27. The dollar touched an intra-day high of ¥111.73 in late January 2001. Such small overshoots are not unusual in the first rally off a low.

A 61.8 per cent retracement was likely to follow. Thus the downside target was either 61.8 per cent from the low or from the shock point, SP1. The targets were thus ¥105.25 and ¥106.02. In the event the dollar fell sharply, to ¥102.06, which was well below the target.

Nevertheless, that low held and the market started to oscillate within a triangle. The last wave of this triangle reached a low at ¥104.77 in early September 2000. More to the point, the weekly closing low in this last stage was ¥106.00. The close is always the most critical price, since it marks a genuine point of balance. It conformed to the principle that learning retraces 61.8 per cent of the move following an information shock.

THE WAVE 4 CORRECTION

One of the advantages of a triangle is that it gives a very clear signal when the market finally breaks out of it. In the system proposed by Elliott, triangles are fourth-wave, or B-wave, phenomena. However, this is by no means an inviolable rule. The dollar–yen rate bears this out. The break was not immediate. An attempt was made in October

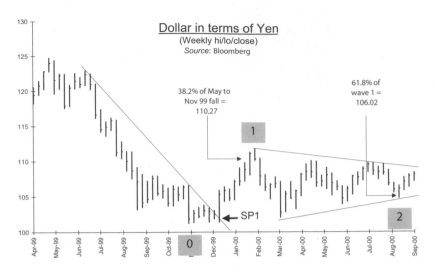

Figure 22.18 The dollar–yen base pattern, 1999–2000

2000, which failed. However, this created waves i and ii of what was to become the main impulse wave (see Figure 22.19). The breakout and the buy signal occurred in late November 2000 at about ¥109.10. There was then a very sharp impulsive rally. As already described, this rally was approximately 261.8 per cent of the widest part of the wave 2 base. Once it had been completed, however, there were three downside targets. The first applied to wave 3 itself. This was 38.2 per cent of wave 3, which was ¥118.36. This was hit almost precisely in late May. However, there were two other important downside targets. These were 38.2 per cent of the whole rally (ie, from 0 to the top of wave 3) and 61.8 per cent of the rally from the shock point (SP2). The former was ¥117.06; the latter was ¥116.15. The virtual synchrony of the two calculations was very powerful. Having had an interim rally, the dollar turned down again. Its weekly closing low in mid-September 2001 was ¥116.58.

THE DOLLAR–YEN BEAR MARKET

The dollar then moved to a new high, thereby completing a five-wave pattern (see Figure 22.20). The buy signal was given on a break of the downtrend in the last phase of wave 4. This occurred at ¥119.68, and is denoted SP3 on the chart. The extent of the subsequent move was, as already mentioned, approximately 161.8 per cent of the depth of

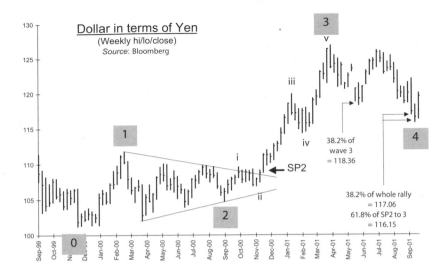

Figure 22.19 The wave 4 correction, April–September 2001

wave 4. The next important question was: when would the bear market be deemed to have begun?

The first potential signal was at a level equivalent to 38.2 per cent of wave 5, which was ¥127.76. The market went through this briefly (to ¥126.40) in March 2002, but closed the week above it. The real clue, however, was the fact that 61.8 per cent of the rally since SP3 was ¥125.59. In other words, the March support was probably indicating the importance of the shock point that triggered wave 5.

Once a market reverses through a 61.8 per cent retracement from a shock point, it has basically rejected the learning that was triggered by that shock point. In other words, once the levels ¥127.76 and ¥126.40 were broken, the dollar was in a bear phase. And so it was. The market subsequently fell towards a level that was 61.8 per cent of the whole 1999–2002 rally.

CONCLUSION

This chapter has explored some of the relationships between information shocks and the golden ratio. It was hypothesized that the golden ratio is intrinsic to the learning process, such that markets are unlikely to retrace more than 61.8 per cent of any rally after an information shock. It was also hypothesized that markets would retain 61.8 per cent of their move since an information shock once learning had

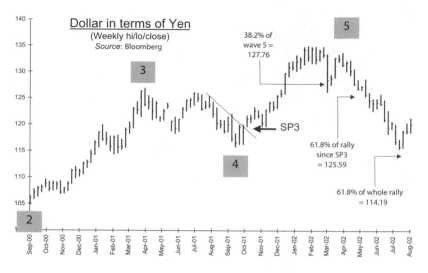

Figure 22.20 The bear phase in dollar–yen, 2002

occurred. A break of either of these two boundaries would likely signal a change in deeper-running fundamentals.

It was demonstrated that this hypothesis seems to work in practice. There is obviously some scope for error in calculating the appropriate boundary levels because fast-moving markets will rarely hit them precisely. On the other hand, the markets will not signal that they have broken a boundary, unless deeper-running fundamentals have indeed started to reverse.

NOTES

1. So if the information shock is accompanied by a price gap in the market, this gap should not normally be filled. This contradicts the old stock market adage that 'gaps are always filled'.
2. Jantsch, Erich (1980) *The Self-organizing Universe*, Pergamon, Oxford.
3. The stop will depend on the user's preferences. One is to place the stop just beyond the turning point. This was the stop favoured by Gartley, who actually made a great deal of money from selling the simple rule as a 'system' during the Depression years. See Gartley, H M (1935) *Profits in the Stock Market*, reprinted (1981) by Lambert-Gann, Pomeroy, Washington. However, this may be too far away from the entry point. Another is to place the stop (eg) 1 per cent away from the entry point. If the stop is triggered, the market may just be over-shooting, so positions should be re-entered as the market drops back below the 61.8 per cent level.
4. See note 3.

5. This does not rule out (and did not rule out) the possibility of a subsequent recession. There was, in fact, a deep recession in 1990–92. The combination of a crash and deep recession tends to occur in the first Juglar cycle after a Kondratyev commodity price high (see Chapter 17).

6. The same conclusion applies to the low in the Dow that was reached in early October 2002. A 38.2 per cent fall from the all-time high of 11,750.28 was 7,260. The market's low on 9 October was 7,197.45, after which the market bounced. It remains to be seen whether this level will eventually be penetrated.

23

The confirmation of buy and sell signals

INTRODUCTION

The greatest constraint on taking the appropriate action in any financial market is doubt. No matter how important a trading signal might appear to be, there is always the possibility that it might be wrong. As important buy and sell signals almost inevitably occur at moments when the vast majority of investors are literally 'the other way', the crowd pressure to ignore the signal or wait for a more certain one is likely to be extremely strong. The first task of any investor, therefore, is to try to reduce their susceptibility to such crowd pressures.

In this context, people who use technical analysis to trade in financial markets will quickly find that their ability to stand out against the herd is increased. This is quite simply because the *raison d'être* of technical analysis is to deduce what the vast majority are indeed doing, so that contrary positions can be taken at the appropriate moment. Nevertheless, it is always essential to try to reduce the element of doubt by applying as many techniques as possible to each particular situation. The interpretation of price patterns is only one of these techniques. Others involve the calculation of price objectives, the calculation of the timing of likely turning points and a direct analysis of investor sentiment and behaviour. In this chapter, we shall examine the idea that we can deduce the exact position of the market in its bull–bear cycle by analysing investor behaviour.

INVESTOR CONFIDENCE AND PRICE FLUCTUATIONS

The starting point to the analysis is the relationship between investor sentiment or investor activity and price fluctuations. It will be remembered that we examined the relationship in some detail in Chapter 8. There it was argued that there is both a limit cycle relationship and a spiral relationship between investor confidence (measured by sentiment or by behaviour) and prices. While a trend is intact, changes in confidence encourage changes in prices, which in turn stimulate changes in confidence and investor activity. However, at a turning point, the following sequence of events occurs:

▌ the 'circular' relationship between prices and confidence begins to break down, changing prices are unable to induce additional changes in investment positions and, accordingly, the market becomes overextended;

▌ investor psychology receives a shock as prices move in the opposite direction to the expectations of the vast majority;

▌ prices move to re-test the levels that were reached just prior to the shock (sometimes prices actually move into new territory during the re-test; sometimes they do not, but, during this phase, confidence in the price trend often appears to run ahead of the actual change in prices, although it does not genuinely return to levels achieved prior to the shock);

▌ finally, prices begin a proper reversal and investor confidence switches with it.

OVEREXTENDED MARKETS AND THE PRINCIPLE OF NON-CONFIRMATION

This analytical framework not only allows investors to understand exactly what is happening at each phase of a full bull–bear cycle, but it also pinpoints exact trading rules that can be used to take advantage of this understanding:

▌ it emphasizes that it is possible to anticipate an energy gap – and, hence, an information shock – when the market becomes overextended in one direction or another;

▌ it highlights the fact that investor psychology becomes damaged
by the shock, so re-tests of the price levels that were reached prior
to the shock can be used to open up new trading positions in the
opposite direction.

In practice, then, the main indicator of an imminent price reversal is a
change in the 'level' of any index that measures either investor
sentiment or investor behaviour. When a trend is intact, the majority
of investors will open up new trading positions, increase their dealing
activity, be prepared to stimulate the momentum of the price trend and
deal in all sectors of the market. However, when a price reversal is
imminent, the relevant confidence indicators tend first to become
overextended, then drop away because investors are simply unable to
open new positions. If the market does then fall, the critical question is
how the confidence indicators respond during subsequent recovery
from the shock. If there is to be a third stage to the reversal, then
investors will be less willing than previously to open up new trading
positions. And if prices actually move out into new territory, but the
confidence indicators do not, then the trend is not confirmed.

These relationships are demonstrated in Figure 23.1. In effect, a
higher-level energy gap is signalled by the performance of the confidence indicators during the fourth and fifth waves of a distorted
lower-level price pulse.

INDICATORS OF INVESTOR BEHAVIOUR

It is therefore important to be able to gauge the disposition of investor
sentiment and the strength of investor activity. The most obvious indicators to use are opinion surveys and liquidity surveys. However,
these can be expensive to create or to buy, and are usually late because
they take time to calculate. A much easier approach is to use simple
mechanical indicators that are readily available from the markets
themselves. These include:

▌ price momentum (for example, percentage rates of change);

▌ price volatility (for example, percentage spread intra-day or intra-
week);

▌ trading volumes (that is, number of bargains or nominal turnover);

▌ open interest and put/call ratios (ie, outstanding positions); and

▌ related market price indices that have a different focus.

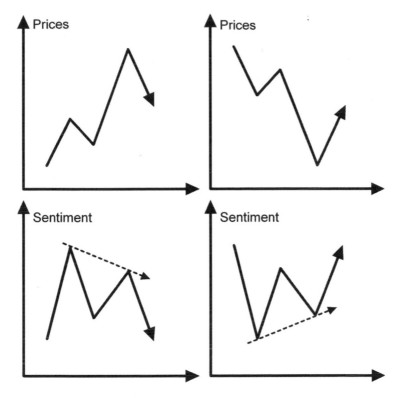

Figure 23.1 The principle of non-confirmation

These do not exhaust the list, but they have the advantage of being either easily calculable or easily available. The first two can be calculated directly from prices themselves, and the rest are usually available from the relevant bourses.

VOLUME AND OPEN INTEREST

Because the rules applying to volume and open interest are essentially the same, we shall analyse them together. Volume is a direct measure of the amount of activity taking place in the market at a particular time. It may be measured either in terms of nominal turnover or the number of bargains. The data may be obtained from the cash markets, futures markets or even the options markets. Indeed, in principle the volume figures for one market for a particular asset may be applied to any of the other markets in the same asset: all that is required is that the data be consistent and the markets be well traded. Hence, for example, in the foreign exchange markets where it is impossible to obtain volume data, it is perfectly acceptable to use volume figures generated by the relevant exchange for an equivalent futures contract.

Open interest, on the other hand, is the total number of outstanding contracts in either the futures or options market that are held by market participants at the end of each day. Although the measure applies to specific futures or options markets, it may also be used for the related securities.[1] Hence, for example, the open interest for the US Treasury long bond futures contract can be used in conjunction with the Treasury cash market.

THE LEVEL OF VOLUME

There are two aspects of open interest and volume that warrant discussion. The first is the general level of the indicators, while the second is the direction of change of those indicators. Let us start with the levels. The level of volume is indicative of people's willingness to deal. This, in turn, reflects traders' attitudes to the market. A low level of volume indicates an unwillingness to open new positions and close old ones. It therefore also indicates some uncertainty about the future direction of the market. Alternatively, a high level of volume is a direct reflection of traders' willingness to open new positions, take profits or close bad positions. It therefore also indicates a high degree of confidence in the future direction of the market.

THE LEVEL OF OPEN INTEREST

In the case of open interest, the level is indicative of the efficiency, or liquidity, of the market. Specifically, it is a measure of the market's ability to absorb new deals at current prices. If open interest is low, then there are very few profits to be taken or bad positions to be closed. A new trade is likely to have a large impact on prices because prices have to adjust in order to induce another dealer to 'go the other way'. At low levels of open interest, therefore, the market is illiquid. If, on the other hand, open interest is high, then there are plenty of profits to be taken and bad positions to be closed. A new trade is likely to have only a very small effect on prices because another dealer is likely to take advantage of the availability of the trade at the current price level. At high levels of open interest, therefore, the market is very liquid.

SUDDEN CHANGES IN THE INDICATORS

The concepts of 'high' and 'low' are, of course, relative. There needs to be a benchmark against which to measure them. In this respect, historical precedent and local market knowledge should provide some assistance. Very often, however, the most important facet of the levels of either open interest or volume is the fact that they change suddenly. This is a clear indication that something is altering in the price–sentiment relationship. In this context, volume is often more important than open interest, but open interest can help to determine the extent of the price reversal that subsequently takes place. Let us therefore analyse the implications of the direction of change in volume and open interest in more detail.

THE DIRECTION OF CHANGE IN VOLUME AND OPEN INTEREST

Both volume and open interest may be taken as proxies for investor confidence in the direction of the prevailing trend. Rising volume suggests a growing awareness of the higher-level trend, and rising open interest indicates a growing commitment to that trend. Falling volume, on the other hand, indicates a spreading inability or unwillingness to pursue the immediate trend, while falling open interest suggests some reversal of sentiment as profits are taken and bad positions are closed out.

CHANGING EMOTIONS DURING THE CYCLE

It will be remembered that while a trend is developing, the limit cycle process between prices and confidence will ensure that investor activity continually strengthens that trend. This implies that, during the trend, volume and open interest should both rise. This occurs whether the price trend is upwards or downwards. At some stage in the limit cycle process, the change in prices will trigger the emotion of fear among investors – either the fear of being left out of the market during a rise or of being left in the market during a fall. Most emotions have a number of different dimensions, but fear is unique in closing the mind to rational thought and focusing the body's energy on physical, mental or social survival. Fearful investors will deal blindly and both volume and open interest should rise sharply. Consequently, the market starts to become overbought or oversold.

SHARP RISES IN VOLUME AND OPEN INTEREST

A sharp rise in volume and open interest essentially undermines the limit cycle between confidence and prices in the short term. In particular, the rise in open interest creates conditions where investors are overstretched and are easily induced to close their positions in response to relatively small changes in price. On the one hand, therefore, investors are unable to marshal sufficient resources to perpetuate the old trend, while, on the other, profit-taking or bear closing may emerge quickly as prices start to reverse. Consequently, the reversal will become self-generating.

THE REVERSAL PROCESS

This is, however, only part of the process. Notice what happens as the reversal gathers pace. Investors close profitable positions and cut out losing ones. Not all of them will react, of course, but many will. This means that, during the first stage of a reversal, open interest will either not rise or will actually fall. At the very least, therefore, the immediate price trend is not being confirmed. At some stage, therefore, prices will begin moving in the same direction as the old trend again and will re-test the levels at which the market became overbought or oversold. It is this re-test that will provide the true indication of the future direction for the market.

VOLUME AND OPEN INTEREST DURING FIFTH WAVES

As we have already seen, a re-test may actually move into new territory. This new high or low is counted as a 'fifth wave', caused by a strong underlying trend. There are four immediate possibilities with respect to the associated movements in volume and open interest:

■ volume and open interest rise into new ground;

■ volume and open interest rise, but not into new high ground;

■ volume rises, but open interest falls;

■ volume and open interest fall.

It follows from the nature of the price–sentiment cycle that if volume and open interest both respond strongly to a new high or low, then the higher-level trend remains intact. Consequently, the damage inflicted by the earlier overbought or oversold condition will have been overcome and the price reversal will have been no more than temporary.

If, however, volume and/or open interest do not manage to rise into new high ground, then a non-confirmation takes place. (This was shown in Figure 23.1.) This means that the damage inflicted on investors' psychology by the initial price reversal was serious and an important trend reversal is about to emerge.

This last conclusion is even more apt if open interest falls during a volume non-confirmation. The implication here is that traders are taking advantage of new price levels to close positions. Confidence in the old trend has therefore already altered and the subsequent price reversal will be strong.

Finally, and in potentially the worst case of all, if prices move into new ground, but volume and open interest fall, then the subsequent price reversal could be quite dramatic. The limit cycle has obviously already broken down completely and investors are in a position to respond with vigour when a new price trend emerges.

VOLUME AND OPEN INTEREST DURING RE-TESTS

Remember that an ordinary, undistorted, re-test of a previous peak is carried out by a wave B, and the re-test of a previous low is carried out by a wave 2. By definition, sentiment during either of these waves is likely to fall short of that which occurred during the preceding impulse waves.[2] This internally weak technical position of the market compounds the likely implications for the upcoming impulse wave. There are then actually three relevant combinations of volume and open interest:

▌ volume and open interest rise;

▌ volume rises, but open interest falls, or vice versa;

▌ volume and open interest fall.

Volume and open interest may well rise together as the sentiment of the previous trend reasserts itself. Usually, however, one or both remain subdued and will not reach the levels attained during that trend.[3]

The real clue to future price movements may, in fact, be given by the performance of open interest. If open interest falls, the evidence suggests that investors are closing positions. This is, of course, true whether volume is rising or falling.

If investors are closing positions, then the implication is that the damage done by the previous shock to the market has not been overcome. The greater is the fall in open interest, the less the market is subsequently able to cope with changes in the supply of, or demand for, stock, and consequently, when an impulse wave materializes, the effect will be dramatic.

THE WIDER IMPLICATIONS OF FALLING OPEN INTEREST

The foregoing analysis highlights the fact that falling open interest (particularly if it is accompanied by rising volume) can provide a very accurate warning of an impending 'third'-wave reversal in prices. In fact, falling open interest can also warn of an impending acceleration in prices just after a price reversal. It is as well to be clear about the difference between the two situations.

Remember that falling open interest essentially restricts the flexibility of the market. The subsequent move is likely to be large because small changes in demand or supply have a large effect on prices, and

Table 23.1 The bull–bear cycle and open interest

Prices	Open interest
1. Bear squeeze	Sharp fall
2. Re-test of low/new low	Rise, but not to new high
3. Beginning of bull	Fall
4. Bull	Rise
5. Overbought set-back	Sharp fall
6. Re-test of high/new high	Rise, but not to new high
7. Beginning of bear	Fall
8. Bear	Rise

large changes in prices then induce a significant change in sentiment, so the process becomes self-generating. Table 23.1 shows the likely fluctuations in open interest during the course of a theoretical bull–bear cycle. Put bluntly, falling open interest occurs when the 'winners' are squeezing the 'losers'. Hence, generally speaking, a sharp fall in open interest marks the 'death' stage of the life cycle of either a bull market or a bear market. It therefore marks the beginning of a significant reversal.

Alternatively, a moderate fall in open interest may mark the 'birth' stage of a new bull or bear trend. It therefore often precedes an acceleration into the main thrust of that trend. Figure 23.2 shows these possibilities (without taking account of high-level trends) within the context of a price pulse.

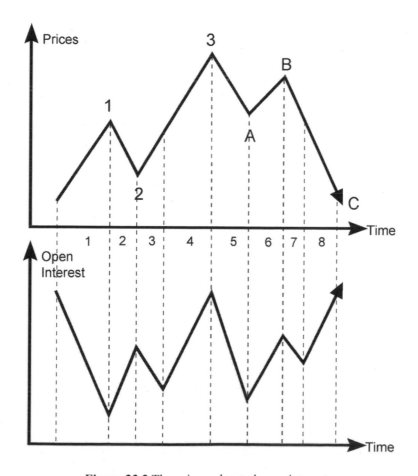

Figure 23.2 The price pulse and open interest

MOMENTUM AND OVEREXTENDED MARKETS

The third analytical tool that can be used to judge the internal strength of a market is a momentum index. Essentially, such an index is a measure of the speed of change in the market. The value of using a momentum measure is actually two-fold. First, the price–sentiment limit cycle suggests that, during an impulse wave, momentum will accelerate. Furthermore, momentum will be at an extreme at the end of these waves – analysts use the terms 'overbought' or 'oversold' to indicate these extremes. Having reached an extreme, the market should reverse itself. If the price pulse is a high-level pulse, the reversal will be immediate, sharp and long-lasting.[4] If, however, the pulse is of a lower order, the reversal will be only temporary.

MOMENTUM AND NON-CONFIRMATION

Second – and if the reversal is only temporary – a momentum measure can be used to judge the strength of the renewed trend. The principle of non-confirmation relies on the idea that the momentum of a market (whether upwards or downwards) will slow appreciably during the final wave (Elliott's 'fifth' wave) that precedes an important reversal (see Figure 23.1 again).

Indeed, this can often be seen in the form of a change in the slope of price movements on the price–time charts during the final wave. Momentum non-confirmations occur both because the short-term limit cycle relationship between prices and confidence is inherently biased (see Chapter 8) and it is, in any case, being gradually over-ridden by longer-term forces. If higher prices are unable to encourage buying or lower prices are unable to encourage selling, a reversal may be imminent.

MEASURES OF MOMENTUM

There are four different measures that can be used as a momentum index:

▎ a simple percentage rate of change, where the current price is expressed as a percentage of the value of an earlier price – the 'earlier' price is always a constant time period (hours, days, weeks, months and so on) away from the 'current' price;

▌ the deviation from a (long-term) moving average – the difference between the current price and the moving average (the moving average has a constant number of data points in it and includes the current price as the last such data point);

▌ a relative strength indicator (RSI), which measures the relationship between price increases and price decreases;

▌ a directional indicator, which directly measures the strength of a trend.

RATES OF CHANGE

Each of the different momentum measures has its own advantages and disadvantages. The percentage rate of change index, for example, is certainly very easy to calculate. Furthermore, it is possible both to use indicators with very short time periods (such as five days) to isolate the momentum of lower degree price pulses and measures with long time periods (such as 12 months) to analyse higher-degree pulses. In order to obtain some idea of what constitutes overbought and oversold, however, it is necessary to have a long history available. Extremes of momentum can then easily be determined by inspection (see Figure 23.3).

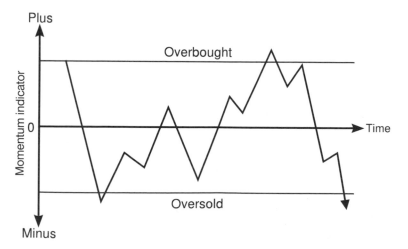

Figure 23.3 Overbought and oversold momentum

DEVIATIONS FROM A MOVING AVERAGE

The use of deviations from a moving average is almost as popular because moving averages are a proxy for the market trend. The theory behind using the deviation from the moving average implicitly relies on the fact that lower-degree price pulses cannot deviate too dramatically from the trend imposed by higher-degree pulses. Consequently, it is possible to test the historic data to find out what constitutes overbought or oversold. Furthermore, a narrowing of the deviation when the market reaches new highs or lows is taken to mean a reduction in the power of the lower-degree pulse *vis-à-vis* the (gradually reversing) higher-degree pulse.

Essentially, there are two possible systems that use moving averages. The first measures the deviation of the current price from an arithmetical moving average of recent prices. This method is very simple, but is not without some imperfections. Specifically, the calculated value of an arithmetical moving average applies to the data at the mid-point of the time period over which it is calculated. Consequently, it is not possible to know the 'correct' value of a moving average that is applicable to today until some time in the future. The system actually works partly because of the idiosyncrasies of the moving average technique itself. The moving average will lag the current price quite significantly. Hence, overbought and oversold conditions occur simply because the moving average has not 'caught up' and non-confirmations occur simply because slowly moving final waves actually do allow the moving average to catch up.

The second form of the moving average system addresses these problems by using two exponentially smoothed moving averages. Exponential smoothing gives a heavier weight to the most recent time periods and a lesser weight to earlier ones. It therefore measures recent crowd pressures, but concentrates its power on recent events. Today's exponential moving average (EMA_t) is calculated as:

$$EMA_t = P_t \times K + EMA_{t-1} \times (1 - K)$$

where:

K = $2/(n + 1)$
n = number of days in moving average
P_t = today's price
EMA_{t-1} = yesterday's moving average.

Subtracting the longer-term exponential moving average from the shorter one results in an indicator that is normally referred to as a 'moving average convergence–divergence' oscillator (MACD). This indicator – originally developed by Gerald Appel in the United States – oscillates slowly as the short-term average converges on, crosses and then diverges from, the longer-term average. The MACD has become one of the primary tools used to judge overbought and oversold conditions and signal non-confirmations.

THE RELATIVE STRENGTH INDEX (RSI)

The RSI was developed by J Wells Wilder in the United States. It measures the relationship between the sum of the daily price increases during a given recent period (usually the last nine days) and the sum of the daily price decreases during the same period. The formula for the measure is given as:

$$\text{Current RSI} = 100 - \frac{100}{1 + \dfrac{\text{Sum of positive changes}}{\text{Sum of negative changes}}}$$

If the sum of all the positive changes during the chosen time period is zero, the ratio in the denominator is also assumed to be zero. However, if the sum of the negative changes is zero, the ratio in the denominator is assumed to be equal to the sum of the positive changes (that is, the sum of the negative changes is assumed to be unity).

The RSI is particularly easy to use. It requires only a very short history, needs no testing to find out what constitutes overbought or oversold and is easy to present graphically. The RSI can oscillate only between values of 0 and 100. Generally speaking, if the value is 20 or less then the market is likely to be oversold; if the value is 80 or more, the market is likely to be overbought. The RSI is also well suited to establishing divergences at market troughs and peaks.[5]

It has to be remembered, however, that the RSI is essentially a short-term trading tool. Hence, a nine-day RSI implicitly assumes that it is unusual for a market to move in one direction for more than eight consecutive trading days. It is nevertheless worth checking the historical data to ensure that uni-directional movements of eight days or more are indeed uncommon. If necessary, the RSI can be calculated using longer time periods.

MOMENTUM TRADING RULES

Whichever method is used to track momentum – whether it be rates of change, deviations from a moving average or the RSI – there are three important rules that should be borne in mind:

▎ Markets can remain overbought for quite a long period of time. As we have already observed, fear of missing further profits (that is, greed) takes time to dissipate. Traders should not therefore react solely to an overbought condition unless there are other grounds for supposing that a reaction is imminent. Errors can be avoided by waiting until the price level and momentum have both started to fall from their overbought level.

▎ Markets tend to remain oversold for relatively short periods of time, because the fear of making losses tends to trigger swift corrective action. Hence, purchases based on oversold criteria will usually yield a profit.[6] Most importantly, non-confirmation of new price highs or lows only occurs when prices themselves (and therefore the momentum index) actually start to reverse.

▎ Many analysts make the mistake of assuming that because prices have moved into new territory while momentum has not, a price reversal is imminent. It is, in fact, often true that either the non-confirmation persists for an extended period of time or momentum eventually catches up with the market.

THE DIRECTIONAL INDICATOR

The fourth momentum indicator – the directional indicator – has a very specific use: it measures the strength of a trend. This is obviously of great value in deciding whether the market is trending or oscillating in a trading range, and in deciding if the trend is pronounced or not. The original work on this index was (again) conducted by J Wells Wilder,[7] although it has been modified by other analysts. The directional indicator (usually known as the DI) is based on the assumption that an up trend exists if today's high exceeds yesterday's high, while a down trend exists if today's low exceeds yesterday's low. The average directional indicator (known as the ADX) is based on the assumption that the more often a market generates a trading range outside the previous day's trading range and the greater are these external trading ranges in relation to the day's total move, then the more powerful is the trend.

The mathematics of the directional indicators is quite complicated and is best produced by computer. Most technical analysis software packages now include them. All the main indicators are 'normalized' in as much as they are multiplied by 100. This means that the numbers oscillate within a range of 0 to 100. For those who wish to observe the calculations directly, the details are included in Wilder's original book and in books such as Alexander Elder's excellent *Trading for a Living*.[8] Here we shall just confine ourselves to the use of the indicators.

The beauty of the DI and the ADX is that, between them, they directly track the evolving power of the crowd. There are two directional indicators – a positive one (+DI), which measures up days, and a negative one (–DI), which measures down days. The positive and negative numbers are averaged over time. If the moving average of the +DI exceeds the moving average of the –DI, then the market is rising. In principle, a buy signal is given if the +DI line crosses the –DI line from below, and, again. The reverse holds true for falling markets.

Meanwhile, the ADX – which is widely regarded as the most important component of Wilder's system – measures the spread between the +DI and –DI lines. In fact, it is a moving average of the spread. Hence, if a trend is evolving in a healthy manner, the ADX line will be rising. This applies whether the trend is up or down. On the other hand, if a trend is running out of steam, the ADX line will begin to reverse. The market is becoming overextended. Importantly, too, the relevant DI line[9] is likely to be signalling a non-confirmation at this point. Finally, if a market is not actually trending, but, instead, is fluctuating horizontally, then the ADX will be falling and is likely to be below both the +DI and the –DI.

THE ADVANCE–DECLINE INDEX

The final set of indices consists of auxiliary indices. These are used to estimate the extent to which all stocks or all sections of the market are participating in a trend. There are two basic auxiliary indices that can be used. The first is an index that is constructed from the daily figures for the number of stocks that have advanced in relation to the number of stocks that have declined. The most popular method of construction is simply to add the net daily advances to, or deduct the net daily declines from, a cumulative figure. The resulting index is known as the 'cumulative advance/decline indicator', or the A/D line. Obviously, such figures are not readily available for all markets, but they are available for stock markets in both the UK and the United States. As they relate to the total number of stocks being traded in the market, they readily provide a good proxy for its internal strength. Hence, if a market price index moves into new ground, but the A/D line does not follow suit, then there is a strong suggestion that trading activity is becoming too speculative and that not all stocks are participating in the movement. Such a non-confirmation does not necessarily mean that it is wrong to participate in the market, but it does mean that the life expectancy of the movement may be limited[10] and that it could be followed by a relatively severe setback.

A SECOND PRICE INDEX

The alternative type of auxiliary index involves the use of a second price index. It must, however, consist of stocks that are entirely different from, but nevertheless related to, those included in the primary index. Hence, in the fixed interest markets, for example, a short-term (interest rate-related) bond index may be used to complement a long bond index. In the US stock market, the Dow Jones Transportation Index may be used to complement the Dow Jones Industrial Index; in the gold market, the price of gold itself may be used to complement a gold mining share index. In all cases, it is reasonable to expect that if a trend is developing in a healthy fashion, both primary and secondary indices should perform together. A divergence between the two indices suggests that a reversal might be imminent.

THE PRINCIPLE OF DIRECT CONFIRMATION: THE DOW THEORY

This chapter has so far covered the basic notion that non-confirmation provides a useful warning of an imminent reversal. The final stage of the analysis is to see how technical indicators can be used to confirm directly the validity of buy and sell signals based on price patterns.

The first technique – which involves the use of an auxiliary price index – was first introduced by Charles Dow.[11] Dow likened movements in the market to the behaviour of the sea: the primary trend in the market (which lasts for at least a year) corresponds to the direction of the tide; the secondary reactions (which last for three to 13 weeks) are the waves, and movements of lesser degree are the ripples on the waves. The first tenet of Dow Theory is that a bull market is formed by a series of rising peaks and rising troughs, while a bear market is formed by falling peaks and falling troughs. The second tenet of the theory is that, as two stock indices are part of the same 'ocean', the tidal action of one must be reflected in the tidal action of the other.

A trend is therefore considered to remain intact until a reversal signal – based on an analysis of the peaks and troughs – is generated. In the first place, a reversal signal consists either of lower highs and then lower lows in what has been a rising market, or of higher lows and then higher highs in what has been a falling market. In other words, a reversal from a top will consist of an initial fall, a rally upwards to re-test the high, and then a drop beneath the low of the initial fall; while a reversal from a trough will consist of an initial rally, a setback to re-test the low, and a rally beyond the high of the first rally. These are shown in Figure 23.4.

At the same time, however, an apparent reversal signal will not be validated unless all sectors of the market are involved. Hence, a second price index, which is separate from but related to the primary index, must confirm the primary index. However, there are two possibilities: one, where the secondary and primary indices are synchronized; and two, where the secondary index diverges from the primary index at what subsequently turns out to be the re-test of the turning point for the primary index. This latter case is shown in Figure 23.5. Here, the secondary index makes a new high or low as the primary

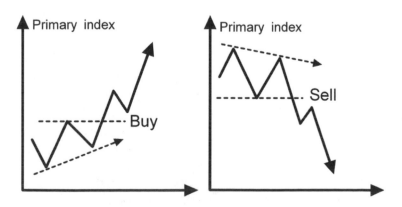

Figure 23.4 Dow Theory reversal signals

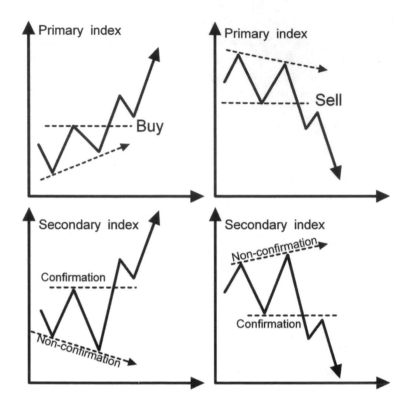

Figure 23.5 Non-confirmation and confirmation in Dow Theory

index re-tests its turning point. This is a non-confirmation. Then, the reversal signal is generated when the secondary and primary indices both move beyond the extremes of the preceding contra- (old) trend corrections. At this stage, the secondary index need not have established a series of rising peaks and troughs (for a bull) or falling peaks and troughs (for a bear).

Quite obviously, these reversal patterns conform to the three-wave archetype that has been explored in earlier chapters. Equally obvious, however, is the fact that the emergence of a three-wave pattern may complete a contra-trend move, rather than signal a change in trend. Dow Theory deals with this problem by paying attention to volumes and by ensuring that the waves that are being tracked are of the correct order of magnitude. Often there will be a high-volume event just prior to the ultimate high or low, and/or during the re-test of the high or low. There should then be a pick-up in volumes as the reversal signal is given. In addition, for a signal to be valid, the time elapse of the initial fall from a high, or rally from a low, must be between three and 13 weeks – never shorter, and seldom longer.

By tradition, Dow Theory buy and sell signals are generated by reference to the Dow Jones Industrial Average and the Dow Jones Transportation Index. A buy signal is shown in Figure 23.6. Industrials reached the low of their massive 2000–02 bear market in October 2002. Transports also made a low at the same time. Both markets then rallied but, when Industrials reached the end of their re-test of the low in March 2003, Transports actually fell to new lows. This was a non-confirmation. However a non-confirmation is not, in itself, a signal: Industrials could, at a later stage, have followed Transports to new low ground. In the event, a buy signal was given on 4 June 2003, when Industrials closed above the peak of their November 2002 rally high. Transports had already risen above their previous contra-trend rally high on 2 May 2003.

The main criticism of Dow Theory is that the signals it provides are very late. However, their importance lies in the fact that they are usually very accurate: an apparent reversal in only one index is often aborted if it is not confirmed by the second index, and a confirmed buy or sell signal indicates that all sections of the market are participating in the move.

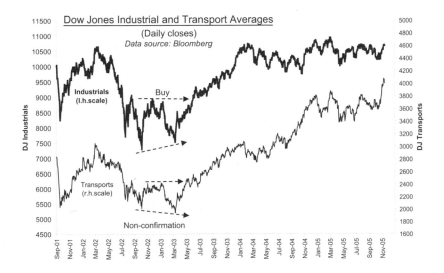

Figure 23.6 Full Dow Theory buy signal

THE PRINCIPLE OF DIRECT CONFIRMATION: OTHER INDICES

Similar conclusions can be drawn from the use of sentiment indicators. If volume, open interest and/or momentum start to confirm a price movement immediately after a price reversal, the reversal is likely to be important. In particular, a sharp change in momentum (to the extent of either becoming very overbought or very oversold very quickly) strongly suggests that the limit cycle relating prices to sentiment has reversed.

CONCLUSION

Let us now summarize the conclusions of this important chapter. The limit cycle relationship between prices and sentiment postulates that a price trend is essentially intact while confidence is improving and the majority of stocks are participating in that trend. Confidence may be represented by a number of different analytical tools, of which the most popular are volume, open interest and momentum. Hence, a trend is intact while all these indicators are still increasing. Such changes are supportive: increasing dealing activity and accelerating momentum (whether up or down) are healthy indications of profits being taken, bad positions being closed and new positions being opened. Sooner or later, however, the confidence indicators will reach excessive levels (often in a surge) that cannot be sustained. They will therefore subsequently tend to contract, even though prices continue to trend. This contraction is strong evidence that an energy gap is appearing. It is therefore non-confirming: prices will need to undergo a contra-trend correction as the overbought or oversold conditions are unwound.

This contra-trend correction may either be swift and temporary or the first stage of a more serious reversal pattern. In either case, the price levels associated with the original overbought or oversold condition will always be re-tested to some degree. If the re-test takes the market to new highs or lows, then the original trend will remain intact unless volume, open interest and momentum are unable to respond. If, on the other hand, the re-test falls short of the initial price turning point, then the market is potentially very vulnerable to a more extended reversal. Hence, either a non-confirmed new high or low (or an unsuccessful re-test) becomes the second stage of the reversal process. The third stage is a dramatic thrust in the direction of the new trend.

These conclusions will cover the majority of situations that investors will meet. There are, however, three other techniques that can be used to ensure against major errors:

■ First, remember that volume and open interest are essentially short-term indicators. It is therefore useful to track at least one long-term indicator.

■ Second, financial markets respond to the influence of the golden ratio and tend to reverse when these influences come into effect; golden ratio-defined price targets may be used to confirm the conclusions from other methods.

■ Third, the impact of limit cycles implies that markets contain a rhythmic beat within their oscillation mechanisms. Cycle analyses may therefore be used to pinpoint the moments in time when excesses of sentiment may be expected to occur. It is therefore to the concepts of golden ratio constraints and time cycles that we next turn.

NOTES

1. An alternative measure is the ratio of puts to calls in the options market. A high ratio reflects a large percentage of open bear positions, and a low ratio reflects a large percentage of open bull positions. The analysis of this chapter can be applied to the put:call ratio.
2. In a normal re-test, the concept of non-confirmation does not apply.
3. There is an important point here that is often missed. Volume and open interest analysis is only applicable to relatively short-term market conditions. It is possible, therefore, to pinpoint long-term reversals only because of an accurate interpretation of the short-term. It is not valid to compare today's open interest or volume with that which occurred, say, two years ago. The market structure is likely to have altered over such a time period.
4. For example, cyclical lows in the Dow Jones Industrial Averages in 1932, 1942, 1949, 1957, 1962, 1966, 1970, 1974, 1978 and 1980 occurred simultaneously with momentum lows. However, it should be added that this does not mean that the low will never be re-tested. The influence of a large cycle just means that the re-test occurs after such a significant time period that it cannot be used for short-term trading.
5. When testing for peaks, the momentum high at the top of wave 3 should be achieved with an RSI of 80 or more. The market will then correct for the overbought condition and the RSI will fall. Prices and the RSI will both subsequently rise again as wave B (the Elliott fifth wave) comes into force. Prices will move into new high ground but the RSI will not. The same argument applies in reverse, of course, when testing for market lows. The momentum low, usually at the end of wave C, should be achieved with an RSI of 20 or less.

The market will then correct for the oversold condition and both prices and the RSI will rise. The subsequent price fall will take the market to a new low, but it will not be confirmed by the RSI.

6.   It is necessary here to be very aware of the relevant degree of pulse that is being traded. If a high-level up trend is in force, the trader should ignore short-term overbought conditions and buy short-term oversold conditions; conversely for a high-level down trend.

7.   The classic work is Wilder, J Wells (1976) *New Concepts in Technical Trading Systems*, Trend Research, Greensboro, South Carolina.

8.   Elder, Alexander (1993) *Trading for a Living*, John Wiley, New York. In my opinion, this is one of the best books on the fundamental applications of technical analysis on the market.

9.   That is, +DI will probably give a non-confirmation at the peak of a bull move, and the –DI will give a non-confirmation at the bottom of a bear move.

10.   Limited, that is, within the context of the hierarchical level being analysed. The last wave of a supercycle pulse may remain unconfirmed for years.

11.   Rhea, Robert (1932) *Dow Theory*, Vail-Ballou, New York.

Part Four

The trader at work

24

The psychology of fear

INTRODUCTION

The foregoing chapters have developed two specific themes relating to financial markets:

▌ group psychology can be used to explain the existence of systemic, non-chaotic order in financial market prices;

▌ as a consequence, technical analysis is an entirely valid method of anticipating future price action.

However, it is one thing to demonstrate the value of technical analysis; it is quite another to convert that information into effective, profitable trading. The difficulty stems from two unavoidable aspects of human psychology. The first is that, no matter how careful an investor has been in analysing a particular market, there is always the possibility that something has been missed. There is, therefore, uncertainty, and uncertainty means that a trader will inevitably experience some degree of anxiety or at least be open to the possibility of experiencing anxiety.

The second problem is that investors tend to identify themselves with their trading positions. That is, their sense of self-esteem and personal well-being become intimately bound up with whether or not the positions make profits or losses. In the case of profits, the associated emotional pleasure is usually considered to be part of the benefits of success; but it is a corollary of this attitude that losses automatically involve a great deal of emotional turmoil. There is therefore a danger that, in the face of any losses, natural low-level anxiety caused by uncertainty will develop into fear. And fear (as demonstrated in Chapter 7) is likely to drive the trader straight into the arms of the crowd.

For most people, therefore, it is impossible to maintain an effective trading performance over long periods of time if high levels of fear and, in turn, stress are being experienced. Sooner or later, the physical and psychological effects will either undermine the individual's health or it will begin to encourage serious trading errors. In both cases, the only logical outcome will be a cessation of trading – whether temporarily or permanently.

A commitment to the use of objective entry and exit signals is a necessary condition for successful trading and investment insofar as it limits the influence of the crowd. However, this commitment is not a sufficient condition. The difficulty is that any system that allows a trader literally to see the recent move in prices automatically exposes that trader to the essential catalyst of the crowd mentality – namely moving prices themselves. It is therefore also necessary for market participants to be able to deal with the psychological damage – whether actual or potential – that accompanies risk-taking. This chapter therefore examines in more detail some of the appropriate methods of limiting fear and of controlling stress while trading.

THE SUBCONSCIOUS MIND

Many people make the mistake of entering financial markets without any objective other than to 'make lots of money'. While quite commendable in itself, such an objective cannot activate the psychological (and physical) mechanisms that contribute to success. Quite simply, the objective of making money means nothing to that part of the mind – the subconscious – which is fundamental to the successful completion of any task that we try to set ourselves.

Our knowledge of the processes that take place within the human mind is, to say the least, incomplete. This is particularly true of the area that is generally referred to as the subconscious – that is, the part of the mind that is beneath[1] (or behind) the conscious mind. The difficulty is that, although we know the subconscious mind is there, we cannot usually access it directly during the course of our ordinary waking lives. Its purpose is to make our regular behaviour as automatic as possible, so that our awareness is free to focus on new information.[2] For example, once a child has learnt to walk, the processes are relegated to the subconscious so that it becomes increasingly unnecessary to concentrate on the actual act of walking. The mind is then freed-up to concentrate on other things. Insofar as it is possible to measure these things, scientists think that the subconscious accordingly accounts for as much as 97 per cent of our mental activity. This is a staggering figure.

The subconscious is, at its most basic, the storehouse for everything that we have ever experienced. However, it is far more than just a memory bank that can be accessed by the computer-like processing properties of the so-called 'logical' part of our mind. It has its own dynamic, linked into the psychosomatic and autonomic nervous systems[3] of the human body, and it profoundly influences our lives with its continuous stream of instructions and imperatives. It has its own objectives – primarily linked to the survival of the physical and psychological matrix of the individual[4] – and unless it is properly instructed to accommodate new purposes, it will instead tend to protect the integrity of its old learnt purposes against any new ones. In short, we are highly unlikely to be able to achieve our own personal objectives unless we can enlist the help of our subconscious. We have to teach the subconscious to accept change.

THE ROLE OF HABITS

The key to understanding the difficulties of initiating change is to understand the role of subconscious habits, particularly defensive ones. Habits are learnt mental, emotional and behavioural patterns that are consistently reproduced in response to specific stimuli. It will be remembered from Chapter 9 that there is a distinct three-phase process to learning. The same process applies to habit formation: an individual responds to a challenge by finding a coping strategy; if the strategy 'works', it eventually becomes embedded in the subconscious; and it is then automatically invoked each time a relevant stimulus occurs. The famous example of Pavlov's dogs is a good case in point. Generally, the purpose of a habit (as with any learnt behaviour) is to minimize energy and free-up the mind to deal with other matters, such as learning something new. However, there are two specific problems with habits: they may be inappropriate to current circumstances and they interfere with the individual's ability to develop alternative strategies.[5]

This is particularly the case with habits that are carried over from childhood. For most people, external behaviour patterns are gradually modified by social interaction, so that early habits are dispersed and replaced. However, there is one area where modification is very, very difficult. This is the area of emotional arousal in response to a perceived threat. The original threat may have been actual or illusory; nevertheless, it would have been treated as real. The brain and sympathetic nervous system then easily lay down pathways through the relatively untrained neuro-physiological network of the child. These pathways are subsequently the easiest to trigger. We shall say a little more about this in the next chapter, where we shall deal with the range of psychological responses to the threats implicit in market fluctuations. Here, however, it just needs to be registered that the first major threat faced by a child (which is almost always to do with their recognition of separateness from the mother) starts to lay down a pattern of automatic and inflexible responses that continue into adult life. The programming therefore begins at an age that is beyond the scope of natural memory recall. Even those who can become aware of the automatic nature of their responses may not find their origin. However, the real tragedy is that most of us are not even aware of these responses in the first place; and, even if we are aware of them, we consider them to be 'natural'. Needless to say, these responses are more than likely to be inappropriate.

THE RESPONSE TO A THREAT

As we saw in Chapter 2, whenever a threat is encountered, the amygdala starts to prepare the nervous system[6] for 'flight or fight'. Under some circumstances, the structure of the mind does appear to allow the forebrain some control over responses.[7] However, that control is dangerously limited. Prior to some individual-specific boundary (largely determined in childhood), the control applies mainly to external responses, but does not deal with the emotions that the amygdala triggers. Beyond the individual-specific boundary, the body receives an injection of adrenalin and enters a full state of threat alert.

Obviously, a great deal can go wrong within this sequence of events. Even a low-level threat will trigger the essence of any habitual emotional response that an individual may have. A higher-level threat will generate a strong emotional arousal, even if the associated physical behaviour is controlled. Unfortunately, failure to use the adrenalin by acting results in a build-up of unresolved tension (stress). Finally, a real shock will spontaneously trigger a full-blooded 'fight or flight' reaction, demanding of a full physical response. This latter response will be a very simple combination of body-oriented instinct and reference-group regulated action.[8,9] Whether it is fight or flight that is the 'path of least resistance', the adrenalin will be used.

STRESS

If we translate these comments into the context of a financial market, it is likely that, at any one moment, large numbers of traders and investors will be experiencing either low-level anxiety because of the continuous threat of making a mistake or stress because a mistake has been made but offsetting physical (that is, dealing) action has not yet occurred. At any one moment in time, then, there is likely to be a great deal of unresolved tension. For each individual, this is likely to be represented by one or more of a number of well-defined physical or psychological symptoms, some of which are shown in Table 24.1.

Table 24.1 Symptoms of stress

Physical	*Psychological*
Shallow breathing	Irritability
Rapid breathing	Loss of self-esteem
Tightness in chest	Inability to concentrate
Sweaty palms	Loss of sexual desire
Clenched rear teeth	Loss of memory
Stomach problems	Nameless fears
Tense muscles	Substance dependency

These symptoms are also likely to be accompanied by negative (that is, unpleasant) emotions of one sort or another. There are, of course, a large number of such emotions that may be experienced, but the most common ones that a trader is likely to experience and have to cope with are fear, anger, frustration, embarrassment and depression. Such emotions use up valuable energy and divert attention away from the solutions to the problem.

THE INFLUENCE OF EMOTIONS

The subject of emotions is actually a very complicated one and any presentation will inevitably oversimplify matters. It is, however, important that a trader has at least an elementary knowledge of the forces at work because, as we shall see, some degree of self-awareness is an important part of the success programme. The main hurdle is that our Western culture does not freely recognize the influence – or even validity – of emotions, particularly in men. Indeed, the situation is so dire that huge numbers of people will, in all honesty, deny that emotions – let alone anxieties – play any role in their decision-making processes. As the analysis evolves, however, it is hoped that the underlying realities will become a little clearer.

Emotions are motivating energies – a 'giving out', as it were. They are invariably aimed at an object. Further, they give meaning to our existence[10] – life without emotions would be no life at all. Emotions are therefore the primary determinants of the what, the how and the why of all activity. This is shown in more detail in Figure 24.1. First, of course, information from the environment is perceived by an individual. Second, it is automatically categorized and placed in a context. This context is the person's beliefs about the structure of the world and about their own function in it. Third, the process of categorization arouses an emotional response. Fourth, the emotions focus energy on a limited number of learnt responses. Fifth, consciousness finally enters the process and helps to determine the appropriate way of carrying out the learnt response.

Figure 24.1 emphasizes the point already made, that the process of stimulus–response is largely handled by the subconscious. In other words, the broad strategy for dealing with a challenge is formed within the subconscious part of the mind. It is only after this point that consciousness enters the process to determine the details of any response. The subconscious mind determines the strategy, the conscious mind determines the tactics.[11]

This means that the widespread conviction that behaviour is consciously determined, and that emotions are therefore only the 'fall-out' from the process, is essentially false. This would probably not matter very much if the process was just an interesting topic for debate among academics. However, the process is actually about the way people understand the world; and if the understanding is at fault, then it follows that the response is likely to be inappropriate.[12] It is this simple fact that explains so much: inappropriate responses result in unexpected outcomes; and unexpected outcomes, in turn, create negative emotions and stress.

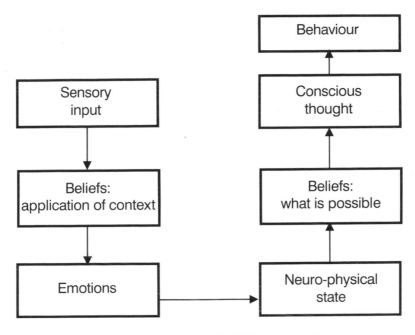

Figure 24.1 The role of beliefs and emotions

BELIEFS AND MEMORIES

As already described, the automatic release of mental energy, which is triggered by the initial stimulus, is filtered through a set of learnt beliefs. Beliefs give meaning to the stimulus. They are the accumulated memories acquired during the processes of socialization, academic learning and personal experience. Furthermore, memories – almost by definition – have emotions attached to them. Memories are, in a sense, the 'bricks' from which our personalities are constructed and emotions are the 'cement' that bind them together. Hence, the stimulus of 'information in context' will activate the emotions that are associated – singly, or in a blend – with the context itself. These emotions may range from being passive and almost imperceptible (such as feelings of comfort) to being active and totally explicit (such as a feeling of blind anger). Whatever their strength, however, the result is that – as emotions are psychosomatic phenomena involving the whole nervous system – a person literally becomes the emotion, or mix of emotions.

Once an emotional environment has been created in the psyche, it should be apparent that the number of appropriate responses becomes limited. An emotion will interact with the person's learnt beliefs about the appropriate way to respond to the original information. For example, anger might find an outlet through either verbal or physical channels, depending on the outcome of previous experiences. The real problem, however, is that the closer an emotion gets to one of the primary ones relating to instincts,[13] the narrower the range of behavioural options becomes. Hence, if the 'fight' emotion is triggered, the 'love' emotion is automatically excluded.

These observations may now be applied to the simple example of a trader who is suddenly confronted by an unexpected change in prices (see Figure 24.2). The first thing that happens is that the unexpected price move is placed into the trader's 'habit of trading' belief system. In other words, the trader recognizes the existence of a missed opportunity or of an unexpected loss. There will immediately be a trace of anxiety.[14,15] If the price movement is a particularly large one, so that the implications are important, the trader is likely to experience fear – either the fear of missing further profits or the fear of making increased losses. The only possible reactions are either to resist the message implicit in the price move (that is, that the adverse trend may continue) or to accept the implications and do something about it. This is a moderate version of the 'fight' or 'flight' response. If the former

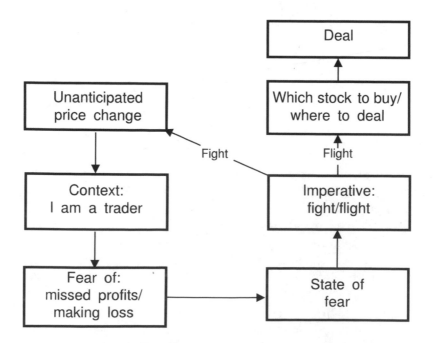

Figure 24.2 The impact of emotions in trading

(that is, the 'fight') response is chosen, then there is obviously a risk that the process is going to continue. In the face of a developing trend, the individual trader is likely to become wound up like a spring until, finally, the 'flight' route is chosen. Only then, when the emotion of fear has finally forced the trader to deal, will consciousness be released to decide which stock will be traded and which broker will be used!

CONCLUSION

The purpose of this chapter has been to emphasize the roles of both the subconscious and of emotions in all our activities. The influence of the subconscious mind means that a great deal of our current behaviour is mechanical. In other words, much of what we do consists of automatic responses to specific stimuli. The advantage of this is that current challenges can be dealt with using a combination of acquired skills, assimilated knowledge and sympathetic biological responses. The problem, however, is that an automatic response is triggered by accessing an associated, emotionally charged memory of some kind. These emotional memories involve instinctual drives, racial, national and family histories, and any previous painful experiences. The emergence of a current emotion may therefore trigger reactions that are no longer appropriate, even though they are based on similar past emotions.

Inappropriate reactions are most likely to occur under conditions that generate anxiety and fear. Our basic reactions to anxiety have usually been programmed into our psyches at a very young age, and most of us are not even aware of them because they are outside of our memory recall. Anxiety is easily triggered once contact is made with trading and investment positions in financial markets. We shall look at this in more detail in the next chapter.

NOTES

1.   The use of the word 'beneath' accords with accepted usage. However, it is more correct to understand the subconscious as being the context within which the conscious mind operates. Furthermore, in terms of motive power, the subconscious is far more powerful than the conscious mind. Research suggests that the subconscious mind accounts for about 97 per cent of the mind's total activity.

2.   The conscious mind appears to be able to keep track of only seven items of information at a time. This implies that the conscious mind is unable to cope with an infinitely complicated world by itself – hence the indispensability of

the subconscious. See Miller, George, *The Magic Number Seven, Plus or Minus Two*, quoted in O'Connor, Joseph, and Seymour, John (1990) *Introducing Neuro-linguistic Programming*, Mandala, London.

3. The psychosomatic nervous system deals with skeletal, muscular and sensory activity. The autonomic nervous system regulates the respiratory, circulatory and other internal organ systems.

4. This incorporates the influences of the individual's particular reference group. The subconscious will contain the belief system of the reference group and will therefore be triggered by a threat to the whole group.

5. The power of habit is partly related to age. When we are young, we are very open to learning. As we become older, we become less open and more rigid: change becomes more difficult to accept.

6. That is, the 'sympathetic' part of the autonomic nervous system, which is linked into the brain stem (see Chapter 2). The sympathetic system stimulates the body by means of the release of adrenalin. This part of the nervous system is to be differentiated from the 'parasympathetic' part of the system, which helps to create calmness by releasing relaxing endorphins.

7. Goleman, Daniel (1996) *Emotional Intelligence*, Bloomsbury, London.

8. An individual threatened by muggers in an alleyway might respond by running away. In a military battle, however, the same individual would likely fight alongside fellow combatants.

9. The point is that the neocortex does not necessarily step in either to control the responses or to re-imagine the external world. Indeed, once primal passions have been aroused, the neocortex may become an active participant in the process because its imaginings can validate and intensify the original emotional response. Out of this specific weakness in the neocortex is born such obscene horrors as human sacrifice and mass genocide.

10. Wilber, Ken (1996) *A Brief History of Everything*, Gill & Macmillan, Dublin, Eire.

11. Obviously, some emotions are more conducive than others to allow conscious thought to operate effectively: a passive sense of well-being, for example, is more likely to accommodate effective communication between people than is, say, an active feeling of anger. The former allows for the wide use of language, reason and intuition, while the latter may tend only to allow a limited range of verbal abuse!

12. This is precisely the criticism that can be levelled against modern economic models – particularly when they are used for economic policy targeting.

13. There is not complete agreement about the set of emotions that can be regarded as primal or instinctive. However, a general list includes fear, anger, lust or joy, sadness, acceptance, trust, disgust, expectancy, anticipation, astonishment and surprise. These emotions correlate with eight fundamental adaptive behaviour patterns that are directed towards survival and reproductive continuity. See Plutchick, Robert (1980) *Emotions: A psychoevolutionary synthesis*, Harper & Row, New York.

14. Other things being equal, that is. The feelings being experienced when the act of perception takes place are of great importance. A person in an open, accepting state will tend to view a reduced range of information as a threat. On the other hand, a person in a closed, isolated state will tend to view a significantly wider range of events as being a threat.

15. There is, in all of us, a basic, deep-rooted belief in the unchanging nature of the world. Our expectations are based on this belief. If outcomes do not match expectations, the implication is that something has changed. This causes anxiety.

25

The troubled trader[1]

INTRODUCTION

The previous chapter pointed the way towards a basic model of personal investment behaviour that starts from a condition of anxiety and progressively winds itself up into high-level fear. Once anxiety begins to roll forward for any reason, it has the potential to create inappropriate actions. Inappropriate actions then result in unexpected, or unwanted, outcomes, which, in turn, create further anxiety. Eventually, the anxiety becomes fear. Persistent anxiety and fear, as we have seen, result in individuals turning to a reference group – in this case, the financial market crowd – for support. Immersion in the crowd reduces an individual's anxiety,[2] but increases the likelihood of major losses.

To be successful in trading and investment, an individual therefore needs to be able to ensure that the vicious circle of anxiety and inappropriate actions does not get a hold. As previously mentioned, one important part of the process is the use of objective entry and exit rules. The other part, however, involves direct management of personal psychological states so that the integrative tendency is not triggered. This is difficult to do, but any countervailing action is better than none.

The first step towards confronting the effects of anxiety was effectively covered in the preceding chapter. This is simply to recognize that the danger exists. The second step, which we shall cover in this chapter, is to understand the specific way that anxiety influences each of us personally. To achieve this understanding, we shall look at the way that different psychological energies blend together to provide basic personality structures. The important point is that each personality 'type' is built around a very specific area of psychological vulnerability – a neurosis. And the third step, which we shall cover in the next chapter, is to implement a strategy for neutralizing the effects of anxiety before it becomes a threat.

THE THREE-PART MIND

In Chapter 2, we discussed Paul Maclean's concept of a triune brain, consisting of the brain stem, the limbic system and the neocortex. In essence, the brain stem deals with instinct, the limbic system deals with emotions and the neocortex handles thought.[3] The first point to make here is that the human mind is dependent on all three parts of the triune brain. The mind is a self-organizing system, just like any other part of nature, and it therefore simultaneously controls, coordinates and consists of the three functions of instinct, emotions and thought.

The second, related point is that, according to analysts such as Oscar Ichazo and Claudio Naranjo,[4] the psychology of each individual is constructed from a blend of these three functions. However, there is strong evidence that there are very subtle differences in the way that we each use them. Hence, some of us are biased towards instinctual activity, others are regarded as being motivated by feelings or emotions and yet others are seen as being thought oriented. It is not always possible to recognize these biases without careful analysis, but, whether they are obvious or not, they do help to determine the essential nature of the personality that we present to the world. Please note that this does not imply any value judgements; it just means that each of us has a bias towards one particular type of motivational energy and away from at least one of the others.

THE PSYCHOLOGICAL MATRIX

While each of us certainly tends to use one aspect of our three psychological areas more than the other two parts, the evidence also suggests that there is an important subsidiary influence involving the other two parts. This suggests that we can define basic psychological matrices in terms of ranked combinations of the biases noted above. Hence, if we denoted each of the separate motivations by a number – 1 for instinct,

2 for emotions and 3 for thinking – we should then be able to designate character traits in terms of numerical combinations, such as 1–2–3, 2–3–1 and so on.

However, the process of determining these numerical combinations is somewhat complicated. First, some people are undoubtedly so dominated by their central motivation of instinct, feeling or thinking that the concept of a 'combination' becomes largely redundant. In these cases, only one descriptive number is relevant. Furthermore, it needs to be emphasized here that, as we are dealing with mechanical behaviour, we are referring to the negative aspect of each of the central drives. Hence, instinct tends to be slothful, feelings tend not to be authentic and based towards image needs, and thinking tends to be a refuge from fear.

Second, where motivations operate more clearly in combination, the 'trailing' motivation (the third number in each combination) is usually so weak that it is only relevant in so far as it identifies a definite imbalance. In these cases, we may as well omit the third number from the combination, leaving just two numbers.

We are therefore going to denote each character 'structure' either by a single number or by a double number. The first step, of course, is to collate the relevant number combinations and, in order to do so, we shall use Figure 25.1. In this diagram, each of the three numbers is placed at one of the corners of a triangle, starting with the number 1 at the top.

BASIC PERSONALITY TYPES

Moving clockwise from the top of the triangle, and bearing in mind our earlier comments, we can make three combinations – 1–2, 2–3 and 3–1. Moving counter-clockwise, we can make another three – 1–3, 3–2 and 2–1. If we then include the solitary numbers, we have another three – 1, 2 and 3. We have therefore arrived at a limited set of nine single paired numbers. These combinations can be arranged into groups as follows:

∎ 1–3 for those who are instinctive, but are also influenced by thought;

∎ 1 for the instinctive;

∎ 1–2 for those who are instinctive, but are also influenced by emotions;

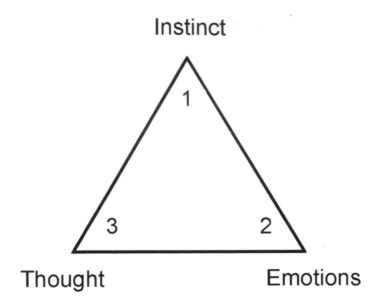

Figure 25.1 The psychological triad

▌ 2–1 for those who are emotional, but are also influenced by instincts;

▌ 2 for those people who are emotional;

▌ 2–3 for those who are emotional, but are also influenced by thought;

▌ 3–2 for those who are thoughtful, but are also influenced by emotions;

▌ 3 for those who are thoughtful;

▌ 3–1 for those who are thoughtful, but are also influenced by instincts.

PRIMARY BEHAVIOURAL CHARACTERISTICS

The second step is to isolate the primary behavioural characteristics of each of these combinations in order to understand what they actually mean in practice. This has been done in Table 25.1. In the area of instinct, the bias involves attitudes towards relationships with the external world. These people are literally 'gut-oriented'. In the area of emotions, the bias relates to feelings. These people are 'heart-oriented'. Finally, in the area of thinking, the bias involves the attitude to action in the world. These individuals are 'head-oriented'. The question now is what these combinations might be saying about someone. What does it mean to be a 1–2-type person or a 3–2-type person?

Table 25.1 Primary behavioural characteristics

Type	Character	Bias
1–3	Instinctive–thoughtful	Overdeveloped relating
1	Instinctive	Out of touch with relating
1–2	Instinctive–emotional	Underdeveloped relating
2–1	Emotional–instinctive	Overdeveloped feeling
2	Emotional	Out of touch with feeling
2–3	Emotional–thoughtful	Underdeveloped feeling
3–2	Thoughtful–emotional	Underdeveloped activity
3	Thoughtful	Out of touch with activity
3–1	Thoughtful–instinctive	Overdeveloped activity

THE GUT-ORIENTED PERSONALITY

Let us look first at the people whose number combination starts with a 1. These are the instinctive, or 'gut'-oriented, people.

The 1–3 people have an overdeveloped willingness to relate to the external world, but their feelings about themselves and their relationships are underdeveloped. They are likely to be self-confident and forceful, and they organize and lead. However, they may be aggressive, sometimes to the point of being destructive.

The 1 people tend to be out of touch with, or unaware of, the way that they relate to their environment. Such people tend to be peaceable and reassuring. However, if they feel threatened, they may withdraw their attention from the threat in order to suppress feelings of anger.

The 1–2 people are going to have an underdeveloped ability to relate flexibly to the world. They are therefore likely to be principled and orderly, responding to the world's requirements. However, they are also likely to have very strong feelings about the need for order and can, therefore, be perfectionists and punitive towards others.

THE HEART-ORIENTED PERSONALITY

Let us now move on to people whose number combination begins with a 2. These are the 'heart'-oriented people, who are defined by the way that their feelings are engaged.

The 2–1 people will have overdeveloped feelings, but their instinctual behaviour tends to be a limiting factor. They will be caring and generous (although potentially possessive and manipulative). If they feel wronged, they may cut off a relationship altogether in order to avoid negative feelings.

The 2 people are out of touch with feelings. Feelings tend to be suspended, while the immediate task is being concluded. These individuals tend to be self-assured and competitive. Under pressure, however, they can be self-centred and hostile.

The 2–3 people will have underdeveloped feelings in the sense that they will not express them directly. Such people tend to express themselves indirectly and therefore tend to be artistic, creative and intuitive. They feel that they are special in some way. However, they can also tend to be introverted and depressive.

THE HEAD-ORIENTED PERSONALITY

Finally, we come to those whose number combination begins with a 3. These are the thinkers, who are 'head'-oriented and who may therefore be defined in terms of their attitude towards activity.

The 3–2 people have an underdeveloped ability to do things. This is not surprising given their neglect of the instinctive functions. Such people tend to be perceptive and analytical in their approach to the world, but they also tend to be somewhat eccentric and, when under pressure, paranoid.

The 3 people are out of touch with doing. That is, they accept without question that activity is required of them. Individuals with this structure are dutiful and likeable. They are also dependent on others and, under pressure, may be self-destructive.

The 3–1 people have a tendency to rush about because their ability to do things is overdeveloped. They spend a lot of time planning future pleasures and are usually accomplished in the sense of having a broad experience of life. However, they can also be very impulsive and somewhat excessive.

THE CHINK IN THE EGO'S ARMOUR

It is, of course, always dangerous to try and place precise labels on human nature. Indeed, the human psyche, when viewed correctly, is actually a process, not a structure. However, the process in each of us tends to get 'stuck', or becomes sluggish, around certain important areas. At some stage – usually before the age of six – we confront our separateness in the world. As Oscar Ichazo puts it, 'a contradiction develops between the inner feelings of the child and the outer social reality to which he must conform'.[5] The resulting trauma then sets up a centre of gravity within the psyche that, in turn, becomes the 'deep-structure' centre around which our personality constellates. According to Mr Ichazo's work, there are only nine possible gravity centres and each, quite simply, is the emotional memory of the trauma and package of responses that the young child used to deal with it.

The result is that the psyche will thereafter always be on the look-out for threats that are similar to the initial, archetypal one. And it will always react with the same distinct package of learnt responses whenever that archetypal threat is encountered. Importantly, however, not only does the psyche tend to react to all conditions of anxiety as if they were similar to the initial trauma, but the automatic nature of the responses is not clearly recognized. If we are aware of them at all, we see the responses as a strength, because they have served us so well in the past.

In fact, however, the responses are also our central weakness. It is absolutely essential to understand this in the context of financial markets. Our automatic responses ensure that we each have a vulnerable spot within our psyches. Financial markets will seek out that vulnerable spot with unerring accuracy and, accordingly, trigger automatic and self-defeating behaviours. It is therefore worth while taking a little time to define these weak spots and the likely response mechanisms in more detail. Then we will have taken a big step towards doing something about them.

BASIC MOTIVATIONS

So, next, we can observe that each character structure has, as it were, two aspects:

▌ a defensive focus of attention;

▌ a likely mode of response to a perceived threat.

In other words, each character trait is like a coordinated radar and weapon response system. It surveys the environment for threat and then responds with an automatic mechanical reaction if a threat is identified. These two extra dimensions to the character traits are shown in Table 25.2.

Table 25.2 Character types and basic motivations

Type	Character	Focus of attention	Response to threat
1–3	Instinctive–thoughtful	Protection	Aggression
1	Instinctive	of	or
1–2	Instinctive–emotional	personal space	withdrawal
2–1	Emotional–instinctive	Protection	Hostility
2	Emotional	of	or
2–3	Emotional–thoughtful	ego	deception
3–2	Thoughtful–emotional	Minimization	Anxiety
3	Thoughtful	of	or
3–1	Thoughtful–instinctive	fear	pretence

The word 'threat' can, of course, mean a number of things. It can, for example, mean a direct physical threat. Here, however, it means a psychological threat. Such a threat is experienced when there is a divergence between expectations (derived from subconscious beliefs) and actual outcomes. In financial markets, therefore, a threat is perceived if expectations of profit are not met. The resultant stress is likely to energize one of a number of possible automatic or compulsive responses.

AVOIDANCE COMPULSIONS

Let us therefore move to the next stage by indicating the details of these compulsions. These are shown in Table 25.3. There is a different compulsion associated with each type of character structure. Each compulsion makes us avoid a particular condition or situation. Hence, for example, a 1–3 person will try to avoid being seen to be weak, while a 3–1 individual will seek to avoid physical or psychological pain.

Table 25.3 Character types and basic avoidance compulsions

Type	Character	Avoids
1–3	Instinctive–thoughtful	Being seen to be weak
1	Instinctive	Getting involved in conflict
1–2	Instinctive–emotional	Any form of imperfection
2–1	Emotional–instinctive	Not being liked/recognized/loved
2	Emotional	Failing in chosen tasks
2–3	Emotional–thoughtful	Being just an ordinary person
3–2	Thoughtful–emotional	Having insufficient data about life
3	Thoughtful	Making any wrong decisions
3–1	Thoughtful–instinctive	Physical or psychological pain

RESPONSE STRATEGIES

The question now arises as to what strategies each individual will adopt when faced with a situation that energizes their avoidance compulsion. That is, what happens when an individual feels threatened?

For each type of person, there is a specific initial defensive response they will make once a perceived threat is encountered. These are shown in Table 25.4. In very general terms, the instinct-oriented people will have to deal with the actual or potential emergence of anger; the feeling-oriented people will have to deal with an impact on their self-esteem; and the thought-oriented people will have to cope with the actual or potential emergence of fear. Hence, for example, a 1–3 individual will avoid being seen to be weak by fighting the source of the threat.

Table 25.4 Initial responses to threats

Type	Avoids	Initial response to threat
1–3	Being seen to be weak	Fight the situation
1	Getting involved in conflict	Withdrawal
1–2	Any form of imperfection	Anger – usually suppressed
2–1	Not being liked/recognized/loved	Dented pride
2	Failing in chosen tasks	Pretend that all's OK
2–3	Being just an ordinary person	Envy the success of others
3–2	Having insufficient data about life	Mental retreat
3	Making any wrong decisions	Fear
3–1	Physical or psychological pain	Make plans to retrieve situation

It is important to be clear that these are basic, or 'core', reactions. Each one will invariably be associated with other responses as part of a reaction 'matrix'. However, each core reaction constitutes a driving force for someone in any situation that is perceived to be a threat. Essentially, we all have a fundamental strategy to avoid the situation that has caused us the most psychological pain in our early lives and every time we are again confronted with one of these situations, we have a deeply ingrained physical, emotional and mental strategy for dealing with the problem.

SOME AWKWARD PERSONAL QUESTIONS

Each person could – with a little introspection – determine their own particular character type from these lists. The reward would be some astounding insights into personal motivations. As a start, it may be helpful to look at the following list of questions. Each question, from 1 to 9, corresponds to one of the personality types shown above. The different variations within each character type are far from complete, so the list only gives an indication of the responses involved. Nevertheless, the questions pinpoint some of the main characteristics of the different types.

If you already participate in markets, simply ask yourself: when I am confronted with a significant loss on an investment position, how do I normally react? If you do not yet trade, ask yourself: when I am confronted with a serious problem, how do I normally react? You should find that you can answer 'yes' to more than one of the questions. However, one of the questions is likely to define very precisely the reaction that matches you best. It will be the reaction that occurs most frequently, but, be warned, it may also be the one that you least wish to admit applies to you.

1. Do you feel an aggressive need to organize something, such as your desk, drawers or other people's behaviour? Alternatively, do you feel very sure that something else nasty is just about to happen but you don't know what it is, and so you don't know what to do? (1–2)

2. Do you feel that the market has let you down and that you don't want anything more to do with it? Alternatively, do you feel like a failure and tend to withdraw from people so that they won't criticize you? (2–1)

3. Do you carry on as if nothing has happened, feeling that it's going to be OK next time? Alternatively, do you feel that things are not quite right, but pretend that things are great? (2)

4. Do you feel that you've made a mess of it yet again and, perhaps, want a drink to avoid getting depressed? Alternatively, do you start to fantasize about winning the lottery? (2–3)

5. Do you ignore the market and concentrate instead on carrying out a piece of research? Alternatively, do you arrange meetings and lunches with contacts or brokers? (3–2)

6. Do you feel cold inside and wish you were somewhere else? Alternatively, do you simply feel that things are going to get very much worse? (3)

7. Do you ignore the immediate problem and start looking for signals or fundamental economic relationships that will ensure you get it right next time? Alternatively, do you think that you're totally inadequate for the job? (3–1)

8. Do you want to break something, throw the telephone down or even hit someone? Alternatively, do you want to make someone else do something they don't want to do? (1–3)

9. Do you feel amazingly relaxed when something goes wrong and wonder what others are making a fuss about? Alternatively, do you just feel like looking after your own needs 'for a change'? (1)

THE THREAT FROM FINANCIAL MARKETS

Now let us look at the situation for these nine character structures within the context of financial markets. Financial markets exhibit three specific characteristics that are relevant to us in the current context. These are that:

▌ they are moving continuously;

▌ there is an ever-present danger of losing money;

▌ they are subject to an infinite variety of influences.

The important point is that each individual is going to be particularly vulnerable to one of these three characteristics of markets – that is, every individual's defensive focus of attention (as indicated in

Table 25.2) is likely to be energized by one of these three characteristics. This will now be demonstrated with reference to Table 25.4.

FINANCIAL MARKETS AND PERSONAL SPACE

The first group of people consists of those who are primarily instinct-
oriented. They will tend to have a very acute sense of self and protect
their personal space. They will seek either to control or avoid anything
that might intrude into this space – especially other people. In order to
maintain their security, the world is mentally classified into two parts:
the part that is unchanging, and therefore unthreatening, and the part
that is active, and is therefore a potential threat.

Financial markets are moving all the time. They are full of unseen
individuals who will deal for reasons that cannot be discerned.
Instinct-oriented individuals will therefore be confronted with that
which they fear the most – namely, an uncontrollable or intrusive
environment. They will react to losses with a desire to fight the market
(1–3) or a withdrawal of attention and emotions (1) or suppressed
anger (1–2).

None of these reactions is appropriate for successful trading. First,
trying to fight the market when it goes against you boils down to
thinking that you are right and the markets are wrong. This may well
be true in the long run, but, as Lord Keynes said, in the long run, we're
all dead. Second, a withdrawal of attention in order to avoid anger
implies continuing to run bad positions, which could make things very
much worse. Eventually, a failure to take account of what has been
going on forces the individual to turn to others for help. Third, the
process of suppressing anger means that important energy resources
are going to be diverted away from coping with the market, stress is
increased and efficient trading is reduced. Ultimately, all that remains
is an overwhelming sense of inadequacy and guilt.

FINANCIAL MARKETS AND THE SELF-IMAGE

The second group of people consists of those who are driven by their
feelings. These individuals are motivated by the need to protect their
self-image and will focus attention on gaining approval from others.
Feelings of low self-esteem are generated when this approval is not
forthcoming. Unfortunately, such feelings of low self-esteem often

derive from the fact that – in Western cultures anyway – we are trained from childhood not to make mistakes. People who have responded the most actively to this sort of training are afraid to make mistakes because it makes them feel unattractive and the natural drive to find out about the world may even become suppressed.

Financial markets continuously present the danger, and the reality, of losing money. In fact, nobody can trade with a 100 per cent success record. Feeling-centred individuals will therefore invariably be confronted with that which they desire least – namely, loss-making trades. The reaction is likely to be a sense of hurt pride (2–1), a false pretence that a problem doesn't exist (2) or envy of others who are more successful (2–3).

Again, none of these reactions is conducive to successful trading in financial markets. Attention is diverted away from coping with the reality of a loss-making trade towards coping with ego problems. First, hurt pride usually triggers hostility towards the market and may involve a withdrawal from a relationship with the market. Second, ignoring the message of the loss and pretending that the position will come right may eventually force the individual to turn to others for emotional support. Third, focusing attention on the success of others, which thereby highlights one's own inadequacies, diverts attention away from solving the problem.

FINANCIAL MARKETS AND FEAR

The third group of people includes those who are characterized by thinking. Individuals in this general category are prone to experience fear very acutely and are therefore motivated by the desire to minimize fear. Such people will focus their attention on information and will be acutely aware of information that constitutes a threat. The greatest threat to security is that of making a loss and individuals who seek to avoid losses are faced with the need to analyse an almost infinite quantity of information.

Financial markets, therefore, confront thought-oriented individuals with precisely the situation they most want to avoid – namely, uncertainty. The result is that they will delay making decisions for as long as possible (3–2), be frozen with fear and ignore threatening information when a decision goes wrong (3) or avoid the issue, either by making plans about future trading or even by doing other things (3–1).

Yet again, none of these reactions is appropriate for successful trading. First, any delay in making a decision is likely to result in either missed opportunities or higher-than-necessary losses. Eventually, the trader may be driven to frenetic action in a vain attempt to recoup the losses. Second, to be frozen by fear when a situation goes wrong means that the situation is likely to become very much worse. Ultimately, relief from fear will only be obtained by an aggressive cutting out of loss-making positions and, thereby, joining the crowd. Third, to pretend that the problem does not exist is merely to delay the day of reckoning. In the meantime, the trader may be forced into a phase of quite obsessive perfectionism in matters unrelated to a loss-making trade in order to avoid dealing with the problem.

THE EMERGENCE OF THE CROWD

So, to summarize, the critical problem is that financial markets are continuously generating all the most potent threats for every single individual all the time. As a result, the maximum number of people are feeling threatened all the time.

Hence, despite promises of infinite wealth for the successful trader, the real experience is different. For the vast majority of people, the actual or potential emergence of losses is likely to generate negative emotions and inappropriate defensive strategies.

It does not take a genius to recognize that the defensive strategies described are unlikely to rectify the situation. Put bluntly, as stress increases, the attitude to dealing becomes less and less rational. Furthermore, personal psychological stability can become severely threatened. Incorrect decisions are therefore likely to mount and personal life satisfaction is likely to deteriorate. Inevitably, the trader will seek relief from the anxiety by identifying with other traders with similar views. In other words, a herd instinct is triggered. Our avoidance compulsions therefore drive us into the welcoming arms of the crowd.

CONCLUSION

This chapter, in a sense, completes a circuit. In earlier chapters we argued that fear was the main catalyst for the formation of a crowd; and we showed how price fluctuations stimulated fear in financial markets and generated ordered price movements. Many people, however, would deny that fear (even fear of missing an opportunity) ever forms part of their motivation to deal. Nevertheless, this chapter has demonstrated that no one is actually immune: what happens is that basic anxiety is hidden from us by automatic avoidance compulsions. Indeed, most of these compulsions do not actually seem to be a response to fear at all. The truth, however, is otherwise.

As a result of the compulsions, an increasing number of people experience a divergence between expectations and outcomes, so anxiety increases. Inevitably, the anxiety (or associated negative emotion) becomes intolerable. At this stage, and whether we realize it or not, most of us end up as part of a crowd. Paradoxically, as part of a crowd, we can then all experience the extremes of naked fear together as the market eventually turns viciously against us. This is the nature of bubbles and crashes.

The question, then, of course, is how can individuals overcome their avoidance compulsions and evade the magnetic pull of the crowd mind so that they can trade successfully in financial markets? As has continuously been emphasized, part of the solution is to adopt a decision-making process – a trading system – that generates buy and sell signals on an objective basis. In principle, the use of a system gives the trader the potential to separate themselves from the herd. However, the use of a trading system is not a sufficient condition for success. It is a necessary condition, but it only provides the working tools. The difficulty is that any system that allows a trader literally to see the recent move in prices automatically exposes that trader to the essential catalyst of the crowd mentality – namely moving prices themselves.

There are two basic possibilities for resolving this problem. The first is to operate directly on the avoidance compulsions themselves. However, this can only be done through an intense and disturbing process of self-observation, which is undoubtedly a life-time process and not necessarily to everyone's taste.

The second possibility is to focus attention instead on minimizing the mismatch between expectations and outcomes (thereby reducing anxiety) and on managing negative emotions when they arise (thereby controlling the integrative tendency). And so, it is to this latter option that we shall turn in the next chapter.

NOTES

1. This chapter is a significantly amended version of an article that first appeared in the winter 1995 edition of *The IFTA Journal*.

2. Psychologically, the individual returns to a state of 'oneness' with a significant other – here, the crowd. This reproduces, albeit in elementary form, the feeling state of an infant in its early relationship with its mother.

3. Maclean, Paul (1979) 'A triune concept of the brain and behaviour', in Boag, T (ed.), *The Hincks Memorial Lectures*, University of Toronto Press, Toronto.

4. See, for example, Ichazo, Oscar (1982) *Interviews with Oscar Ichazo*, Arica Institute Press, New York. Mr Ichazo is the source of a new perspective on human development, which places the human psyche in the wider context of universal consciousness. Unfortunately, his work is still largely unpublished – mainly because he is not in favour of his work being used outside the context of personal consciousness development. However, and for better or worse, the essential elements of his insights have been made more widely available via the writings of Claudio Naranjo and Helen Palmer. The former willingly admits his debt to Mr Ichazo; the latter apparently does not. For those who are interested in finding out more – particularly from a clinical perspective – I have no hesitation in recommending Claudio Naranjo's book (1994) *Character and Neurosis*, Gateways/IDHHB, Nevada City, California.

5. Oscar Ichazo, op. cit.

26

The psychology of
success

INTRODUCTION

In this chapter, we shall address the basic personal requirements for successful trading and investment. The analysis will be conducted from the point of view of someone who wishes to embark on a career where personal account trading is essentially the sole source of income. If supplementary sources of income are available, then so much the better.

The strong message – which cannot be stressed enough – is that success is directly related to our willingness to accept complete responsibility for our activity in, and response to, markets. In this way, we can never be – and we can never regard ourselves as being – victims. Markets do not 'happen' to us, they do not 'make' us trade, they do not 'make' us miserable and stressed. Markets just are. It can therefore be no one's task other than our own to ensure that we are fully prepared to participate in this constantly moving and risky, but exciting and ultimately rewarding, environment.

BASIC REQUIREMENTS

In order to counteract the problems associated with anxiety and stress, it is necessary to adopt both an attitude and a lifestyle that are

conducive to regular participation in financial markets. This is particularly true where trading is the sole (or main) source of income. First,
a trader must be quite clear about their goals, or objectives, when
making a commitment to trade markets regularly. Second, the trader
must be able to sustain the energy necessary to maintain that
commitment. Third, the trader must have a suitable method for
achieving their pre-determined objectives (see Figure 26.1).

GOAL-SETTING

Stress and negative emotions are essentially caused by a divergence
between expectations concerning an outcome and the actual outcome
itself – either people don't get what they want or they get what they
don't expect. This is shown in Figure 26.2. Not only is the area representing 'achievements' much smaller than the circle representing
'expectations', but it also lies partly outside of that circle.

There is an old proverb that says if you aim at nothing, that's
exactly what you will hit. The implication is that it is vital to aim at
something specific. There is, however, very little general understanding of how this should be done.

The most effective way of establishing objectives is known as
'goal-setting', or outcome-setting. Establishing goals has two clear
results:

■ it significantly reduces the likely gap between what is expected
and what actually occurs and, therefore, contains stress in such a
way that it is manageable;

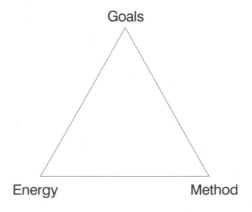

Figure 26.1 Trading prerequisites

Figure 26.2 The cause of anxiety and stress

▍ the technique actually increases an individual's capabilities to a significant extent by focusing energy on achievable results.

In Figure 26.3, these results are represented by the closer correlation between the circles representing 'expectations' and 'achievements' and by an increase in the size of the circle representing 'achievements'.

GOALS FOR THE TRADER

Because of the intensely personal nature of goal-setting, it is not appropriate to analyse the range of potential objectives relating to personal needs, family needs and career needs in great detail here, but it is possible to make some general points. The important starting point is to find out

Figure 26.3 The advantages of goal-setting

what it is that actually motivates you as an individual. Towards what do your desires point?[1] Quite simply, if you follow your deepest desires (when these have been properly elucidated), you will harness the most powerful energy available to you.[2] The second step is to place these desires into a philosophical framework to ensure that there is no incompatability between your needs and those of the community in which you live and work.[3] The third step is to make a plan of action, along the lines of the goal-setting procedures that will be outlined shortly.

If your family and social contexts are, indeed, amenable to a trading career, then the relevant goals narrow down to deciding whether or not your trading income is adequate and you are emotionally satisfied by the processes of trading. In fact, the question of the adequacy of your income can be further subdivided into whether or not you are financially secure and your trading methods are profitable (see Figure 26.4).

The three goals of successful trading, financial security and emotional satisfaction are actually contingent on one another: each is impossible without the others. Thus, there will be no financial security without successful trading; there will be no successful trading without emotional satisfaction; and there will be no emotional satisfaction without financial security.

PRACTICAL CONSIDERATIONS

It would be great if it was always going to be possible to start trading with a huge profit that then set you up for the rest of your career. In practice, however, the reality is likely to be a little bit more prosaic.

Figure 26.4 The trader's goals

The best advice that can be given is that it is absolutely essential to pace yourself in the early period. Even rockets that are headed for the stars need to go through a process of acceleration before they can leave the Earth's orbit.

It will be very important to establish, from the outset, exactly what level of income you are aiming for. This requires that you actually analyse your outgoings in some detail so you know before you start what costs you need to cover. It goes almost without saying that you will need to be practical about this. It may be necessary to start a trading career by amending your lifestyle (temporarily) in order to cut your costs. Once you have done this, your income requirements are likely to be more achievable.[4]

This, of course, raises the issue of what capital you have available to start on a trading career. This is a very personal decision. As a rule of thumb, for traders with no other source of income, it is probably necessary to assume that you will be able to make at least 20 per cent per annum on your capital outlay. Hence, if your income requirements are £20,000 per annum, then you probably need to start with a capital outlay of £100,000. In good years, you are likely to earn considerably more than this, but in a bad year you could earn less. The problem is that you may start with a difficult year. For example, through no fault of your own, trading conditions may just be very difficult, with low volatility.

The inherent riskiness of trading suggests that a measured approach is appropriate. There is, in fact, a strong case for starting to trade in small amounts while actually pursuing another profession. In this way you can learn without risking very much. Do you, for example, yet have the experience to trade effectively? It may only take a year or two to learn how to be able to go through the mechanics of trading, but it may take up to five years to learn whether or not you are able to cope with the trading environment. Further, do you understand fully the technical issues involved in the market(s) in which you intend to trade? The technical and legal aspects of trading are becoming increasingly complicated and need to be learnt and implemented carefully.

If you start with care, you will establish the base – in terms of both finance and experience – from which you can achieve serious results.

THE FIVE ASPECTS OF EFFECTIVE GOAL-SETTING

These practical considerations will need to be incorporated into your goal-setting procedures. They are designed to ensure that the subconscious mind knows what to expect – that is, the subconscious is programmed with new, practical, beliefs about the future so that it can help rather than hinder you. For example, if you do not actually believe that you can trade markets successfully, then you will simply not be able to trade markets successfully.

The central issue is clearly to define the desired outcome itself. This outcome will be a combination of internal experiences and external behaviours that represent the desired state. For example, it may be to become a successful trader. There are, in fact, five distinct conditions that must be met in order to establish a goal that will be effective for you:

▮ It must be stated in the positive rather than in the negative. It is important to be precise about exactly what is required, rather than merely eliminate undesirable conditions. The subconscious probably already knows what you don't want anyway, which is why it keeps projecting negative emotions at you.

▮ It must be ecological – in the sense of being consistent with your relationships with other people, with your environment and, indeed, with your beliefs about life. In other words, it must fit completely and naturally into your life and preserve balance.

▮ It must be stated in terms of a relevant context. Your subconscious will need to know exactly when, where and with whom you want the outcome. The realization of the goal must be placed within an effective time frame. Obviously a goal that is to be realized within the space of a few months is going to generate more energy than one that is to be realized within an ill-defined number of years. However, the time period must be practical. Doubling your income in two years is a more practical objective than doubling it within one month.

▮ It must be defined in terms of a sensory experience. It is important that you know what it will be like to have the outcome. Hence, you should be able to visualize what it will be like to have the outcome. You should be able to see, hear and feel it in as much detail as you can.

▮ It must be within your power to initiate and maintain the resources necessary to produce the outcome. If you are unable to produce the resources or effect the necessary changes in the environment, then the project will not get off the ground. It would, for example, not be practical to trade a market without sufficient capital.

CONVERTING DESIRES INTO ACTUAL BELIEFS

These five conditions for defining an outcome are also the five steps that must be taken in order to programme the subconscious. If you commit yourself to goal-setting, then it is necessary to go through the five conditions outlined above, in sequence, one at a time. Further, at each stage of the goal-setting procedure, the subconscious must be fully engaged so that it will automatically accept the goal as being a valid call on its energy. In this way, desires become beliefs.

Much has been written about this mysterious process in recent years.[5] At one level, the very act of defining achievable out-turns in a positive way transmits important information to the subconscious memory. At another level, however, there is strong evidence to suggest that certain techniques significantly enhance the process. These techniques are visualization, writing and affirmations.

VISUALIZATION

The subconscious does not communicate with the conscious mind via language: it communicates instead in images and feelings. Hence, the simple act of visualizing a goal as clearly as possible, with all its associated sensations, is treated by the subconscious as if it were reality. This is because imagination and memory actually share the same neurological circuits. Visualization, in effect, creates a new reality for you, so your nervous system and your emotions will behave as if your visualized situation already existed. Consequently, the visualized goal will quickly sink into your subconscious as a strong belief. All that then remains is to transfer the belief from the inner mind to outer reality.

To be really effective, it is recommended that the five steps outlined above are completed in one session (although the session can be repeated). You should take as much time as possible and be in as relaxed a state as possible. Most authorities, in fact, recommend that the session be started by using a simple breathing exercise. Breathe deeply for a few minutes, all the while concentrating just on the drawing in and flowing out of the breath. This has the benefit of both diverting the mind's attention away from non-relevant issues and actively slowing down the brain's basic rhythm. If the hoped-for future state is experienced in the mind's eye in full detail – complete with sights, sounds and smells – while in a relaxed state, it is more likely to become the expected state than if you are tense.

Start by defining the desired outcome. It may be something like 'I want to be a trader who earns £XX,000'. Keep it simple, so that queries and questions do not immediately arise. If all you have to start with is a behaviour or state that you don't want, then ask yourself what it is that you would rather have. This avoids the spiral into asking 'Why?' and blaming external circumstances.

Having stated the goal to yourself, check that you really do want it. Ask yourself specifically 'Will I now accept this goal?' If the answer is an unequivocal 'Yes', then you're on your way, but watch for any doubts that may emerge, particularly those that start 'Yes, I want the goal, but . . .'. If there are any doubts, go back to stating the goal in a way that takes care of the doubt.

When you have a clear 'yes', state to yourself, in the clearest possible way, the time when your goal will be achieved, the place where it will be achieved and with whom it will be achieved.

Then – and this is the crucial stage – visualize the goal in full detail. See it as being your reality.

Finally, confirm to yourself your own part in moving towards the goal. See yourself gathering the necessary resources and completing the necessary tasks. Again, see it as your reality.

It may actually be necessary to conduct this exercise more than once. Often it is helpful to have someone – such as a trained practitioner in neuro-linguistic programming – to help you through the exercise. The results undoubtedly warrant the effort.

WRITING DOWN AND AFFIRMATIONS

The process of visualization can be supplemented and enhanced by two powerful reinforcing techniques. The first is simply to write your goals down on a piece of paper once you have completed the five-step process described above. The act of committing the goal to paper helps to ensure that the subconscious recognizes your sense of purpose.

The second technique is designed to help the subconscious to continually orientate itself towards the goals that you have already set yourself. This technique involves the use of affirmations. Simply put, an affirmation is a statement, made to yourself, that affirms a particular condition to be true. The affirmation is made regularly to yourself, out loud if possible. Hence, for example, the simple statement 'Every day I trade according to my system trading rules' will be a powerful reinforcement to your goal of doing so.

There are, however, a few important rules to be followed when setting affirmations for yourself. The first thing to remember is that they can be used only to manage beliefs, they cannot be used to manage emotions (which are determined by beliefs). You will achieve very little by telling yourself that you're feeling generous when in fact you are angry. You would need to focus on the belief that is causing the anger.

The second thing is that the affirmation should be positive and personal. It should be couched in language that asserts a particular reality as definitely being true for you and does not implicitly leave an unanswered question. There is little value in either leaving yourself out of the affirmation ('life is great!' – for whom?) or in just excluding undesirable conditions ('my life is not bad!' – then what is it?) Such statements have little or no effect on the subconscious. Third, the statement should (if possible) be in the present tense ('I am an effective trader') or, if it is in the future, include a time target ('I shall have an income of £20,000 per annum by my next birthday'). Otherwise, the mind will simply dismiss the affirmation as sheer nonsense. The point is, you have to believe in it.

Goal-setting, combined with the act of committing the goal to paper and then backing it up with appropriate affirmations, is very simple. All that it requires is that you put aside a little time to implement the process. It is an understatement to say that your life could be transformed as a result. Those who have persisted with it have confirmed that it is a very powerful technique.[6]

STRATEGY FOR ACHIEVING GOALS

Once a goal (or set of goals) has been set and started to become part of a person's belief system, it is important to concentrate attention on the process of achieving that goal. Goals belong to the future; the process is the immediate task in hand. Business plans are all well and good, but it is also necessary to marshal the necessary human, mechanical and financial resources into a cohesive strategy in order to achieve the plan.

The diversion of focused attention towards process is, in fact, critical. This is because there is an important difference between goals and process that is often missed: goals are targets, not achievements;

and it is achievements that attract and manipulate emotional energy. If, therefore, attention is focused on what can be achieved now, huge energy resources can (and will) be released from unfulfilled desires and from unpleasant emotions that, instead, can be used to deal with the tasks of the moment. You will begin to live closer to the present.

STRATEGIES FOR TRADERS

The question for the trader in this context is whether or not it really is possible to divorce the longer-term goal of profitable trading from the potentially traumatic short-term effects of incurring losses. The answer lies in the making of two specific commitments. The first is the commitment to use a technical trading system (the 'method') that provides automatic entry and exit criteria and incorporates money management principles. This will encourage you to remain disengaged from the emotional contagion of the marketplace and encourage you to limit your risk. The second commitment is to the adoption of an attitude towards yourself (the 'energy maintenance') that is supportive of trading. The basic need is to maintain your energy levels in order to cope with the inevitable shocks and vicissitudes of the markets.

METHOD

The basic requirements for a successful trading technique are shown in Figure 26.5. They involve a technical trading system, the use of stops and the spreading of risk.

In the first place, it is essential to use a trading system that generates automatic entry signals. These signals may be taken as suggestions rather than as fixed instructions, but they reduce uncertainty by eliminating the need to search for further confirming information.

Second, it is essential to use 'stops' to exit a trade. Stops are levels at which profits must be taken or losses realized once the market begins to move in the opposite direction to that required. Stops should be regarded as instructions to deal and should not be cancelled or altered. Their use will reduce stress by ensuring that, as far as is possible, losses are not allowed to become too large to handle and profits are not allowed to erode unnecessarily.

Finally, trading with specific amounts of capital, in more than one market, should help to spread risks so that the overall effect of the

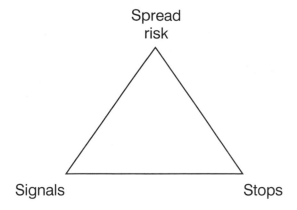

Figure 26.5 The method

volatility of profits and losses is reduced. In this way, ultimate success is not dependent on the profitability of the last trade. Consequently, your emotional fluctuations are also kept to a minimum.

A practical example of a profitable short-term trading methodology, which uses the three criteria outlined above, is set out in Chapter 27.

ENERGY

The final requirement is to maintain energy. By this is meant that the successful trader needs to have the ability to maintain the energy and concentration levels that are essential to pursuing profits in a fast-moving, high-risk operating environment (see Figure 26.6).

It is usually accepted as being logical that a successful trading career requires clear thinking, physical energy and emotional freedom. The point that is often missed, however, is that physical, mental and emotional health are required constantly. Even highly successful traders are likely to suffer from 'burnout' and thereby suffer from loss of income and/or ill health if they do not incorporate a regimen of good health into their overall strategy.

PHYSICAL HEALTH

It seems to be a widespread belief (at least in the West) that good health is something you either have or you don't have. In other words, it's a

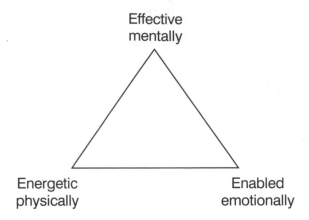

Figure 26.6 Energy

question of luck. While there is inevitably an element of truth in this view, it is far from being the whole story. Quite simply, if a suitable amount of care is taken, then the chances of becoming ill are significantly reduced. Unfortunately, it is on the question of overall health that most traders suffer from myopia. Indeed, the trading culture often requires that traders pay relatively little attention to the basic principles of personal healthcare. High-fat foodstuffs (often eaten at speed) and alcohol, combined with long trading hours and a sedentary lifestyle, are the hallmarks of modern financial operators.

It is, of course, extraordinarily difficult to overcome the peer group pressures that operate in financial markets, but, ultimately, it is a question of balance. If sufficient care is taken with diet, exercise and recreation, then the body itself will try to remain healthy.[7] It is, after all, its natural condition.

MENTAL AND EMOTIONAL HEALTH

Physical health is, however, only a part of the solution – mental and emotional health are equally important. There are, of course, many facets to this particular subject, but the central feature of a balanced personality is the willingness to accept the truth about a given situation. If there is a gap between beliefs about the world and the reality, then the result is likely to be inappropriate expectations and, hence, a divergence between expectations and outcomes. Such a divergence results in psychosomatic stress and negative emotions. In some circumstances, a failure to recognize the truth of a situation is likely to yield obvious and dramatic results. As an example, if somebody is going to make a physical attack on you, it is important to your survival that you should recognize the threat straight away. Treating overt hostility as an act of friendship is a sign either of madness or of saintliness. The problem, however, is that the gap between beliefs and reality can be very subtle. If, for example, somebody makes a friendly approach to you, it is not always certain that you will recognize it as such. You may assume that there is an ulterior motive. Indeed, it is all too easy to mistake a friendly gesture for a threat of some sort.

These examples are, of course, only two from among many possibilities, but it is obvious that a divergence between beliefs and reality can be the cause of great discomfort. We have already argued that the process of goal-setting can significantly reduce the problem, but, of course, this does not eliminate it entirely. It is still necessary to deal with shorter-term (strategic) objectives, and these objectives may be expected but not met. The result is likely to be stress.

STRESS

There are two points to be made here. First, the emergence of signs of stress (including negative emotions) can be a very useful item of information. They point unerringly to the presence of a weakness in the strategy for achieving your goals. For example, a series of losses that eventually becomes too stressful will point to a problem with the trading system.

The second point – one that is all too often missed – is that stress and negative emotions may be related to problems that have occurred in the distant past and, as such, may be inappropriate to the present. Each of our personal experiences – particularly as children – helps to create in us a set of beliefs that we subsequently use to guide our lives. We have already mentioned that beliefs – which give the world meaning for us – are trapped in a sort of emotional glue. Some of these emotions are empowering in the sense of channelling energy into productive use. Others, however, are decidedly disempowering in that they divert energy away from the task of maintaining a high degree of personal well-being. This is particularly true if the emotions are being suppressed in some way.

The trouble is that the negative emotions of our childhood are not only suppressed during childhood, but they are also easily invoked during adulthood.[8] As children, most of us develop defensive habits to deal with our specific fears, but they are usually inappropriate to the changing world in which we live. Hence, when a habit fails to work, very strong emotional reactions are generated. We discussed this point in some detail in the last chapter and confirmed that our 'natural' habits are, in fact, something of a hindrance when dealing in financial markets. We observed that the emotions that were most likely to be associated with these habits were fear, hostility, anger and frustration. Modern psychoanalytical theory suggests that these primary habits and their associated emotions may be reduced, or even eliminated, by bringing them out into consciousness.

It is probably fair to say that research into the dynamics of consciousness is only just beginning to reveal the healing power inherent in the ability of the conscious mind to concentrate on parts of the subconscious. Goal-setting confirms that it is possible to manipulate the subconscious into accepting instructions from the conscious mind, rather than the other way around. This in itself is a massive step forward. However, potentially more important is the possibility of altering the nature of our defensive habits by focusing attention on their causes. The focused conscious mind can act like a micro-surgical laser beam in separating today's reality from yesterday's memories and, as a result, the former is not polluted by the influence of the latter. There are various ways of reducing the persistent demands of old habits,[9,10] but the solution, quite simply, is a careful analysis of our beliefs about ourselves and relationships in, and with, the world.

RELAXATION TECHNIQUES

It was earlier observed that deep breathing can be used to establish a state that is particularly helpful for visualization techniques. In essence, the brain's rhythms harmonize and slow when we do this, and research has shown that it has a wonderfully relaxing effect on the metabolism of the whole body. Now, one of the symptoms of stress is shallow breathing. The breath is taken in high in the chest and the lungs are rarely fully emptied. Obviously this is appropriate to a short period of fast breathing, when the body is oriented towards coping with a threat. However, if shallow breathing persists for extended periods of time, the body tends to become de-oxygenated. This adds to the overall stress levels.

A direct corollary of this is that slow and deep breathing can elim-inate many of the physical and mental symptoms of stress. Accordingly, a commitment to even a short period of slow and deep breathing each day – preferably in the morning, before the day's work has begun – can have profound and far-reaching effects. A large number of books have been written on this subject and it is worthwhile investing in one of them and then implementing its recommendations.[11]

CONCLUSION

Genuine survivors in financial markets – that is, individuals who are able to make a living by trading successfully over sustained periods of time – are likely to be the sorts of people who pay attention to their physical and psychological health. Unfortunately, however, the majority of people who trade markets will not do this until a stress-related crisis of some sort forces them to change.

In the meantime, it cannot be emphasized enough that, at the very least, genuine success in trading markets involves the adoption of a trading system. Without the discipline of such a system, the very best efforts are likely to be doomed to failure. It is, therefore, to the subject of trading systems we turn next.

NOTES

1. A useful starting point here is to ask yourself four questions:

    What would I do if I no longer had to worry about money?
    What would I do if I only had six months to live?
    What would I do if success were guaranteed?
    What have I achieved that has given me satisfaction and a feeling of impor-tance?

    In answering these questions, you will get a very clear indication of your primary motivations.

2. The late Joseph Campbell used to encapsulate this truth in the advice 'follow your bliss'. See, for example, Cousineau, Phil (1990) *The Hero's Journey: The world of Joseph Campbell*, HarperCollins, New York.

3. Essentially, this means undertaking to participate in the society within which you live and work. See, for example, Peck, M Scott (1978) *The Road Less Travelled*, Simon & Schuster, New York.

4. Ideally, your income from guaranteed sources (such as from bonds) should completely cover your budgeted living expenses. Then you are independent. Your trading capital should then be a separate issue, so that a bad trading period will not interfere with your basic requirements.

5.   See, for example, Bretto Milliner, Charlotte (1988) *A Framework for Excellence*, Grinder & Associates, Scotts Valley, California. This book should be available from any bookshop that stocks a range of books on neuro-linguistic programming (NLP). See also O'Connor, Joseph, and Seymour, John (1990) *Introducing Neuro-Linguistic Programming*, Mandala, London.

6.   See, for example, Alder, Harry (1994) *NLP: The new art and science of getting what you want,* Piatkus, London.

7.   There are many excellent books that address the problem of achieving balance in the area of health. See, for example, Chopra, Deepak (1990) *Perfect Health*, Bantam Books, London.

8.   See, for example, Miller, Alice (1983) *The Drama of Being a Child*, Faber & Faber, London.

9.   Peck, M Scott, op. cit.

10. One of the clearest analyses of the beneficial effects of self-observation is contained in Krishnamurti, J (1954) *The First and Last Freedom*, Victor Gollancz, London.

11. An ideal and practical approach to stress is the excellent book by Loehr, James (1997) *Stress for Success*, Times Books, New York. For a more traditional view, see Markham, Ursula (1989) *Managing Stress*, Element, Shaftesbury, Dorset.

27

The mechanics of success

INTRODUCTION

The use of a trading system is essential for success. The discipline that it imposes simultaneously keeps a trader (relatively) immune from the emotional contagion of the marketplace and enables decisions to be made on the basis of objective criteria. There are, of course, almost infinite numbers of systems that can be used, depending on your personal preferences and the technology that is available to do the task. The falling prices of very powerful personal computers and the ready availability of automatic datafeeds make it possible for an individual to compete in sophistication with some of the biggest financial houses. It is not, however, essential to use such technology. It can be just as rewarding to track markets using nothing more than graph paper – indeed, it can be validly argued that such an approach would actually give you a better 'feel' for the market. Be that as it may, there are three basic criteria for effectiveness that need to be spelt out:

■ a system needs to be profitable;

■ it needs to be proven;

■ it needs to be personalized.

SYSTEM EFFECTIVENESS

These three criteria are not mutually exclusive. The point of drawing attention to them is that you – as the trader – have to be satisfied that the trading system being used actually meets your requirements. A system that leaves areas of significant doubt will not serve the goals of financial security and emotional well-being. It is also important to be comfortable with the operations of the system.

It goes almost without saying that a system has to be able to generate profits, but there are two related issues that need to be addressed. The first is whether the system is going to be used to supplement other sources of income or is to be the sole source of income. In the former case, the resources devoted to the initial research need not be burdensome; in the latter case, however, a significant amount of time and (often) money does need to be spent in choosing a suitable system.

The second issue that needs to be considered is whether you want to undertake a highly active trading profile in a limited number of markets or deal less frequently, but in a large number of markets.

Once these objectives are clear in your mind, then the effort can be made to establish a profitable system. In the initial stages, profitability obviously has to be tested on the basis of historical data. However, obviously, the real test of a system is its actual performance under live conditions. Any system will inevitably be buffeted by trends that are longer-term than those for which the system was designed. It is at such times, after a period of underperformance, that subjective (and invariably fatal) panic overrides can be forced into play. It is important, therefore, to test out the system in real time – but, initially, without making a massive financial commitment. This will help to ensure that the system itself can cope with the actual speed and volatility of the markets being traded, and that you can cope mentally and emotionally with those periods of time when the system generates losses.

This problem of coping is an important one and should not be underestimated. In Chapter 24, it was argued that the emotional strain of dealing with losses might, in the final analysis, simply be too much. It is for this reason that care should be taken to ensure that the system is the 'right' one in terms of feel and familiarity. Obviously, this is very subjective, but then so it should be because it is a question of confidence and commitment. For example, most traders are more likely to trust a system that they have designed themselves than one that is essentially a 'black box' signal generator. This is not to say that the latter are ineffective – far from it. It is just that such systems inevitably raise strong doubts when they start to make losses, because the cause of the losses may not be apparent straight away.

SYSTEM DESIGN

An effective system – that is profitable, proven and personalized – needs to have three elements:

▌ it should generate potential entry signals;

▌ it should define specific exit points;

▌ it should allow the spreading of risk.

There are obviously quite a few possibilities here, so, in order to expedite the task of explaining the system requirements, we shall use a simple example. The example is a short-term trading system that can be used in almost any liquid market. It is an effective system, but is not perfect. Its value here is only to demonstrate some of the ideas involved. All that is required is access to a price series, where each price is registered regularly at an hourly interval. If it is possible to record the spread of prices during the course of an hour – and therefore record the highest price, lowest price and last ('closing') price for each hour – so much the better. It is assumed that these prices, and the associated indicators, can be plotted in graphical form.

The trading signals for this system are generated at the end of each hour's price movement (the closing price is the important one). If a bar chart recording hourly spreads is used, then it is possible to check for warnings of an imminent signal by observing the behaviour of the current price and comparing it with potential end-period signal levels.

THE SYSTEM STRUCTURE

The first task is to calculate two arithmetical moving averages – namely, a 26-hour moving average of the hourly closing prices and the hourly equivalent of a 21-day moving average of such prices (that is, 21 times the trading hours in a day). The shorter average highlights the short-term trend and the longer one relates to the longer-term, more slow-moving, trend. Both averages are used to determine whether the current price is bullish or bearish within a particular time frame. A current price above a moving average will be bullish; a price below the moving average will be bearish.

Although it is unnecessary in a simple system such as this, the moving averages can be supplemented by an 'average directional indicator' (ADX). This was discussed in Chapter 23. The ADX gives an indication as to whether or not the market is actually trending.

The second task is to calculate a momentum indicator that will give you both an indication of reversals in momentum and a tool to recognize non-confirmations. The most popular momentum indicator in modern markets is the 'moving average convergence–divergence (MACD) line', which we also discussed in Chapter 23.

This indicator measures the difference between two moving averages. When plotted as a graph, the line oscillates slowly up and down as the two averages first diverge from each other, then converge on each other and finally cross over one another. The original version uses exponential moving averages, so that more weight can be given to recent time periods than to older ones. However, quite acceptable results can be obtained by using simple arithmetical averages. The recommended time periods for the two moving averages are 13-hour and 34-hour.[1]

When the MACD indicator is rising, the implications are positive for prices: if the indicator is less than zero (that is, the 13-hour average is still below the 34-hour average), then the market is only potentially bullish; if the indicator is greater than zero (that is, the 13-hour average is above the 34-hour average), then the market is actually bullish. The converse holds true if the MACD indicator is falling: if the indicator is above zero, then the market is potentially bearish; if the indicator is less than zero, then the market is actually bearish.

The third task is to calculate an indicator known as the 'signal line'. This indicator is a moving average of the MACD line. Again, the best type of average for this purpose is an exponential average, but acceptable results can be obtained by using an ordinary arithmetical average. The recommended period for this average is eight hours.[2] In principle, a definite recommendation to enter a trade is generated whenever the MACD line crosses the signal line.

Once the mechanics for calculating these averages have been established, all that is necessary is to set out a basic set of entry and exit rules, then use them. These rules are obviously variable, but one particularly useful set of rules is given below.[3]

THE ENTRY RULE

A position is opened when the MACD line breaks the signal line and one of the following supplementary (or confirming) signals occurs:

▌ momentum has not confirmed the recent price low (in the case of a buy signal) or high (in the case of a sell signal);

■ the last price crosses the 26-hour moving average in the same direction as the momentum signal;

■ the last price signals a break-out from a valid price pattern;

■ the price is reversing away from a golden ratio objective.

THE EXIT RULES

Half of the trading position should be closed when the price hits a target calculated from golden ratio expansions or contractions, and if one of the following criteria is also met:

■ the golden ratio target is also at a support/resistance level;

■ momentum is diverging from the movement in absolute prices;

■ momentum is at an extreme and the ADX is not rising.

All (remaining) open positions should then be closed if either a pre-determined stop loss is triggered or if the MACD line breaks the signal line in the opposite direction to the trade.

CLOSING AND REVERSING POSITIONS

If the current price is above the (hourly equivalent of the) 21-day moving average, then closing a short position automatically implies opening a long position. Thus, if the current price is below the 21-day moving average, then closing a long position implies opening a short position. Otherwise, the normal entry/exit rules apply.

It is also worth emphasizing that reversals away from the golden ratio objectives can be used to anticipate this effect.

INVESTMENT FUNDS

Within the context of this short-term trading system, it is advisable to use a 'standard' amount of funds for each trade. This standard unit should be used every time a signal is given. However, there are two practical alternatives. The first is to allocate half of the standard amount whenever the MACD entry signal (the primary momentum signal) is given. The rest of the funds can then be allocated when one of the supplementary signals is generated. The second alternative is to wait and allocate all the funds when a full set of signals (a primary signal, plus a supplementary signal) is produced. This alternative might, in any case, be usefully adopted when markets are particularly volatile.

If an average directional indicator is being used, some of the directional uncertainty is removed. Accordingly, full amounts can be allocated if the ADX line is rising, while half units should be used if it is falling.

THE THREE-WAVE MARKET MAP

The entry and exit signals can be used without reference to longer-term trends. However, the knowledge that all price patterns are based on the price pulse introduces tremendous scope for adding a valid subjective dimension to trading decisions.

The archetypal nature of the price pulse means that a clear three-up/three-down base or top pattern is likely to emerge just prior to a higher-order impulse wave.[4] The pattern can be used to construct a market map of the future, with appropriate objectives calculated from golden ratio expansions. Quite obviously, the larger this pattern, the more powerful the subsequent impulse wave is likely to be. The map will help determine whether or not longer-term investment positions ought to be opened, and, if so, what amount of money ought to be allocated to the trade.

If the emergent pattern is considered to be particularly strong – that is, if the pattern has taken some time to develop and there are grounds for supposing that the fundamental background picture is changing – then serious consideration should be given to committing some multiple of the basic investment unit to the trade. This multiple should then be invested when a short-term trading signal is generated. If required, the amount may be split into two equal units, so that half is invested on the primary signal and the rest allocated to the supplementary signal.

It follows that shorter-term exit signals should not trigger a full closing off of all positions. This should only occur when the calculated objective is hit.

SPREADING RISK

Part of the mechanics of success involves spreading risk, so that a loss does not incapacitate your trading programme. There are two basic ways of doing this. The first is to trade in either a number of markets or in a number of different stocks in the same market. The point is that the variety should be sufficient to ensure that any losses are going to be more than offset by profits elsewhere, but the variety should not be so great that you cannot cope with all the information and activity.

The second way of spreading risk is to distribute it over time, rather than across markets or stocks. In other words, it may be more acceptable to wait for those trades where you expect the outcome to be particularly dynamic (because of a significant base or top pattern). The idea would be to keep a close watch on a number of different markets, but only trade when conditions are right.

MONEY MANAGEMENT

Whichever approach is suitable for you, there are two cardinal money management rules that need to be obeyed[5]. The first is that no trade should allow you to lose more than 10 per cent of your capital. If you are trading equities, bonds or currencies, a 'stop loss' (see below) should be triggered well before the 10 per cent limit is hit. Suitable adjustments should be made for leveraged futures positions. In options markets, no more than 10 per cent of your capital should be placed on a single trade because there is a chance that the option may expire worthless. The 10 per cent rule should also be applied to 'recovery' situations – where the company has been facing severe financial difficulties, but is now considered to be over the worst.

The second money management rule is that no more than 20 per cent of your capital should be placed in a single investment. This will ensure that, if you are spreading your risk across markets or stocks, you should be able to hold at least five positions.

If these rules are adhered to, then it will be possible to weather stormy times and still be able to take maximum advantage of profitable trading opportunities when they present themselves.

OPENING POSITIONS

We shall now discuss the signals themselves in a little more detail. The entry rules essentially rely on a reversal in momentum (the MACD line) to establish the basic signal. However, it is still possible that the reversal will be too short-term to provide a profitable trading opportunity – hence the use of supplementary or confirming signals. The first signal relies on the concept of 'non-confirmation' that we analysed in Chapter 23. If the primary momentum signal is being given on a reversal from a price extreme, and there has been a non-confirming divergence between the price extreme and the MACD line, then the signal has a greater chance of being valid.

The second supplementary signal relies on the argument that the moving average approximates the trend in the market, and that a penetration of the moving average therefore indicates a change in trend. However, the signal has a greater chance of being valid if the moving average itself is in the process of reversing.[6] The use of a moving average in this way is particularly useful when the primary momentum signal has been generated under very choppy trading conditions.

The third signal allows for the break out from congestion areas, holding patterns, recognizable reversal patterns and trend lines. These patterns are the basis of much traditional technical analysis. In a sense, they are late signals because prices will already have moved some way before the signal is given. Nevertheless, such signals may constitute the last piece of information in the movement away from an area of very volatile price action.

The fourth signal covers those cases where the price has reached a valid price objective and is reversing away from it. First, the price may have achieved a retracement objective of 38.2 per cent or 61.8 per cent of the previous move, and may be moving back into the main trend. An MACD entry signal should catch such a renewed trend. Indeed, it is particularly powerful for the 61.8 per cent retracement, where the market has re-tested the previous high or low. Second, the price may have reached a golden ratio objective for an impulse move and may be reversing into a new trend. The MACD entry signal should allow you to catch the beginnings of this new trend, too.

CLOSING POSITIONS

It is all very well entering trades successfully, but it is obviously also important to ensure that subsequent profits are not allowed to erode unnecessarily and that any losses are kept to an absolute minimum. To this end, the need to follow strict rules about closing positions cannot be emphasized enough.

As discussed earlier, there are psychological influences that encourage traders to take profits too early and realize losses too late. There is also the related problem of identifying with trading positions so that self-esteem becomes dependent on the outcome of the trade. Both of these sets of problems can be reduced, or even eliminated, by adopting rigid exit criteria.

STOPS

The cardinal rule is that every trade must be accompanied by a precisely defined set of exit rules. In other words, when a trade is entered, a clear decision has to be made about the conditions under which the trade must be closed. There are actually two situations to be addressed. The first of these concerns the emergence of a loss on a trade. The question to be answered is, when is the trade definitely wrong so that it is necessary to stop the loss? The answer depends partly on the circumstances under which the trade was opened. Has the original reason for entering the trade been aborted? Was the entry signal so temporary as to be false? However, the answer also depends partly on what level of losses can be absorbed for any one trade. This is a particularly important consideration in volatile markets, such as foreign exchange.

As already indicated, at no stage should more than 10 per cent of your capital be at risk on any one trade. A loss in excess of this amount will seriously damage your ability to continue trading. The level at which a stop loss must be triggered should be determined at the time that the trade is opened. Once a stop loss level has been determined, it should neither be cancelled nor altered.

MECHANICAL EXIT SIGNALS

The second situation to be considered is the more fortunate one relating to the conditions under which profits must be taken. Mechanical exit rules will ensure that profits are regularly 'booked' and will also encourage you not to feel frustrated or annoyed if the maximum profit is missed. You never go broke taking profits, however small those profits may be. Having taken a profit, you can then move on to the next trading opportunity without undue concern about how successful (or unsuccessful) you've been.

CALCULATED TARGETS

One of the powerful messages from this book is that mechanical exit rules are substantially enhanced by incorporating calculated targets. This is because such targets help to avoid the premature closure of winning trades and can help generate an exit signal close to the point of maximum profit. The only targets considered here to be valid are those calculated from the golden ratio. Nevertheless, they should not be used by themselves, simply because there are always various possibilities. Consequently, only half the position should be closed when a valid target is reached and then only if one of three other supportive conditions is met – that is, either the calculated target must previously have been associated with a price reversal or there is a potential divergence between prices and price momentum or the market is very overbought or oversold.

HIGHER-LEVEL TRENDS

When calculating the potential targets, there is one very important consideration that must be taken into account. This is that the energy from the current level of the price pulse is derived from, or qualified by, the energy of higher-level pulses (see Chapter 5). Golden ratio objectives for the short-term trend will usually work, but may be quickly washed away by the power of the superior trend. This implies that two factors need to be taken into account. First, the power of higher-level trends may cause prices to undershoot or overshoot objectives. Usually, the objectives are very precise, but a leeway of +/– 1 per cent should be allowed. Second, the influence of higher-level trends means that you will need to be aware of the longer-term context within which you are operating. Reference to recent important turning points in the 21-day moving average of prices (see below) will usually provide a very good indication of this context.

However, when there is some uncertainty – for example, when it is not immediately clear whether or not the market is just beginning a correction to the most recent phase of a trend or is just about to begin a major reversal – the correct approach is to be cautious, follow the golden ratio signal on half of the position and be ready to re-enter the market when a valid entry signal is generated. It may even be fair to say that the real power of the application of calculated targets probably only comes with experience.

FINAL EXIT

Exit rules based on the golden ratio objectives will be very effective for a large number of – or even on most – occasions. However, once the market begins to reverse away from a target, then (whether or not any of the supportive conditions have been met) open positions should be closed when the MACD line cuts the signal line. No other factors need to be taken into account.

CLOSING OLD POSITIONS AND OPENING NEW ONES

There are two possible problems with these exit rules. First, if there has been some uncertainty over the level of the price pulse being traded, there may be occasions when positions are, in effect, closed prematurely. If the dealing rules are followed consistently, then this should not actually matter too much as a re-entry signal will inevitably be generated when the underlying trend re-asserts itself.

Second, there are occasions when the short-term trading system does not immediately show whether or not the closing of an old position should be accompanied by the opening of a new one in the opposite direction. In order to circumvent this uncertainty, it is a good idea to use a much longer moving average to define the background trend of the market. Without doubt, one of the best averages for this purpose is a simple arithmetical 21-day moving average. If hourly charts are being used, then it is a simple matter to convert the 21-day average into the corresponding hourly average. The market trend is then defined by the current price in relation to the moving average:

■ if the price is above the average, and the average is rising, then the trend is bullish;

■ if the price is below the average, and the average is falling, then the trend is bearish.

The rule for opening and closing positions is then quite simple:

■ if the market trend is bullish, then closing shorts implies opening new longs;

■ if the trend is bearish, then closing longs implies opening new shorts.

As indicated above, using moving averages in this way may be supplemented by using an average directional indicator. If the ADX is rising, then the market trend (whether up or down) is intact. Under these circumstances, closing contra-trend trades should be accompanied by the opening of pro-trend trades. If the ADX is falling, then the market is not trending and a more circumspect approach is required.

CONCLUSION

The basic system outlined in this chapter is far from being the last word in profitable trading systems. The aim here has been to indicate how a profitable trading system can be developed. For the individual trader, great insights can come from just trying to develop a personalized trading system. Furthermore, backtracking through all the historical signals and identifying their validity encourages great confidence in the system.

However, it should be clear from the analysis that profitability is likely to be enhanced by a genuine understanding of how markets behave, and by use of the golden ratio to determine price objectives. These, in turn, encourage patience while natural forces evolve and encourage confidence that expectations will be fulfilled. These are two of the primary advantages of goal-setting, which we outlined in Chapter 26.

NOTES

1. Different analysts use different time periods for the calculation of the exponential moving averages. The original ones recommended by Gerald Appel were 12-period and 26-period averages respectively. The author's own researches suggest that 13-period and 34-period averages may give better results.
2. Many analysts use nine-period averages.
3. This particular trading system has been used by the author and is one that has been refined over a long period of time.
4. See Chapter 12.
5. These rules are for general guidance only. In modern, highly leveraged markets, great care needs to be taken with risk control. One of the best books on the subject is Elder, Dr Alexander (2002) *Come Into My Trading Room*, John Wiley, New York.
6. The moving average signal is unlikely to be correct if it is generated when the moving average is still moving sharply against the direction indicated by the signal.

28

Summary and conclusions

An analysis of universal laws can provide us with an explanation of stock market dynamics. The need individuals have to obey universal laws and participate in greater wholes is the key to a fuller understanding of all social, economic and political activity. In the current context, it allows us to 'explain' the stock market phenomenon by forcing us to adopt the assumption of non-rational crowd behaviour by market participants.

The important point to remember is that the ownership of investment positions in the pursuit of stock market profits creates a 'crowd' mentality. The decision to make an investment (or disinvestment) may have been arrived at rationally, but, once a financial exposure exists, so does the potential for stress and fear. Price behaviour becomes the arbiter of investment decisions and price movements can therefore trigger responses from investors that have a large non-rational dimension. This non-rational response is the binding force in the crowd situation.

Once a crowd has been created, it has a life cycle of its own. In the context of a financial market, the crowd's behaviour during this life cycle can be measured by changes in prices and sentiment. The former can be tracked using price–time charts, while the latter can be judged by plotting variables such as volume, open interest or momentum.

While a crowd exists, it has natural metabolic rhythms that have both an internal and an external dimension. The internal rhythms are, by definition, specific to the particular crowd and are reflected in regular, cyclical fluctuations that can be found in the price–time charts. At the same time, however, the crowd has to oscillate in a limit cycle relationship with its social and economic environment. Some of the environmental oscillations are themselves 'regular', and so the crowd oscillates in harmony with these external rhythms because, essentially, it has 'learnt' to do so. In both these situations, where the fluctuations are regular and continuous, it is possible to use observed cycles to forecast the timing of turning points in financial market prices.

Most of the environmental oscillations, however, will appear as 'shocks' to the crowd. They may consist of either pro-trend information or contra-trend information – pro-trend information encourages existing trends; contra-trend information generates a correction; both generate a three-stage fluctuation as the crowd seeks to assimilate the information.

This three-wave response is the basis of what we have called the 'price pulse'. Each phase of the price pulse is defined by the golden ratio and its derivatives. The golden ratio has long been recognized as an intrinsic part of nature in terms of both the relationship between different aspects of the same spatial structure and the growth and learning processes of that structure. It follows that price movements in financial markets are subject to the 'constraints' of the golden ratio and it is therefore possible to forecast the extent of price movements using this ratio.

Finally, the alternating up and down movements created by the combination of rhythmic cycles and contra-trend shocks are reflected in a limited number of price patterns. These have long been identified by traditional technical analysis and can be used to deduce trading signals that have a low risk of being incorrect and a high probability of being profitable.

Of course, no system is perfect. There will be occasions when the messages being given are either inconclusive or conflicting. On these occasions, investors should not anticipate reversals if to do so means 'moving away from base'. At the simplest level, this implies that long-term investors should always stay in the market until definite sell signals are given, and that short-term investors should always stay out of the market until definite buy signals are generated. On most occasions, however, technical analysis will confirm the presence of a reversal while it is in the process of developing.

The crucial requisite for wealth accumulation is for a trader to be properly positioned for large market movements. It is important to remember that large movements are created, essentially, by the failure of the majority of investors to anticipate all developments fully, and by the consequent reaction *en masse* to largely unforeseen events.

Substantial price movements simply cannot occur if everybody is getting the market right all of the time. Technical analysis focuses attention on what the majority of investors are doing at any given moment, while simultaneously enabling successful investors to stand aside from the crowd mentality. It is a rational approach to a non-rational environment.

Hence, technical analysis should, at the very least, ensure that no major mistakes are made. When used properly, the techniques will not give strong buy signals just prior to a price collapse, nor strong sell signals just prior to a rally. More generally, there are always clear warning signals that a terminal juncture is approaching and these signals subsequently translate into some form of appropriate buy or sell signal just prior to the major part of the relevant impulse wave.

It has been the objective of this book to show that technical analysis is an accurate and theoretically justifiable method of forecasting behaviour in financial markets. Only putting theory into practice will, however, demonstrate the validity of the technique. Investors who follow the rules outlined in this book should, after a little experience, find that it is entirely possible to embark on a long-term programme of accumulating wealth.

Index